135#

THE ESSENTIALS OF MACROECONOMIC ANALYSIS

The essentials of MACROECONOMIC ANALYSIS

Richard A. Bilas
California State College, Bakersfield

Frank J. Alessio
University of Arizona

1974

BUSINESS PUBLICATIONS, INC.   Dallas, Texas   75224
Irwin-Dorsey International   London, England   WC2H 9NJ
Irwin-Dorsey Limited   Georgetown, Ontario   L7G 4B3

© BUSINESS PUBLICATIONS, INC., 1974

All rights reserved. No part of this publication may be reproduced, stored in a retrieval system, or transmitted, in any form or by any means, electronic, mechanical, photocopying, recording, or otherwise, without the prior written permission of the publisher.

First Printing, January 1974

ISBN 0-256-01242-3
Library of Congress Catalog Card No. 72-96526
Printed in the United States of America

TO CATHY, DAVID, AND AMI—
  someday they will understand why
AND TO PEGGY

Preface

The authors' purpose in this book is to treat in a clear and concise but rigorous manner the fundamentals of macroeconomic analysis. To accomplish this we begin with a few simple and unsophisticated models of the determination of the level of national income. We gradually add refinements to the models until we develop a three sector model in which the price level is a variable. At this point we begin to examine rigorously the relationship between the supply of money and the price level. The theoretical models then become the background for an examination of macroeconomic policy.

As with most textbooks, this one developed from a series of lectures given by the authors over the past several years at Georgia State University, California State College, Bakersfield, and the University of Arizona. We owe a considerable debt to J. M. Keynes upon whose work we, as those before us, build. However, we would be remiss in not indicating initially that we have been greatly influenced by the work of Don Patinkin and Martin Bailey. Furthermore, the work of Milton Friedman, too, is reflected in the text.

As is always the case in a textbook of this type, it could not have appeared in its present form without the aid of many friends and colleagues. To professors Ansel M. Sharp of Oklahoma State University, Dennis R. Starleaf of Iowa State University, Jack L. Robinson and J. Kirker Stephens of the University of Oklahoma, and Stephen L. McDonald of the University of Texas at Austin we extend our thanks. These gentlemen reviewed the material at various stages and convinced us to leave our pet hobby horses on several occasions. Errors of omission and commission are, however, the responsibility of the authors. We extend our thanks also to LaNell Osburn and Peggy Alessio, without whose secretarial support the manuscript never would have been completed. Finally, Eugene DeGiorgio was a capable assistant in putting together the index.

December 1973
RICHARD A. BILAS
FRANK J. ALESSIO

Contents

1. **Introduction** 1

   What is macroeconomic theory? Why study macroeconomic theory? The approach of this book. What to expect in this book.

2. **Some national income accounting** 7

   Two approaches to the measurement of national product. The notion of value added. Net versus gross investment. The calculation of gross and net national products in the United States. National income, personal income, and disposable personal income. Current and constant gross national product. Price indexes. Some weaknesses of price indexes. Interpreting the national income accounts.

3. **Equilibrium analysis** 24

   Simple macroeconomic equilibrium. The stability of simple equilibrium. A more complicated look at equilibrium—A view ahead.

4. **The simple mechanics of income determination** 31

   A simple model of income determination. The simple multiplier. Temporary and permanent expansions. Deflationary, expansionary, and inflationary gaps.

5. **The level of consumption** 54

   The historical record. Classical and Keynesian theory. Three theories of the consumption function: *Absolute Income Theory. Relative Income Theory. Permanent Income Theory.* Other factors.

6. **The level of investment** 76

   Investment and the rate of interest. Investment and the level of national income. Investment and the change in the level of income. Investment

x   Contents

and the wage rate. Technology and the level of investment. Some empirical evidence.

7. **The role of the government** 95

The historical perspective. The role of the government sector in raising the level of income. The balanced budget multiplier. Multipliers with constant tax receipts. Tax receipts fluctuating with income.

8. **Money and the rate of interest** 117

The transaction-precautionary demand for money. The speculative demand for money. The total demand for money. Some empirical evidence. The supply curve of money. Money market equilibrium.

9. **The goods and services sector and the money market combined** 135

The *IS* curve. The *LM* curve. Equilibrium revisited. Changes in equilibrium—Fiscal policy. Changes in equilibrium—Monetary policy. Changes in equilibrium—Other policies.

10. **The price level** 153

The price level and the expenditures sector. The price level and the monetary sector. The price level as a variable in the monetary sector.

11. **The employment sector—Equilibrium reestablished** 164

The employment sector. Walras' law and equilibrium. Disturbances to equilibrium.

12. **The rate of interest: Real or monetary?** 182

The employment and expenditure sectors are self-contained. The interest rate as a real phenomenon. The interest rate as a monetary phenomenon. The interest rate as a real and a monetary phenomenon.

13. **Additions to the model—The real balance effect** 190

The real balance effect and the level of consumption. The real balance effect and the employment sector. Real balances and the monetary sector. A digression on Say's law.

14. **Some further additions to the model** 203

Consumption and the rate of interest. Real investment as a function of the level of real income. Real investment and the real wage rate. The bonds market. A note on money creation.

15. **The international sector** 222

The import function. Fixed and flexible exchange rates. Adjustment with a fixed exchange rate. Adjustment with a flexible exchange rate.

Contents   xi

16. **Aggregate supply**   236

The relationship between real output and the price level. An alternative approach to aggregate demand. Aggregate demand and aggregate supply combined. The employment function. The relationship between real output, the price level, and aggregate demand.

17. **Inflation**   257

Demand-pull inflation. Cost-push inflation. Employment and the price level. Inflationary equilibrium. The effects of inflation.

18. **Keynesian and Classical economics: The fundamental difference**   273

The wage stop. The quantity theory of money. The Monetarist—Neo-Keynesian controversy.

19. **Some growth economics**   291

The required rate of investment. The warranted rate of growth. Some general comments on growth models. Neoclassical growth theory. Economic growth and technical progress.

20. **A view of macroeconomic policy**   310

Fiscal policy. Monetary policy. Wage and price controls. Fiscal lags, monetary lags, and fine tuning.

Selected references   329

Index   337

1 Introduction

THERE are two basic branches of economic analysis. One branch deals, in the main, with the theory of individual economic units and is usually called *microeconomic theory*. The second branch deals with broad economic aggregates and is usually called *macroeconomic theory*. While microeconomics deals with the problems of allocation and distribution, macroeconomics deals with the determination of the level of national income. We will deal exclusively with the theory of income determination in this volume.

WHAT IS MACROECONOMIC THEORY?

Macroeconomic theory attempts to explain, analyze, and examine the interrelationships between such variables as output, employment, interest, money, and prices. These are the key variables that determine the level of economic activity, and the level of national income, in a society. Therefore, macroeconomic theory analyzes the performance of the economy as a whole.

In the final analysis we will be examining the problems of inflation, unemployment, and growth. We will not be dealing with the problems of a single firm, a single worker, or a single consumer. Instead, we will be examining the problems of broad—aggregate—sectors of the economy: consumption, investment, government spending and taxing, and monetary policy. We will not be dealing with the problems of a poor family alone. Instead, we will be examining the problem of raising the level of income for the economy as a whole. We will not be dealing with the selection of an appropriate price to charge for a single product. Instead, we will be examining the price level, how it changes, and the effects of these changes. We will not be dealing with the selection of the appropriate amount of labor to hire in the production of a particular product. Instead, we will be looking at the level of employment for society as a whole.

It is interesting to note that macroeconomics differs significantly from the other branch of economic analysis—microeconomics. Those factors which microeconomics generally takes as given, macroeconomics views as important variables. For example, in microeconomics it is generally assumed that the level of total output of society is given. In macroeconomics, this is a value to be determined. What is taken as given in macroeconomics is that which is to be determined in microeconomics. For example, in macroeconomics it is usually assumed that the distribution of output is given, while in microeconomics this is something to be determined. The emphasis in macroeconomics is quite different from the emphasis in microeconomics.

This is not to say that we can always make such a sharp distinction between macroeconomics and microeconomics. From a macroeconomic point of view, society is better off as the level of output increases and the level of employment increases. That is to say, as society approaches the point of full capacity—the point at which all resources available are fully utilized—it is better off. From the point of view of microeconomics, society is better off when resources are allocated optimally given full capacity. Hence, we must talk of both full capacity and optimum allocation.

Whereas a relatively simple distinction can be made between microeconomics and macroeconomics, there is a distinction within the framework of macroeconomics that is less simple, more important, and somewhat controversial. It is the distinction between Classical macroeconomic theory and Keynesian macroeconomic theory—each with its own model of income determination. We will view both Keynesian and Classical models. Although there are some similarities in the two types of models, you will see that there are such significant differences that accepting one usually implies the rejection of the other.

Most of our task, however, will be concerned with two macroeconomic questions. What influences and determines the level of prices and hence the value of money? What is the relationship between money, employment, output, and production? We will look at these questions from both the Keynesian and Classical points of view, and note the differences and similarities of the two approaches.

WHY STUDY MACROECONOMIC THEORY?

It is one thing for us to answer the question of what is macroeconomic theory; it is another thing, and probably more important to our readers, for us to answer the question of why we study macroeconomic theory. The answer is simple. We study macroeconomic theory in the hope of discovering means to improve our standard of living: raising the levels of income and employment, and stabilizing price inflation. We study macroeconomic theory to understand why the level of unemployment is as high as 25 percent of the labor force, as it was in the United States during 1933, or as low as 3.5 percent, as it was during 1969. We study macroeconomic theory to understand why prices are rising by as much as 7 percent per annum during 1970, or by as little as 1 percent during 1962. We study macroeconomic theory to understand why national income is growing as rapidly as 4 percent per annum during 1964, or as slowly as 2.7 percent per annum during 1971. Thus, we study macroeconomic theory to understand and explain what causes the changes in these basic economic conditions.

Even though understanding the causes of changes in basic economic conditions is an important reason for studying macroeconomic theory, it is not the only reason. An equally important reason is the formation of *macroeconomic policy*. Once we determine the forces or variables, such as the money supply, which precipitate changes in economic conditions, these variables become policy tools that can be used to alter economic conditions in predictable ways. In other words, macroeconomic theory tells us not only what causes changes in economic activity, but also how economic activity can be influenced, changed, and controlled through overt macroeconomic policy. Therefore, we study macroeconomic theory to discover how to reduce the level of unemployment, to reduce the rate of price inflation, and to raise the rate of growth in national income. Actions which are designed to produce these changes in unemployment, price inflation, and income are labeled macroeconomic policy. Effective macroeconomic policy cannot be formulated without understanding the essentials of macroeconomic theory.

THE APPROACH OF THIS BOOK

Our goal—simply defined—will be to understand the circular flow of goods and services shown in Figure 1–1. In the upper portion of

FIGURE 1–1

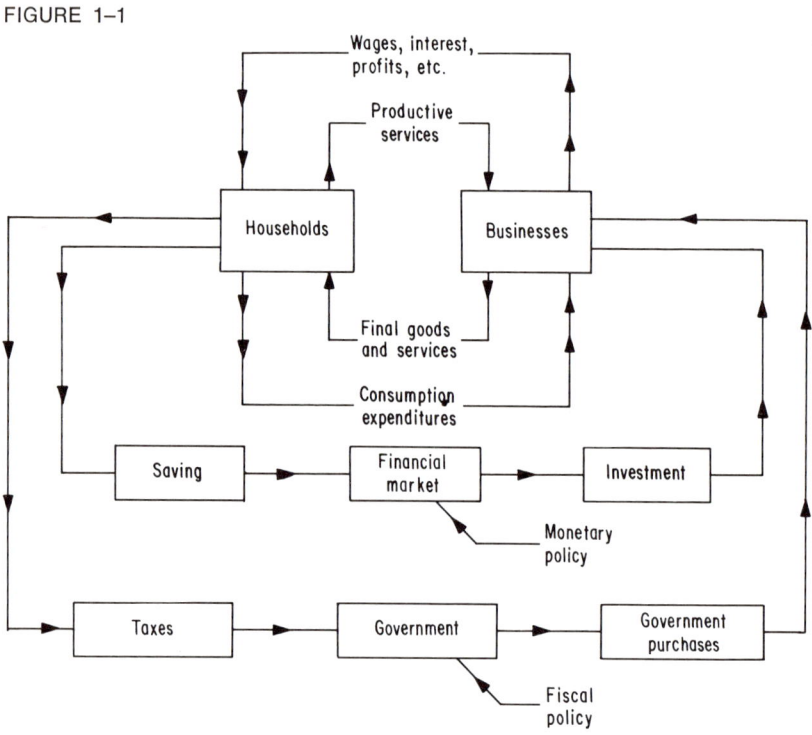

the figure, we note that the incomes of the households come from business firms in return for productive services necessary to produce final goods and services. These incomes, in the aggregate, interestingly make up the national income. We will not be so much concerned with this upper portion of the circular flow. However, we will refer to it again in the next chapter when the essentials of national income accounting are reviewed.

In the lower portion of the figure, we note that consumption expenditures flow from households to businesses. In return, the households receive final goods and services. Households receive the output of the firms. Furthermore, we note that not all household income is spent on final goods and services. Some of the income is saved, channeled through the financial market—banks and other financial institutions—and lent to business firms to finance investment expenditures. Also, we note that some of the household income is paid to the government as taxes, and is respent by the government on goods and services from the business sector. Finally, in the lower portion of the figure, we note that macroeconomic policy—in the form of *monetary policy*—influences the flow of saving into investment, and macroeconomic policy—in the form of *fiscal policy*—influences the flow of household tax payments into government expenditures. In this book we will not be concerned with the composition of these flows, but rather with the size of the flows.

We may view the circular flow of goods and services in two manners. We may employ *partial equilibrium analysis,* or we may employ *aggregate equilibrium analysis*. Partial equilibrium analysis deals with individual markets and will be used occasionally in this volume. However, most emphasis will be placed on aggregate equilibrium analysis. Aggregate equilibrium analysis deals with interrelated markets or sectors and reflects the high degree of interdependence in an economic system. We will attempt to stress the important interdependence between output, employment, the price level, the rate of interest, and the supply of money.

It is more or less traditional to study economic theory in a static sense. That is to say, one usually assumes that all forces affecting a variable do so at the same point in time. For the most part we will employ this method of analysis. Thus, we will look at the value of variables at various points in time and will compare these values over time. However, in general, we will not view the time path of these variables. That is to say, we will not note how the values of the variables change over time. The movement of the values of variables over time is in the realm of dynamic analysis. To be sure, we will at several points view dynamic analysis, but the primary emphasis will be on static analysis.

WHAT TO EXPECT IN THIS BOOK

In this volume we will attempt to view the determination of the level of economic activity. To do so, we will look primarily at three sectors of the economy. We will look first at the goods and services or expenditure sector. We will then shift our attention to the money market or the monetary sector. Finally, we will look at the employment sector or the labor market. Throughout the analysis (of these three sectors), we will attempt to make meaningful policy suggestions based on economic theory. In addition to our view of these three sectors, we shall also look at such topics as inflation, growth, and unemployment. Finally, we will attempt to compare Keynesian and Classical models.

Before entering into a discussion of macroeconomic theory, however, it is first necessary to examine some fundamental concepts. In Chapter 2, therefore, we will look at some national income accounting to gain an insight into the concepts of income, output, and the price level. In Chapter 3 we will discuss briefly the idea of macroeconomic equilibrium. With this material behind us, we will then be able to discuss macroeconomic theory in a more meaningful manner. Thus, we now turn to the concepts of income and output and the circular flow of Figure 1–1.

2 Some national income accounting

SINCE MACROECONOMIC ANALYSIS studies the determination of the level of income, one major element in this branch of economic theory is the definition of national income. National income is a rather loose term that is often defined as the money value of all final goods and services produced by an economy during a given period of time. The various measures of "national income" or "national product" are *gross national product, net national product, national income, personal income, and disposable personal income*. In this chapter, we shall examine these national income accounts.

TWO APPROACHES TO THE MEASUREMENT OF NATIONAL PRODUCT

We begin our examination of these national income concepts by attempting to measure net national product (NNP) by the *flow-of-product approach*. Please examine the lower part of Figure 1–1 of the previous chapter. When discussing Figure 1–1, we noted that money flowed from households to business firms in exchange for goods and services. These consumption expenditures are part of the net national product of the economy. They represent, for example, the dollar value of the consumption of oranges, bread, beer, income tax services, and so on purchased by the public during the accounting period. However, we also noted that households often think in terms of future consumption (i.e., saving) as well as current consumption. That is to say, individuals often devote part of their income to saving and investment. Consequently, instead of drinking beer now they may wish to save the "beer money" and invest it in the necessary equipment to help produce more beer for future consumption. In this manner, households not only engage in current consumption activities, but they also engage in future consumption or saving; and finance net investment. Thus, we may say that net national product is the sum total of consumption expenditures plus net investment expenditures. These net investment expenditures may take the form of equipment, buildings, or even inventories to be used for future consumption.

In addition to consumption and net investment expenditures by households and businesses, we must also include expenditures for goods and services on the part of the government—state, local, and federal. In one sense, these are expenditures that would have been made by households in the absence of a government sector. Thus, we include in net national product all government payroll expenditures plus the goods and services that governments purchase from private industry.

Finally, we note that not all purchases of goods and services in this country are made by nationals of this country, and not all purchases made by us are for goods and services produced in this country. Purchases of our goods and services by foreign nationals are called exports, while our purchases of foreign goods and services are called imports. Since exports represent the sale of domestically produced commodities, they are added to net national product. Since imports represent the purchase of foreign-produced commodities, they are subtracted from net national product (after all, we did not produce those goods and services). Hence, we speak of a *net foreign balance* which is, in the simplest sense, exports less imports.

Thus, we arrive at a measure of expenditures on final goods and services called net national product which is simply consumption expenditures plus net investment plus government expenditures on goods and services plus the net foreign balance. This is what we really mean by the consumption expenditures in the lower portion of Figure 1–1.

Rather than look at the *flow-of-product approach,* we may also look at the *income or earnings approach* to the measurement of net national product. To do this please examine the upper part of Figure 1–1. In that portion of the figure, productive services flowed from households to business firms in return for wages, interest, profits, and so forth. The sum of wages, interest, profits, and so on that flow from the business firms is the total cost of the output produced by businesses. Since these costs are paid to the public, they are the earnings of the factors of production used to produce the output consumed by the households. Wages represent the return to labor, interest the return to capital, rent the return to land, and profits the return to the entrepreneur for taking a risk. That which is left over after all payments have been made to labor, land, and capital is profit. Thus, we may say that net national product may also be defined as the total factor earnings that are the costs of producing society's final goods and services during a given period of time.[1]

We now have two ways of measuring net national product, and both yield the same result. The income of a society during a given accounting period consists of the goods and services produced by it during that period. For every dollar of current output there is a dollar claim upon the output created. If total claims on producers during the production process are less than the value of output, the residual is profit—the return to the entrepreneur. Thus, we may say that total income and total net product are the same thing looked at from two different points of view. The income approach uses the upper portion of Figure 1–1, while the flow-of-product approach uses the lower portion of the figure.

THE NOTION OF VALUE ADDED

The problem of measuring the dollar value of final goods and services is rather complicated since the final output of one firm may well become the input for another firm. Consequently, if we simply took all final products and added their values together we would have overstated total final output because of the many intermediate products included. We would be guilty of double counting if we used such a procedure. To eliminate this double counting, we use the "value added" approach.

The concept of value added is most easily explained with the aid of a simple example. Suppose that we consider a simple economic system which produces only bread. This system produces all the necessary ingredients for the production of bread, but the only final product it produces is bread. We assume that there are four parts to the pro-

---
[1] This measure of net national product is a bit naïve. As we will see presently, we must include indirect business taxes in the measure of net national product.

duction process. First wheat is produced, then flour, then dough, and finally bread. Table 2–1 provides a numerical example. Wheat is produced and sold to the flour maker for $4. Since there was no production prior to that of wheat, the wheat producer added value of $4

TABLE 2–1

Production process	Sales		Cost of intermediate goods		Value added (wages, rents, etc.)
Wheat.......	$ 4	–	$ 0	=	$ 4
Flour.......	6	–	4	=	2
Dough	12	–	6	=	6
Bread.......	20	–	12	=	8
	42	–	22	=	20

to society's output: The value added by the wheat producer is $4. When the flour maker finishes his work, he sells the flour to the dough maker for $6. The flour maker paid $4 for the wheat, and sold the flour to the dough maker for $6. The value added by the flour maker is $2. When the dough maker finishes with the flour, he sells his product to the bread maker for $12: The value added by the dough maker is $6. The bread maker works the dough and produces $20 worth of bread: The value added by the bread maker is $8.

Total sales is $42; but this includes many intermediate products and, thereby, represents more than final products alone. Indeed, the $42 represents the value of *all* output produced. If we subtract from $42 the cost of intermediate goods, we have the value of all final goods or $20. Naturally, in our example, this $20 is the sales of bread. In this simple economy, the sum of all the values added, equals the value of all final output. Thus, if we add the values added of the wheat producer, the flour maker, the dough maker, and the bread maker, we also arrive at $20—the final value of goods and services.

To avoid double counting a value added approach must be employed. It is possible when using the flow-of-product approach to consider only final goods and services, but, when the earnings or income approach is used, the compilation of net national product requires that the value added approach be used. Also, by this approach, the statistician does not include the purchases of materials and services from other firms because those dollars will get properly counted in net national product from the income statements of the other firms.

NET VERSUS GROSS INVESTMENT

Thus far we have been talking about net national product and, as such, we are able to consider only net investment—investment required to produce more in the future. However, there is also investment necessary to replace worn-out capital equipment—replacement investment. Gross investment, therefore, represents not only new investment but also all replacement investment.

Since the difference between gross investment and net investment is replacement, and since replacement investment equals depreciation or capital consumption allowances, gross national product (GNP) is therefore net national product plus the capital consumption allowances.

According to accounting convention, capital consumption allowances not only consider depreciation but they also consider the decline in money value of capital assets due to obsolescence. For national income purposes we only wish to consider depreciation and not obsolescence. Thus, we must understand that since capital consumption allowances are an overstatement of depreciation, net national product will be an understatement if we merely subtract capital consumption allowances from gross national product. National income accounting usually does not correct this discrepancy.

THE CALCULATION OF GROSS AND NET NATIONAL PRODUCTS IN THE UNITED STATES

With the use of Table 2–2, we may look at a calculation of national output in the United States in 1970. Figures are in billions of dollars, and are presented in the table in the form of the earnings approach only.

Please examine Table 2–2 closely. Wages and other supplements include the employer's contribution to social insurance. Corporate profits are comprised of dividends, taxes on the profits, those profits which are not distributed to shareholders, and an inventory adjustment factor. The inventory adjustment is simply a means whereby profits during the year are adjusted for price changes during the year. They are windfall gains or losses, not production gains or losses. Finally, indirect business taxes have been entered since these are sales and excise taxes that can be passed onto the consumer. For example, a firm may produce a product which it would normally sell for $1.

TABLE 2-2*

Wages and other employee supplements		$599.8
Net interest		33.5
Rent income of persons		22.7
Indirect business taxes		92.1
Income of unincorporated enterprises		67.6
Corporate profits before taxes		76.5
Dividends	$25.2	
Undistributed profits	18.6	
Corporate profits taxes	37.6	
Inventory valuation adjustment	−4.8	
Net National Product		892.2
Capital consumption allowances	84.3	
Gross National Product		976.5

* In billions of dollars.
Source: *Federal Reserve Bulletin*.

The production of this item creates an equal amount of wages, rent, interest, and profits. If the government places a 5 percent sales tax on the item, the seller will simply add 5 percent to the price of the product. Thus, the price of the item will be $1.05. This five cents must be paid out to the government and, in this sense, it is not earned income by any of the factors of production. However, it must be considered in the determination of the level of national output, since the tax is used in the determination of market prices.

We may also look at a calculation of national output in the form of the flow-of-product approach. Table 2–3 shows these calculations for 1970. The sum of these expenditures is the same as the sums given in Table 2–2. The two approaches yield the same measure. We do indeed have two different methods of measuring net national product and gross national product.

TABLE 2-3*

Personal consumption		$616.7
Durable goods	$ 89.4	
Nondurable goods	264.7	
Services	262.6	
Government purchases of goods and services		220.5
Net private domestic investment		51.4
Net foreign investment		3.6
Net National Product		892.2
Capital consumption allowance	84.3	
Gross National Product		976.5

* In billions of dollars.
Source: Federal Reserve Bulletin

NATIONAL INCOME, PERSONAL INCOME, AND DISPOSABLE PERSONAL INCOME

As was mentioned earlier, there are other measures of national output or income. We have seen the difference between gross national product and net national product. We must now perform a few manipulations on net national product to develop other measures of national product.

National income (also called national product at factor cost) represents net national product with indirect taxes and business transfers removed. Business transfer payments are those payments which are not current production expenses. Typically, business transfer payments are in the form of a "reserve for bad debts" or a "reserve for gifts to nonprofit institutions, and individuals." One example of a business transfer payment is the cash prize awarded by a corporation for promotional purposes (e.g., The Readers Digest's Sweepstakes). Even though the prize money is a current business expense, it is not a payment to a factor of production. Neither indirect business taxes nor business transfer payments are payments to factors of production, and, therefore, are not part of factor cost. Likewise, any surplus (profit) earned by government enterprises (government agencies which sell their output of goods and services to cover a substantial part of their operating expenses) plus any subsidies received by them must be removed from net national product to arrive at national income. In 1970, with net national product at $892.2 billion, national income was $800.1 billion. We have seen (Table 2–2) that indirect business taxes were $92.1 billion. Business transfer payments were $3.6 billion. The surplus of government enterprises less subsidies was $ − 1.8 billion and there was a statistical discrepancy of $−1.8 billion.[2] Thus, by subtracting $92.1, $3.6, and $−1.8 from net national produce, we arrive at national income.

Another measure is personal income. Personal income is a measure of the income received by households. It is national income less the contributions made to the social security system by individuals, less corporate income taxes, less undistributed corporate profits, plus any government and business transfer payments (workmen's compensation, for example). In 1970, the level of personal income in the United

---

[2] This discrepancy is due to the two different ways of calculating net national product.

States was $801 billion.[3] Note that we include business transfer payments since the "reserve for bad debts" and the "reserve for gifts" represent personal income to someone.

Disposable personal income measures the amount of personal income that is available for expenditures. It equals personal income less personal taxes. In 1970, personal taxes were $116.3 billion, so disposable personal income was $684.8 billion. Personal outlays such as personal consumption expenditures and consumer interest payments amounted to $634.6 billion in 1970, so the residual of $50.2 billion must be personal savings.

Obviously, we have not toiled through the national income accounts just for the fun of it. Instead, we have examined all the various measures of national income because the exercise leads to a crucial economic relationship which we will use time and time again in subsequent chapters. In the preceding paragraph, we noted that the part of disposable personal income that is not used for consumption expenditures (ignoring consumer interest payments) is savings. Therefore, we conclude that the part of current income not consumed is saved, or:

(2.1) $$Y - C = S,$$

where Y is some measure of national income (e.g., gross national product or disposable personal income), C is consumption, and S is savings. Equation (2.1) represents an important accounting identity, and an important economic relationship, and we will return to it throughout this book.

In Figure 2–1, we have summarized the material covered in the previous sections. The column on the extreme left-hand side of the figure represents gross national product. Subtracting capital consumption allowances, we arrive at net national product which appears in the second column from the left. We note that the difference between gross national product and net national product is the same as the difference between gross investment and net investment. To arrive at national income, we subtract indirect business taxes. The third column then, represents national income and we have indicated those items of importance which when added together will determine national income. These items are wages, interest, rents, proprietor's income (income of unincorporated enterprises), and corporate profits.

---

[3] Usually personal income is less than national income. The year 1970 was somewhat exceptional in this respect.

2 / Some national income accounting 15

FIGURE 2-1

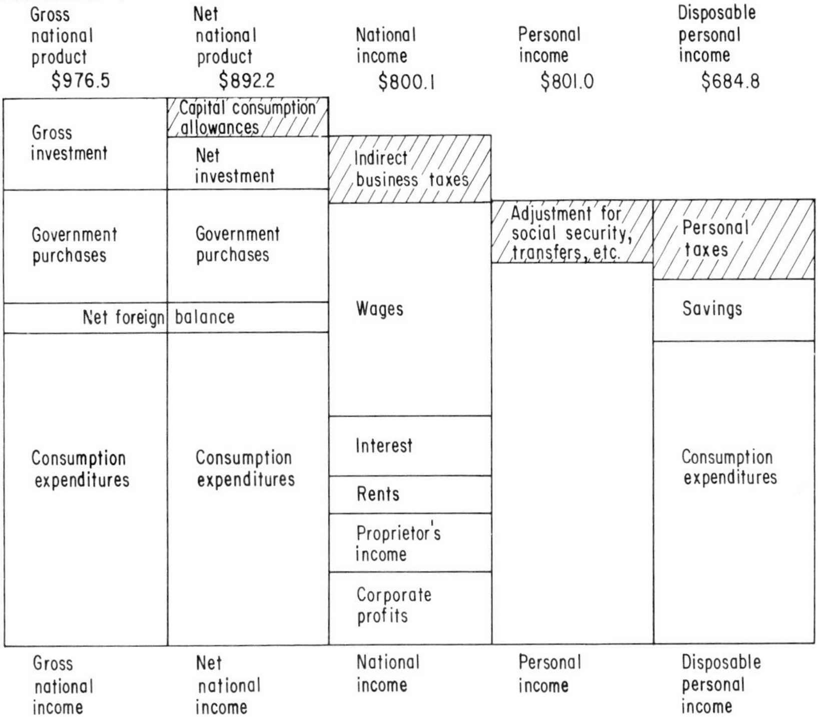

Gross national product $976.5	Net national product $892.2	National income $800.1	Personal income $801.0	Disposable personal income $684.8
Gross investment	Capital consumption allowances			
	Net investment	Indirect business taxes		
Government purchases	Government purchases		Adjustment for social security, transfers, etc.	Personal taxes
Net foreign balance		Wages		Savings
Consumption expenditures	Consumption expenditures	Interest		Consumption expenditures
		Rents		
		Proprietor's income		
		Corporate profits		
Gross national income	Net national income	National income	Personal income	Disposable personal income

In the fourth column from the left, we have determined personal income. To arrive at personal income from national income, we subtract corporate taxes, social security contributions, and undistributed corporate profits. We then add in transfers. To attain the final column—disposable personal income—we subtract personal taxes. We note, in the final box, that disposable personal income is made up of savings and consumption expenditures. These consumption expenditures have, in effect, been carried along from the first box on the left-hand side.

CURRENT AND CONSTANT GROSS NATIONAL PRODUCT

We have seen that the value of final production in the economy, or gross national product as we have defined it, is equal to the sum of all expenditures on final goods and services during an accounting

16   The essentials of macroeconomic analysis

year. In other words, gross national product is the *dollar* value of all final goods and services produced in the economy, with each unit of final output valued at its current market price. Thus, when we say that the gross national product for the United States for 1970 is $976.5 billion, we have identified *GNP valued in current dollars* (at current market prices).

Suppose that we could look into the future. Specifically, suppose that we predict—with absolute certainty—that GNP for the United States for 1984 is to be $1,952.4 billion. In other words, GNP is expected to double over the 14 years. What does it mean? In what sense has GNP doubled? Has the economy produced twice as many final goods and services in 1984 as it did in 1970? Or has the market price of each unit of final output doubled over the time span? Either the increase in the number of goods and services produced, or the increase in the market price of each unit of output produces a doubling of GNP in current dollars. This happens because there are two components in the valuation of GNP: the number of units of each output produced, and the market price of each unit of output.

The point can be made clear with the use of a simple example. Assume that the economy produces only four goods, with a specified quantity (Q_a, Q_b, Q_c, Q_d) and current market price (P_a, P_b, P_c, P_d) for each. GNP in current dollars would equal:

(2.2) $GNP = P_a \times Q_a + P_b \times Q_b + P_c \times Q_c + P_d \times Q_d,$

since this summation is nothing more than the dollar value of all final goods produced. By our calculations, GNP for 1970 equaled:

(2.3) $GNP(1970) = P_a(1970) \times Q_a(1970) \times P_b(1970) \times Q_b(1970)$
$+ P_c(1970) \times Q_c(1970) + P_d(1970)$
$\times Q_d(1970) = \$976.5$

and GNP for 1984 is predicted at:

(2.4) $GNP(1984) = P_a(1984) \times Q_a(1984) + P_b(1984) \times Q_b(1984)$
$+ P_c(1984) \times Q_c(1984) + P_d(1984)$
$\times Q_d(1984) = \$1,952.4.$

After some thought, it seems quite probable that the increase in GNP over the 14-year period would be the result of combined increases in final output (the Qs for 1984 are expected to be larger than those for 1970) and increases in market prices (the Ps for 1984 are expected to be larger than those for 1970). Therefore, since the *P*s have risen as well as the *Q*s, the doubling of GNP cannot be viewed as a doubling of the quantity of final goods produced. It is only a doubling of the dollar value of final goods.

What has been the increase in the number of final goods produced? When we have answered this question, we will have identified *GNP valued in constant dollars* (at constant market prices). And we will have identified the increase in *real* production in the economy: the change in the *Q*s alone. We will have eliminated the influence of price inflation on the measure of GNP. The result—GNP in constant dollars—is a truer measure of the volume (value) of final goods and services produced in the economy.

PRICE INDEXES

To make the adjustment from a current dollar to a constant dollar value of GNP, we must construct a *price index* and "deflate" the current dollar measure of GNP. A price index is an "average" price: not the price of a single good or service, but the average price of all goods and services used in the analysis. Unfortunately, constructing a price index is not a simple task. It is difficult because the prices of different commodities change over time by different amounts—prices do not change proportionately, some rise by 10 percent while others rise by 20 percent while others may fall by 3 percent. A price index must account for all of the various changes in the prices of the various commodities.

It is difficult to construct a price index for a second reason. How do you weight the different commodities whose prices have changed by different amounts? For example, suppose that we look at two goods, A and B, whose prices have increased by 100 percent (from $0.05 to $0.10) and by 10 percent (from $0.20 to $0.22), respectively. The average price increase is 55 percent. If a consumer purchases some quantity of A but not B, his price level—his cost of living—has risen 100 percent. If he purchased B only, it would have risen 10 percent. If he had purchased one unit of each commodity, his price level would have increased by 28 percent. Calculate the change: $\frac{0.32 - 0.25}{0.25} = 0.28$. Thus, we see that the increase in the price index varies as the quantity of each commodity purchased varies. To calculate the true price index, each price change must be weighted by the quantity of the respective commodity purchased, as in our last example.

At this point, a simple exercise may clarify the notion and calculation of a price index. Examine Table 2–4. It lists the prices paid for

TABLE 2–4

Product	P_1	P_2	P_3	Q_1	$P_1 Q_1$	$P_2 Q_1$	$P_3 Q_1$
A	$0.05	$0.10	$0.05	5	$0.25	$0.50	$0.25
B	0.10	0.20	0.22	8	0.80	1.60	1.76
C	0.07	0.14	0.16	6	0.42	0.84	0.96
D	0.09	0.18	0.15	7	0.63	1.26	1.05
					$2.10	$4.20	$4.02

our four goods—A, B, C, and D—in three different time periods. It also lists the quantity of each good sold in the first time period, and the total dollars spent in each time period. Suppose that we wish to construct an index of prices based on Table 2–4 in order to show what has happened "on the average" to these prices over time. This is a problem similar to that facing the statisticians employed by the U.S. Bureau of Labor Statistics when they attempt to investigate changes in consumer prices with the use of the consumer price index, with one very important difference. When the Bureau of Labor Statistics estimates the consumer price index, it faces an economy composed of many more than four goods. Since it cannot quickly and accurately acquire data on the prices and quantities of all goods and services in the economy, the Bureau works with a representative "market basket" of commodities. It hopes that the increase in the price of this "basket" of commodities reflects the increase in the overall price level. In other words, from the market basket, the Bureau constructs a "representative" consumer price index.

Let us assume that our four products are a representative market basket. Prices in the first time period are given in the column labeled P_1, similarly for P_2 and P_3. It is a simple matter to compare prices in the first time period with those in the second time period. Since all prices have doubled, we may assume that the price level has doubled also. But it is not as simple to compare prices in the second time period with those in the third time period. Two prices have gone up, and two prices have gone down. Has the price level changed? Applying weights will yield an answer. To obtain the price index, we must weight each commodity by the quantity of that commodity sold. Remembering this, we proceed with our calculation of the price index.

During the first time period the total number of dollars spent on the four items was $2.10. In the second period the number of dollars spent doubled to $4.20. We would have expected this since all prices doubled. Thus, we may say:

$$(2.5) \qquad I_1 = \frac{\$2.10}{\$2.10} \times 100 = 100,$$

where I_1 is the price index in the first period, and

$$(2.6) \qquad I_2 = \frac{\$4.20}{\$2.10} \times 100 = 200,$$

where I_2 is the price index in the second period. Finally, the price index in the third period is:

$$(2.7) \qquad I_3 = \frac{4.02}{2.10} \times 100 = 191.$$

Prices fell in period three compared with period two, but they rose in period three compared with period one.

Now we can use our price index to deflate national income. The procedure is simple: divide the current dollar value of national income for the given year by the price index for that year. If the money value of national income (national income valued in current dollars) is $1,000 during the first time period, and stayed the same through the next two time periods, the real value of national income (national income valued in constant dollars) would fall during the second time period and rise (above its value in the second period) during the third time period. Calculating these changes we obtain:

$$(2.8) \qquad \text{GNP}_1 = \frac{1{,}000}{100} \times 100 = \$1{,}000,$$

$$(2.9) \qquad \text{GNP}_2 = \frac{1{,}000}{200} \times 100 = \$500,$$

$$(2.10) \qquad \text{GNP}_3 = \frac{1{,}000}{191} \times 100 = \$524.$$

Thus, even though money national income remained constant at $1,000 during the three time periods, the real value of national income changed. It fell, then it rose. As we noted earlier, national income valued in constant dollars gives a more useful measure of the performance of the economy than national income in current dollars.

Table 2–5 summarizes some recent data on GNP in both current and constant dollars.

TABLE 2–5

	GNP current (billions)	GNP constant (billions)
1955	$398.0	$438.0
1956	419.2	446.1
1957	441.1	452.5
1958	447.3	447.3
1959	483.7	475.9
1960	503.7	487.7
1961	520.1	497.2
1962	560.3	529.8
1963	590.5	551.0
1964	631.7	580.0
1965	681.2	614.4
1966	749.9	658.1
1967	793.9	675.2
1968	864.2	706.6
1969	929.1	724.7
1970	976.5	720.0

Source: *Federal Reserve Bulletin.*

SOME WEAKNESSES OF PRICES INDEXES

Price indexes are used not only to adjust GNP from current dollars to constant dollars, but they are also used independently to view the course of inflation (a rise in prices in general) or deflation (a fall in prices in general). Since several "official price indexes" are available (e.g., the consumer price index and the wholesale price index), care must be exercised in the choice of a price index. If our task were to measure the behavior of the price level of consumer goods, we would have little interest in using an index designed to measure costs in the construction industry. However, even with the choice of a consumer price index to measure behavior of the price level of consumer goods, additional care must be exercised. If we wish to measure cost of living changes for poor income families, we would not want to use an index which included items from the market basket consumed by upper middle-class families. Hence, some systematic effort must be made to include in the index only those items that are typical of the kinds of goods with which we are concerned.

These several problems are minor, however, compared to those problems which are inherent in the very nature of index numbers. Generally, index numbers have an upward bias. That is to say, index numbers tend to overstate price increases and understate price decreases. Hence, price indexes tend to overstate the magnitude of inflation. The reasons for the overstatement are simple. Almost all index numbers are constructed in the manner in which we constructed ours above. Suppose that we have two goods, each of equal importance, and we wish to construct an index. Suppose further that the price of one of these goods doubles in year 2 compared with year 1—the base year. Assume that the price of the other good is cut in half. We would expect no change in our price index. However, it can easily be shown that the price index in period 2 has risen relative to that of period 1. Using our method of constructing a price index, assuming that prices in the first period were $1 for each good, and assuming a weighting of unity for each commodity we obtain:

$$(2.11) \quad I_2 = \frac{1 \times 2 + 1 \times \frac{1}{2}}{1 \times 1 + 1 \times 1} \times 100 = \frac{2.5}{2} \times 100 = 125.$$

The method that we have used is basically that of constructing an arithmetic average and thus we obtain the upward bias. We could avoid this bias if we were to use the notion of a geometric average but this method is rather complicated and is seldom used.[4]

It should be clearly understood that in the construction of our index numbers we have used base year weights. Recall from Table 2–4 that we used quantities in the first period to serve as weights. This method will once again produce an upward bias in our index numbers. For example, if prices rise we can expect the consumer to consume relatively less of those products whose prices rose the most and relatively more of those products whose prices rose the least. Unfortunately, using base year weights we have attached too much importance to those products whose prices have risen most and too little importance

---

[4] If we were to use the geometric mean in this simple example we would have:

$$I_2 = \left[\sqrt{\frac{(1 \times 2)(1 \times \frac{1}{2})}{(1 \times 1)(1 \times 1)}} \right] 100 = 100.$$

This method would indeed yield the true change in the price level of the second period compared with the first period.

to those products whose prices have risen least. There is another source of upward bias. Of course, if given year weights were used the bias would be in the downward direction.

Implicit in our derivation of price indexes has been the idea that consumer's tastes remain unchanged over time. Such is hardly the case. By assuming tastes constant, however, we can say that price changes come about because of changing conditions on the supply side of the market. With changes on the supply side of the market, we can say unambiguously that lower prices will be associated with higher quantities and vice versa. Using base year weights, there is an upward bias in our index numbers. However, if we allow for changing tastes, then higher prices will usually be associated with larger quantities and so, with base year weights, there would be a downward bias in the index numbers. Since there are changes on both the supply and demand sides of any market, it is difficult to assess the direction of the bias at any point in time—but there will be a bias. Most economists seem to believe, by the way, that the "official" price indexes are biased upward by both the use of the arithmetic average type of construction and the base weight problem.

There are other possible reasons for the belief that the major price indexes have an upward bias. It is argued that adequate allowances for changes in quality are not made. The Bureau of Labor Statistics does make changes for improvements in quality which cause price changes, but they do not make changes for improvements in quality which are not reflected in price changes. A prime example is improved medical services. If improvements in medical care are not reflected in price changes, these improvements are not reflected in the consumer price index. For example, a shorter period of time to recover from an illness is not reflected in the price index despite the fact that this would represent a definite improvement in the quality of medical services.

Finally, there is said to be a bias connected with the introduction of new products. The Bureau of Labor Statistics does make substitutions of new products for old ones. The argument, however, is that there is too much delay in introducing these new products into the index. Hence, at a period of time during which the price of a new product is falling due to the introduction of mass-production techniques, it is left out of the index. However, during a period of time when price is rising due to increases in demand, the product is included. Thus, there is another source of upward bias.

How strong the biases in our index numbers really are is very difficult to determine. However, the biases do exist, and care should be used in putting too much faith on the story told by index numbers.

INTERPRETING THE NATIONAL INCOME ACCOUNTS

We will use the concepts of national income in all of the analysis that follows, but we must use them with caution, for the concepts of national income, especially gross national product and net national product, can be misleading. One reason that they are misleading is that they do not count all economic activity. Our discussion has assumed that all market transactions involving goods and services are included in the calculation of national income. The assumption is incorrect. Some market transactions are excluded. For example, sales of "used" goods and services are excluded from national income because they do not reflect production in the current year. Since they were included in national income when originally produced, including them again would be double counting. In addition, market transactions involving illegal transactions, such as dope peddling and illegal gambling, are excluded from national income because they have been "forbidden" by society. Finally, please recall that transfer payments are excluded from some measures of national income (gross national product, net national product, and national income), but included in other measures (personal income and disposable personal income). Why? Thus, the national income accounts exclude many of the economic transactions which occur during the year.

Dollar measures of national income are misleading for another and possibly more important reason. Although national income accounting tells us something about the *quantity* of goods and services produced in the economy, it tells us little about the *quality* of life in the economy. GNP, for example, includes the production of undesirable goods as well as desirable goods. It includes expenditures on such undesirables as junk mail, napalm, billboards, and television commercials. Furthermore, it neglects the disagreeable by-products of our industrialized society—pollution, congestion, and noise. Although these may not be undesirable or disagreeable to all members of our society, their production and presence increases the frustration and misery of many people. Our point is simply that national income accounting does not account for any of the misery or frustration.[5]

Please be cautious when using the concepts of national income.

---

[5] For an interesting discussion of this point, see "Measuring the Quality of Life," *The Wall Street Journal,* May 18, 1972.

3 Equilibrium analysis

EQUILIBRIUM is usually defined in economics as a position of rest, or as a state of balance between opposing forces, or as a state requiring no change over time. Consequently, in equilibrium, there are no forces at work which would change the values assigned to the variables in the problem. Every time period is an exact duplicate of the previous time period. Conversely, disequilibrium is usually defined in economics as a position of change, or as a state of imbalance between opposing forces, or as a state requiring change over time. Each successive time period differs from the preceding time period. Our analysis is essentially equilibrium analysis. We will view equilibria, examine and describe their characteristics.

SIMPLE MACROECONOMIC EQUILIBRIUM

At the core of macroeconomic analysis are the questions: What determines movements in the level of national income: What determines the equilibrium level of national income? Before we can answer these questions completely, we must understand the concept of *macroeconomic equilibrium*.[1]

Suppose that we have an economy comprised of two decision-making units, consumers and producers. In this simplified economy, the

---

[1] An excellent discussion of the concept of equilibrium can be found in F. Machlup, "Equilibrium and Disequilibrium: Misplaced Concreteness and Disguised Politics," *Economic Journal,* March 1958, pp. 1–24.

consumers, households and individuals, make all the consumption decisions, while producers make all the investment decisions. Obviously, these assumptions are unrealistic. Businesses as well as households consume and save; households as well as businesses invest. Nevertheless, it is analytically simpler to make the artificial separation. It will not affect the results of our analysis.

The necessary condition for each group to establish equilibrium independent of the other group is easily stated. For consumers (savers) to be in equilibrium, they must actually consume (save) the amount that they intended to consume (save). Thus, equilibrium among consumers (savers) requires:

(3.1)
intended S = actual S, or
ex ante S = *ex post* S, or
planned S = unplanned S,

where S represents savings. For producers (investors) to be in equilibrium, they must actually invest the amount that they intended to invest. Equilibrium among producers (investors) requires:

(3.2)
intended I = actual I, or
ex ante I = *ex post* I, or
planned I = unplanned I,

where I represents investment.

What do these equilibrium conditions mean? How are the terms defined? From the previous chapter, we know that savings is defined as that portion of income which is not consumed. It is the portion of current income which is stored or held in some fashion. Usually, it is held in the form of real and financial assets: real estate, bank accounts, stocks, and bonds. It is held in order to earn interest income and capital gains, or as a reserve against unforeseen contingencies. Investment is the purchase of a capital good which is to be used to produce other goods and services. Usually, investment expenditures are purchases of machinery and other equipment; but they are also defined to include residential and nonresidential construction expenditures (because they produce a future stream of services), and net changes in business inventories (because they are available to be sold during future time periods).

We saw in Figure 1–1 of Chapter 1 that investment expenditures must be financed out of current savings. The dollar value of investment expenditures actually made during the time period must equal the dollar value of actual savings. The equality occurs because both actual savings and actual investment equal the portion of income that is not spent on consumption. Do not misunderstand. The statement that the dollar values of savings and investment are equal does not mean that savings and investment are identical conceptually. They are not, even though most people treat them as identical. Remember that an act of saving is the purchase of a capital asset to be used as a store of wealth. Whereas, an act of investment is the purchase of a capital asset to be used as a factor of production. For example, when an urbanite buys an acre of country land to hold in speculation of capital gains, he is saving. When a farmer buys an acre of country land to raise corn, he is investing. It is a narrow, but significant distinction.

From equations (3.1) and (3.2) and the fact that we defined savings and investment as equal in an *ex post* manner, we can develop an equilibrium condition for the economy as a whole. We know that:

(3.3) $$ex\ post\ I = ex\ post\ S.$$

Substituting equations (3.1) and (3.2) into (3.3) we obtain:

(3.4) $$ex\ ante\ S = ex\ ante\ I.$$

An economy is in equilibrium when intended savings equals intended investment. With a little work, the equilibrium condition given by equation (3.4) can be understood. Suppose that the level of national income is $50 billion: with households planning to consume $40 billion and planning to save $10 billion, and business firms planning to invest $5 billion. If household consumption plans are fulfilled (and there is no reason why they should go unfulfilled in our example), actual consumption will equal $40 billion and actual savings will be $10 billion. Since *ex post* savings and investment must be equal, actual investment is $10 billion. Households are in equilibrium but business firms are not. Business firms were forced to accumulate inventories in the amount of $5 billion, and were forced, thereby, to invest $5 billion more than they had intended. With $50 billion of national income, businesses expected households to consume $45 billion of goods and services, and therefore, produced $45 billion of output. However, households consumed only $40 billion. The difference, $5 billion, is the unintended accumulation of inventories or unintended investment. Since business firms were forced to invest more than they intended, they are not in equilibrium (reexamine equation

[3.2]). Thus, the economy is not in equilibrium because intended savings exceeds intended investment.

Suppose, on the other hand, that with the same intentions and the same level of income, *ex post* or actual savings equals $5 billion. Thus, *ex post* or actual investment is $5 billion. Producers are in equilibrium, but consumers are not since they are only saving $5 billion when they had intended to save $10 billion. Again, the economy is not in equilibrium because intended saving exceeds intended investment. Equilibrium for the economy requires that intended savings equals intended investment. It requires that both consumers (households) and producers (business firms) have their intentions fulfilled simultaneously. That is the sense of equation (3.4). Equation (3.4) is nothing more than a restatement of the definition of equilibrium given at the beginning of the chapter.

Since one sector can be in equilibrium while the other is not, we must inquire as to how intended savings and intended investment are brought into equality, and how the economy is brought into equilibrium. The economy is brought into equilibrium by changes in the level of national income, and this equilibrating process is what we will study throughout this volume.

THE STABILITY OF SIMPLE EQUILIBRIUM

Table 3–1 helps to explain how changes in the level of national income induce changes in intended (*ex ante*) savings and intended

TABLE 3–1*

National income	Consumption	Intended savings	Intended investment	Unintended investment or inventory change
$260	$220	$40	$10	$+30
230	200	30	10	+20
200	180	20	10	+10
170	160	10	10	0
140	140	0	10	−10

* In billions of dollars.

(*ex ante*) investment which, in turn, move the economy toward equilibrium. Assume that the level of intended investment remains constant at $10 billion, but that the level of intended savings changes as the level of income changes. Specifically, we assume that the level of intended savings increases with increases in income. The reason is simple: Since consumers have earned more income, they are likely to consume more and save more.[2] Using Table 3-1, suppose that the level of national income equals $260 billion and the level of intended savings equals $40 billion initially. Since intended savings is greater than intended investment, the economy is not in equilibrium. Indeed, $260 billion worth of output has been produced, but only $230 billion of it has been sold—$220 billion as consumption and $10 billion as intended investment. Consequently, inventories must increase by $30 billion. There is $30 billion of unintended investment. When inventories accumulate unintentionally, the level of output (production) is usually adjusted downward. As production declines, employment and income fall also. If national income falls to $230 billion and consumption to $200 billion, intended savings will decline—in our example—to $30 billion. There would still be an unintended increase in inventories of $20 billion, but the unintended accumulation is less than it was previously (by $10 billion). Nevertheless, intended savings still exceeds intended investment. There is still disequilibrium, but the disequilibrium is smaller than it was previously ($20 billion instead of $30 billion). Once again, production and employment and income decline. Intended savings declines, and the disequilibrium between savings and investment narrows. Each adjustment in income brings the economy closer to equilibrium. When national income has decreased to $170 billion, intended (*ex ante*) savings equals $10 billion and, thereby, equals intended (*ex ante*) investment. There is no additional accumulation of inventories—at least unintentionally. The economy has reached equilibrium.

What would happen if the initial level of national income had been $140 billion instead of $260 billion? There would be disequilibrium; but it would be characterized by underproduction rather than overproduction, intended investment would exceed intended savings. Production, employment, and income would rise until savings rose into equality with investment. Equilibrium would be restored.

The point to note is that there is always a movement toward the level of output at which the levels of intended savings and intended investment are equal. However, it is the change in the level of income that induces the change in the level of intended savings. Therefore,

---

[2] The specific relationship between savings and investment and income will not be discussed here. We will look at these relationships in the next chapters.

we say that the equality between savings and investment is brought about by changes in the level of income. Since the level of national income falls when intended savings is greater than intended investment causing savings to fall into equality with investment, and since national income rises when intended investment is greater than intended savings causing savings to rise into equality with investment, the economy always gropes toward the level of income at which intended savings equals intended investment. Therefore, we say that the equilibrium is stable.

A MORE COMPLICATED LOOK AT EQUILIBRIUM—A VIEW AHEAD

Our view of the equilibrating process was seriously oversimplified. We looked only at the consuming and investing sectors of the economy. By doing so, we have limited our analysis to the goods and services sector of the economy. We have been concerned only with the decision-making units which determine the level of goods and services in the economy. We have not considered the money market or the labor market. To be sure, for an economy to be in macroeconomic equilibrium, it is necessary that the level of intended savings and the level of intended investment be equal. This, however, means only that the goods and services, or expenditure, sector is in equilibrium.

The other sectors in the economy must also be in equilibrium for the economy to be in equilibrium. As we shall see, it is possible for the goods and services sector to be in equilibrium while another sector is not. Accordingly, the economy is not in equilibrium. We will examine the equilibrium characteristics of the other sectors in the coming chapters.

In those chapters, we will consider equilibrium in the money market. Since the level of the money supply influences the level of income as well as the level of consumption, it is necessary that we look closely at this market. Since labor is necessary to produce output and since labor receives income which is spent on the goods and services that have been produced, it is necessary that we look at the labor market in some detail. Finally, we will look at the bonds market—since bonds represent a substitute for money. While we will not pay as much attention to the bonds market as we will pay to the other sectors, you should not believe that it is less important than the others. Thus, we do admit that our analysis in this chapter has been naïve—purposely naïve—to look only at a single sector in a highly interdependent economic system. Our analysis in the chapters that follow will utilize a more complicated approach than that presented in this chapter.

CONCLUDING NOTE

Now that we have completed an introductory view of our economic system, we can proceed to build a macroeconomic model to determine the equilibrium level of national income. It is to this matter that we turn our attention in the next chapter.

4 The simple mechanics of income determination

IN THE PRECEDING CHAPTERS, we defined various items in the national income accounts and we discussed the concept of equilibrium. We will now develop some simple models which will determine equilibrium levels of national income. These simple models will relate the equilibrium level of national income to consumption, investment, and savings. We will later expand the models to include many more variables such as the rate of interest, the price level, the money supply, and the wage rate.

A SIMPLE MODEL OF INCOME DETERMINATION

Let us assume that consumption expenditures depend only on the level of income, or:

(4.1) $$C = C(Y).$$

Y may represent national income, net national product, gross national product, or disposable personal income. Let us assume a very simple economy in which disposable personal income and gross national product are identical. That is to say, we will consider a private closed economy. There is no government, no exports, and no imports. We will also assume that there is a direct relationship between income and consumption such that C increases as Y increases. We will, however, assume that although consumption increases as income increases, it does so by a smaller amount. Some of the increase in income is diverted to savings. Hence, we say:

(4.2) $$0 < \frac{\Delta C}{\Delta Y} < 1,$$

where $\frac{\Delta C}{\Delta Y}$ is called the *marginal propensity to consume* or the MPC. The MPC is the proportion of any increment in income which is diverted by individuals to consumption expenditures.

If we assume for simplicity a linear relationship between consumption and income, we may develop a linear consumption function:

(4.3) $$C = a + bY$$

where b is the marginal propensity to consume, and a is some positive number representing the level of consumption when the level of national income is zero. It should be intuitively clear that even at a zero level of national income there will be some positive level of consumption. In such circumstances, consumption expenditures will be financed from past savings. Thus, if $a = \$60$ billion and $b = \frac{3}{4}$, when the level of income is $300 billion, the level of consumption will be $285 billion. When income rises to $400 billion, the level of consumption increases to $360 billion. Note that the increase in income is $100 billion, but the increase in consumption is only $75 billion, or $\frac{3}{4}$ of $\Delta Y = \$100$ billion. Graphically, a linear consumption function is shown in Figure 4–1. In this figure, we measure consumption expenditures on the vertical axis and national income levels on the horizontal axis. The slope of the consumption function is $\frac{\Delta C}{\Delta Y}$ or b.

FIGURE 4–1

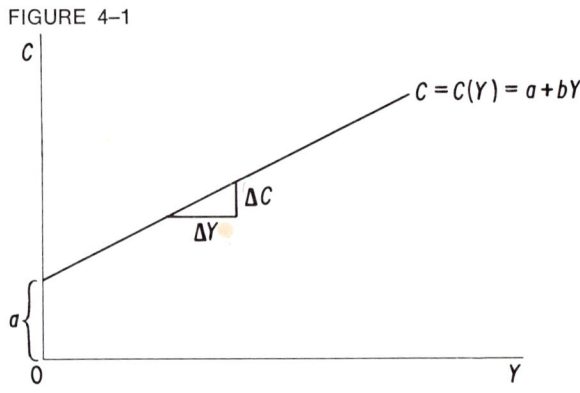

Suppose that we define the average propensity to consume (APC) as simply consumption divided by income or $C(Y)/Y$. If we assume a linear consumption function, we know that MPC is constant as the level of income changes, however, the APC falls as the level of income rises. This proposition may be demonstrated with the aid of Figure 4–2. For example, with income at the level Y_1, the average

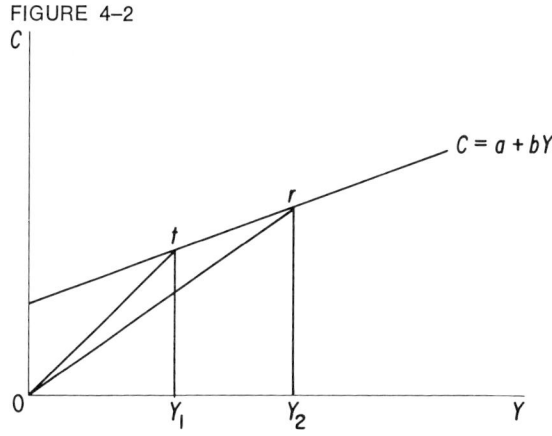

FIGURE 4–2

propensity to consume is $tY_1/0Y_1$ which is the slope of line $0t$. When the level of income increases to Y_2, APC becomes $rY_2/0Y_2$, or the slope of the line $0r$. Since the slope of $0r$ is less than the slope of $0t$, we note that APC falls as the level of income rises given a linear consumption function.

From an earlier discussion, we know that disposable personal income is comprised of consumption expenditures as well as savings. We can demonstrate this fact graphically in Figure 4–3. National income (disposable personal income in our simple economy) is plotted on the horizontal axis, consumption and savings (S) are plotted on the vertical axis. Since $Y = C + S$, the graph of this relationship must be represented by a straight line emanating from the origin at an angle of 45°.

Suppose that we superimpose Figure 4–1 on Figure 4–3 in Figure 4–4. Figure 4–4 also contains a savings function. Since savings is merely that part of disposable personal income not consumed, we simply subtract consumption from income to obtain savings. Thus, in the figure, when the level of income is zero, the level of savings

FIGURE 4-3

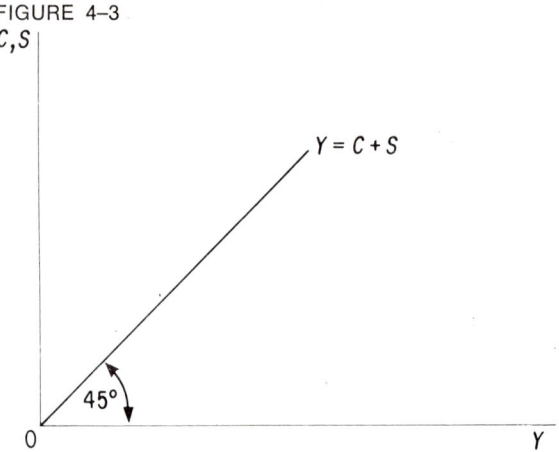

will be zero minus a or $-a$. When the level of income is Y_3, the level of savings will be $Y_3 - C_3 = -S_2$. When the income level increases to Y_1, it is just matched by the level of consumption so that the level of savings is zero. As income increases above Y_1, consumption will also increase, but by relationship (4.2) we know that the increase in consumption will be less than the increase in income, and so we find a positive level of savings. At income level Y_2, the level of savings will be $Y_2 - C_2 = S_1$. We have derived the savings function, and we should note that the slope of this function equals $(1 - b)$ and is called

FIGURE 4-4

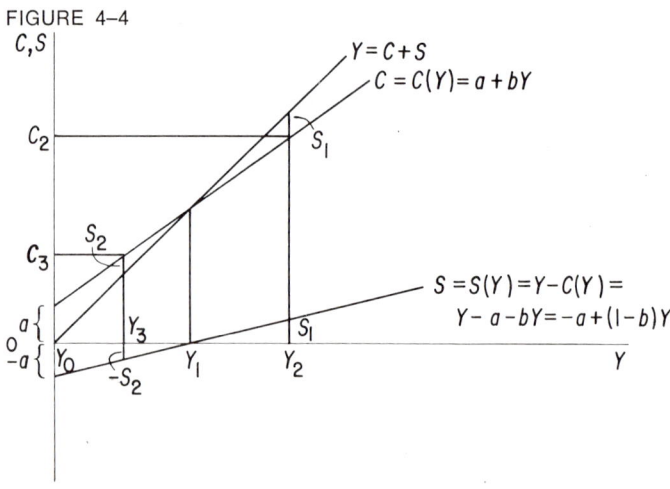

the *marginal propensity to save* or MPS. As might have been expected, the marginal propensity to consume plus the marginal propensity to save is equal to one. This follows very naturally from our knowledge that consumers make only two decisions—the decisions to save and to consume. Consumption plus savings must use all their income.

In Figure 4–4 we have, in effect, derived also the equation of a linear savings function. We repeat this operation here. Since

(4.4) $$Y = C + S,$$

we may solve for S and obtain:

(4.4a) $$S = Y - C.$$

From (4.3) it follows that:

(4.5) $$S = Y - a - bY$$

or, rearranging the terms on the right-hand side,

$$S = -a + (1 - b)Y,$$

where $(1 - b)$ is the slope of the savings function. It is equation (4.5) that we have plotted as the savings function in Figure 4–4.

An example may help explain the point. Please examine Table 4–1 and Figure 4–4. All our calculations are based on equations (4.3)

TABLE 4–1*

a	Y	MPC	C	MPS	S	ΔY	ΔC	ΔS	$\Delta(C+S)$
$60	$ 0	¾	$ 60	¼	$-60				
60	100	¾	135	¼	-35	$+100	$+ 75	$+25	$+100
60	240	¾	240	¼	0	+140	+105	+35	+140
60	380	¾	345	¼	+35	+140	+105	+35	+140

* Dollars in billions.

and (4.5). Assume that the level of consumption expenditures when income equals zero, a, is $60 billion. When national income is zero, consumption equals $60 billion and savings equals —$60 billion. Consumers are drawing down their past savings by $60 billion to buy goods and services for current consumption. This corresponds to point Y_0 in Figure 4–4. When national income is $100 billion, consumption equals $135 billion and savings equals —$35 billion. Consumers are still consuming out of past savings, but by a smaller amount. This corresponds to point Y_3 in Figure 4–4. When national income is $240 billion, consumption equals $240 billion and savings equals zero. Consumers are consuming all of their current income. This corresponds to point Y_1 in Figure 4–4. Finally, when national income is $380 billion, consumption equals $345 billion and savings equals $35 billion. Consumers are saving some of their current income. This corresponds to point Y_2 in Figure 4–4. It is important to note that, in each case, income increased by a larger dollar amount than either consumption or savings alone, while the change in consumption plus savings equaled the change in national income. This happens because the MPC and the MPS are each less than unity, and because the MPC plus the MPS sum to unity.

Let us now introduce investment. Assume, for the moment, that intended investment is constant. That is to say, we assume that, at all levels of income, the level of investment will be $\bar{I}$. We will modify this assumption at a later point. For now, we employ it only as a simplifying assumption. From an earlier discussion, we recall that the level of income equals the level of consumption expenditures plus the level of intended investment expenditures. Thus, we say:

(4.6) $$Y = C + \bar{I}$$

or

$$\bar{Y} = a + b\bar{Y} + \bar{I},$$

where $\bar{I}$ is the given level of intended investment.

Solving for Y, we obtain:

(4.7) $$\bar{Y} - b\bar{Y} = a + \bar{I}$$
$$(1 - b)\bar{Y} = a + \bar{I},$$

and

$$\bar{Y} = \frac{a + \bar{I}}{1 - b}$$

where $\bar{Y}$ represents a particular level of income consistent with a, b, and $\bar{I}$. $\bar{Y}$ is the equilibrium level of income and is examined more carefully with the aid of Figure 4–5.

In the previous chapter, we said that an economy is in equilibrium when intended savings and intended investment are equal. Equilibrium exists only at income level $\bar{Y}$ in Figure 4–5. At income level Y_2, the level of intended savings is zero, but the level of in-

FIGURE 4-5

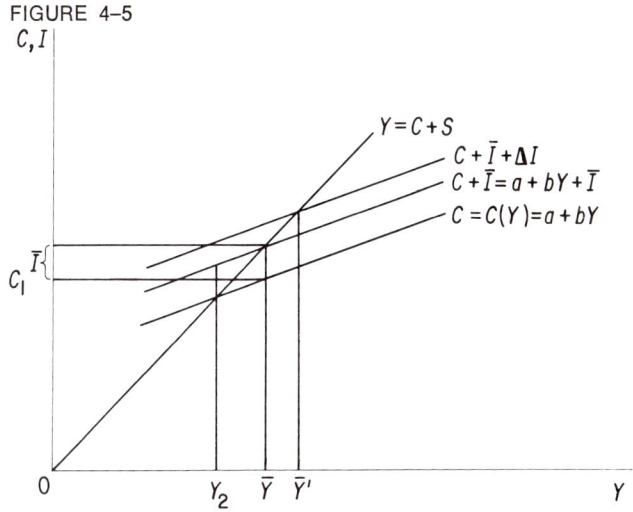

tended investment (at all income levels) is $\bar{I}$. Investment is greater than savings, and equilibrium is not achieved. At income level $\bar{Y}$, however, intended savings and intended investment are equal. At that income level, savings is equal to $\bar{Y} - C_1$. This is $\bar{I}$—the level of investment. The economy is in equilibrium. Savings and investment in an *ex ante* sense are equal.

Once again, an example may be helpful. Assume that $\bar{I}$ equals $20 billion, a equals $60 billion, and b (the MPC) equals $\frac{3}{4}$. Then, according to equation (4.7), $\bar{Y}$ equals $320 billion. When $\bar{Y}$ is $320 billion, consumption (given by equation [4.3]) equals $300 billion and savings (given by equation [4.4a]) equals $20 billion. Since $\bar{I}$ equals S, $\bar{Y}$ is indeed an equilibrium level of national income.

We may, of course, view the results obtained in the previous paragraphs by looking at the savings function. This is done with the aid of Figure 4-6. At all levels of income, the level of investment is equal to $\bar{I}$. From Figure 4-5, we see that the level of savings is zero at income level Y_2. This we have indicated in Figure 4-6. At income level $\bar{Y}$, savings and investment are equal. The economy is in equilibrium. We must recall that $\bar{I}$ represents the level of intended investment, for our equilibrium condition requires that intended investment equals the level of intended savings. Suppose that producers produce only income level (output level) Y_2—below $\bar{Y}$. At that income level, savings is zero, intended investment

FIGURE 4-6

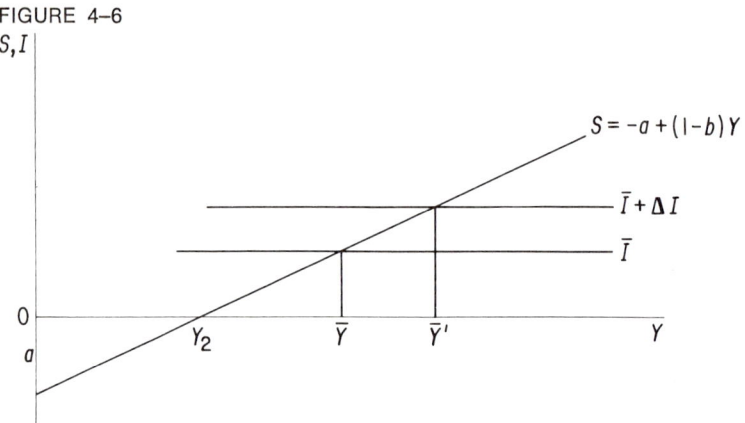

is $\bar{I}$, and consumption is Y_2. Thus, consumption plus investment will be $Y_2 + \bar{I}$. There will have to be a reduction in inventories on the part of businessmen. There will be unintended inventories in the amount of $-\bar{I}$. On the other hand, suppose that the level of income were above $\bar{Y}$. Consumption plus investment would be less than Y. There would be unintended investment in inventories on the part of businessmen. Equilibrium cannot exist in this case or in the former case. In this case, realized investment is greater than intended investment due to unintended inventory accumulation; while, in the previous case, realized investment is less than intended investment due to the unintended inventory decumulation. Equilibrium only obtains when realized investment (actual investment) equals intended investment. This only occurs at income level $\bar{Y}$. Equilibrium only occurs when:

(4.8) $$S = -a + (1-b)Y = \bar{I}.$$

Since this final point should now be well understood, we will dispense with the formality of referring to intended savings and intended investment. Rather, we will simply refer to savings and investment—recognizing that equilibrium will obtain only when they are equal in the *ex ante* or intended sense.

THE SIMPLE MULTIPLIER

Suppose that the level of investment increases from $\bar{I}$ to $\bar{I}'$. It should be clear that the level of national income will increase, also.

Assume that $\bar{I}' - \bar{I} = \Delta I$—that the change in $\bar{I}$ equals ΔI. Referring back to Figures 4–5 and 4–6, we see that the level of income rises, as a result, to $\bar{Y}'$. It is important to note how much the level of income rose compared to the change in the level of investment—ΔI. The new level of income may be expressed as:

(4.9) $$\bar{Y}' = \frac{a + \bar{I}'}{1 - b}$$

following the procedure employed to obtain equation (4.7). We know that $\bar{Y}'$ in equation (4.9) is greater than $\bar{Y}$ in equation (4.7), since $\bar{I}'$ is greater than $\bar{I}$. Let us, therefore, subtract the smaller $\bar{Y}$ from the larger $\bar{Y}'$. We obtain:

(4.10) $$\bar{Y}' - \bar{Y} = \frac{a + \bar{I}'}{1 - b} - \frac{a + \bar{I}}{1 - b},$$

$$\Delta Y = \frac{\bar{I}' - \bar{I}}{1 - b},$$

$$\Delta Y = k\Delta I,$$

where $k = \dfrac{1}{1-b} = \dfrac{1}{1-\text{MPC}}$. For fairly obvious reasons, k is known as the multiplier. For example, if the marginal propensity to consume is $3/4$ then $k = 4$. Hence, if investment increases by $5 billion income will increase by $20 billion—or a multiple of the increase in income. The level of income has been "multiplied up" by the increase in the level of investment expenditures in the economy.

There are alternative methods of more closely examining the simple multiplier concept. We may view the concept graphically as in Figure 4–7. In the figure, we have drawn a linear consumption function, a consumption function plus investment level $\bar{I}$, and finally a consumption function plus investment level $\bar{I}'$. View the graph from the lowest curve to the highest. With the level of investment $\bar{I}$, the equilibrium level of income is $\bar{Y}$. After the increase in investment to the level $\bar{I}'$, the level of income increases to $\bar{Y}'$. Since the slope of any of the three *expenditure curves* drawn is less than 1, i.e., less than the slope of the 45° line, it follows that $\Delta Y > \Delta I$. The multiplier is at work. When the initial equilibrium is disturbed by the increase in investment, there is an increase in desired expenditures at income level $\bar{Y}$. There is a movement from r to s. The additional expenditure raises income to the level at t. At this increased level of income, individuals increase their desired expendi-

FIGURE 4-7

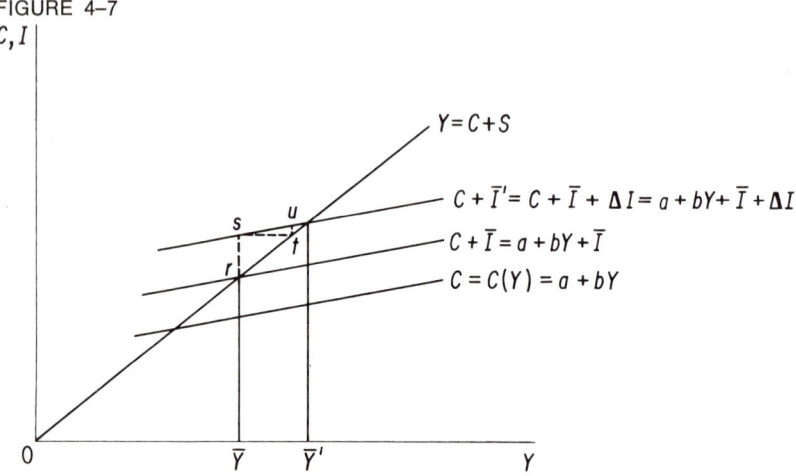

tures to the level at u, and so income again is increased toward the level $\bar{Y}'$. This continuous increase in desired expenditures, and hence income, multiplies up the level of income.[1] Interestingly and importantly, the multiplier works in the negative direction as well as in the positive direction. When the level of investment falls the level of income will be multiplied down. The multiplier works just as effectively in both directions.[2]

The common sense of the multiplier may be seen with the aid of a numerical example. Suppose that I decide to build an addition on my house at a cost of $1,000. To build this addition, suppose that I employ heretofore unemployed resources. The $1,000 that I spend to build the addition will induce a secondary expansion of national income over and above the initial $1,000 expenditure. Let us assume that the marginal propensity to consumer is ¾, or 0.75. The $1,000 that I pay to the carpenters, plumbers, electricians, and so on, will become their income. They, in turn will spend 75 percent of this income. Hence, consumption increases by $750. However, the process does not stop there. This consumption spending becomes new income to the grocer, the baker, and so forth. They then spend 75 percent of the $750 or $562.50. This money becomes the income of other members of society, and they spend 75 percent of the $562.50 on

---

[1] Since $st = rs$ it follows that $\bar{Y}' - \bar{Y} = \Delta Y > rs = \Delta I$.

[2] An algebraic derivation of the simple multiplier is given in the appendix to this chapter.

consumption expenditures, i.e., they spend $421.88. This money becomes the income of another group, and they, in turn, spend 75 percent of this income. The process continues indefinitely. Total income increases by $1,000 + $750 + $562.50 + $421.88 + . . . until income increases to an amount equal to the multiplier times the initial increase in expenditures. In our case, since the multiplier equals 4, income will increase to $4,000. This multiplier process is demonstrated schematically in Figure 4–8.

FIGURE 4–8

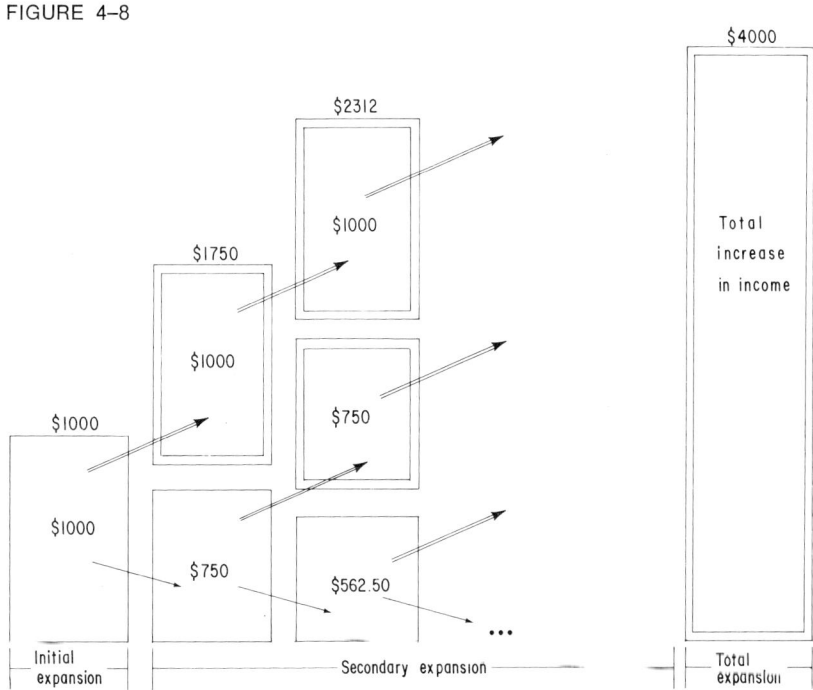

An additional point is in order. We have noted that income is multiplied up or down when the level of investment changes. Suppose, however, that the level of investment remains constant but the entire consumption function shifts up. That is to say, suppose that the marginal propensity to consume does not change, but rather the level of consumption at the zero level of income does change. That is, suppose that everyone consumes more on the average than they did previously. The new consumption function will be parallel to the old one. Of course, the consumption function could shift up in a fashion such that the new consumption function would not be parallel to the old one. Such a shift means that the slope of the consumption function (the MPC) has changed also. We will ignore such shifts in this volume and deal only with parallel shifts.[3] Again the multiplier will work. Given the consumption function and a level of investment of $\bar{I}$, the level of income will be $\bar{Y}$ as determined in equation (4.7). With an upward shift in the consumption function as suggested above, the new equilibrium level of income may be stated as:

$$\bar{Y}' = \frac{a' + \bar{I}}{1 - b},$$

where a' is greater than a. Thus, if we note that $\bar{Y}'$ is greater than $\bar{Y}$ we may obtain:

$$\bar{Y}' - \bar{Y} = \frac{a' + \bar{I}}{1 - b} - \frac{a + \bar{I}}{1 - b}$$

(4.12)
$$\Delta Y = \frac{a' - a}{1 - b}$$

$$\Delta Y = \frac{\Delta a}{1 - b}$$

$$\Delta Y = k \Delta a.$$

The level of income is multiplied up once again.

Perhaps a clearer picture may be made looking at the above analysis graphically. Given the original consumption function and the investment level $\bar{I}$, the equilibrium level of income is $\bar{Y}$ in Figure 4–9. The upward shift in the consumption function causes the expenditure line to shift up as well since the level of investment is assumed constant at all levels of income. The new level of income is $\bar{Y}'$. Since the slopes of all the expenditure lines are the same (being less than 1), it follows that the increase in income is greater than the increase in consumption at all levels of income. The multiplier has again worked to raise the level of income.

---

[3] If the marginal propensity to consume were to increase, then following the above procedure we would find that:

$$\Delta Y = \Delta k(a + \bar{I}).$$

If the marginal propensity to consume were to increase, and the level of consumption at the zero level of income were to increase, we would find that

$$\Delta Y = \Delta k \bar{I} + k'a' - ka$$

where k' is the new multiplier and a' the new level of consumption at the zero level of income.

FIGURE 4-9

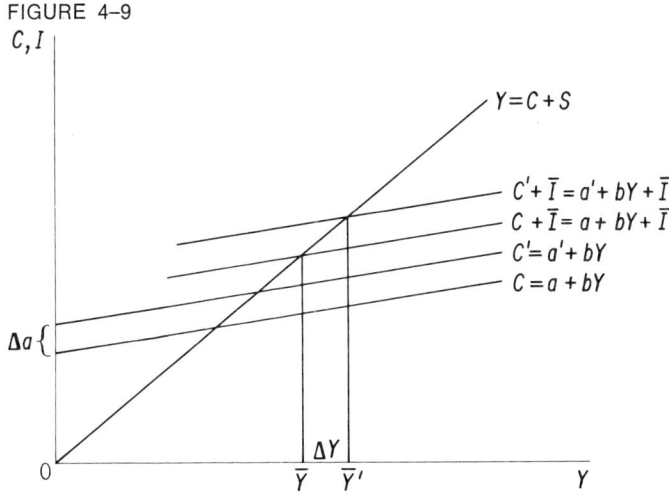

TEMPORARY AND PERMANENT EXPANSIONS

The new equilibrium level of national income in Figure 4–9 was supported by an increase in total expenditures from $a + bY + \bar{I}$ to $a' + bY + \bar{I}$ as a result of increased consumption expenditures. We have implicitly assumed that the shift in consumption expenditures is permanent—that the higher level of spending is maintained forever. However, this need not be so. The rise in consumption expenditures could be temporary only—a higher level of spending in this time period which subsequently returns to its original level. In the case of a permanent increase, the resulting increase in output and income is permanent also; and, in the case of a temporary increase, the resulting increase in output and income is only temporary. Examining each case adds a new dimension to the multiplier process.

Let us examine a case of temporary expansion first. Since expenditure, income, and output changes take place through time, we can break our analysis into "representative" time periods of equal, but unspecified, length. We call them "rounds." See Table 4–2. Assume that in round 1 the economy is at an equilibrium level of income equal to $300 billion. Consumption expenditures equal $285 billion, intended investment equals $15 billion, and total desired expenditures (the sum of consumption plus intended investment) equal $300 billion. In round 2, we disturb the equilibrium by injecting an additional $10 billion of consumption expenditures—an increase in total con-

TABLE 4-2*

Round	C	ΔC	C' = C + ΔC	I	Total desired expenditures	Y	ΔY	Unintended inventory changes
1	$285	$ 0	$285	$15	$300	$300	$ 0	$ 0
2	285	10	295	15	310	300	0	−10
3	285	7.5	292.5	15	307.5	310	10	+ 2.5
4	285	5.6	290.6	15	305.6	307.5	7.5	+ 1.9
5	285	4.2	289.2	15	304.2	305.6	5.6	+ 1.4
6	285	3.2	288.2	15	303.2	304.2	4.2	+ 1.0
7	285	2.4	287.4	15	302.4	303.2	3.2	+ 0.8
8	285	1.8	286.8	15	301.8	302.4	2.4	+ 0.6
.	.	.	.	.	.	.	.	.
.	.	.	.	.	.	.	.	.
.	.	.	.	.	.	.	.	.
∞	285	0	285	15	300	300	0	0
Cumulative change		$40					$40	

* Dollars in billions.

sumption from $285 billion to $295 billion. This increase in consumption expenditures is a once for all-time exogenous increase. It will not occur again. All subsequent changes in consumption and investment are induced by the initial exogenous change. Graphically, we could picture the exogenous change as an upward shift in the consumption function followed by a downward shift back to its original position. Intended investment remains constant through all rounds. Consequently, total desired expenditures in round 2 jump to $310 billion. If we assume that producers do not anticipate changes in consumer expenditures, but simply produce an amount equal to last period's production plus any unintended change in inventories during the last period, output during round 2 remains at $300 billion. Since current expenditures now exceed current output, the excess demand for consumer goods must be supplied out of inventories. Thus, producers experience an unintended decrease in inventories equal to −$10 billion. Obviously, the economy is no longer in equilibrium.

By our assumption, in round 3 producers expand output by $10 billion—they produce $310 billion of goods and services. Since $310 billion of output creates $310 billion of income (recall the circular flow of Chapter 1), consumption in round 3 (given by equation [4.3] and the ensuing discussion) equals $292.5 billion and total expenditures equal $307.5 billion. Consumption expenditures have increased by $7.5 billion. However, this increase was induced by the expansion in production, and was not the result of a second exogenous shift in the consumption function. With current total expenditures at $307.5 billion current output exceeds current expenditures. The excess supply of goods and services forces an unintended inventory accumulation of $2.5 billion. Again, the economy is in disequilibrium.

In round 4, producers contract output by $2.5 billion to $307.5 billion. Income falls to $307.5 billion, consumption expenditures to $209.6 billion and total expenditures to $305.6 billion. Nevertheless, expenditures are still less than output. Inventories are still accumulating unintentionally. In round 5, producers contract output again; but, the contraction is smaller than in round 4 ($1.9 billion rather than $2.5 billion). In this manner, the levels of output and income decline continuously until round ∞. In round ∞, output and income have contracted by enough so that the initial levels of consumption and intended investment are just sufficient to support the level of production. The economy has returned to the equilibrium of round 1.

The process discussed above, and given in Table 4–2, is summarized schematically in Figure 4–10. The point to note is that the *cumulative*

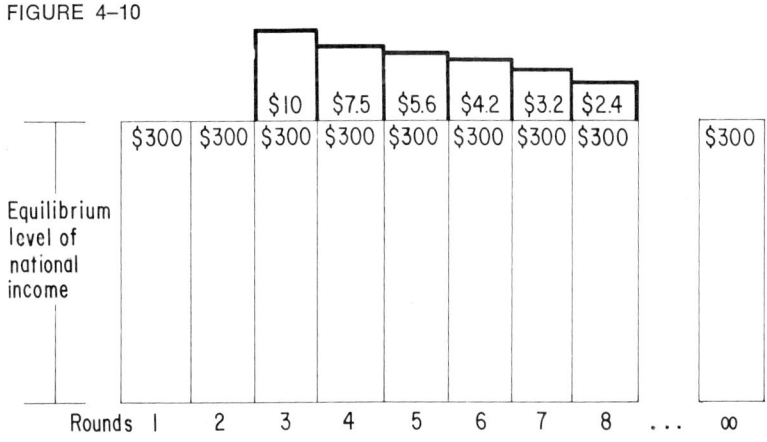

FIGURE 4–10

increase in expenditures and income over all rounds equals $40 billion. The once-for-all-time exogenous increase in consumption expenditures has induced diminishing rounds of consumer spending which created a *cumulative* increase in income equal to four times the initial increase in consumption, but did not raise output and income to permanently higher levels. The increase in income, like the increase in consumption, is temporary only. In a temporary expansion, the multiplier process given in equations (4.10) and (4.12) summarizes the *cumulative* effect on income.

If the consumption function shifts upward and remains at the new, higher level round after round, the initial equilibrium level of income will be replaced by a higher equilibrium level. This is the result shown in Figure 4–9 as the movement from $\bar{Y}$ to $\bar{Y}'$.

We can describe the movement of the economy to the higher equilibrium level of national income by a simple extension of our previous analysis. In round 2 of Table 4–2, we assume that consumption expenditures rose temporarily by $10 billion. In the present case, however, we assume that the $10 billion increase in consumption expenditures is permanent—it will repeat round after round. Thus, in round 2 the level of consumption expenditures increase by $10 billion. In round 3, the level of consumption expenditures increase by another $10 billion plus the $7.5 billion induced by the increase in round 2, or by $17.5 billion. In round 4, consumption expenditures increase by another $10 billion plus the $7.5 billion induced by the increase in round 3 plus the $5.6 billion induced by the increase in round 2, or by $23.1 billion. In each round, the level of national income increases by the amount of the change in consumption expenditures in the previous round. Thus, income increases to $310 billion in round 3, to $317.5 billion in round 4, to $323.1 billion in round 5 and so on until the level of national income eventually increases by $40 billion to $340 billion. It is a permanently higher equilibrium level of income.

The process is summarized in Table 4–3, and in Figure 4–11. The point is that a permanent upward shift in the consumption function has induced continuous rounds of additional spending which created a *total* increase in income equal to four times the initial increase in consumption. The increase in income, like the increase in consumption, is permanent. In a permanent expansion, the multiplier process given in equations (4.10) and (4.12) summarizes the *total* effect on income.

DEFLATIONARY, EXPANSIONARY, AND INFLATIONARY GAPS

We can now utilize some multiplier analysis to define and explain the concepts of deflationary, expansionary, and inflationary gaps. Also,

4 / The simple mechanics of income determination 47

TABLE 4–3*

Round	C	ΔC	C' = C + ΔC	I	Total desired expenditures	Y	ΔY	Unintended inventory changes
1.....	$285	$ 0	$285	$15	$300	$300	$ 0	$ 0
2.....	285	10	295	15	310	300	0	−10
3.....	285	17.5	302.5	15	317.5	310	10	− 7.5
4.....	285	23.1	308.1	15	323.1	317.5	7.5	− 5.6
5.....	285	27.3	312.3	15	327.3	323.1	5.6	− 4.2
6.....	285	30.5	315.3	15	330.5	327.3	4.2	− 3.2
7.....	285	32.9	317.9	15	332.9	330.5	3.2	− 2.4
8.....	285	34.7	319.7	15	334.7	332.9	2.4	− 1.8
.....	.	.	.	.	.	.	.	.
.....	.	.	.	.	.	.	.	.
.....	.	.	.	.	.	.	.	.
∞.....	285	40	325	15	340	340	0	0

* Dollars in billions.

we will get a preliminary peek at the role of multiplier analysis in the formation of macroeconomic policy. Suppose that we have an economy characterized by all of the assumptions introduced in this chapter: there is no government sector, no exports or imports; the level of income equals the sum of consumption plus investment expenditures; consumption expenditures are based on a linear consumption function; intended investment is not affected by changes in con-

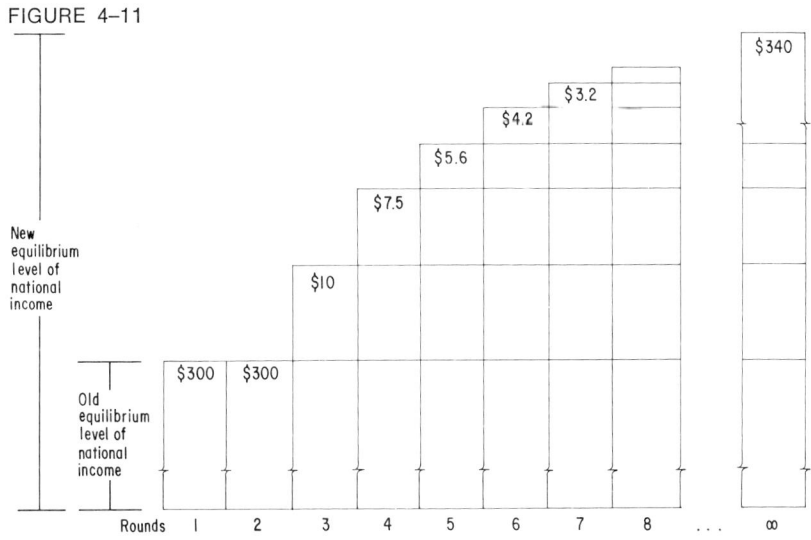

FIGURE 4–11

sumption expenditures or income; and, the level of savings is based on a linear savings function. Consequently, we can summarize our economy in the four following equations (which we have seen before):

(4.6) $\quad Y = C + I,$
(4.3) $\quad C = a + bY,$
(4.5) $\quad S = -a + (1 - b)Y,$
$\quad\quad\quad I = \bar{I},$

where all symbols are as defined earlier. You should be familiar with them.

Let us assume that a equals \$60 billion, b equals ¾, and $\bar{I}$ equals \$36 billion. Under these circumstances, what is the level of national income? According to equation (4.7) national income equals $(60 + 36)/(1 - ¾)$, or \$384 billion. This level of income is represented by $\bar{Y}$ in Figure 4–12. What is the level of consumption? According to equation (4.3), consumption expenditures equal (\$60 billion + (¾)\$384 billion), or \$348 billion. What is the level of

FIGURE 4–12

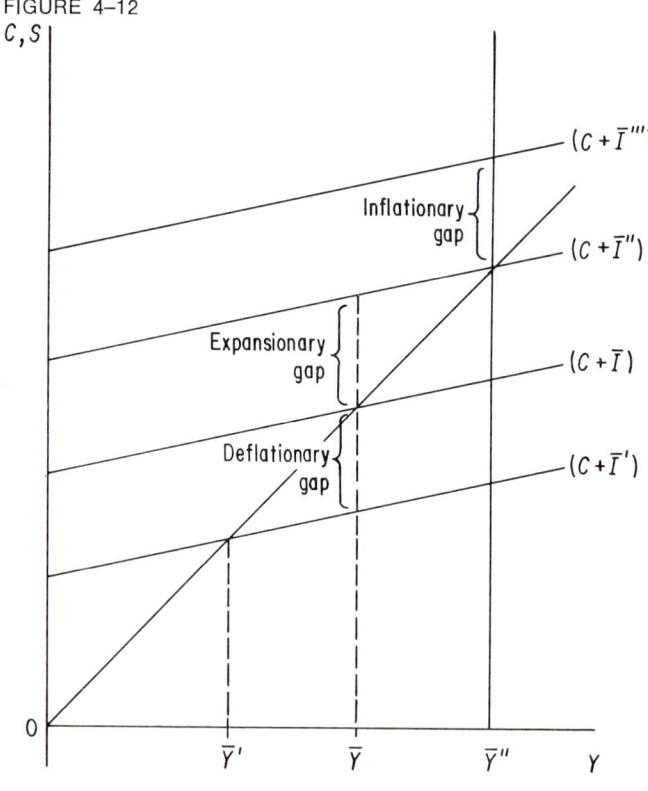

savings? According to equation (4.5), savings equals ($-\$60$ billion + ($\frac{1}{4}$)$384 billion), or $36 billion. Given this information, is $\bar{Y}$ an equilibrium level of income? It is! Savings equals intended investment—there are no forces of change operating in the economy.

Let us now assume that the level of intended investment falls from $\bar{I}$ to $\bar{I}'$, from $36 billion to $32 billion. All other things remaining, for a moment, constant. What is the new value of total expenditures? Since total expenditures equal the sum of consumption plus investment spending, total expenditures now equal ($348 billion + $32 billion), or $380 billion. In Figure 4–12 $(C + I)$ shifts downward to $(C + \bar{I}')$. The vertical distance between the two functions is equal to the reduction in investment spending, or $4 billion. We call this vertical distance a *deflationary gap*. Total expenditures are now less than total production which remains, momentarily, at $384 billion. Savings exceeds intended investment $(S > \bar{I}')$. Under these conditions, we know that the level of income must decline. The equilibrium level of national income will deflate, or shrink. How far will it deflate? It will deflate until savings falls into equality with intended investment. It will deflate by $16 billion to a lower equilibrium level of national income equal to $368 billion. This level of national income is represented by $\bar{Y}'$ in Figure 4–12. In other words, income deflates by four times the size of the reduction in investment. Therefore, in a deflationary gap, we say that income deflates by an amount equal to the multiplier (k) times the reduction in total spending. In this case, investment expenditures fell, but the same analysis would hold for a reduction in consumption expenditures.

Suppose we assume, instead, that the level of intended investment rises from $\bar{I}$ to $\bar{I}''$ from $36 billion to $40 billion. All other things remaining, for a moment, constant. What is the new value of total expenditures? Total spending now equals ($348 billion + $40 billion), or $388 billion. In Figure 4–12 $(C + \bar{I})$ shifts upward to $(C + \bar{I}'')$. The vertical distance between the two functions is equal to the increase in investment, or $4 billion. We call this vertical distance an *expansionary gap*. Total expenditures are now greater than total production which remains, momentarily, at $384 billion. Savings is less than intended investment $(S < \bar{I}'')$. Under these conditions, we know that the level of income must rise. The equilibrium level of national income will expand, or increase. How far will it expand? It will expand until savings rises into equality with intended investment. It will expand by $16 billion to a higher equilibrium level of income equal to $400 billion. This level of national income is represented by $\bar{Y}'''$ in Figure 4–12. In other words, income expands by four times the size of the increase in investment. Therefore, in an expansionary gap, we say that income expands by an amount equal to the multiplier (k) times the increase in total spending. Again, the analysis is identical for increases in investment or consumption expenditures.

Let us now assume that the equilibrium level of national income given by $\bar{Y}'''$ is a *full-employment level of income*—the level of income at which all factors of production seeking to be employed are employed. In this sense, $\bar{Y}'''$ represents the maximum production of goods and services possible in our economy. Suppose that the level of intended investment rises once again, from $\bar{I}''$ to $\bar{I}'''$. In Figure 4–12, $(C + \bar{I}'')$ shifts upward to $(C + \bar{I}''')$. The vertical distance between the two functions is called an *inflationary gap*. The reason is obvious. Total spending exceeds total production. However, by our full-employment assumption, production cannot expand beyond $\bar{Y}'''$. All the additional demand for goods and services, given by $(\bar{Y}''' - \bar{Y}'')$ cannot be supplied. Since the excess demand cannot be satisfied, it will force the price level to rise. Therefore, in an inflationary gap, we say that the production of goods and services cannot be increased, and real (constant dollar) national income cannot expand; however, nominal (current dollar) national income expands—but the expansion is pure price inflation.

We can use the concepts of deflationary and expansionary gaps to preview the role of multiplier analysis in macroeconomic policy. Suppose that the economy was initially at a less-than-full-employment level of national income—for example, $\bar{Y}$. Furthermore, suppose that we desire to achieve full employment. Therefore, we must move the economy from $\bar{Y}$ to $\bar{Y}''$. How do we do it? We do it by creating an expansionary gap, by expanding total expenditures on consumption or investment. By how much must total expenditures increase? They must increase by an amount equal to $(\bar{Y}'' - \bar{Y})/k$, where k represents the multiplier. For example, if $\bar{Y}''$ equals $400 billion, $\bar{Y}$ equals $384 billion, and k equals 4, total income must increase by $16 billion. However, with a multiplier equal to 4, $16 billion of additional income can be created by only $4 billion of additional expenditures: $(400 - 384)/4$, or $4 billion. Note how important our multiplier has become. It identifies the multiple increase or decrease in spending which is required to increase or decrease national income by the desired amount. Unfortunately, our simple multiplier is an overstatement of reality. We will see why in later chapters.

CONCLUDING NOTE

In this chapter we have discussed a simple model of income determination. It is on this model that we will build in the following chapters. As we expand the model by considering more variables, it will be seen that the problem of determining an equilibrium level of income is no simple matter. Indeed, the problem will become a most complicated one. In the next chapter, we will examine the consumption function in more detail.

APPENDIX

We may also examine the simple multiplier concept algebraically. Suppose that investment changes by ΔI. Immediately, there is an initial increase in income from $C + \bar{I}$ to $C + \bar{I} + \Delta I$. Call the increase in income $\Delta_1 Y$. $\Delta_1 Y$ is the difference between the original level of income $\bar{Y}$ and the immediate income level, call it Y', determined by $C + \bar{I} + \Delta I$. From equation (4.3), say that given income level $\bar{Y}$, the level of consumption is C_1 and, given income level Y', the consumption level is C'. C' will naturally be greater than C_1 since Y' is greater than $\bar{Y}$. Thus, we may subtract the smaller level of consumption from the larger, or:

(4.13) $$C' - C_1 = a + bY' - a - b\bar{Y}$$

or

$$\Delta_1 C = b \Delta_1 Y.$$

Since b is known to be less than unity, equation (4.13) shows quite clearly that the change in consumption is less than the change in income.

The increase in investment has brought about an increase in income and this increase in income has caused an increase in consumption. However, there are more increases to come. The initial increase in consumption also increases income. Just as my consumption dollars become someone else's income, some of those income dollars become consumption dollars, and hence someone else's income, and the cycle is repeated again and again. Thus, we may say that:

(4.14) $$\Delta_1 C = \Delta_2 Y.$$

Since the marginal propensity to consume is less than 1, when $\Delta_2 Y$ income dollars are "used" by the consumer some will find their way into additional consumption dollars. Thus, it follows that:

(4.15) $$\Delta_2 C = b \Delta_2 Y,$$

or substituting from (4.12)

$$\Delta_2 C = b(\Delta_1 C).$$

But from equation (4.13) we obtain:

(4.16) $$\Delta_2 C = b(b \Delta_1 Y) = b^2 \Delta_1 Y.$$

Thus,

(4.17) $$\Delta_2 C = b^2 \Delta I,$$

since we initially assumed that the change in investment, ΔI, brought about a change in income on the order of $\Delta_1 Y$.

Now, this new level of consumption, $\Delta_2 C$ becomes someone else's income, or:

(4.18) $$\Delta_2 C = \Delta_3 Y.$$
(4.19) $$\begin{aligned}\Delta_3 C &= b \Delta_3 Y \\ &= b(\Delta_2 C) \\ &= b(b^2 \Delta_1 Y) \\ &= b^3(\Delta_1 Y) \\ &= b^3 \Delta I.\end{aligned}$$

We may repeat this process over and over again. After i repetitions we have:

(4.20) $$\Delta_i C = b^i \Delta I \text{ where } i = 1, 2, \ldots,$$

We are now in a position to obtain the total change in income that results from an increase in investment of ΔI. We merely have to sum all the changes in income contributed by each successive step just outlined. The total change in income is:

(4.21) $$\Delta Y = \Delta_1 Y + \Delta_2 Y + \cdots + \Delta_i Y.$$

From above we note,

(4.22)
$$\Delta_1 Y = \Delta I \text{ and}$$
$$\Delta_2 Y = \Delta_1 C = b\Delta_1 Y = b\Delta I \text{ and}$$
$$\Delta_3 Y = \Delta_2 C = b^2 \Delta_1 Y = b^2 \Delta I \text{ and}$$
$$\cdots \quad \cdots \quad \cdots \quad \cdots$$
$$\Delta_i Y = \Delta_{i-1} C = b^{i-1} \Delta_1 Y = b^{i-1} \Delta I.$$

We may conclude[4]:

(4.23) $\quad \Delta Y = \Delta I + b\Delta I + b^2 \Delta I + \cdots + b^{i-1} \Delta I + \cdots$
$$= \Delta I (1 + b + b^2 + \cdots + b^{i-1} + \cdots), \text{ or}$$
$$\Delta Y = \Delta I \left[\frac{1}{1-b} \right].$$

Since $\dfrac{1}{1-b} = k$, we have:

(4.24) $\quad\quad\quad\quad\quad\quad \Delta Y = k \Delta I.$

We have viewed the multiplier as a step-by-step process, and once again concluded that an increase in investment will "multiply up or down" the level of income.

The results of equation (4.24) are identical with those of equation (4.10).

---

[4] To solve equation (4.23) we use the formula for summing an infinite series

$$S = \frac{a}{1-r}$$

where S is the sum, a the first term and r the ratio between terms.

5 The level of consumption

IN THE LAST CHAPTER we developed a simple theory of national income determination. We concluded that the economy tends toward a level of national income equal, in equilibrium, to the sum of consumption plus investment expenditures. We discovered that the level of total spending supports the level of national income. Therefore, we must look more closely at the determinants of total spending. In this chapter, we will examine the determinants of the level of consumption. We will examine investment expenditures and government spending in the following chapters.

THE HISTORICAL RECORD

In Chapter 4, we assumed that the level of consumption expenditures is dependent upon the level of income. We assumed that consumption increases as income increases. Furthermore, we assumed that the increment to consumption, although positive, is less than the increase in income. Finally, we assumed that the proportion of current income allocated to current consumption declines as income increases. In precise economic terminology, we assumed that the marginal propensity to consume (MPC) is greater than zero but less than unity, and constant; while the average propensity to consume (APC) falls with each rise in income. Consequently, our consumption-income relationship is linear, in the form:

(5.1) $$C = a + bY.$$

The question that we must consider is: Does the available statistical evidence validate our assumptions about the consumption function? Since income is not the only factor influencing consumption, since consumption is likely to be affected by such factors as past income, expected future income, price expectations, asset holdings, taxes, the distribution of income, and a host of sociological factors, we might expect the consumption-income relationship to be relatively weak. Therefore, we must determine the strength of the relationship between consumption and income; or, said in a more precise manner, we must determine how strongly consumption and income are correlated. The historical data, usually called time series data, for consumption and disposable personal income for the period 1929 through 1970 are presented in Table 5–1.

The consumption and disposable personal income data, excluding the period 1942 through 1946,[1] are plotted in Figure 5–1 as a *scatter diagram:* for each level of disposable personal income, the corresponding level of consumption is identified. The data in the scatter diagram allow us to test the strength of the consumption-income relationship. A straight line which best reflects the long-run correlation between consumption and disposable income is "fitted" to the data by a statistical technique called regression analysis.[2] The resulting regression line, and the equation explaining the slope and position of the regression line, represents the correlation between consumption and disposable income over the long-run period 1929 through 1970.[3] Thus, the regression line and regression equation are statistical estimates of the *long-run consumption function*. The regression analysis yields a long-run consumption function equal to:

(5.2) $$C = 7.6 + .90Y, \quad R - .94,$$

where Y represents disposable personal income, and R represents the *coefficient of correlation* which indicates the strength of the relation-

---

[1] The period 1942 through 1946 has been excluded because it corresponds to the years of World War II which, as a result of resource scarcity and consumer rationing, introduces a serious statistical bias to the case.

[2] An elementary explanation of regression analysis can be found in Michael J. Brennan, *Preface to Econometrics* (2d ed.; New York: Southwestern Publishing Company, 1965), pp. 308–52.

[3] As you have probably noticed, not all points lie precisely on the regression line, although most lie very close to it. The vertical distance between the regression line and any point not on the line represents the influence of all factors other than disposable personal income on consumption expenditures. The evidence indicates that all the other factors, taken as group, are not as significant as income.

TABLE 5–1*

Year	Disposable personal income	Personal consumption expenditures	Average propensity to consume
1929	$150.6	$139.6	.93
1930	139.0	130.4	.94
1931	133.7	126.1	.94
1932	115.1	114.8	.99
1933	112.2	112.8	1.05
1934	120.4	118.1	.98
1935	131.8	125.5	.95
1936	148.4	138.4	93
1937	153.1	143.1	.94
1938	143.6	140.2	.98
1939	155.9	148.2	.95
1940	166.3	155.7	.94
1941	190.3	165.4	.87
1942	213.4	161.4	.76
1943	222.8	165.8	.74
1944	231.6	171.4	.74
1945	229.7	183.0	.79
1946	227.0	203.0	.89
1947	218.0	206.3	.95
1948	229.8	210.8	.92
1949	230.8	216.5	.94
1950	249.6	230.5	.92
1951	255.7	232.8	.91
1952	263.3	239.4	.91
1953	275.4	250.8	.91
1954	278.3	255.7	.92
1955	296.7	274.2	.92
1956	309.3	281.4	.91
1957	315.8	288.2	.91
1958	318.8	290.1	.91
1959	333.0	307.3	.92
1960	340.2	316.1	.93
1961	350.7	322.5	.92
1962	367.3	338.4	.92
1963	381.3	353.3	.93
1964	407.9	373.7	.92
1965	434.4	398.4	.91
1966	456.3	418.0	.91
1967	477.5	430.1	.90
1968	499.0	452.7	.91
1969	513.5	469.3	.90
1970	531.5	475.9	.89

* In billions of 1958 dollars.
Source: *Economic Report of the President*, January 1972.

FIGURE 5-1

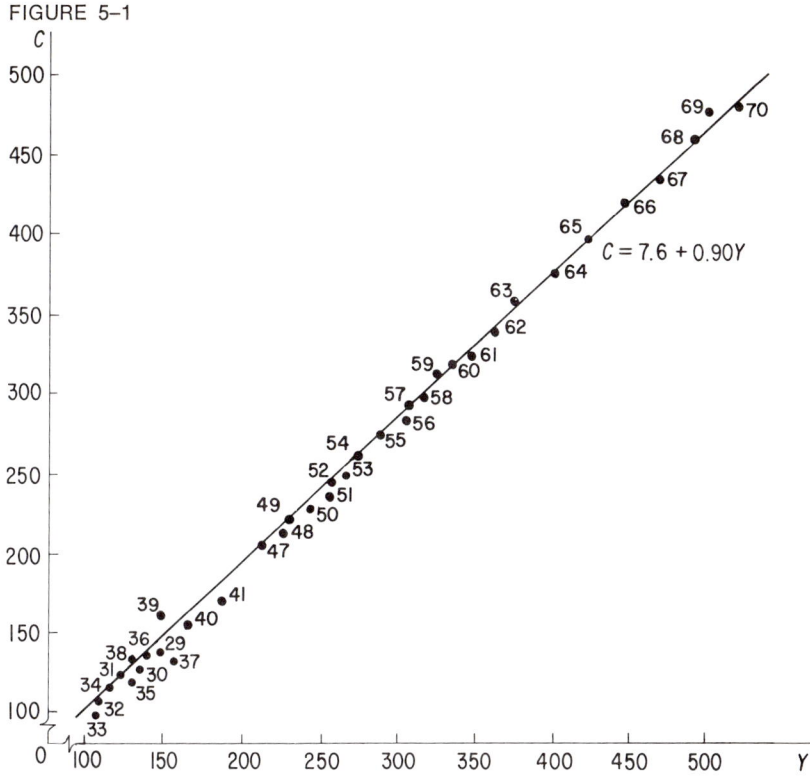

ship between the two variables. A coefficient of correlation equal to .94 means that 88 percent of the variation in the level of consumption expenditures over the period 1929 through 1970 is due to variations in the level of disposable personal income.[4] In addition, equation (5.2) says that, on the average and over the long-run, 90 cents of every additional dollar of disposable income was spent on consumption goods and services. Finally, since our statistical consumption function is linear, the APC should decline as income increases. Therefore, the statistical evidence appears to validate our consumption-income assumptions.

However, lest we become prematurely overconfident about our assumptions, some additional statistical investigating should be undertaken. Suppose that we break the data in Table 5-1 into two subperiods, 1929, through 1941 and 1947 through 1970, and compute

[4] If $R = .94$ then $R^2 = .88$. R^2 is called the *coefficient of determination*.

regression equations—statistical consumption functions—for each subperiod. The regression analysis yields two *short-run consumption functions* equal to:

(5.3) $C(1929 - 1941) = 41.8 + 0.76Y(1929 - 1941)$, and
(5.4) $C(1947 - 1970) = 27.3 + 0.88Y(1947 - 1970)$.

The corresponding regression lines are shown in Figure 5–2.

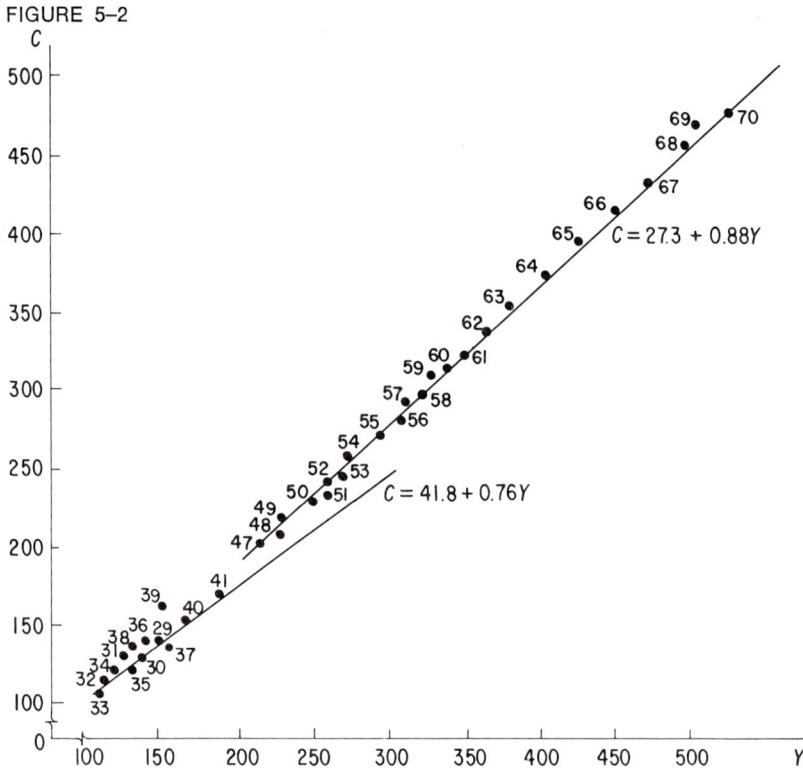

FIGURE 5-2

What does the new evidence suggest about the consumption-income relationship? It suggests that the consumption function is shifting upward, and becoming steeper, through time. Look at the evidence. First, note that the intercept of equation (5.3) is greater than that of equation (5.4); i.e., $41.8 billion is larger than $27.3 billion—the regression line for equation (5.4) would cut the vertical axis in Figure 5–2 below the regression line for equation (5.3). Second, note that the MPC of equation (5.3) is less than that of equation (5.4); i.e., .76

is smaller than .88—the regression line for equation (5.4) has a steeper slope than the regression line for equation (5.3). Clearly, the short-run consumption function is shifting upward, and becoming steeper, through time. We will discuss the possible causes of the upward drift later in this chapter.

As the consumption function rotates upward, the value of the APC increases, approaches the value of the MPC, and tends to become numerically constant. This proposition can be demonstrated with the help of Figure 5–3. (You may need to review the diagrammatic defini-

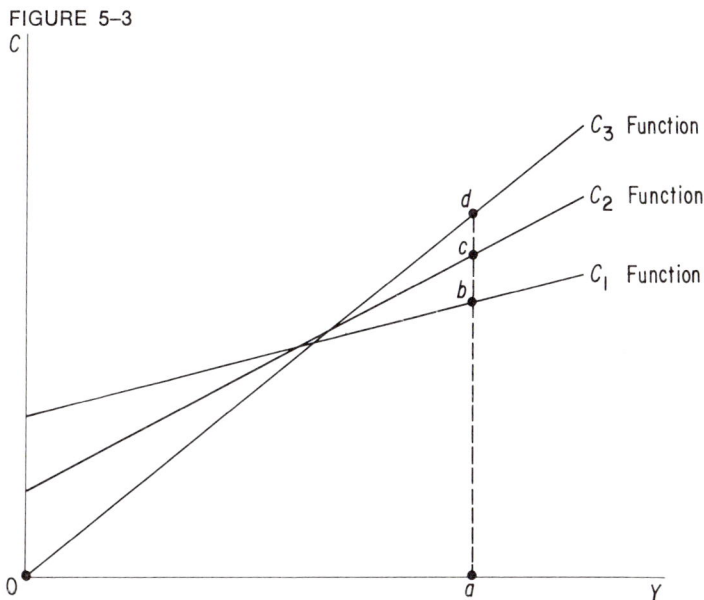

FIGURE 5-3

tion of the APC given in Chapter 4.) At point b on the consumption function identified as C_1, the APC is equal to the ratio $ab/0a$. At point C on the consumption function identified as C_2, the APC is equal to $ac/0a$. At point d on the consumption function identified as C_3, the APC is equal to $ad/0a$. Since ab is less than ac which is less than ad, the APC is increasing as the consumption function becomes steeper. As the slope of the consumption function becomes steeper, and its intercept falls to the origin, the value of the APC equals that of the MPC. When curve C_1 has rotated to curve C_3, the MPC equals $ad/0a$ and the APC equals $ad/0a$. Obviously, they are equal. Furthermore, along a linear consumption function, when the MPC and the APC are equal, the value of the APC is constant—it does not change as the level of income changes. You should be able to prove it.

Since the evidence suggests that the consumption function is rotating upward over the long run, the APC must be increasing and approaching a constant value. In any case, it is not declining. In fact, the APC data shown in Table 5–1 reveal that it has been relatively constant over the long run—remaining, in normal years, in the neighborhood of .89 to .95. Therefore, our assumption that the APC declines as income increases is valid only when our analysis is limited to the short run. Over the long run, we must modify our assumption to account for a relatively constant average propensity to consume.

What general conclusions can be reached regarding the consumption-income relationship? First, the evidence indicates that the primary determinant of consumption expenditures is the level of income. Thus, we can say that consumption is primarily a function of income. Second, the MPC is indeed positive and less than unity. Third, there are two consumption functions, a short-run consumption function and a long-run consumption function. The short-run consumption function is characterized by a declining APC (as income increases); while the

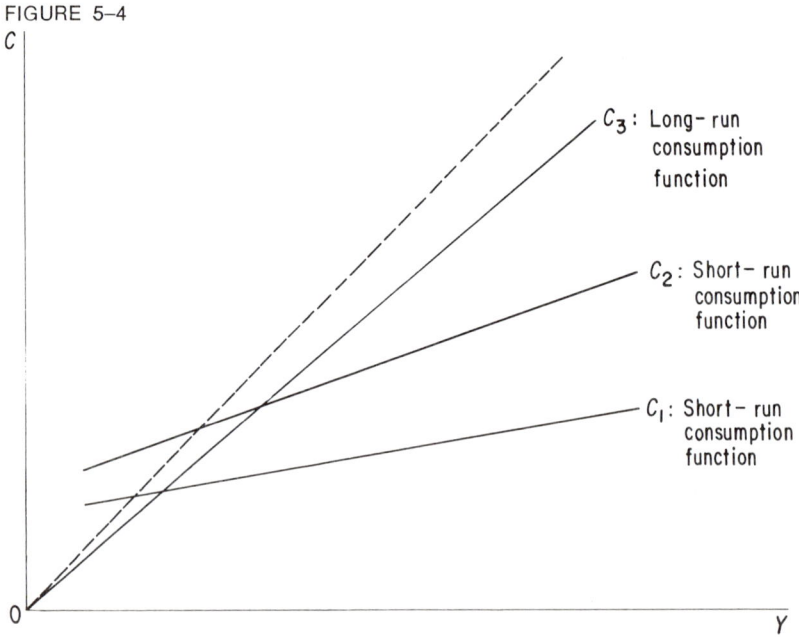

FIGURE 5–4

long-run consumption function is characterized by a constant APC (as income increases). Fourth, the short-run consumption function tends to shift upward and steepen in slope over time. These conclusions are summarized in Figure 5–4. To understand the diagram, you must remember the time dimension. Functions C_1 and C_2 represent short-run consumption functions, with average propensities to consume which decline as income increases. Function C_3 represents a long-run consumption function, with an average propensity to consume which remains constant as income increases. We will explain the theories relating the short-run and long-run consumption functions in the remainder of this chapter.[5]

CLASSICAL AND KEYNESIAN THEORY

In Chapter 1 we noted that there are two schools of macroeconomic theory, Classical and Keynesian. The consumption function provides us with a first glance at one of the differences between Classical and Keynesian macroeconomics. We are interested in the difference between the two views for a more important reason than historical nit-picking. The Keynesian rejection of the Classical assumptions about the consumption function marks the starting point of modern economic theory.

Classical economists argued that the level of consumption expenditures is determined largely by the rate of interest. Variations in consumption and savings are the result of variations in the rate of interest: as the rate of interest increases, consumption out of current income decreases and savings out of current income increases. The Classical rationale is easily stated. They theorized that the ultimate goal of every consumer is to maximize utility within the limits of his income and resources. He must decide whether he receives more utility from consuming his income during the current time period, or from consuming part of his current income presently and saving the remainder for consumption during future time periods. They argued that the decision to consume more and save less, or consume less and save more, is made on the basis of the level of current prices, expected price changes, and the rate of interest. If the interest rate is high, and prices are expected to remain stable, the utility maximizing consumer has an

---

[5] An excellent treatment of the consumption function can be found in Michael K. Evans, *Macroeconomic Activity*, (New York: Harper and Row, Publishers, 1969), Chaps. 2 and 3.

incentive to postpone current consumption in order to save. The incentive is simply the prospect of earning interest income and, thereby, the lure of higher levels of consumption in the future. After all, if prices remain constant, every dollar of current savings held at interest yields more than a dollar's worth of future consumption. Accordingly, the higher the rate of interest—assuming stable prices—the greater is the incentive to save. The lower the rate of interest, the greater is the incentive to consume. Thus, according to Classical theory, the levels of consumption and savings are largely determined by the level of interest rates.

Keynesian economists argue that the level of consumption expenditures is determined primarily by the level of income. They theorize that consumption changes with income and is relatively unaffected by interest rates. They argue for the existence of marginal and average propensities to consume. They insist that the MPC is positive and less than unity, and that the APC declines as income increases. Finally, they argue that, at very low levels of income, consumption expenditures may even exceed income. Does the argument sound familiar? It should because our consumption functions, which are based on income, are Keynesian rather than Classical.

THREE THEORIES OF THE CONSUMPTION FUNCTION

Earlier in this chapter, we discussed two consumption functions, a short-run consumption function and a long-run consumption function. We noted that, along a short-run consumption function, total consumption increases by less than total income (that is why the APC declines as income increases). Along a long-run consumption function, total consumption increases in equal proportions with total income (that is why the APC remains constant as income increases). Thus, we say that the consumption-income relationship is nonproportional in the short run, but proportional in the long run.

One of the major debates in modern economic theory centers around the question of which relationship—proportional or nonproportional—is correct. There are three alternative theories. The *Absolute Income Theory* argues that the proper relationship between consumption and income is nonproportional and is characterized by a short-run consumption function, but that this function shifts upward over time giving the statistical appearance of a proportional relationship. The *Relative Income Theory* and the *Permanent Income Theory* argue, for different reasons, that the proper relationship is proportional and is characterized by a long-run consumption function, but that short-run deviations produce the statistical appearance of a nonproportional relationship. We will examine each of the three alternative theories.

Absolute Income Theory

According to the Absolute Income Theory (AIT) the level of consumption expenditures depends on the *absolute* level of income, with the APC declining as the absolute level of income increases.[6] Since the level of national income grows over time, the AIT concludes that the APC should diminish continuously. Thus, the AIT argues that the consumption-income relationship is nonproportional. In Figure 5–4, as income increases over time, consumption should follow the nonproportional function identified as C_1. However, we saw that the statistical evidence suggests otherwise. The evidence indicates that, over the long run, consumption follows the path of the proportional function identified as C_3.

To rationalize this difference between theory and reality, the proponents of the AIT argue that there are upward shifts in the nonproportional consumption function—for example, the shift from C_1 to C_2 in Figure 5–4—caused by changes in factors other than income. They argue that the upward shifts are the result of such factors as: consumers spending a larger portion of any given level of income than was historically normal because of the increased accumulation of wealth that has accompanied U.S. economic development; people becoming less frugal, and spending a larger portion of current income, as they migrate from rural to urban communities (there is some statistical evidence suggesting that the MPC of urban workers is higher than that of farmer workers); and, households spending more at every level of income in order to purchase newly introduced consumer goods which they regard as "necessities." The AIT argues that these factors have caused the short-run, nonproportional consumption function to shift upward in a manner that creates an illusion of proportionality, and, thereby, obscures the basic nonproportional relationship. Thus, the AIT argues that it is the influence of these factors (other than

---

[6] The development of the Absolute Income Theory is usually credited to A. Smithies, "Forecasting Postwar Demand: I," *Econometrica*, January 1945, 1–14.

income) which causes changes in consumption and income to appear proportional ; but, if all other things were held constant, consumption and income would vary nonproportionally.

Relative Income Theory

According to the Relative Income Theory (RIT), the level of consumption expenditures is not determined by the absolute level of income but by the *relative* level of income, with the APC declining as *relative income* increases and remaining constant as absolute income increases.[7] More specifically, the RIT argues that the level of consumption spending is determined by the household's level of current income relative to the highest level of income it previously earned. Therefore, we can say that:

$$(5.5) \qquad C = aY + b\left(\frac{Y_h}{Y}\right)Y,$$

where C represents the current level of consumption expenditures, Y represents the current level of income, Y_h represents the highest level of income previously earned, and a and b represent numerical constants which relate income to consumption.

From equation (5.5), we can establish the two major conclusions of the RIT. First, when a household (and all households in the aggregate) experiences a temporary, short-run increase in current income above its previous peak level of income, it increases its consumption expenditures by an amount which is less-than-proportional to the increase in current income. Consequently, when current income rises relative to peak income, the APC declines and the increase in total consumption expenditures is *not proportional* to the increase in total income.[8] Second, when a household (and all households in the aggregate) experiences current and peak income growing by the same per-

---

[7] The development of the Relative Income Theory is usually credited to J. S. Duesenberry, *Income, Savings, and the Theory of Consumer Behavior* (Cambridge, Mass.: Harvard University Press, (1949).

[8] The proposition that an increase in current income relative to previous peak income causes the APC to decline can be demonstrated mathematically. Assume that the following conditions hold during the current time period (t):

$$C_t = C_t,$$
$$Y_t = Y_t, \text{ and}$$
$$Y_{ht} = Y_t.$$

Therefore, total consumption expenditures are:

centage amount, it increases its consumption expenditures by an amount which is proportional to the increase in current income. Consequently, the APC remains constant and the increase in total consumption expenditures is *proportional* to the increase in total income.[9]

$$C_t = aY_t + b\left[\frac{Y_{ht}}{Y_t}\right]Y_t, \text{ and};$$

The APC equals:

$$\frac{C_t}{Y_t} = a + b,$$

since $Y_{ht} = Y_t$. Now let current income increase in time period $(t+1)$ by g percent while the previous peak level of income remains constant (current income rises relative to peak income). Under these assumptions:

$$Y_{t+1} = (1+g)Y_t,$$
$$Y_{ht+1} = Y_{ht} = Y_t, \text{ and}$$
$$C_{t+1} = aY_{t+1} + b\left[\frac{Y_{ht}}{Y_{t+1}}\right]Y_{t+1}.$$

The APC now equals:

$$\frac{C_{t+1}}{Y_{t+1}} = a + \frac{b}{(1+g)},$$

which is less than C_t/Y_t since g is greater than zero. Therefore, an increase in current income relative to peak income causes the APC to decline, which means that the increase in total consumption expenditures is not proportional to the increase in total income.

[9] The proposition that an equiproportional increase in current and peak income leaves the APC constant can be demonstrated mathematically. Assume that the following conditions hold during the current time period $(t+1)$

$$C_{t+1} = aY_{t+1} + b\left[\frac{Y_{ht}}{Y_t}Y_t\right], \text{ and}$$

$$\frac{C_{t+1}}{Y_{t+1}} = a + \frac{b}{(1+g)}.$$

Assume that current income and peak income both increase during time period $(t+1)$ by g percent (current income does not rise relative to peak income). Under these assumptions:

$$Y_{t+2} = (1+g)Y_{t+1}, \text{ and}$$
$$Y_{ht+2} = (1+g)Y_{ht} = (1+g)Y_t$$

Therefore;

$$C_{t+2} = aY_{t+2} + b\left[\frac{(1+g)Y_t}{(1+g)^2 Y_t}\right]Y_{t+2} \text{ and}$$

$$\frac{C_{t+2}}{Y_{t+2}} = a + \frac{b}{(1+g)},$$

which is equal to C_{t+1}/Y_{t+1}. Therefore; equiproportional growth in current and peak income leaves the APC constant, which means that the increase in total consumption expenditures is proportional to the increase in total income.

Thus, according to the RIT, changes in current consumption are not proportional to the changes in current income only when current income rises relative to previous peak income. If current and peak income grow together, changes in consumption are always proportional to the changes in income. This is the argument of the RIT.

We can demonstrate both conclusions with a simple numerical example. Suppose that we are able to examine the consumption behavior of a household whose previous peak income (Y_h from equation [5.5]) equals $10,000. Also, suppose that we vary the household's level of current income (Y from equation [5.5]) by $2,000 increments from a level of $6,000 to $14,000, assuming that the change in current income is temporary and does not alter the peak level of income. Finally, if we assume that a equals 0.20 and b equals 0.40 (from equation [5.5]), we can calculate the household's level of consumption and APC for each level of current income. We see that, as current income rises relative to peak income, the APC declines and the level of consumption expenditures increases less-than-proportionally with the level of current income. This information is summarized in Table 5–2, and illustrated in Figure 5–5. Thus, according to the proponents

TABLE 5–2

Current income Y	Peak income Y_h	Consumption expenditures $C = aY + b(Y_{h/Y}) \cdot Y$	Average propensity to consume C/Y
$ 6,000	$10,000	$5,200	0.866
8,000	10,000	5,600	0.700
10,000	10,000	6,000	0.600
12,000	10,000	6,400	0.533
14,000	10,000	6,800	0.485

of the RIT, it is an increase in current income relative to peak income which gives rise to the short-run, nonproportional consumption function.

Suppose that we examine the consumption behavior of another household whose peak income equals $10,000, and whose current income equals $10,000 also. Furthermore, let us assume that the household's level of current income increases by increments of 10 percent from $10,000 to $14,641, assuming that each change in current in-

FIGURE 5-5

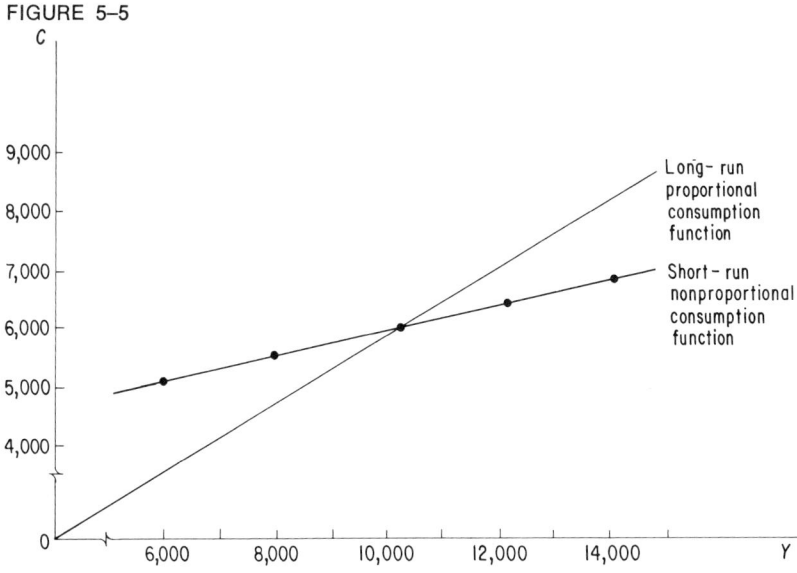

come is permanent and causes peak income to increase by the same percentage amount. Please notice that the change in peak income lags behind the change in current income. The lagged change in peak income occurs because it takes the household some time to realize that the change in current income is permanent rather than temporary. With a equal to 0.20 and b equal to 0.40, our calculations show that, as current income rises proportionally with peak income, the APC remains constant and the level of consumption expenditures increases proportionally with the level of current income. This information is summarized in Table 5-3, and illustrated in Figure 5-5. Thus, accord-

TABLE 5-3

Current income Y	Peak income Y_h	Consumption expenditures $C = aY + b(Y_h/Y) \cdot Y$	Average propensity to consume C/Y
$10,000	$ 9,090	$6,000	0.600
11,000	10,000	6,200	0.563
12,100	11,000	6,820	0.563
13,310	12,100	7,502	0.563
14,641	13,310	8,252	0.563

ing to the proponents of the RIT, it is continuous growth in current income—and, thereby, growth in peak income by the same percentage rate—which gives rise to the long-run, proportional consumption function.

There is a final point to note about the Relative Income Theory. It works for decreases as well as increases in the level of current income. When used to analyze decreases in current income relative to peak income, the RIT reveals a fundamental psychological "law" of consumption. As current income falls relative to peak income, each household (and all households in the aggregate) is forced to reduce its level of consumption. However, the reduction in consumption is less than the reduction in income. Consumers attempt to maintain as much of their previous level of consumption—or standard of living—as possible. They prevent consumption from declining too far by drawing down their past savings. In this way, the reluctance to reduce consumption spending in proportion to the loss in current income acts as a ratchet which keeps the economy from slipping backward and losing all its previous gains in income and standard of living. We call this the *ratchet effect,* and you can see it operate by working backward through Table 5–2 and the short-run consumption function of Figure 5–5. The evidence shows that consumers have followed a ratchet pattern in four post-World War II recessions.

Thus, the RIT argues that it is the temporary deviations in current income from peak income which have caused short-run, nonproportional variations in consumption and income, and have obscured the basic, long-run relation between consumption and income. The RIT is fundamentally different from the AIT. The RIT explains away the short-run consumption function as a result of temporary deviations in current income, while the AIT explains away the long-run consumption function as the result of factors other than income on consumption. Yet, both theories acknowledge the existence of separate short-run and long-run consumption functions.

Permanent Income Theory

According to the Permanent Income Theory (PIT), the level of consumption expenditures is not determined by absolute or relative levels of income but by the level of *permanent income,* with the APC out of permanent income remaining constant as permanent income increases and the APC out of current income declining as current income increases above permanent income in the short run.[10] Although it sounds similar to the Relative Income Theory, there is a significant difference. The PIT argues that *permanent consumption* is proportional to *permanent income;* while the RIT argues that, in the long run, *current consumption* is proportional to *current income.* The difference is more than semantic.

Let us examine the difference between permanent income and current income. Ask yourself these questions: what measure of income determines a household's level of consumption spending? What is the appropriate time dimension? Does consumption depend on income earned today, this week, this month, or this year? Do consumption expenditures actually vary upward and downward from month to month as household income varies or do consumption expenditures seem to be insulated, in reality, from short-run variations in the current flow of income? Common sense and most family budget studies tell us that the appropriate measure of income is an average of the amounts received in the current year and the preceding year, or an average of the amounts received in the current and preceding years and the amount expected in future years. The measure of income determined as an average of current, past, and future incomes is called permanent income.

The PIT uses the concept of permanent income, and rejects current income, as the basis for consumption expenditures. However, we are still begging the essential question: What is the time horizon of permanent income? How far back into past income and forward into future income does permanent income reach? Obviously, the answer is different for every individual and every household. The time horizon for each household, or individual, is determined by the minimum length of time that a past level of income must be experienced to be believed permanent, and by the degree of certainty in the expectations of future levels of income. The longer is the experience span required, the farther back in time the past income component must go. The greater is the degree of certainty, the farther forward in time the future income component will go. The required experience span and the degree of certainty in expectaions are influenced by a host of socioeconomic

---

[10] The development of the Permanent Income theory is usually credited to M. Friedman, *A Theory of the Consumption Function* (Princeton, N.J.: Princeton University Press, 1957).

factors as health, education, job security, accumulated wealth, and so forth. Thus, the time horizon for determining permanent income is usually greater than one year but less than the life span of the household (or individual).

Since permanent income is defined as an average of current, past, and future incomes, a household's level of current income may be larger or smaller than its permanent income. Explaining a divergence between permanent, and current income is simple. Current income, according to the PIT, is divided into two components: a permanent income component and a *transitory income* component, such that:

$$(5.6) \qquad Y = Y_p + Y_t,$$

where Y represents current income, Y_p represents permanent income, and Y_t represents transitory income. Consequently, current income is greater or less than permanent income as transitory income is positive or negative. For example, suppose that a household wins a cash prize in a legal lottery. Since the cash prize was not fully anticipated and since it is not likely to be won by the household regularly, it represents positive transitory income. Instead, if a household experience a loss in income due to a temporary illness or work layoff, the loss represents negative transitory income. In the first case, current income rises above permanent income. In the second case, current income falls below permanent income. According to the PIT, the transitory income components are expected to cancel out (i.e., sum to zero) over the time horizon used to compute permanent income, but are present always in shorter time periods.

Similarly, the PIT argues that current consumption is divided into two components: permanent consumption and *transitory consumption,* such that:

$$(5.7) \qquad C = C_p + C_t,$$

where C represents current consumption, C_p represents permanent consumption, and C_t represents transitory consumption. Obviously, current consumption is larger or smaller than permanent consumption as transitory consumption is positive or negative. Furthermore, the PIT uses a peculiar definition of consumption—current, permanent, and transitory alike. The PIT excludes the purchase of consumer durable goods (e.g., automobiles, and refrigerators) from the definition of consumption. It defines consumption as spending on services and nondurable goods plus depreciation on consumer durable goods. The net addition to the household's stock of durable goods is defined, by the PIT, as savings. We will note the importance of this definition of consumption shortly. (By the way, both the AIT and the RIT include the purchase of durable goods in their definitions of consumption.)

Using these definitions, we can be more specific about the meaning of the PIT. The PIT argues that permanent consumption is proportional to permanent income—that the basic relationship is summarized by a proportional consumption function. In other words, the APC out of permanent income (i.e., the ratio C_p/Y_p is constant). Furthermore, the value of the APC (whether it is large or small) depends on the level of interest rates, the ratio of "nonhuman" to total wealth (i.e., "nonhuman" plus "human" wealth) and tastes. Thus we can summarize the consumption function of the PIT in the following equations:

(5.8) $$C_p = bY_p,$$

or

(5.8a) $$\frac{C_p}{Y_p} = b,$$

where b represents the APC (and the MPC) out of permanent income. Please note that the PIT requires that b is positive but less than unity, and constant. All other variables were defined earlier. Equations (5.8) and (5.8a) are shown in Figure 5–6. In Figure 5–6, the slope of the consumption function is less than the 45° line because b is less than unity. The ratio $ad/0a$ equals the ratio $ec/0e$ because the APC out of permanent income is constant. The consumption function of this figure portrays a proportional relationship between C_p and Y_p.

If we examine equations (5.8) and (5.8a) and Figure 5–6 closely, we find a startling conclusion of the PIT. The PIT argues that the ratio C_p/Y_p is independent of Y_p itself—the APC out of permanent income does not change as Y_p changes. If all households had the same tastes, faced the same interest rates, and had the same ratio of "nonhuman" to total wealth, each would spend exactly the same proportion of its permanent income on consumption—regardless of its position on the income distribution scale. A "rich" household is supposed to consume the same proportion of its permanent income as a "poor" household. Startling indeed! For example, suppose that

FIGURE 5-6

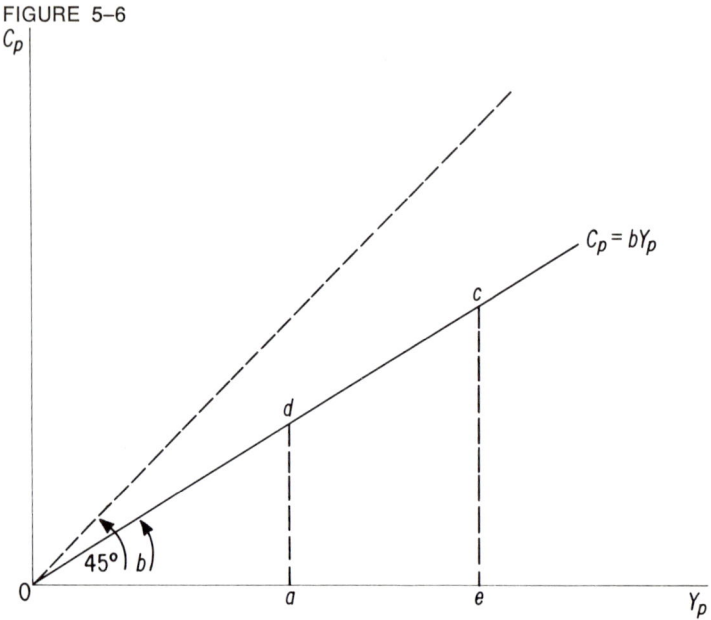

we have two households which are identical in every respect except for the level of permanent income. Suppose that each household consists of four members, that one household receives $5,000 of permanent income, and the other household receives $10,000 of permanent income. According to the PIT, if the poorer household spends all of its income on consumption (i.e., has an APC equal to unity), then the richer household would spend all its income on consumption too. If the richer household saves 10 percent of its income (i.e., has an APC equal to 0.90), then the poorer household would save 10 percent of its income also. This conclusion seems improbable. Most economists would argue that the pressures for present consumption are greater at lower levels of income. Consequently, it seems unlikely that a poor household would save the same proportion of its income as a wealthy household.

Furthermore, suppose that each household experienced a 25 percent increase in permanent income. According to the PIT, the wealthier household would consume 90 percent ($2,250) of its $2,500 gain, and the poorer household would consume 90 percent ($1,125) of its $1,250 gain. Again, the conclusion seems improbable. Most economists would argue that the wealthy household would save a larger proportion of its increase in income than the poorer family. Therefore, contrary to the PIT, we expect low-income households to consume a larger proportion (and save a smaller proportion) of their incremental income than high-income households. One explanation for the divergence between what we expect to happen and what the PIT argues will happen lies in the PIT's definition of consumption. If low-income households spend a significant percentage of their additional income on consumer durable goods, and since the PIT defines purchases of durables as savings, the proportion of incremental income saved (through purchases of durables) by low-income households may be close to the proportion saved by high-income households.

Another controversial conclusion of the PIT is that transitory consumption is not related to transitory income. When a household experiences a transitory decline in income, its consumption expenditures do not decline too. Likewise, when a household experiences a transitory increase in income, its consumption expenditures do not increase too. According to the proponents of the PIT, unexpected changes in income do not produce changes in consumption; instead, they produce equivalent changes in savings. In the jargon of the PIT, the MPC out of transitory or "windfall" income is zero, and the MPS out of transitory or "windfall" income is unity. Remember that, in the PIT, the purchase of consumer durable goods is counted as savings. To the extent that households spend "windfall" income on boats, autos, refrigerator-freezers and the like, transitory income would be "saved."

If current consumption is uncorrelated to transitory income, the consumption-income relationship is nonproportional in the short run. For example, suppose that b of equation (5.8) equals 0.90, the permanent income of a particular household equals $10,000, and its level of permanent consumption equals $9,000. Now let the household experience a transitory loss in income of $1,000, causing current income to decline to $9,000 (from equation [5.6]). The level of consumption does not decline too, rather it remains at $9,000 and the APC increases. Instead, let the household experience a transitory gain in income of $1,000, causing current income to rise to $11,000 (again from equation [5.6]). Once again, the level of consumption remains at $9,000. Note that the APC declines as income increases. The "windfall" gain must, according to the PIT, go into additional savings or into the purchase of consumer durable goods. Thus, if consumption and transitory income are uncorrelated, the short-run relationship between consumption and income is nonproportional.

Since the PIT argues that the proper consumption function relates permanent consumption to permanent income, it concludes that the long-run consumption-income relationship is proportional. Changes in permanent income give rise to proportional changes in permanent consumption. Furthermore, since the PIT argues that permanent consumption and transitory income are uncorrelated, it concludes that the short-run consumption-income relationship is nonproportional. Both conclusions are illustrated in Figure 5–7.

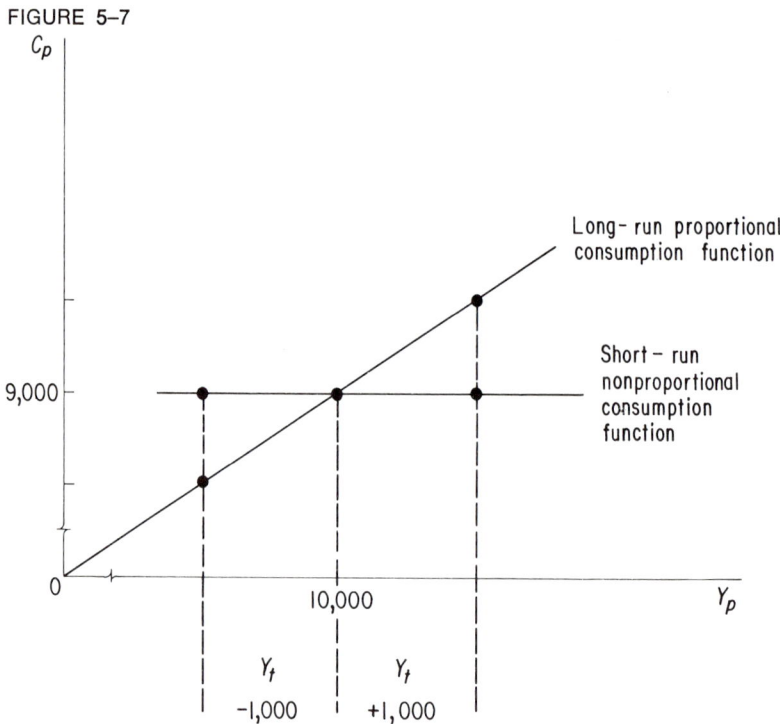

FIGURE 5–7

The PIT explains the existence of two consumption functions in a manner similar to the RIT. However, the two theories are not identical, nor are they comparable. The RIT is based on a relationship between current consumption and current income; while the PIT is based on a relationship between permanent consumption and permanent income. It is interesting to note that the differences between the PIT and the RIT are still the source of considerable controversy among economic theorists.

A minor problem now faces us. Shall we employ a long-run consumption function or a short-run consumption function? Since our task is to analyze changes in economic activity when income levels rise as well as fall, it will be easier to employ the notion of the short-run consumption function. Hence, we will use throughout this book a linear consumption along which the average propensity to consume falls as income rises.

OTHER FACTORS

Thus far we have assumed that the level of consumption is dependent upon the level of income, however defined. This assumption is an obvious oversimplification. There are factors other than income which affect the level of consumption expenditures. Although none of these factors, is as important as income, our discussion of the consumption function would be incomplete without them. Nevertheless, since the material in this chapter has been relatively difficult, it seems prudent to postpone our discussion of the more significant of these other factors—interest rates, price expectations, and accumulated wealth—until later chapters where we can examine each one in detail. Consequently, we will discuss the influence of interest rates on consumption in Chapter 13, prices and price expectations in Chapter 9, and wealth in Chapter 12.

CONCLUDING NOTE

In this chapter, we took a long, and sometimes tedious, look at the consumption function. We saw that the statistical evidence suggests the existence of two functions: a short-run (nonproportional) consumption function and a long-run (proportional) consumption function. We examined three alternative theories which attempt to explain the relationship between the two consumption functions. Finally, we decided to concentrate our attention on the short-run consumption function because our basic task is to understand the causes of short-run variations in national income and employment.

In the next chapter, we look at the factors which determine the level of investment expenditures.

6 The level of investment

IN THE PRECEDING CHAPTERS we have assumed that the level of investment was independent of the level of income. Indeed, we implicitly assumed that the level of investment was constant and, as such, was independent of all variables. Clearly, this is an oversimplification. The level of investment does fluctuate, and there are many variables—such as the interest rate, the level of income or output, the wage rate, the level of technology, and the corporate tax rate—which influence the size and frequency of the fluctuations. In this chapter, we will look at these variables.

INVESTMENT AND THE RATE OF INTEREST

The decision to invest in machinery, for example, depends upon whether or not the expected rate of return on the machine is greater than the cost of borrowing the necessary funds, or, if the funds are already available, the cost of the earnings lost by purchasing the machine rather than lending out the funds. The principle sounds simple, but it is actually complicated. Ask yourself the question: How do you estimate the expected returns to and costs of a machine which may not yield a return at all for n years and starting with the $(n+1)$st year yields a return which differs every year?

In order to answer the question properly, we must restate the principle. The decision to invest in a machine (or a building, or inventories) depends upon whether or not the investment is expected to yield more revenue over its lifetime than it costs to purchase and operate: i.e., depends upon whether it is expected to add to total profits. If the expected total revenue exceeds the total cost, the machine should be purchased. Again, the principle sounds deceptively simple. Ask the question: Since a machine usually has a lifetime which extends over a number of years, how do you know the revenue it will earn in future years? What is the present value (i.e., today's value) of all the future returns? Once we know the answers, the machine should be purchased if the *present value* of the returns exceeds the cost.

For example, suppose that we expect (through market surveys, and econometric forecasting) a particular machine to yield a return of R dollars (e.g., $100) in each of the next n years. Therefore, we expect the total net returns from the machine over the next n years to be:

$$R_1 + R_2 + R_3 + \cdots + R_n + J$$

where J represents the scrap or salvage value of the machine after n years of use. Using this information, we can calculate the present value of the stream of returns:[1]

$$(6.1) \quad V = \frac{R_1}{(1+i)} + \frac{R_2}{(1+i)^2} + \cdots + \frac{R_n}{(1+i)^n} + \frac{J}{(1+i)^n},$$

where V represents the present value of the stream of returns, and

---

[1] We can demonstrate the method for calculating the present value of an asset. Suppose that the rate of interest is i, and I lend you $100. In one year, I will receive from you $100 + 100i$ or $100 (1 + i)$. We may say, in general, that if the amount of money lent is P_0, the lender will receive at the end of one year:

$$P_1 = P_0(1+i).$$

If that new sum is loaned out for another year, the amount returned at the end of that year is:

$$P_2 = P_1(1+i) = P_0(1+i)(1+i) = P_0(1+i)^2$$

Following this procedure, a loan for n years would return:

$$P_n = P_0(1+i)^n.$$

Thus, we may conclude that a claim that in n years will return P_n dollars may be sold today for exactly P_0 dollars, or:

$$P_0 = \frac{P_n}{(1+i)^n}.$$

P_0 is the present value of the claim.

Let us now consider the present value of a bond. Instead of a single claim

i is some appropriate interest rate. Furthermore, suppose that the machine initially cost C dollars (e.g., \$1,000) to purchase. If i equals 0.05 and J equals zero, then we have:[2]

(6.2) $$V = \frac{100}{(1.05)} + \frac{100}{(1.05)^2} + \cdots + \frac{100}{(1.05)^n},$$

$$V = \frac{100}{0.05} \approx 2{,}000 \text{ as } n \text{ gets very large.}$$

Since V approaches \$2,000 and $C = \$1{,}000$, the decision to invest is a simple one. Since the present value of the expected income stream is greater than the cost of the machine, the entrepreneur should invest. Furthermore, note that with an explicit life of a machine and known returns, V is easy to calculate. Hence, V can easily be compared to C.

Now let us return to our original statement about the decision to invest. We said that the rational entrepreneur will invest in a machine whenever the rate of return exceeds the cost of borrowing, or, in the absence of borrowing, the opportunity cost of the available funds. If the rate of return is r and it is the same as the rate at which money can be borrowed, then it is a matter of indifference whether funds are used to purchase a machine or to lend out to obtain interest payments. However, if $r > i$, where i is the rate of interest and r the rate of return, then the machine should be purchased even if it is necessary to borrow funds to do so.

We are still begging the essential question: Since a machine is expected to earn a stream of returns over a number of years, how do we calculate the current, expected rate of return to the machine? To do it, we must know three things about the machine: its stream of returns $R_1, \ldots, R_n$, its initial cost C, and its scrap or salvage value J. The expected rate of return to the investment is simply the *discount rate* which exactly equates the value of all expected future earnings to the initial cost of the machine. We say that:

---

collectible at some specified future date, a bond represents a series of claims collectible at different times in the future. Assume that each year a coupon can be cashed in for a fixed sum R. When there are no more coupons left (when the bond has reached maturity), the bond may be cashed in for its par value, J. Today's value of the bond is merely the present value of the sum of all the discounted future returns plus the discounted value of the maturity value. The present value of the bond may be given by equation (6.1).

[2] The solution to (6.2) requires the summing of an infinite series with the use of the formula: $S \frac{a}{(1+r)}$; where S is the sum of the series, a, the first term in the series, and r the ratio between terms.

$$(6.3) \quad C = \frac{R_1}{(1+r)} + \frac{R_2}{(1+r)^2} + \cdots + \frac{R_n}{(1+r)^n} + \frac{J}{(1+r)^n},$$

where r is the expected rate of return to the investment. You should recognize that r would be the discount factor in a present value problem (compare equation [6.3] with equation [6.1], and with the equations in footnote 1). In economic jargon, we say that r is the *marginal efficiency of capital* (MEC):[3] it is the expected rate of return; it is the discount rate which exactly equates the value of all expected returns to the initial cost of the investment.

Let us consider a simple example. Suppose that a decision must be made whether to invest in a machine with an infinite expected life. Further suppose that the return is $100 per year and the initial cost of the machine is $1,000. Since the machine has an infinite life expectancy, there is no salvage value to consider. Thus

$$(6.4) \quad 1{,}000 = \frac{100}{(1+r)} + \frac{100}{(1+r)^2} + \cdots + \frac{100}{(1+r)^n},$$

$$1{,}000 = \frac{100}{r},$$

$$r = 0.10.$$

If $i = 0.05$, so that lending $1,000 yields a $50 return, it is wise to invest in the machine. The return from the machine, or the MEC, is twice as great as the interest payment, since $r = 2i$. It should be clear that r is quite difficult to calculate, particularly in cases in which the returns differ from year to year and when the life expectancy is not infinite. Also, it should be clear that when r is greater than i, V will exceed C. The two statements are equivalent. Compare the examples summarized in equations (6.2) and (6.4).

Now that we understand the principle governing the decision to invest, we must ask an additional question: How many machines should the rational entrepreneur purchase? How much investment should take place? The answer is simple. As long as the MEC (r) is greater than the rate of interest (i), or as long as the present value of the stream of future returns (V) exceeds the cost (C), investment should take place. Suppose that a business manager sees an array of potential investment projects available to his firm. Since each investment project is different, each has a different stream of returns, a

---

[3] J. M. Keynes, *The General Theory of Employment, Interest, and Money* (New York: Harcourt, Brace and World, Inc., Publishers, 1936), p. 135.

different initial cost, a different present value, and a different rate of return (MEC). Suppose that the firm can borrow an unlimited supply of funds at a constant interest rate. Using this information, the business manager can array each investment project according to the amount by which its r (MEC) exceeds i; after all, the greater is the rate of return above the cost of borrowed funds, the more profitable is the investment. Such a situation is illustrated in Table 6–1. Clearly, investment project one is more profitable than invest-

TABLE 6–1

Investment projects	$(r - i)$
1.	(0.10 − 0.05) = 0.05
2.	(0.08 − 0.05) = 0.03
3.	(0.05 − 0.05) = 0
4.	(0.04 − 0.05) = −0.01
5.	(0.03 − 0.05) = −0.02

ment project two, project two is more profitable than project three, and so on. How many investment projects should the business manager undertake? He should invest in project one because it adds more to the firm's revenues than it does to costs, and, thereby, increases the total profits of the firm. He should invest in project two for the same reasons. He is indifferent about project three because it adds equally to revenues and costs, and, thereby, leaves the total profits of the firm unchanged. He should not invest in projects four and five because they add more to costs than to revenues, and, thereby, decrease the total profits of the firm. Therefore, the maximum number of investment expenditures is three—the rational businessman will not invest beyond project three because r (MEC) is less than i. Therefore, investment should take place to the point where the marginal efficiency of capital (r) equals the cost of borrowing (i).

Let us now note what happens as the rate of interest falls. It should be apparent that when the rate of interest falls from, say, 5 percent a year to 3 percent a year, investment opportunities with rates of return just over 3 percent a year become profitable, whereas before the fall in the rate of interest these investment opportunities were unprofitable. Under these circumstances, the businessman should increase his level of investment up to, but not beyond, investment project five.

Thus, we conclude that as the rate of interest falls the level of investment will increase, assuming that the MEC remains unchanged. Hence, we may depict graphically an investment function relating the level of investment to the rate of interest in Figure 6–1. In the

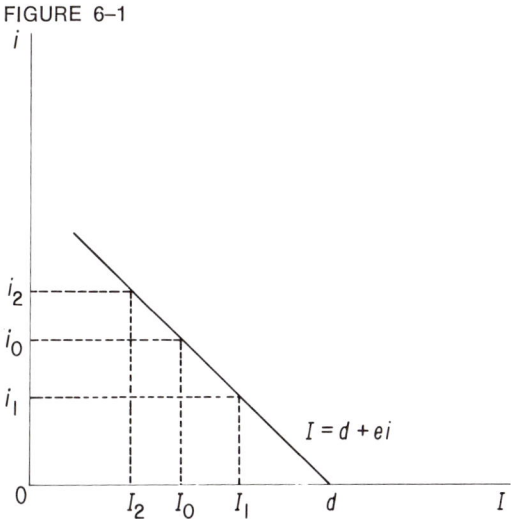

FIGURE 6–1

figure, we have drawn a linear investment function for simplicity. The equation of such an investment function is:

(6.5) $$I = d + ei,$$

where d is positive and e is negative. The fact that e is negative indicates that the level of investment increases as the rate of interest falls, and the fact that d is positive shows that when the rate of interest falls to zero the level of investment will reach some maximum level, d.

We can now view a line of causation running from the rate of interest to the level of investment, and from the level of investment to the level of income and the level of consumption. As the interest rate falls, the level of investment increases. Given the consumption function, the equilibrium level of national income must rise. When the level of income increases so, of course, does the level of consumption. In Figure 6–2 we show an increase in the level of income and consumption brought about by a decrease in the rate of interest. In the figure, we note that two expenditures lines, or aggregate demand functions, have been drawn. The lower one is based upon the given

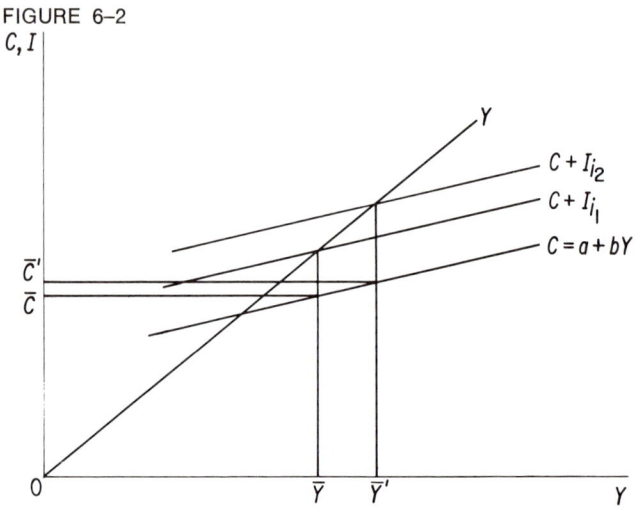

FIGURE 6-2

consumption function, and the level of investment generated when the interest rate is i_1. The higher aggregate demand function is based upon the given consumption function, and the level of investment generated when the interest rate has fallen to i_2. Note that the level of income has increased from $\bar{Y}$ to $\bar{Y}'$, while the level of consumption has increased along the consumption function from $\bar{C}$ to $\bar{C}'$. You should note that the equilibrium level of income has risen simply because the level of investment has increased, and the full multiplier effect obtains. This analysis differs from the earlier analysis of the increase in income only in that we have indicated what might have brought about the upward shift in the investment function, when looking at the income-expenditure approach to the determination of equilibrium levels of national income.

INVESTMENT AND THE LEVEL OF NATIONAL INCOME

There is no reason to confine ourselves to considering the rate of interest as the only determinant of the level of investment. We may, for example, assume that as the level of national income increases, investment opportunities become more plentiful and so the level of investment, for any given rate of interest, will increase. Thus, we would note an outward shift in the investment function of Figure 6–1. Likewise, if the level of national income were to fall, the investment function would shift to the left telling us that at all levels of the interest

FIGURE 6-3

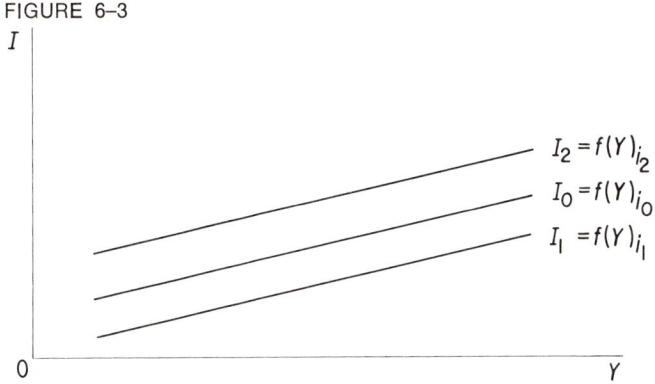

rate, the level of investment will go down. This, of course, comes about from the apparent lack of investment opportunities.

We may graphically view the relationship between the level of investment and the level of national income in Figure 6–3. In the figure, we have assumed a given level of the rate of interest, in this case i_0. If the interest rate were to increase to i_1, the investment function of the figure would fall to I_1; or if the interest rate were to fall to i_2, the investment function would shift upward to I_2. We might also note the relationship between this new investment function, the consumption function, and the equilibrium level of national income. Such a relationship is depicted in Figure 6–4. It should be noted in the

FIGURE 6-4

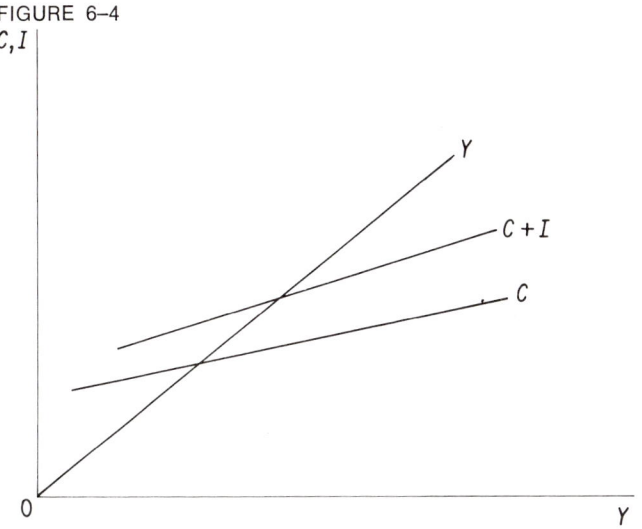

figure that the slope of the new aggregate demand function is greater than the slope of the consumption function. The reason for this should be obvious. Investment no longer is independent of the level of income. Indeed, we have assumed, as shown in Figure 6–3, that investment increases as the level of national income increases. Thus, the aggregate demand function $(C + I)$ will be steeper than the consumption function.

We can demonstrate that the new aggregate demand function is steeper than the consumption function. Let the new aggregate demand function equal:

$$(6.6) \qquad C + I = a + bY + (d + ei + fY)$$
$$= (a + d + ei) + bY + fY$$
$$= (a + d + ei) + (b + f)Y.$$

The term in parentheses on the right-hand side of equation (6.6) represents the investment function with a given level of the rate of interest, and where f is positive to show that investment increases with income. We note, in the final expression of equation (6.6), that when the level of income is zero, the level of aggregate demand is either positive or negative depending upon the value of e. We would, of course, expect $(a + d + ei)$ to be positive under "normal" circumstances. Since f is positive, it is clear that the slope of this aggregate demand function, $(b + f)$, is greater than the slope of the consumption function, b. Hence, the position of the aggregate demand function of Figure 6–4 relative to the consumption function of the same figure is appropriate.

INVESTMENT AND THE CHANGE IN THE LEVEL OF INCOME

While it is interesting to view investment as a function of both the rate of interest and the level of national income, it is also necessary to think of the level of investment as dependent upon the rate of interest and the change in the level of national income from one period to the next. We call this relationship the *accelerator principle*. When viewing the relationship between the level of investment, the interest rate, and the change in the level of income we leave the world of static analysis and enter the world of dynamic analysis. That is to say, we now view the movements of variables over time, rather than looking at them at a moment in time.

Since every level of output is produced by some combination of labor and capital, and if the amount of available labor is specified and held constant, there is some optimal level of the capital stock. The optimal level of the capital stock is that level, given the existing labor force, which produces output most efficiently. To the extent that business firms attempt to be as efficient as possible, the optimal level of the capital stock is also the desired level of the capital stock. Clearly, the existing level of capital stock may be equal to, less than, or greater than the desired level, which is nothing more than the level of capital stock that the business sector of the economy seeks to reach. Let us assume that the desired level of capital stock depends upon the level of national income and the rate of interest. Thus, we say:

(6.7) $$K^d = u + vY + zi,$$

assuming a linear relationship among the variables. In order to attain the desired level of capital stock (if it has not been reached), investment or disinvestment must take place. Just how rapidly firms wish to reach the desired level of capital stock determines the volume of investment. Suppose the speed of adjustment can be represented by a fraction, α, of the difference between the desired level of capital stock and the actual level. This fraction, α, simply shows that fraction of the difference between the desired level of capital stock and the existing level of capital stock which business firms, in general, wish to make up during a single accounting period. Therefore, we say:

(6.8) $$I = \alpha(K^d - K),$$

where K is the existing level of capital stock. For simplicity assume that $\alpha = 1$. Then, we have, by substituting equation (6.7) into equation (6.8):

(6.9) $$I = u + vY + zi - K.$$

However, since $\alpha = 1$, adjustment was complete in the previous period. Hence,

(6.10) $$K_t = K^d_{t-1},$$

or the actual capital stock in period t is the same as the desired level of capital stock in period $t - 1$. Hence,

(6.11) $$\begin{aligned} I_t &= u + vY_t + zi_t - K^d_{t-1} \\ &= u + vY_t + zi_t - u - vY_{t-1} - zi_{t-1}, \end{aligned}$$

substituting equation (6.10) and equation (6.7) into equation (6.9). We may rewrite equation 6.11 as:

(6.11a) $$I_t = v(Y_t - Y_{t-1}) - z(i_t - i_{t-1}).$$

If the interest rate is somehow held constant, the only way for investment to increase is for income to increase at an increasing rate. For example, if in period $t = 0$, $Y = \$100$ and in period $t = 1$, $Y = \$105$ and assuming $v = 4$, the level of investment in period $t = 1$ is \$20. If now in period $t = 2$, Y increases to \$110, investment will remain at \$20. Why? For the level of investment to increase, the level of income will have to increase in period $t = 2$ to something greater than \$110. It follows that if the growth of national income slows down, investment will suffer an absolute decline even though the level of income has risen. If $Y = \$110$ during period $t = 2$ and grows to \$113 during period $t = 3$, the level of investment (given by equation [6.11a]) actually falls to \$12. Calculate the change. If the growth of income speeds up, the level of investment will increase. If $Y = \$113$ during period $t = 3$ and grows to \$120 during period $t = 4$, the level of investment rises to \$28. Again, calculate the change. Thus, the level of investment expenditures seems to be very sensitive to changes in the growth rate of income.

The coefficient v is the increment in capital stock required to increase the level of output by one unit. v is sometimes called the *capital-output ratio*. For example, if four units of capital are required to increase output by a single unit, the capital to output ratio (v) is 4. It is this relationship which creates the strong link between the level of investment and the growth of income. It is this relationship which gives rise to the *accelerator effect,* or *accelerator principle.*

We may look a bit more closely at the accelerator effect with the aid of a numerical example. Let us define induced investment as investment demanded for the sole purpose of providing additional capacity to produce a larger output. Autonomous investment, on the other hand, is investment demanded for the purpose of improving the method of producing a given level of output. Suppose that the capital-output ratio is 2 (i.e., $v = 2$), and suppose that the marginal propensity to consume is ½. For simplicity, we will ignore the rate of interest, and, therefore, we assume that:

(6.12) $$I_t = v(Y_{t-1} - Y_{t-2}),$$

where I is the level of induced investment. Note that this statement is somewhat different from that presented in equation (6.11). In equation (6.12) we assumed a somewhat different time lag than that indicated in equation (6.11). The reason for this will become apparent shortly. Finally, let us assume that we have the following consumption relationship:

(6.13) $$C_t = C_{t-1} + b(Y_{t-1} - Y_{t-2}).$$

Equation (6.13) merely indicates that today's consumption depends upon yesterday's consumption and the change in income over the previous two periods, and assumes that a linear relationship exists between these variables. The linear relationship is assumed, as usual, for simplicity only.

Suppose, in period $t = 0$, that autonomous investment is \$10 and consumption \$90. Thus, income in the period is $(C + I) = \$100$, ignoring the government sector. Suppose, in period $t = 1$, that autonomous investment increases to \$15. Assuming that consumption remains at \$90, the level of national income rises to \$105.[4]

We now employ equations (6.12) and (6.13) to obtain the values found in Table 6–2. For example, to determine income in period

TABLE 6–2

Time period	Autonomous investment	Induced investment	Consumption	Income
0........	$10	$ 0	$ 90.0	$100.0
1........	15	0	90.0	105.0
2........	15	10.0	92.5	117.5
3........	15	25.0	98.8	138.8
4........	15	42.6	109.5	167.1
5........	15	56.6	123.7	195.3
6........	15	56.4	137.8	209.2
7........	15	27.8	144.8	187.6
8........	15	–43.2	134.0	105.8

two, it is first necessary to determine the level of induced investment. Substituting the appropriate values into equation (6.12), we have:

(6.14) $$I_2 = 2(105 - 100) = 10.$$

To determine the level of consumption, we substitute the appropriate values into equation (6.13) and obtain:

---
[4] Since consumption depends upon the change in income over the previous two periods, we have assumed that this change will not be present initially. Rather, this effect will not be felt until period $t = 2$.

(6.15) $C_2 = 90 + \frac{1}{2}(105 - 100) = 90 + 2.5 = 92.5$.

Thus, the level of income in period two is $(15 + 10 + 92.5)$, or $117.5.

We see from Table 6–2 that the increase in autonomous investment causes income to increase which, in turn, induces investment to take place. The level of national income is "accelerated" and "multiplied" up, but eventually, as the level of income increases less rapidly, the level of induced investment falls and so the level of income itself begins to fall. Investment depends upon the rate of change in income, and determines the level of income. Investment is, thus, something of a two-edged sword.

There are some rather interesting implications that can be derived from our accelerator analysis. Suppose, for example, that the increase in national income between periods $t = 0$ and $t = 1$ is brought about not by an increase in autonomous investment but by an increase in government expenditures. Suppose that the increase in government expenditures is $5. Suppose that in period $t = 0$, the level of government expenditures is $10, and in all periods thereafter the level of government expenditures is $15. We are merely assuming that the autonomous investment column of the table is replaced by government expenditures, and the level of autonomous investment is constant. The level of income increases, and the accelerator effect takes over. Assuming that the new level of government expenditures is maintained in the future, the level of income will rise and then fall, if we assume that the increase in government expenditures does not stimulate autonomous expenditures by the private sector of the economy. If the private sector relies on the government sector to increase the level of national income, we find that the level of government expenditures will have to rise continuously. "Pump priming" must occur.[5] However, in times of a depression, when most economists argue that increases in government expenditures are desirable, it is altogether possible that the accelerator effect will not work. With excess capacity, as in a depression, there is no reason to believe that the private sector will be stimulated by government expenditures. There is no reason for business firms to add to their productive capacity in the face of existing excess capacity.

However, this is not to say that the accelerator model is useless.

---

[5] While the results will differ somewhat for different values of v and b, the direction of the movements in the variables will be the same.

On the contrary, the model provides one explanation of the turning points of the income cycle. The process is illustrated in Figure 6–5.

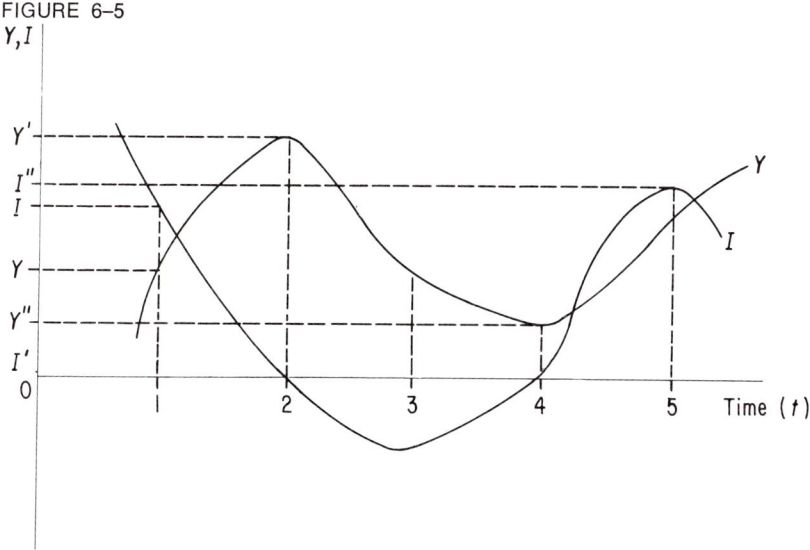

FIGURE 6-5

Suppose that the level of income grows, but at an ever slower rate, from Y to Y' over the period $t = 1$ to $t = 2$, peaking at Y'. Y' is an upper turning point in the income cycle. Since income is increasing at a decreasing rate, the accelerator principle tells us that the level of investment is declining: for example, from I to I' over the same time period. Beyond the upper turning point, the level of income begins to decline (as if the economy were in a recession or depression). As income falls from Y' to Y'' over the period $t = 2$ to $t = 4$, the rate of decline changes. Income declines at an ever faster rate from $t = 2$ to $t = 3$, and at an ever slower rate from $t = 3$ to $t = 4$. The change in the rate of decline in income is important. When it is decreasing at an ever faster rate (as if the economy was depressing at a faster and faster rate), the accelerator principle says that the level of investment actually becomes negative as the economy fails to replace worn-out capital goods. When the level of income is decreasing at an ever slower rate (as if the economy was depressing at a slower and slower rate), the accelerator principle says that the level of investment begins to increase again. At the precise point where the rate of decline in income switches from an ever faster to an ever slower rate, investment reaches its lowest point. It is a lower turning point in the investment cycle. Beyond this point, investment expenditures increase.

Furthermore, as the level of investment begins to expand, the multiplier says that aggregate demand and income will grow too. Eventually, the income cycle reaches its trough (at $t = 4$) or lower turning point. Please note that the lower turning point in the investment cycle occurs before the lower turning point in the income cycle. Similarly, an upper turning point in the investment cycle (at I'' and $t = 5$) leads the upper turning point in the income cycle. Thus, if no other factors in the economy change autonomously, the accelerator principle can be used to explain the turning points in the income cycle.

INVESTMENT AND THE WAGE RATE

If we assume that the wage rate rises and the level of employment does not fall, we know that the wage bill must increase. For any particular producer, such a situation might make a particular investment less profitable than if the wage rate had not risen.[6] This would also be true in the aggregate. To raise the wage rate and assure that the wage bill will increase, we merely assume that the labor supply curve remains fixed and all changes occur on the demand side of the market. In Figure 6-6 we view the aggregate labor market.[7] In the figure,

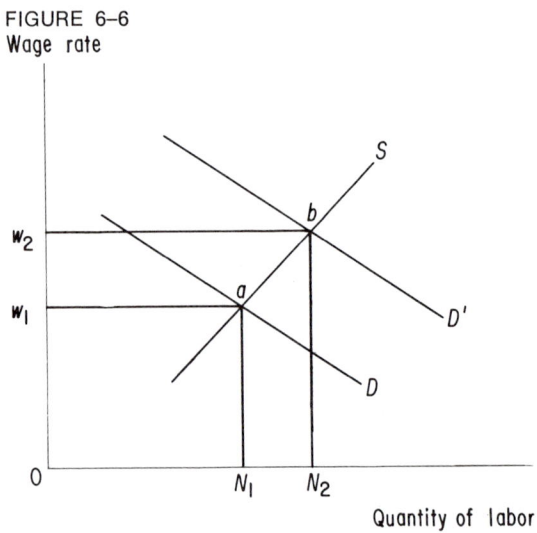

FIGURE 6-6

---

[6] Naturally, profitability depends upon the use of and, hence, the total cost of all factors of production as well as revenues from the investment.

[7] We will examine more closely the meaning of the aggregate labor market in a later chapter.

FIGURE 6-7

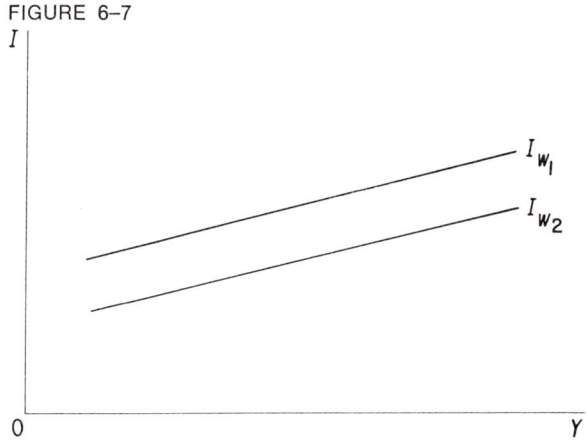

with demand curve D and supply curve S, the equilibrium wage rate is w_1 and the equilibrium quantity of labor hired and supplied is N_1. The total wage bill, therefore, is given by the rectangle $0w_1aN_1$. With an outward shift in the demand for labor, given the supply curve, the wage rate rises to w_2 and the equilibrium quantity of labor hired increases to N_2. The total wage bill increases to $0w_2bN_2$. If we assume that the increase in the wage bill causes less investment to take place, the aggregate investment function will shift down in Figure 6-7 causing the aggregate demand function of Figure 6-8 to shift downward too. The net result is that the equilibrium level of national income will fall, if there are no other changes in the economy. We shall return

FIGURE 6-8
Aggregate demand

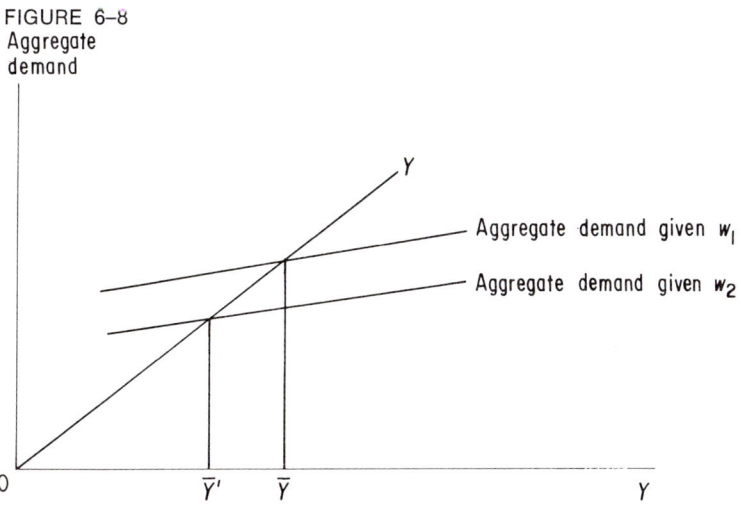

to this problem in a later chapter, and see that there are possibilities for an increase in income despite the fact that the wage rate has risen. A relevant question to ask is: Why did the demand curve for labor shift to the right? The answer to this question may well explain the possibility of an increase in the level of national income.

TECHNOLOGY AND THE LEVEL OF INVESTMENT

We must mention in passing that it is also true that technological change will influence the level of investment. Inventions may make existing capital equipment obsolete. In such a case, there will be an outward shift in the investment function of Figure 6–1. Of course, not all technological change will work in this direction. Some inventions will clearly be of a capital saving type, and so will make possible the replacement of existing capital by equipment that represents a smaller investment outlay than the capital replaced. This will not usually be the case, however.

SOME EMPIRICAL EVIDENCE

Most attempts to estimate the relative statistical significance or importance of the various factors which are thought to influence the level of investment expenditures have produced uncertain results. Nevertheless, a complete discussion of the investment function requires that we look at some of these results. Most recent studies have attempted, through regression analysis, to correlate changes in investment expenditures with changes in such variables as the quantity of output (the accelerator principle), the rate of price inflation, the rates of interest paid on debt instruments (bonds) and equity instruments (stocks), the corporate tax rate, and the investment tax credit.

In order to compare the relative strength of the variables, we examine the sensitivity or *elasticity of investment* to each of the variables individually. The elasticity of investment measures the percentage change in investment expenditures induced by a given percentage change in one of the independent variables; for example, the elasticity of investment to output measures the percentage change in investment induced by every percentage change in output—if this elasticity equaled four (4), then every 1 percentage point increase in output would produce a four (4) percentage point increase in investment.

The elasticity coefficients derived from some regression equations (you should review the meaning of regression analysis given in Chapter 5) from the period 1953 through 1968 are summarized in Table 6–3.[8]

TABLE 6–3

Percentage change in dependent variable		Percentage change in investment expenditures
Output	10.0	7.6–9.0
Price inflation	10.0	1.6
Interest rate (bonds)	10.0	−3.6
Interest rate (equities)	10.0	−1.6
Corporate tax rate	10.0	−3.9
Investment tax credit	10.0	0.7

These elasticity coefficients are easily interpreted. Over the period 1953 through 1968, the coefficients indicate that: each 10 percent increase in output resulted in a 7.6 to 9 percent increase in investment; each 10 percent increase in the rate of price inflation resulted in a 1.6 percent increase in investment; each 10 percent decrease in the interest rate paid to debt and equity instruments resulted in a 3.6 percent and a 1.6 percent increase in investment, respectively; every 10 percent decrease in the corporate tax rate resulted in a 3.9 percent increase in investment; and every 10 percent increase in the investment tax credit resulted in a 0.7 percent increase in investment.

Using these elasticity coefficients, we can state several tentative, uncertain conclusions about the relative importance of each variable on the level of investment expenditures. Over the period 1953 through 1968, changes in the level of output was the most significant factor influencing the level of investment expenditures. The corporate tax rate was the second most significant variable, followed by the interest rate paid on bonds, followed by the rate of price inflation and the interest rate paid on equities. The investment tax credit was the least significant variable.

We must now ask the question: Is our theory of investment demand, summarized in equation (6.11a), validated by the statistical evidence? The evidence suggests that the accelerator principle dominates the investment demand function. Furthermore, it suggests that the rate

---

[8] C. W. Bischoff, "Business Investment in the 1970s: A Comparison of Models," *Brookings Papers*, Vol. 1 (1971).

of interest, at least the rate paid to bonds, is important also. Both are included in equation (6.11a). However, the evidence also suggests that a complete investment demand function must include the corporate tax rate as a variable. Accordingly, we must modify equation (6.11a) to include the influence of the corporate tax rate. If we assume that the level of investment expenditures and the corporate tax rate are linearly related, the investment demand equation becomes:

(6.16) $$I_t = v(Y_t - Y_{t-1}) + z(i_t - i_{t-1}) + w(c_t - c_{t-1}),$$

where c represents the corporate tax rate, and where w is a negative number. As the corporate tax rate falls, there will be an outward shift in the investment function of Figure 6–1.

CONCLUDING NOTE

In this chapter we examined the determinants of the level of investment. One of the key variables in the determination of the level of investment was the rate of interest, another was the corporate tax rate. In later chapters, we will look at the factors determining interest rates, and influencing corporate tax rates. However, before we do so, we must complete our discussion of the components of aggregate demand. Therefore, we turn our attention to the influence of government spending on the level of national income.

7 The role of the government

THE ROLE of the government has become increasingly significant over the past few decades. A large part of the total demand for goods and services in the economy consists of purchases made by groups working through the government. In this chapter, we will examine the impact of these government purchases on the level of national income.

Since our analysis concentrates on government purchases, we are not concerned with the activities of agencies, such as the Postal Service, which are considered to be "government enterprises" and are included in the national income accounts as business enterprises. Nor are we concerned with government transfer payments, for they do not represent a part of the government's demand for current output—although they do affect private demand. Our analysis is limited to government purchases of (demand for) goods and services. In a sense, we are concerned with "government consumption." However, in fact, we are not talking about consumption at all; instead, we are talking about "government production." After all, the government sector merely combines the services of labor, land, and capital which it purchases from the private sector of the economy, and, in turn, produces services that are either given away or sold to consumers and other producers.

THE HISTORICAL PERSPECTIVE

One view of the importance of government purchases in the circular flow of economic activity is seen by examining the growth of government purchases over the past three decades, and by looking at the increase in the percentage of gross national product which is accounted for by government purchases. This information, based on constant dollar GNP, is summarized in Figures 7–1 and 7–2. The data indicate

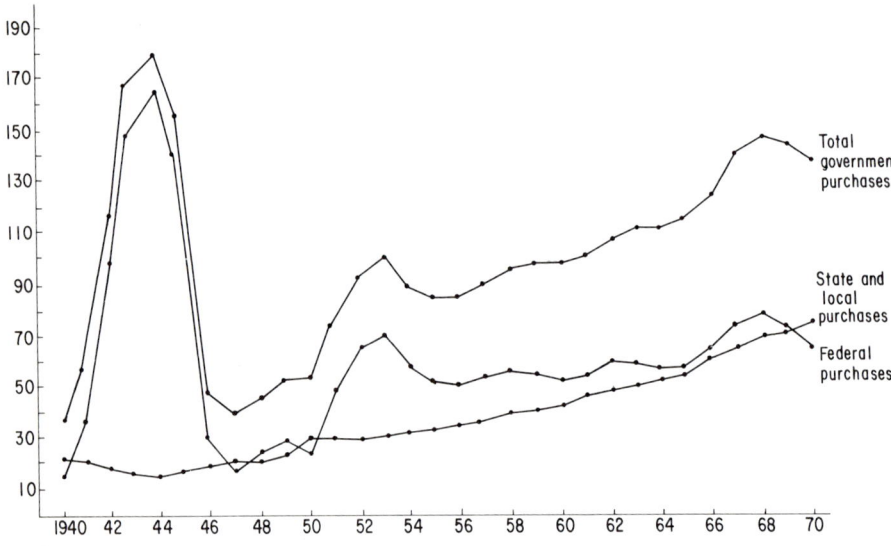

FIGURE 7–1
Government purchases of goods and services (in billions of 1958 dollars)

Source: *The Economic Report of the President*, January 1972.

clearly that the total volume of government purchases has risen steadily since the end of World War II. By year-end 1970, government purchases of goods and services accounted for more than 19 percent of GNP. Purchases by all levels of government—federal, state, and local—as a percent of GNP rose by nearly 4 percentage points over the period 1940 through 1970. Therefore, we can say that government purchases have become an increasingly important source of total spending—at least over the long run.

Another view of the importance of government purchases in the circular flow of economic activity is seen by dividing GNP into two components, private sector GNP and government sector GNP. This information, for the calendar year, 1970, is summarized in Figure 7–3. During 1970, 21.2 percent of all wages paid to workers in the economy were paid by the government sector to its employees. In

FIGURE 7–2
Government purchases of goods and services as a percent of gross national product (in 1958 dollars)

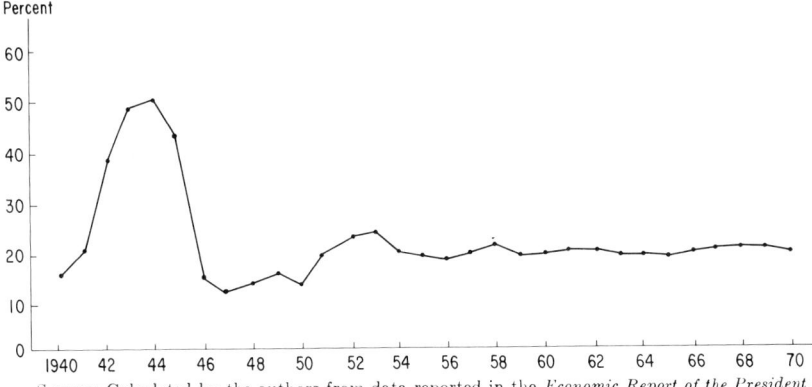

Source: Calculated by the authors from data reported in the *Economic Report of the President* January 1972.

other words, more than one fifth of all wages originated in government payrolls. Also during 1970, 20.6 percent of all employment in the economy originated in the government sector. In other words, more than one fifth of all jobs were government service jobs. Once again, we can say that all sectors of government have become increasingly important sources of economic activity.

Thus, in absolute terms, the government sector—federal, state, and local governments—exerts significant influence on the level of eco-

FIGURE 7–3
Government wages and employment, 1970 (percent of total)

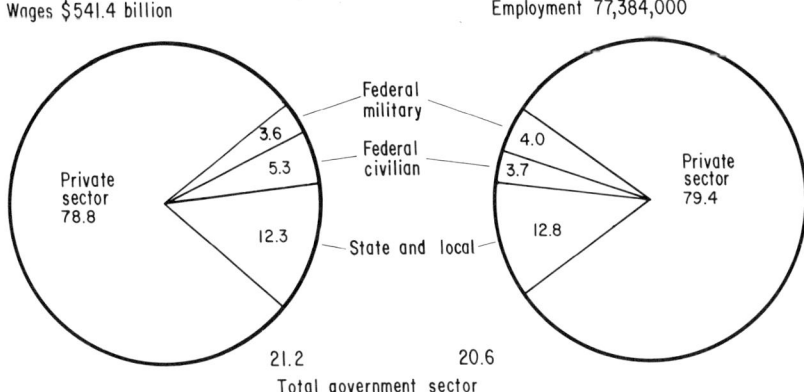

Source: *The Federal Budget: Its Impact on the Economy* (New York: The Conference Board, Inc. 1973).

THE ROLE OF THE GOVERNMENT SECTOR IN RAISING THE LEVEL OF INCOME

In Chapter 4, we noted that it was possible to raise the level of national income by either an increase in the level of investment or by an upward shift in the consumption function. It is also possible to raise the level of national income through government action. If we expand our economy to include the government sector, we say that:

(7.1) $$Y = C + I + G,$$

where G represents the level of government purchases. Equation (7.1) says that total spending in the economy is now comprised of three components: consumption expenditures made by the private sector (C), investment expenditures made by the private sector (I), and consumption and investment expenditures made by the government sector (G). Assuming that government purchases are constant regardless of the level of national income, we know that the equilibrium level of national income is $\bar{Y}$. It is shown in Figure 7–4. In the figure, we have drawn the short-run consumption function of Chapter 5, and have assumed for simplicity that the level of investment is constant at all levels of income. By the analysis of Chapter 4, the equilibrium level of national income would be only $\bar{Y}'$; but

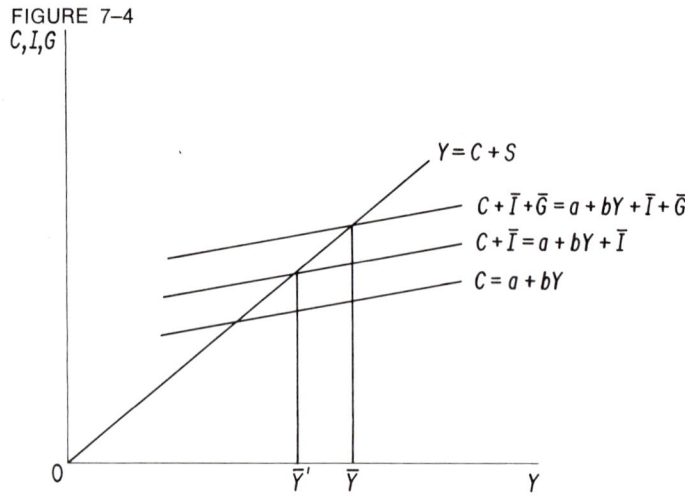

FIGURE 7–4

since we have added government expenditures, $\bar{G}$, the equilibrium level of income has reached $\bar{Y}$.

You may recall from Chapter 4 that we examined a problem in which the full-employment level of income was $400 billion, but the equilibrium level of income was only $384 billion. There was a deflationary gap. Appropriate government action could raise the equilibrium level of income to the full-employment level, and eliminate the deflationary gap. Indeed, with a marginal propensity to consume of ¾, all that is needed is an increase in the level of government expenditures of $4 billion—assuming that there are no leakages—so our multiplier analysis tells us.

Let us be more general. Suppose, when the level of government expenditures is $\bar{G}$, the level of national income is $\bar{Y}$. Following the procedure developed in equation (4.7) of Chapter 4, we know that:

$$(7.2) \qquad \bar{Y} = \frac{a + \bar{I} + \bar{G}}{(1 - b)}.$$

Let us now suppose that the level of government expenditures increases to $\bar{G}'$. The level of national income increases to:

$$(7.3) \qquad \bar{Y}' = \frac{a + \bar{I} + \bar{G}'}{(1 - b)}.$$

Since the level of income has risen, we may subtract equation (7.2) from equation (7.3) to obtain the change in income. Accordingly,

$$(7.4) \qquad \bar{Y}' - \bar{Y} = \frac{a + \bar{I} + \bar{G}'}{(1 - b)} - \frac{a + \bar{I} + \bar{G}}{(1 - b)},$$
$$= \frac{\bar{G}' - \bar{G}}{(1 - b)},$$
$$\Delta Y = \frac{\Delta G}{(1 - b)},$$
$$\Delta Y = k \Delta G,$$

where ΔY represents the change in national income, ΔG represents the change in government expenditures, and k is the multiplier. Once again, our simple multiplier analysis obtains.

Graphically, we note in Figure 7–5 that, when the level of income is $\bar{Y}$, there is a deflationary gap that must be filled in order for full employment to be achieved. At the full-employment level of income, the size of the deflationary gap is rs. An increase in the level of government expenditures by the amount rs will multiply up the level of income to the full-employment level, $\bar{Y}'$. Hence, by

FIGURE 7-5

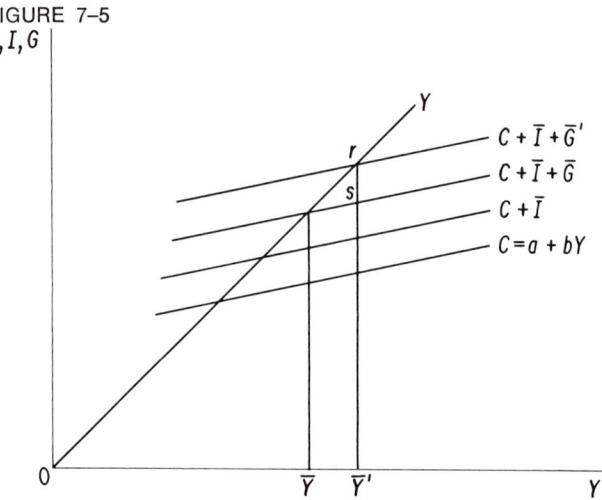

increasing the level of government expenditures to $\bar{G}'$, the full-employment level of national income will be reached. Please note that government expenditures increased by less than the subsequent increase in national income.

THE BALANCED BUDGET MULTIPLIER[1]

Unfortunately our analysis is not quite complete. We have ignored too much. If investment opportunities improve as income grows, the investment function is likely to shift upward as a result of increased government spending—as we saw in Chapter 6. If society feels that it should consume more out of every level of income because of an increased feeling of affluence as income grows—as we saw in Chapter 5, the consumption function is also likely to shift upward as a result of increased government expenditures. Thus, when the government spends more, not only does the government expenditure function shift upward, but the private sector expenditure functions are likely to shift upward as well. Therefore, it appears that our previous analysis has underestimated the impact of government spending on the level of national income.

However, appearances can be deceiving. In order for the government to increase its expenditures, it must raise additional revenue.

---

[1] The materials contained in this section as well as the next several sections draw heavily on the work of Martin Bailey. See his *National Income and the Price Level* (2d ed.; New York: McGraw-Hill Book Co., 1971), chap. 9.

It can raise the additional revenue in three ways: tax revenues can be increased; government bonds can be sold; or money can be printed and circulated. We will ignore temporarily the latter two methods of financing government expenditures, and concentrate in this chapter on raising revenue through increased taxes.

Let us assume initially that the government conducts its business with a continuously *balanced budget*. That is to say, for every dollar spent by the government, a dollar is raised through taxes. Under this assumption, we say:

(7.5) $$C = a + b(Y - T) = a + b(Y - G),$$

where T represents taxes, and $(Y - T)$ represents disposable income. Please note that consumption is now based on income net of taxes, i.e., disposable income. Since the budget is continuously balanced, we may substitute G for T as we have done on the right-hand side of equation (7.5).

Given equation (7.1), we may substitute equation (7.5) into equation (7.1), and assuming a given level of investment and government expenditures, we obtain:

(7.6) $$Y = a + b(Y - \bar{G}) + \bar{I} + \bar{G},$$
$$Y = a + bY - b\bar{G} + \bar{I} + \bar{G},$$
$$Y - bY = a + \bar{I} + \bar{G} - b\bar{G},$$
$$\bar{Y} = \frac{1}{(1-b)}(a + \bar{I} + \bar{G} - b\bar{G}),$$

where $\bar{Y}$ is a particular level of income. Suppose that the level of government expenditures increases to $\bar{G}'$. The new equilibrium level of income is:

(7.7) $$\bar{Y}' = \frac{1}{(1-b)}(a + \bar{I} + \bar{G}' - b\bar{G}').$$

Subtracting equation (7.6) from equation (7.7), we obtain:

(7.8) $$\bar{Y}' - \bar{Y} = \frac{1}{(1-b)}(a + \bar{I} + \bar{G}' - b\bar{G}' - a - \bar{I} - \bar{G} + b\bar{G}),$$
$$= \frac{1}{(1-b)}(\bar{G}' - \bar{G} + \overline{bG'} - \overline{bG}),$$
$$= \frac{1}{1-b}(\bar{G}' - \bar{G})(1-b),$$
$$\Delta Y = \Delta G.$$

The level of national income increases only by the increase in government expenditures. Under the assumption of a continuously balanced budget, each dollar of additional government spending creates only one additional dollar of income. Therefore, we can say that the balanced budget multiplier has a value of one (unity). It appears that our previous analysis has overestimated the impact of government expenditures on the level of national income.

It is not difficult to understand why the balanced budget multiplier equals unity, and to understand the source of our analytical overestimation. Simply ask the question: What is the source of the tax revenues? Who pays the taxes? The private sector of the economy pays the taxes. Each dollar of revenue gained by the government is a dollar of taxes paid by the private sector. Therefore, it might, at first glance, appear that the level of income will not change as a result of increased government spending matched by an equal increase in tax revenues. If private consumption were entirely replaced by public or government consumption, government spending would not raise the level of national income. However, while it is true that private consumption is replaced to some extent by government consumption, it is not completely replaced. Some of the additional taxes paid by the private sector are paid out of savings, in order to protect the current level of consumption. Consequently, because an increase in government spending which is financed by an increase in taxes does not reduce private consumption by the full amount of the tax, government spending can be expansionary. However, because some part of the additional government spending is offset by a reduction in private spending as the private sector pays more taxes, government spending is not as expansionary as we previously thought.

Let us see why savings decreases, as well as consumption, when the level of taxes increases. If we assume that the marginal propensity to consume equals ¾, we know that every dollar of additional income creates $0.75 of additional consumption and $0.25 of additional saving. It follows that every dollar loss in income produces a $0.75 reduction in consumption and $0.25 reduction in saving. Thus, for each dollar taxed away from the private sector, $0.75 would come from private consumption and $0.25 from private savings. Hence, we may conclude that the consumption function shifts downward due to an increase in taxes, causing the expenditure function to shift downward also. However, the increase in government expenditures causes the expenditure function to shift upward, and the overall effect is a net upward shift in the expenditure function of society and a net increase in the level of income.

A simple numerical example illustrates the point. Let us continue to assume that the marginal propensity to consume out of disposable income is ¾. Now suppose that the government increases its level of spending and taxes simultaneously by $10 billion. Faced with an additional tax bill of $10 billion, the private sector reduces its level of consumption by $7.5 billion and its level of savings by $2.5 billion. Consequently, total expenditures have increased by $2.5 billion: the $10 billion of additional government expenditures less the $7.5 billion of reduced private consumption expenditures. Furthermore, the level of income increases by $10 billion.

These results are demonstrated graphically in Figure 7–6. Assume

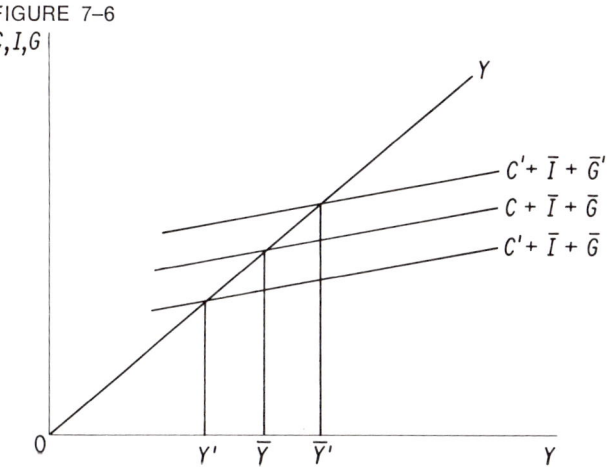

FIGURE 7–6

that the initial equilibrium level of income is $\bar{Y}$. With an increase in taxes, the aggregate expenditure function shifts downward, causing the equilibrium level of income to fall to Y'. With an increase in government expenditures exactly equal to the tax increase, the aggregate expenditure function shifts back upward causing the equilibrium level of income to rise to $\bar{Y}'$. The downward shift in the expenditure function was equal to $b\Delta T$ ($7.5 billion) at all levels of income, while the upward shift in the same function amounts to $\Delta T(=\Delta G) = \$10$ billion at all levels of income. Since the consumption function shifts down by $b\Delta T$, the change in consumption at all levels of income is equal to the marginal propensity to consume times the change in taxes. This change will naturally be less than $\Delta T = \Delta G$ since the marginal propensity to consume is less than one.[2]

We can demonstrate the result in a more formal manner. If the level of government expenditures increases by the amount ΔG and the level of taxes increases by the amount ΔT, the level of income is multiplied up due to the additional expenditures by an amount equal to:

(7.9) $$\Delta Y_1 = k\Delta G.$$

Simultaneously, the level of income is multiplied down due to the additional taxes by an amount equal to:

(7.10) $$\Delta Y_2 = kb\Delta T.$$

Assuming a continuously balanced budget, $\Delta G = \Delta T$ and the total change in the level of income is found by subtracting equation (7.10) from equation (7.9):

(7.11) $$\Delta Y_1 - \Delta Y_2 = \Delta Y = k\Delta G - kb\Delta T,$$
$$= k(\Delta G - b\Delta G),$$
$$= k(1 - b)\Delta G.$$

Since $k = 1/(1-b)$, we see that:

(7.12) $$\Delta Y = \Delta G.$$

Therefore, we conclude that an increase in government spending financed entirely by increased taxes causes national income to expand. Also, we conclude that—as a first approximation—the *balanced budget multiplier* equals unity.

Our conclusion that the balanced budget multiplier equals unity has an interesting implication for macroeconomic policy. If the level of national income is below the full-employment level, additional government spending which is financed dollar for dollar by additional taxes can close the deflationary gap. The desired increase in income and employment is achieved with a balanced budget, thereby avoiding the pitfalls—real or imaginary—of *deficit spending*. However, as we

---

[2] It must be noted that government expenditures in our example do not mean government transfer payments. If taxes are used to finance government transfer payments, the level of disposable income will not change and there will be no multiplier effect.

7 / The role of the government

noted previously, our conclusion (that the balanced budget multiplier equals unity) must be viewed with caution for it is based on a crude model of income determination. It ignores the fact that taxes rise with income, and that private sector consumption and investment functions are affected by government expenditures. Once these factors are taken into consideration, the value of the balanced budget multiplier falls below unity. Nevertheless, our analysis is sufficiently rigorous to show that a balanced budget is fiscally expansionary, not fiscally neutral as commonly thought.

It is also interesting to note that if the level of government expenditures remains the same with a balanced budget, but there is an upward shift in the consumption function or in the investment function, the level of income is multiplied up in the usual manner. Suppose, for example, that the level of investment increases at all levels of income to $\bar{I}'$. Then we know that the new level of income may be given as:

$$(7.13) \qquad \bar{Y}'' = \frac{1}{(1-b)}(a + \bar{I}' + \bar{G} - b\bar{G}).$$

Subtracting equation (7.6) from equation (7.13), we see that the change in income is:

$$(7.14) \quad \bar{Y}'' - \bar{Y}' = \frac{1}{(1-b)}(a + \bar{I}' + \bar{G} - b\bar{G} - a - \bar{I} - \bar{G} + b\bar{G})$$

$$\Delta \bar{Y}' = k\Delta I,$$

where $\Delta I = \bar{I}' - \bar{I}$, and represents the change in investment expenditures. The simple multiplier obtains.

Suppose that households value government expenditures as income. For example, "free lunches" provided at jobs or in schools may be regarded as income to the private sector because this form of government expenditure releases private dollars previously spent on the lunches for other activities. The provision of parks is another example. If individuals count the consumption component of government expenditures in their own consumption, the consumption function becomes:

$$(7.15) \qquad C + G_C = a + b(Y - T + G) = a + bY,$$

where G_C is government consumption. Therefore,

$$(7.16) \qquad C = a - G_C + bY.$$

Substituting into equation (7.1) and assuming a given level of investment, we have:

(7.17) $$Y = a - G_C + bY + \bar{I} + \bar{G},$$

for a particular level of government expenditures. Solving equation (7.17) for $\bar{Y}$, we find:

(7.18) $$\bar{Y} = \frac{1}{(1-b)}(a - G_C + \bar{I} + \bar{G})$$

$$= \frac{1}{(1-b)}(a + \bar{I} + G_I),$$

where

$$G_I = G - G_C,$$

and represents the investment component of government expenditures. It follows that if there is a shift in the aggregate expenditure function brought about by a change in either a or $\bar{I}$, the simple multiplier will obtain. For example, if the level of investment were to increase to $\bar{I}'$, the level of income would increase by $\Delta \bar{Y} = k \Delta I$.

Suppose that there is an increase in the level of government consumption expenditures. With government consumption substituting for private consumption, there will be no increase in the level of national income. Why is this so? We note immediately that G_C does not appear in equation (7.18). Hence, a change in G_C can have no effect on a change in the level of income. The logic is quite simple. If government consumption increases and individuals consider government consumption to be a substitute for private consumption, the level of consumption will remain the same. Private consumption expenditures will fall by exactly the same amount by which government consumption expenditures increased. Since the overall level of consumption expenditures has remained the same, the level of national income should not rise. The composition of consumption has, of course, changed: Public consumption expenditures have risen relative to private consumption expenditures.

However, suppose there is an increase in the level of government investment. Specifically, let us assume that the level of government investment increases, and the budget remains balanced. The new equilibrium level of national income is:

(7.19) $$\bar{Y}' = \frac{1}{(1-b)}(a + \bar{I} + G_I'),$$

where G_I' is the higher level of government investment. If we subtract (7.18) from equation (7.19), we find:

(7.20) $$\bar{Y}' - \bar{Y} = \frac{1}{(1-b)} (a + \bar{I} + G_I' - a - \bar{I} - G_I)$$
$$\Delta Y = k\Delta G_I.$$

Once again the simple multiplier obtains. This result may be a bit difficult to understand. However, the increase in government investment is viewed by consumers as an increase in income even though it is financed by taxes. The depressing effect of the taxes has been offset by those individuals who produce the additional government investment.

MULTIPLIERS WITH CONSTANT TAX RECEIPTS

Let us now remove the balanced budget notion, and assume only that the government holds tax receipts at a given level. There is no guarantee that taxes and government expenditures are equal. In fact, it is rarely the case. Thus, we say:

(7.21) $$C = a + b(Y - \bar{T}),$$

where $\bar{T}$ represents the given level of tax revenues. As we noted earlier, the introduction of taxes into our analysis means that consumption is determined by the level of disposable income. Thus, in Figure 7–7, the consumption function relevant to our analysis is C'

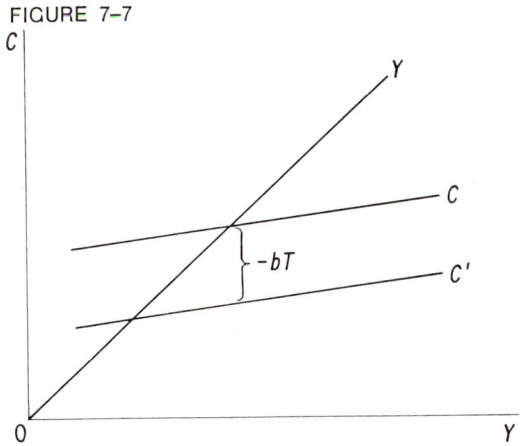

FIGURE 7–7

rather than C. Once again, the consumption function has shifted downward at all levels of income by the amount $b\bar{T}$, just as in our analysis of Figure 7–6.[3]

Given a particular level of investment, $\bar{I}$, and a particular level of government expenditures, $\bar{G}$, we obtain:

(7.22) $$Y = a + bY - b\bar{T} + \bar{I} + \bar{G}.$$

Solving for $\tilde{Y}$, we find:

(7.23) $$\tilde{Y} = \frac{1}{(1-b)}(a + \bar{I} + \bar{G} - b\bar{T}),$$

where $\tilde{Y}$ represents the equilibrium level of income. Now suppose there is an upward shift in either the consumption function, or the investment function, or both. As usual, we assume that the shift is such that the new aggregate expenditure function is parallel to the old function. For simplicity, let us assume that only the consumption function shifts upward. The level of income will increase. The new level of income is:

(7.24) $$\tilde{Y}' = \frac{1}{(1-b)}(a' + \bar{I} + \bar{G} - b\bar{T}).$$

The change in income is:

(7.25) $$\tilde{Y}' - \tilde{Y} = \frac{1}{(1-b)}(a' - a) = k\Delta a,$$

where Δa represents the upward shift in the consumption function. As might have been expected, the simple multiplier again prevails.

In the previous section, we examined a problem in which individuals assumed that government expenditures were part of their income, and that government consumption was part of their consumption. Let us look at a similar analysis in this section, and let us also assume that they count taxes actually paid as a reduction of their private income.

The consumption function is now written:

(7.26) $$C + G_c = a + b(Y - \bar{T} + \bar{G}).$$

---

[3] Assuming that taxes are initially zero at all levels of income, and then a lump-sum tax is imposed, the consumption function will shift down at all levels of income by bT or $b\Delta T$ since T and ΔT will be the same in this case.

Thus, solving for the level of income:

(7.27)
$$Y = a + b(Y - \bar{T} + \bar{G}) - G_c + \bar{I} + \bar{G},$$
$$(1 - b)\bar{Y} = a + \bar{I} - b\bar{T} + bG_c + (1 + b)G_I,$$
$$\bar{Y} = \frac{1}{(1-b)}(a + \bar{I} - b\bar{T} + bG_c + (1+b)G_I).$$

It should now be relatively clear that if there is a change in the private sector such that the aggregate expenditure function shifts upward in a parallel manner (i.e., if a increases, or if I increases by the same amount at every level of income), the simple multiplier effect prevails—as it did in the analysis leading up to equation (7.25). However, as one might expect, the simple multiplier effect does not prevail when there is a change in government consumption (G_c), or government investment (G_I).

Suppose that there is an increase in government consumption. According to equation (7.27), income increases by an amount:

(7.28)
$$\Delta Y = \frac{b}{(1-b)} \Delta G_c,$$
$$= \left[\frac{1}{(1-b)} - 1\right] \Delta G_c,$$
$$= (k - 1)\Delta G_c,$$

where the multiplier is now $(k - 1)$. Obviously, the multiplier associated with changes in government consumption $(k - 1)$ is smaller than the multiplier associated with private sector spending (k). Why? The reason is simple. Since individuals view government consumption as a substitute for private consumption, the expansionary impact of an increase in government consumption is offset to some extent by the reduction in private consumption which it has replaced. For example, if the multiplier (k) equals 4, a $100 billion increase in government spending creates—all other things remaining constant—$400 billion of additional income. However, if the increase in government spending is in fact an increase in government consumption, the initial $100 billion increase in government consumption simply replaces an identical amount of private sector consumption. Since all other things do not remain equal, the net increase in income is only $300 billion: $400 billion less $100 billion. Income of $100 billion is lost due to the reduction in private consumption. The multiplier (k) is reduced to $(k - 1)$.

The conclusion has an interesting economic implication. It says that private sector consumption is more expansionary (contractionary) than government consumption. Each additional dollar of private consumption creates more income than an additional dollar of government consumption.

Unfortunately, to make the analysis even more complicated, the opposite is true of increases in government investment expenditures. They are more expansionary (contractionary) than private investment expenditures. Suppose that there is an increase in government investment. From equation (7.27) we know that the subsequent change in income is:

$$
\begin{aligned}
(7.29) \quad \Delta Y &= \left[\frac{(1+b)}{(1-b)}\right] \Delta G_I, \\
&= \left[\frac{1}{(1-b)} + \frac{b}{(1-b)}\right] \Delta G_I, \\
&= (k + k - 1) \Delta G_I, \\
&= (2k - 1) \Delta G_I,
\end{aligned}
$$

where the multiplier is now $(2k - 1)$. Obviously, the multiplier associated with government investment expenditures $(2k - 1)$ is larger than the multiplier associated with private sector spending (k). This is due in large measure to the desire of the private sector to spend a large proportion of the income derived from the government investment, which is additional to the respending of the income received by the productive services that supply the investment.

Under the assumption of constant tax receipts, our conclusions about the impact of equal autonomous increases in private consumption expenditures (as shown in equation [7.25]), in government consumption expenditures (as shown in equation [7.28]), and in government investment expenditures (as shown in equation [7.29]) on the

FIGURE 7-8

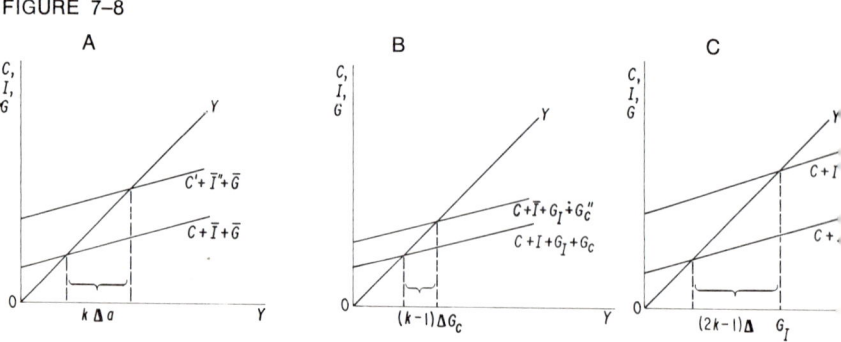

level of national income are illustrated in Figure 7–8, parts A, B, and C, respectively. The diagrams show that an additional dollar of government investment generates more additional income than an additional dollar of private consumption, which, in turn, generates more additional income than an additional dollar of government consumption. The macroeconomic policy implication is obvious.

TAX RECEIPTS FLUCTUATING WITH INCOME

In general, budgets are not balanced and tax receipts are not held constant. Instead, tax receipts vary directly with income. Let us assume that tax receipts vary with income in a linear manner. We say:

(7.30) $$T = tY$$

where t represents the tax rate, and is, therefore, a number whose value lies between zero and unity. Whereas, in our previous discussions of taxes, we noted that the consumption function would shift parallel downward, we now note that when taxes vary with income the consumption function will rotate to the right and downward as income increases, as illustrated in Figure 7–9. If the consumption function before taxes is identified by C, then the consumption function after an income-based tax is imposed looks like C'. The logic is straightforward. Suppose that, along consumption function C, the marginal pro-

FIGURE 7–9

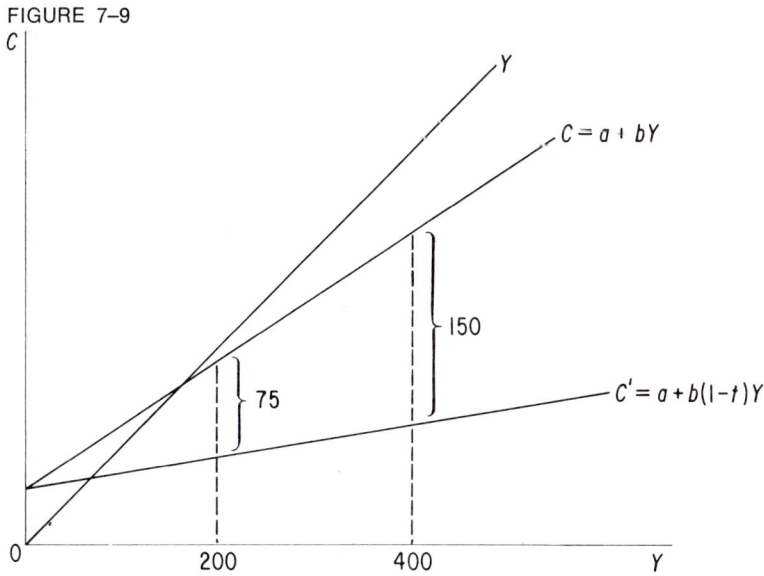

pensity to consume is ¾, and the tax rate (t from equation [7.30]) is ½. When the level of income is zero, there are no tax revenues. However, when the level of income is $200 billion, tax revenues equal $100 billion, and disposable income equals $100 billion. With a fall in disposable income of $100 billion, consumption will fall by $75 billion. Thus, at income level $200 billion, C' lies $75 billion below C. When the level of income is $400 billion, tax revenues equal $200 billion, and disposable income equals $200 billion. Thus, at an income level of $400 billion, C' lies $150 billion below C. Therefore, we conclude that the vertical distance between C and C' increases as income increases. The consumption function rotates downward and to the right.

✗ As a result of the downward displacement of the consumption function, the slope of C' is less than the slope of C. This proposition can be demonstrated using methods similar to those employed in previous sections of this chapter. Using equation (7.30), we write the consumption function as:

(7.31)
$$\begin{aligned} C &= a + b(Y - tY), \\ &= a + bY - btY, \\ &= a + b(1 - t)Y. \end{aligned}$$

The slope of the new consumption function is $b(1-t)$ which is less than b. Along consumption function C, the slope is ¾—the MPC. Along consumption function C', the slope is ⅜. As a result, every change in expenditures—private as well as government—now induces a smaller change in the level of national income than it did when taxes were assumed to be independent of income.

When tax revenues change proportionally with income, the impact of changes in the level of expenditures on national income is dampened, and the value of the multiplier is reduced. Disregarding any feedback between government expenditures and private consumption decisions, and given a level of investment ($\bar{I}$) and a level of government expenditures ($\bar{G}$), the equilibrium level of national income—when taxes vary proportionally with income—is determined by substituting equation (7.31) into equation (7.1). Consequently,

(7.32)
$$\begin{aligned} Y &= a + b(1-t)Y + \bar{I} + \bar{G}, \\ \bar{Y} &= \frac{1}{1 - b(1-t)}(a + \bar{I} + \bar{G}), \\ \bar{Y} &= k''(a + \bar{I} + \bar{G}) \end{aligned}$$

where k'' is the new multiplier. Clearly k'' is less than k since $b(1-t)$ is less than b. Applying the principles used throughout the chapter, we see that, with an increase in government expenditures, the level of income rises by k'' times the change in government expenditures. With a shift in either the consumption function or the investment function or both, income also increases by k'' times the change. The impact of the multiplier is dampened because taxes rise with income leaving less disposable income to finance additional national income.

A numerical example illustrates the point. Let us assume initially that the marginal propensity to consume (b) equals ¾, and the tax rate (t) is zero. Accordingly, every dollar of additional government spending creates $3 of additional consumption and $4 of additional national income. The impact of a $100 billion increase in government expenditures is summarized in Table 7–1. Instead, let us assume that,

TABLE 7–1*

ΔG	$C = b \Delta Y$	$T = t \Delta Y$	$Y = k \Delta G$
$100	$ 0	$0	$100.00
0	75.00	0	75.00
0	56.25	0	56.25
0	42.19	0	42.19
0	31.64	0	31.64
0	23.73	0	23.73
0	17.80	0	17.80
0	13.35	0	13.35
0	10.01	0	10.01
0	7.51	0	7.51
0	5.63	0	5.63
.	.	.	.
.	.	.	.
.	.	.	.
$100	$300.00	0	$400.00

* In billions of dollars.

although the marginal propensity to consume (b) remains at ¾, the tax rate (t) rises to ⅓. Accordingly, every dollar of additional government spending creates $1 of additional consumption, one third of a dollar of taxes, and $2 of additional national income. The impact of a $100 billion increase in government expenditures is summarized in Table 7–2. The $200 billion loss in national income, comparing the totals of Table 7–1 with those of Table 7–2, is the direct result of $66.66 billion of income (i.e., $200 billion of potential expenditures)

TABLE 7-2*

ΔG	$C = b(1-t)\Delta Y$	$T = t\Delta Y$	$Y = k''\Delta G$
$100.00	$ 0	$33.33	$100.00
0	50.00	16.50	50.00
0	25.00	8.25	25.00
0	12.50	4.13	12.50
0	6.25	2.06	6.25
0	3.12	1.03	3.12
0	1.56	0.52	1.56
0	0.78	0.26	0.78
0	0.39	0.13	0.39
0	0.19	0.06	0.19
0	0.08	0.03	0.08
.	.	.	.
.	.	.	.
.	.	.	.
$100.00	$100.00	$66.66	$200.00

* In billions of dollars.

being taxed away from the private sector as income increases. Thus, the introduction of an income-based tax dampens the multiplier effect.

Again, as in other sections of this chapter, we now assume that individuals value government expenditures as income, and government consumption as private consumption. Under these conditions, and assuming that tax rates fluctuate with income, we find the consumption relationship:

(7.33) $$C = a + b(1-t)Y + bG - G_C.$$

Thus, the equilibrium level of income, $\bar{Y}$, is:

(7.34) $$\bar{Y} = \frac{1}{1 - b(1-t)} (a + \bar{I} + (1+b)G_I + bG_C).$$

With a shift in the private expenditure function, the level of income changes by:

(7.35) $$\Delta Y = k'' \Delta X,$$

where ΔX represents the change in private expenditures.

With an increase in the level of government consumption, the level of national income increases by:

(7.36) $$\Delta Y = k'' b \Delta G_C,$$

while an increase in government investment causes national income to increase by:

(7.37) $$\Delta Y = k''(1 + b)\Delta G_I.$$

Once again our multiplier analysis points to the same macroeconomic policy implication: government investment expenditures are more expansionary than private sector expenditures which, in turn, are more expansionary than government consumption expenditures. A comparison of the multipliers given in equations (7.35), (7.36), and (7.37) demonstrates the point. Since b is positive but less than unity, the multiplier for government consumption ($k''b$) is smaller than the multiplier for private sector expenditures (k'') which is smaller than the multiplier for government investment ($k''(1 + b)$). Consequently, an additional dollar of private sector spending is more expansionary than an additional dollar of government consumption, but less expansionary than an additional dollar of government investment.

CONCLUDING NOTE

In this chapter, we examined several multipliers under various assumptions about budgetary rules. During our examination, we saw the strong influence that government spending exerts on the level of economic activity. A brief look at the historical record told us that the government sector provides a significant, and growing, portion of the total demand for the goods and services available in the economy. In addition, our analysis of the government sector demonstrated that balanced budgets are always fiscally expansionary, that government investment expenditures are more expansionary (contractionary) than private sector spending, and that government consumption expenditures are the least expansionary (contractionary) of all.

However, our analysis of the impact of government spending on income and employment was incomplete. It avoided several issues. It made no judgments, and stated no opinions, about the appropriate size of the government sector, or the appropriate role of government agencies. Our analysis did not attempt to answer the questions: What should the government do? How big should the government sector be? These are questions which each informed citizen must answer for himself. Our analysis answered one question only: What is the impact of the government sector on the level of national income?

Furthermore, our analysis ignored many of the feedbacks from the government sector to the private sector. Although it did assume that government expenditures affect private sector consumption, it ignored—for example—the impact of government investment on private sector investment.[4] Also, it ignored the effect of government taxes on the incentives of the private sector.[5] Our analysis avoided any discussion of deficit spending[6]—other than our examination of the balanced budget multiplier. Finally, our analysis ignored the money creating powers of the government, and their impact on the level of economic activity. We will examine this problem in a later chapter.

We now put aside the government sector, for a short time only, in order to complete our analysis of the determinants of aggregate demand. Accordingly, in the next chapter, we turn our attention to the demand for money and the determinants of the rate of interest.

---

[4] A discussion of these influences can be found in: Wallace E. Oates, *Fiscal Federalism* (New York: Harcourt Brace Jovanovich, Inc., 1972).

[5] Ibid.

[6] Ibid.

8 Money and the rate of interest

In Chapter 6, we viewed the rate of interest as a principle determinant of the level of investment. Furthermore, we noted that there was a definite link between the rate of interest and the market value of an asset. This was the nature of the discounting problem which we examined in Chapter 6. Therefore, we might conclude that the rate of interest, since it is related to the market value of assets, is determined in a manner similar to other prices; i.e., through the demand for and supply of the particular product. Consequently, we could argue that the rate of interest is determined by the demand for and the supply of interest-bearing assets. Alternatively, we could argue that the rate of interest is determined by the demand for and the supply of money. Both approaches to determining the rate of interest lead to the same conclusions. After all, the logical alternative to holding money is holding bonds and other interest-bearing assets. Consequently, when there appears to be an excess demand for bonds, there must be an excess supply of money seeking to be transferred into bonds. In this chapter, we shall examine the money market, the relationship between the money market and the bonds market, and the determination of the rate of interest.

THE TRANSACTION-PRECAUTIONARY DEMAND FOR MONEY

An individual, or business firm, rarely finds that its income and expenditures are perfectly synchronized. In fact, income tends to accrue less continuously than expenditures; i.e., income is received less frequently, expenditures are made more frequently. The need to bridge the gap between income and expenditures, and to finance day-to-day transactions, gives rise to a *transactions motive* for holding cash. However, this alone is not a sufficient economic reason for holding cash balances. The transactions needs of individuals and business firms could be financed by liquidating—at the appropriate time—real assets or financial assets.

Why would a rational individual or business firm hold assets which must be liquidated to finance expenditures when they could simply hold cash instead? Cash is more convenient. The reason is clear: there is a "cost" to holding idle cash balances. It is an *opportunity cost*. It is the interest income foregone by not holding interest-bearing assets, and it can be measured by the interest rate paid on default-free financial assets. Therefore, as long as the rate of interest paid on default-free assets is greater than zero, no individual or business firm would hold cash balances to meet transactions requirements—provided that the brokerage fee for liquidating the assets, usually called the *transactions or transfer cost*, does not exceed the interest payment. When the interest payment is not large enough to cover the transactions cost and to compensate the individual for any inconvenience incurred during the transfer process, no individual or business firm would hold financial assets to meet transactions requirements. Therefore, it is the existence of transactions costs, together with the gap between income and expenditures, which give rise to the *transactions demand for money*.

The influence of the interest rate and transactions costs on the transactions demand for money is easily explained.[1] Let us assume that the brokerage fee, or transactions cost, for liquidating interest-bearing assets is fixed at 6 percent of the market value of the asset being liquidated (for example, it would cost $6 to liquidate a bond with a market value of $100). When the interest rate is 6 percent or less, the cost of liquidating assets equals or exceeds the interest income earned by the assets, and it is rational to hold money to satisfy transactions requirements. Therefore, we say that the transactions

---

[1] For a more comprehensive discussion on the role of interest rates and transactions costs on the transactions demand for money, see W. J. Baumol, "The Transactions Demand for Cash: An Inventory Theoretic Approach," *The Quarterly Journal of Economics*, November 1952; and J. Tobin, "The Interest Elasticity of the Transactions Demand for Cash," *The Review of Economics and Statistics*, September 1956.

demand for money is completely interest inelastic at interest rates equal to or below the brokerage fee;[2] i.e., any increase in the interest rate will not induce a movement from cash into interest-bearing assets. What happens at interest rates greater than 6 percent? The interest income earned by financial assets exceeds the transactions costs, and there is some inducement to move out of cash into interest-bearing assets. Furthermore, as the interest rate rises farther and farther above the brokerage fee, the inducement to move into interest-bearing assets increases. Therefore, we can say that the transactions demand for money becomes increasingly interest elastic as the interest rate rises farther above the brokerage fee; i.e., each increase in the rate of interest above the brokerage fee induces an ever larger movement from cash into interest-bearing assets. Thus, we hypothesize that the transactions demand for money is not very responsive to changes in the rate of interest at relatively low rates of interest, but becomes increasingly responsive at relatively high rates of interest. A demand curve for transactions balances which portrays these elasticity characteristics is shown in Figure 8–1. Clearly, the transactions demand for money

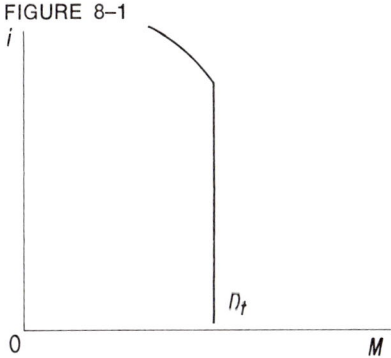

FIGURE 8–1

becomes increasingly interest elastic at higher rates of interest.

A second reason for holding money is to guard against emergencies. There is always the possibility that an unexpected need to increase expenditures will arise, and since expected future receipts can never

---

[2] Elasticity is defined as the percentage change in a dependent variable divided by the percentage change in an independent variable. When the percentage change in the dependent variable is less than the percentage change in the independent variable, we say that the relationship is inelastic. In this case, we assume there is no change in the dependent variable when the independent variable changes.

be known with certainty, there is a *precautionary motive* for holding cash. As with the transactions demand for cash, the demand for precautionary balances will be interest inelastic over low-interest rates. At high enough rates of interest, of course, the demand for precautionary cash balances falls as individuals and business firms place money into earning assets. In this sense, the *precautionary demand for money* is nothing more than a variant of the transactions demand for money.

Even though the transactions and precautionary demand for money are interest inelastic at low levels of the interest rate, the demand for transactions balances increases as the level of national income increases. As the level of national income increases, more transactions take place in an economy, and so the demand for money balances to cover these transactions increases also. The relationship between the level of national income and the demand for transactions-precautionary purposes is shown in Figure 8–2. In the figure, we have as-

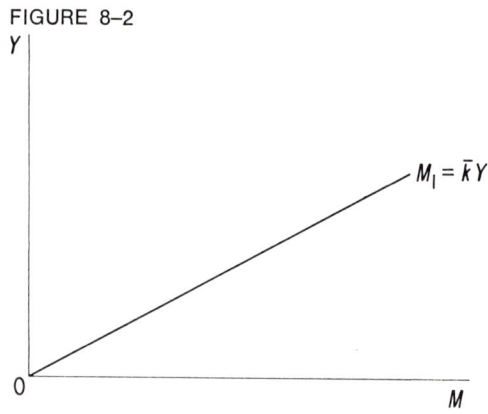

FIGURE 8–2

sumed that at a zero level of national income there are no transactions, and so the demand for transactions-precautionary balances is zero. Also we have simplified matters a bit by assuming that the demand for transactions-precautionary balances increases linearly with income.

The equation describing the transactions-precautionary demand curve of Figure 8–2 is:

(8.1) $$M_1 = \bar{k}Y,$$

where M_1 represents the transactions-precautionary demand for money, Y represents the level of income and $\bar{k}$ represents the percentage of national income over which society wishes to keep command in money form.³ This is the Cambridge k, and we shall return to it in a later chapter when we discuss the quantity theory of money. For the moment, we merely note that equation (8.1) represents the pre-Keynesian concept of the demand for money. In this sense, equation (8.1) represents the Classical demand for money. According to Classical theory, the demand for money was related to the level of national income, not to the rate of interest—at least in the usual ranges of the rate of interest.

THE SPECULATIVE DEMAND FOR MONEY

We have just seen that a basic reason for holding cash balances is to satisfy the transactions-precautionary demand for money. However, the transactions-precautionary demand does not explain the existence of all idle cash balances—individuals and business firms do hold cash balances in excess of transactions-precautionary requirements. The demand for cash balances in excess of transactions-precautionary needs is called the *speculative demand for money*, and it is an important link in the Keynesian break away from the Classical theory of the demand for money.[4]

According to Classical theory, an individual or business firm had no reason to hold idle cash in excess of transactions-precautionary requirements. If they did, they would lose the interest-bearing assets. This Classical conclusion assumes that investors hold their interest-bearing assets to maturity, and are, therefore, unaffected by future rises in the interest rate.

However, Keynesian theory argues that this assumption is overly restrictive. Investors may be forced to, or elect to, liquidate assets before the maturity date. Furthermore, each investor holds expectations as to future movements in interest rates. According to Keynesian theory, if the investor expects future interest rates to rise appreciably and expects to be forced to liquidate his assets before the maturity date, he will hold money instead of interest-bearing assets. If he expects

---

[3] This $\bar{k}$ should not be confused with the k used in describing the simple multiplier. Tradition has it that a "k" is used to describe both concepts.

[4] For a more comprehensive discussion of the speculative demand for money, see J. Tobin, "Liquidity Preference as a Behavior towards Risk," *Review of Economic Studies*, February 1955; and L. S. Ritter, "The Role of Money in Keynesian Theory," in Deane Carson (Ed.), *Banking and Monetary Studies*, (Homewood, Ill.: Richard D. Irwin, Inc., 1963.)

future interest rates to fall and expects to be able to liquidate his assets before the maturity date, he will hold interest-bearing assets instead of money. (We will see why this is so shortly.) Since the expectations of future movements in interest rates is purely speculative, the demand for cash balances to be held in excess of transactions-precautionary requirements—due to expectations of a future rise in interest rates—is called the speculative demand for money.

The speculative demand for money is best understood by examining the relationship between the interest rate and the market price of a bond. Suppose that the market price of a bond is $100, and the interest rate paid on the bond is 6 percent per annum. The bond can be redeemed in one year for $106. The calculation is simple: $100 + 0.06 ($100) = $106, or more generally:

(8.2) $$B_t + iB_t = B_t(1 + i) = B_{t+1},$$

where B_t represents the purchase price of the bond, i represents the interest rate, and B_{t+1} represents the redemption value of the bond one year after its purchase. Therefore, if the purchase price of the bond is $100 and the interest rate is 6 percent, the redemption price of the bond is $106.

Now let us reverse the logic of equation (8.2). Suppose that the redemption price of the bond is given at $106, and the interest rate is given at 6 percent. What is the current purchase price of the bond, B_t? According to equation (8.2), the current purchase price is:

(8.3) $$B_t = \frac{B_{t+1}}{(1 + i)},$$
$$= \frac{\$106.00}{(\$1.06)} = \$100.00.$$

Now assume that the interest rate paid on new bonds falls from 6 percent to 4 percent per annum during the year, while the rate on the old bond remains at 6 percent. What is the new purchase price of the old bond? Since the yield on the old bond is fixed at $6, equation (8.3) says that the new purchase price of the old bond is:

(7.4) $$\bar{B}_t = \frac{\$106.00}{(\$1.04)} = \$101.92.$$

Therefore, we conclude that as interest rates fall, bond prices rise; and, as interest rates rise, bond prices fall.

As interest rates rise and bond prices fall, the investor who liquidates his bond before its maturity date experiences a *capital loss*. He is forced to sell the bond at a price below the price he paid for it. Conversely, as interest rates fall and bond prices rise, the investor who liquidates his bond before its maturity date experiences a *capital gain*. He is able to sell the bond at a price above the price he paid for it.

Now the essence of the speculative demand for money is that the investor's expectations of future changes in the interest rate create expectations about future capital gains and losses, and give rise to changes in the demand for money. A current fall in the interest rate creates expectations of a future rise, while a current rise in the interest rate creates expectations of a future fall in the rate of interest. If the interest rate rises, investors transfer out of money into bonds because they expect a future decline in the interest rate and a possible capital gain. Conversely, if the interest rate falls, investors transfer out of bonds into money because they expect a future rise in the interest rate and a possible capital loss. Therefore, we conclude that the speculative demand for money increases as the interest rate falls. The relationship between the interest rate and the speculative demand for money is shown in Figure 8–3, where the demand function for speculative balances is labeled M_2.

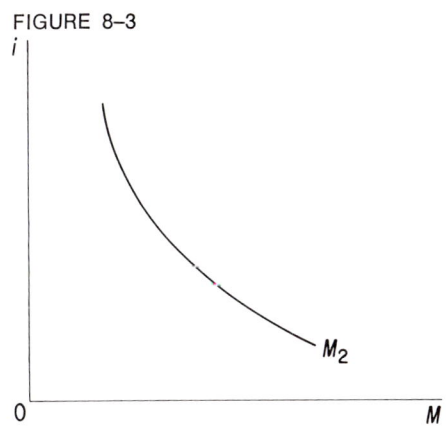

FIGURE 8–3

The equation describing the speculative demand curve of Figure 8–3 is:

(8.5) $$M_2 = L_2(i),$$

where M_2 represents the speculative demand for money, and $L_2(i)$ is functional notation describing an inverse relationship between the speculative demand for money and interest rates.

It is often argued that the demand curve for speculative balances becomes perfectly elastic at very low rates of interest.[5] In other words, at very low rates of interest, there is a *liquidity trap*. The logic behind this argument is quite simple. When the rate of interest falls to a very low level, it becomes perfectly clear that the only place the rate of interest can go is up again. When there is perfect certainty that the rate of interest will go up, no one wishes to purchase bonds and everyone moves into money. If the rate of interest is sure to rise, then it follows that bond prices will fall. When bond prices fall, all bondholders take capital losses. Hence, no one will wish to stay in bonds and, so, there will be an infinitely elastic demand for money at the low-interest rate—since money is the only close substitute for holding bonds.

Of course, there is an equally logical counter argument to the existence of the liquidity trap. To have an infinitely elastic demand for money means there must be an infinitely elastic supply of bonds at the same interest rate. However, any individual or business firm who plans an infinite supply of bonds at some low rate of interest must be unconcerned with the obligation to make interest payments on the bonds. With an infinite supply of bonds, even at a low rate of interest, the interest payment obligation will also be infinite. Thus, if the quantity of bonds supplied is infinite at any positive rate of interest, it must be infinite at all rates of interest for the interest obligation will always be infinite. It follows, therefore, that the demand for money for speculative purposes is infinitely elastic at all rates of interest. As a matter of fact, there would also be an infinitely elastic demand for commodities at all rates of interest if there is an infinite supply of bonds. Those who wish to get out of bonds, wish to get into something else—anything else. Commodities are just as good a substitute for bonds as is money in this sense. Naturally, we would not expect to observe an infinitely elastic demand for speculative balances at all rates of interest. This is illogical and so, therefore, is the liquidity trap.

THE TOTAL DEMAND FOR MONEY

We may now put together the transactions-precautionary demand for money and the speculative demand for money to form the *total*

---

[5] For perfect elasticity, the percentage change in the dependent variable divided by the percentage change in the independent variable will be infinite.

FIGURE 8-4

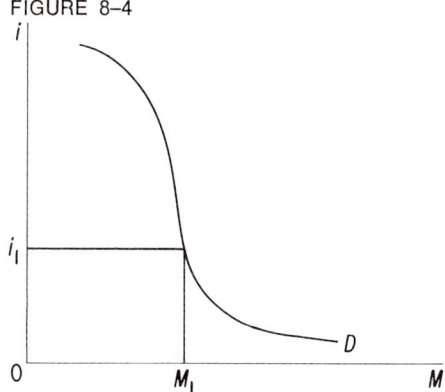

demand for money. We do so graphically in Figure 8-4 by adding together horizontally the demand curves of Figures 8-1 and 8-3. The demand curve D is negatively sloped throughout. We have exaggerated in the figure to show the influence of both the transactions-precautionary demand and the speculative demand. In future graphs, we will merely depict the demand curve as a negatively sloped function.

Unfortunately, we have ignored the influence of the level of national income in Figure 8-4. Since the transactions-precautionary demand for money depends on the level of national income, we must include this in our conclusions summarized in Figure 8-4. We do so rather simply. Let us add the transactions-precautionary demand from equation (8.1) to the speculative demand for money from equation (8.5). We have:

(8.6) $$M_d = \bar{k}Y + L_2(i),$$

where M_d represents the total demand for money, and $L_2(i)$ represents the speculative demand for money. In a more general sense, we say:

(8.7) $$M_d = L_1(Y) + L_2(i),$$

where $L_1(Y)$ represents the transactions-precautionary demand. Finally, we state:

(8.8) $$M_d = L(Y, i),$$

where we simply say that the demand for money depends upon the rate of interest and the level of national income. To depict equation (8.8) graphically, however, presents a problem.

Our problem is solved by examining Figure 8–4 more closely. What would happen to the demand for money at any interest rate, say i_1, when the level of income increased? In the figure, the quantity of money demanded at interest rate i_1 is clearly equal to M_1, but we have not specified the level of national income. Suppose it is Y_1. What happens to the quantity of money demanded at interest rate i_1 when the level of income increases to Y_2? There is no change in the quantity of money demanded for speculative purposes, since we know from our previous discussion that the sepculative demand is independent of the level of income. However, when the level of national income increases, we know that the quantity of money demanded for transactions-precautionary purposes increases also. Thus, we have a point on a new demand curve for money. By changing the rate of interest and following the same procedure, we may trace out all points on a new demand curve for money. Thus, when considering equation (8.8) we may trace out a family of demand curves for money, each related to a different level of national income as shown in Figure 8–5.

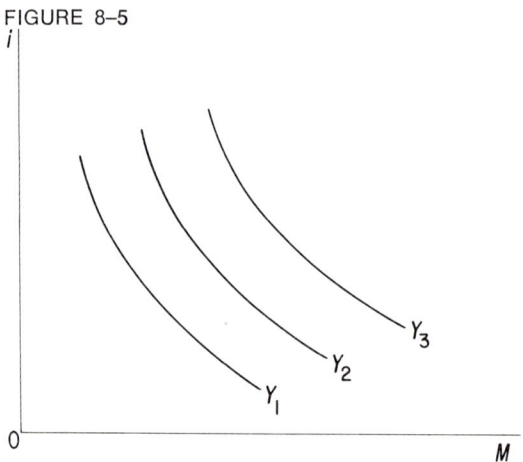

FIGURE 8–5

In the figure, we have drawn three particular demand curves of the family of demand curves. Note that the total demand curve for money shifts to the right as the level of national income increases. Contrariwise, the demand curve for money shifts to the left as the level of national income decreases.

SOME EMPIRICAL EVIDENCE

Our discussion of the demand for money should have prompted you to ask several empirical questions. How sensitive is the demand for money to changes in the rate of interest? Is there a liquidity trap? How sensitive is the demand for money to changes in the level of national income? Fortunately, we can answer these questions, and at the same time, test the validity of the demand for money functions given in equations (8.7) and (8.8).

There are several statistical studies of the demand for money in the economic literature. Most of these studies have tried to determine how strongly changes in the demand for money are correlated to changes in interest rates and national income, and have utilized regression analysis to do so (a summary explanation of regression analysis is given in Chapter 5). One study, performed on a demand for money function similar to equation (8.7), used time series data for the period 1900 through 1958 to estimate a regression equation equal to:[6]

(8.9) $\ln M_d(1900-1958) = a - 0.95 \ln i(1900-1958) + 1.1 \ln Y(1900-1958)$
$R = 0.99$,

where $\ln M_d$ represents the log—to the natural base e—of the demand for money, $\ln i$ represents the log—to the natural base e—of the interest rate, $\ln Y$ represents the log—to the natural base e—of national income, and R represents the coefficient of correlation.

What does equation (8.9) suggest about the strength of the relationship between the demand for money and interest rates and national income? It suggests that each 10 percent change in the interest rate (for example, a change from 5 percent to 5.5 percent) produced a 9.5 percent change in the demand for money over the period 1900-58. A rise in the interest rate by 10 percent produced a fall in the demand for money by 9.5 percent. Also, it suggests that each 10 percent change in the level of national income (for example, a change from $500 billion to $550 billion) produced an 11 percent change in the demand for money over the same period. A rise in national income by 10 percent produced a rise in the demand for money by 11 percent. Finally, it suggests—by examination of the coefficient of correlation—that 98 percent of the variation in the total demand for money over

---
[6] A. H. Meltzer, "The Demand for Money: The Evidence from the Time Series," *Journal of Political Economy*, June 1963. Other estimates can be found in M. Friedman, "The Demand for Money: Some Theoretical and Empirical Results," *Journal of Political Economy*, August 1959.

the years 1900 through 1958 was due to the variations in the level of interest rates and national income. Consequently, the demand for money function given in equation (8.7) appears to have some statistical validity: the demand for money is primarily determined by interest rates and national income, with the demand for money rising as interest rates fall and rising as national income rises.

Another study—using interest rates as the only variable in the demand for money function—was performed for the period 1909 through 1958, and produced a regression estimate of equation (8.5) equal to:[7]

$$(8.10) \qquad \frac{M_d}{Y} = a + 0.008(1/i)$$

$$R = .91,$$

where M_d/Y represents the proportion of national income held as idle cash balances, i represents the level of interest rates, and R represents the coefficient of correlation.

What does equation (8.10) suggest about the demand for money function? It suggests that the interest elasticity of the demand for money function is higher at low-interest rates, and lower at high-interest rates—but never perfectly elastic.[8] Can you derive this conclusion from equation (8.10)? Consequently, it appears that the slope of the total demand for money function becomes flatter as the level of interest rates declines—just as we drew it in Figures 8-3 and 8-5. Thus, we conclude that the demand for money functions summarized in equations (8.7) and (8.8)—and our theoretical discussion that proceeded them—appear to be valid.

THE SUPPLY CURVE OF MONEY

Although we have gained a fairly complete understanding of the demand for money function, we have not yet reached the point where we are able to determine the equilibrium rate of interest. We have

---

[7] H. A. Latane, "Cash Balances and the Interest Rate: A Pragmatic Approach," *Review of Economics and Statistics,* November 1954.

[8] For empirical investigations of the existence or nonexistence of the liquidity trap, see J. Tobin, "Liquidity Preference and Monetary Policy," *Review of Economics and Statistics,* Vol. 29 (1947); and D. Laidler, "The Rate of Interest and the Demand for Money-Some Empirical Evidence," *Journal of Political Economy,* Vol. 74 (1966).

not yet looked at the supply side of the money market. It is to this that we now turn.

The monetary authority is responsible for determining the supply of money in an economy.[9] By *money supply*, we mean simply the sum total of currency and bank deposits held by the nonbank public. Since the simplest assumption to make regarding the money supply is to assume it is exogenously determined by the monetary authority and is not responsive to changes in the interest rate, this is the assumption we will make. It will not bias our conclusions seriously. Hence, we depict the money supply curve as a vertical line in Figure 8–6.

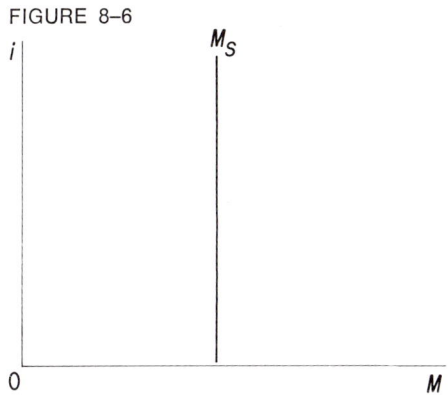

FIGURE 8–6

The money supply curve is assumed to be, for our purposes, completely interest inelastic.

The assumption that the money supply curve is completely interest inelastic is something of an oversimplification. Generally, the monetary authority does not act in such a manner as to keep the money supply constant at all levels of the interest rate. To begin with, the monetary authority usually permits the quantity of money to change in relation to changes in the level of income over time. Also, in the short run the monetary authority generally permits the supply of money to increase, or decrease, in line with general business conditions. In bad times, for example, businesses usually try to reduce inventories, and

---

[9] On the supply of money function, see K. Brunner, "A Scheme for the Supply Theory of Money," *International Economic Review*, January 1961, and K. Brunner and A. Meltzer, "Some Further Investigations of Demand and Supply Functions for Money," *Journal of Finance*, May 1964.

repay bank loans. By so doing, demand deposits at commercial banks fall and the money supply is reduced. Banks generally regard expansion in bad times as risky, so they welcome the chance to reduce their commitments to businesses. During good times, on the other hand, inventories accumulate and firms are in no hurry to curtail loans. Also, banks are eager to make loans during good times. The point is that demand deposits increase, and the money supply increases. While it is true that the monetary authority could follow policies which would keep the money supply constant during bad times and good times alike, they rarely pursue such a policy. It follows, therefore, that the money supply function should be positively sloped and not vertical as the curve of Figure 8–6.

Furthermore, it must be emphasized that the assumption that the money supply curve is completely interest inelastic implies that commercial banks are "loaned up." By law, banks in this country must hold in reserve approximately 20 cents for each dollar of deposits. The other 80 cents is loaned to customers. The amount actually held in reserve depends upon the bank and its location. Suppose that a bank, or the banking system in general, is holding 25 cents in reserve for each dollar of deposits when banks are required to hold only 20 cents on the dollar. There are *"excess reserves."* Thus, banks have extra money to lend to customers. As the interest rate increases, banks will lend out these excess reserves. Furthermore, if the reserve requirement were to change, excess reserves may be created, or, on the other hand, banks may lose excess reserves. Lowering the reserve requirement will create excess reserves, if banks are "loaned up," and so as the interest rate rises more loans will be made. However, if the reserve requirement is increased, and banks are "loaned up," reserves will have to be found. Loans will, in all probability, have to be called in. For analytical simplicity, we will assume banks are "loaned up," hold no excess reserves by choice, and therefore, are unresponsive to changes in the rate of interest.

We will see, in the chapters that follow, that the positively sloped supply curve and the vertical curve yield the same general results; and since the vertical supply curve is easiest to work with, we will use it. Thus, we say that the supply function of cash balances is given by:

(8.11) $$M_s = \bar{M}$$

where $\bar{M}$ is the exogenously determined supply of money.

MONEY MARKET EQUILIBRIUM

We are now able to bring together the two sides of the money market. In so doing, we will be able to determine the equilibrium stock of money, and the equilibrium rate of interest. In Figure 8–7,

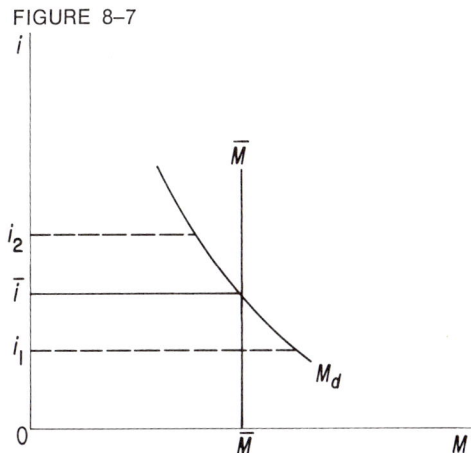

FIGURE 8–7

we note that the equilibrium stock of money is the given stock ($\bar{M}$) while the equilibrium rate of interest is $\bar{\imath}$—the rate of interest at which the supply of money just equals the demand for money.

An important point to note about the money market equilibrium is that it is a stable equilibrium. If the actual interest rate is above the equilibrium rate, market forces will force the actual rate to fall. If the actual interest rate is below the equilibrium rate, market forces will force the equilibrium rate to rise. In both cases, the actual interest rate tends toward equality with the equilibrium rate.

The point is important. Suppose that the equilibrium interest rate—the rate at which the supply of and demand for money are equal—is given as $\bar{\imath}$ in Figure 8–7. Suppose that the monetary authority declares, for an unspecified reason, that at the existing level of national income, interest rates should be pegged at i_1—below the equilibrium interest rate of $\bar{\imath}$. According to Figure 8–7, when the interest rate is pegged at the artificially low level of i_1, the demand for money exceeds the supply of money. The demand for cash balances is greater than the available supply. What is likely to happen? The individuals and business firms who demand these excess cash balances will liquidate some of their bondholdings; i.e., they will sell bonds in order to gain the desired additional cash. Their attempt to sell bonds causes the supply of bonds to rise relative to the demand for bonds. Bond prices fall, and interest rates rise. Moreover, interest rates continue to rise until there is no excess demand for money—until the equilibrium interest rate $\bar{\imath}$ has been restored. Similarly, when the interest rate is pegged at the artificially high level of i_2, the supply of money exceeds the demand for money. The individuals and business firms who have extra cash attempt to reduce their cash balances by purchasing bonds. Their attempt to purchase bonds causes the demand for bonds to rise relative to the supply. Bond prices rise, interest rates fall, and interest rates continue to fall until there are no excess cash balances remaining—until the equilibrium interest rate $\bar{\imath}$ has been restored. The point, of course, is that the money market, like any other market is cleared through market forces.[10] If erroneous prices, or interest rates, are somehow set, they will not prevail. The interest rate is determined by the forces of supply and demand. The money market is in equilibrium when:

(8.12) $$\bar{M} = M_d = L(Y,i).$$

However, this does not mean that the interest rate is fixed forever, under all circumstances, at $\bar{\imath}$. Indeed, the equilibrium of the money market can be disturbed by the monetary authority in such a way so as to induce a permanent increase or decrease in the equilibrium rate of interest. Suppose that the monetary authority wishes to lower the equilibrium interest rate—perhaps to stimulate investment spending and raise the level of national income. How can it induce a lower interest rate? It can force the equilibrium interest rate downward by increasing the supply of money. In Figure 8–8A, the money supply curve given by M_1 would shift rightward to M_2. With the larger money supply, the old equilibrium interest rate, i_1, is too high—there is an excess supply of money. Under these circumstances, as we have seen, the equilibrium interest rate eventually falls to i_2. By creating an excess supply of money at the old interest rate, and disturbing the money

---

[10] We might note at this point that if the supply curve of money were positively sloped, implying, of course, that banks can affect the money supply, an increase in the demand for money (an outward shift in the demand curve like a movement from curve Y_1 to curve Y_2 in Figure 8–5) would raise interest rates and so commercial banks would grant more loans, and thereby increase the money supply. Such an action would have an expansionary effect on the economy.

FIGURE 8-8

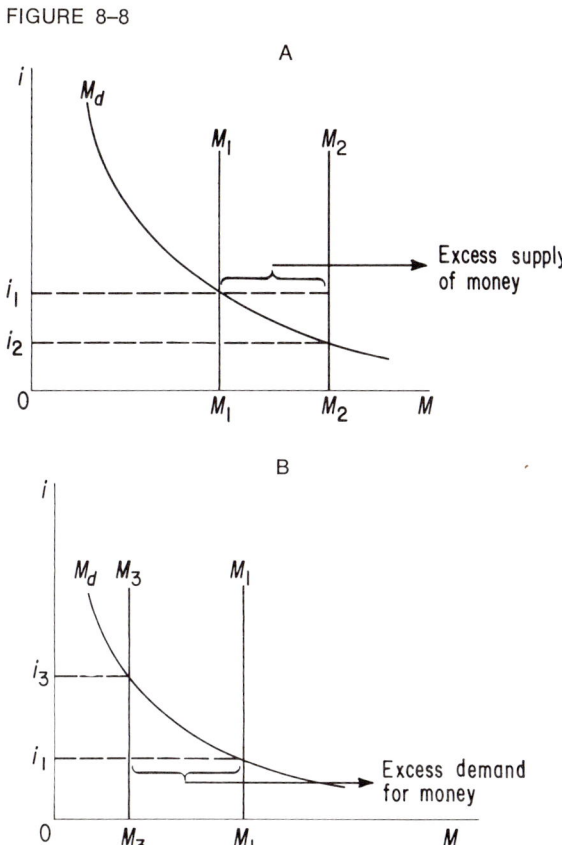

market equilibrium, the monetary authority has forced the level of interest rates to fall from i_1 to i_2.

Instead, suppose that the monetary authority wishes to raise the equilibrium interest rate—perhaps to reduce investment spending and curtail price inflation. How can it induce a higher interest rate? It can force the equilibrium interest rate upward by reducing the supply of money. In Figure 8–8B, the money supply curve given by M_1 would shift leftward to M_3. With the smaller money supply, the old equilibrium interest rate, i_1, is too low—there is an excess demand for money. Under these circumstances, as we have seen, the equilibrium interest rate eventually rises to i_3. By creating an excess demand for money at the old interest rate, and disturbing the money market equilibrium, the monetary authority has forced the level of interest rates to rise from i_1 to i_3.

However, in both cases, our description of the interest rate adjustments are incomplete. If the change in the money supply and the interest rate produces a change in national income, as we will see in the next chapter, the demand for money will change and so will the equilibrium level of interest rates—a change that we have ignored. Although we will cope with this difficulty in a later chapter, it will not alter our conclusions that the equilibrium rate of interest is determined by the interaction of the supply of and demand for money, and that the equilibrium rate of interest is that rate which equates the two money market functions.

CONCLUDING COMMENT

In this chapter, we examined the relationship between the demand for and supply of money and the rate of interest. Also, we noted that there is a relationship between the rate of interest, money and the level of national income. In Chapter 6, we noted that there was a relationship between the rate of interest, the level of investment, and the level of national income. It is now time to relate national income and the rate of interest in a more formal manner. It is to this task that we turn in the next chapter.

9 The goods and services sector and the money market combined

In Chapters 4, 5, 6, and 7 we considered the goods and services sector of the economy, and in the last chapter we viewed the money market. We can now combine these two sectors, and obtain an aggregate equilibrium view of the economy.

THE *IS* CURVE

In Chapter 6, we discovered that there exists a line of causation running from the rate of interest to the level of investment and, ultimately, to the level of national income. We found that when the interest rate fell, the level of investment increased and this, in turn, increased the level of national income. Thus, we concluded that when the rate of interest fell, the equilibrium level of national income rose; and when the rate of interest rose, the equilibrium level of national income fell. Such was the essence of Figure 6–2 in Chapter 6, and the discussion centering around that figure.

Our discussion implies that we can portray the relationship between the interest rate and the equilibrium level of national income graphically, as shown in Figure 9–1. The functional relationship between the rate of interest and the level of national income is given by the curve labeled *IS*. We call this the *IS curve,* and it is simply a locus of points of equilibrium interest rates and equilibrium levels of national income. At any point on the *IS* curve, the level of intended savings is equal to the level of intended investment.

FIGURE 9-1

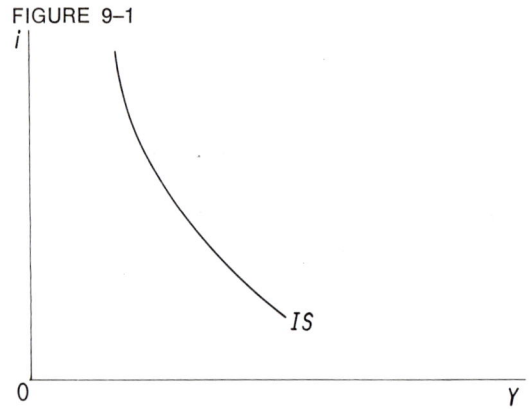

The economic interpretation of the *IS* curve—the sense in which intended savings and intended investment are equal along the *IS* curve, and the nature of the equilibrium values of income and the interest rate—is best understood by examining its derivation. The derivation of the *IS* curve is demonstrated in Figure 9–2. In the figure, we have drawn an investment function in panel (a). In panel (b), we have drawn a straight line emanating from the origin at a 45° angle. Since investment is to be measured along the horizontal axis of this panel and savings along the vertical axis, it follows that every point on the line must represent points at which intended savings and intended investment are equal. This is our equilibrium condition. In panel (c), a savings function is given. Given the investment function, the equilibrium condition, and the savings function, it is simple to construct the *IS* curve in panel (d).

Choose an interest rate i_1. At that rate of interest, the level of intended investment will be I_1. For equilibrium to obtain, the level of savings must equal the level of investment, and so we determine S_1 in panel (b). Given the consumption function and, hence, given the savings function, the level of savings S_1 is consistent with income level Y_1. Therefore, we now know that with interest rate i_1, the level of national income required for equilibrium to prevail is Y_1. The relationship between i_1 and Y_1 determines point *a* in panel (d). Choose another interest rate—say i_2. Given the investment function, the level of intended savings must be S_2 as determined in panel (b). The savings function of panel (c) shows that savings level S_2 is consistent with income level Y_2, and so combining i_2 and Y_2 we obtain point *b* in

FIGURE 9-2

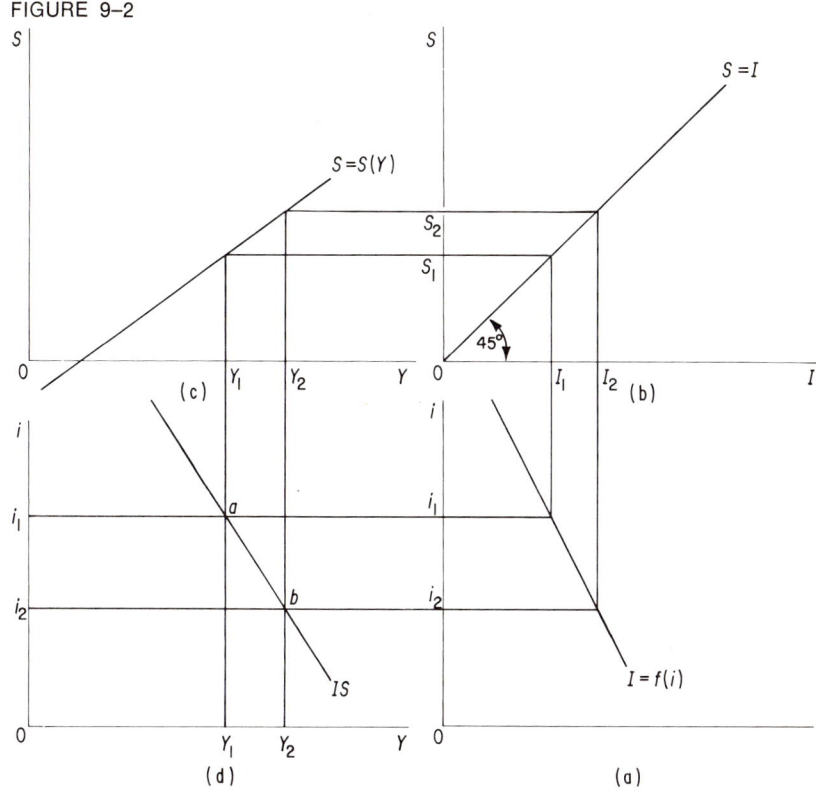

panel (d). Proceeding in this manner, we are able to develop the entire *IS* curve, and to see that is shows the rates of interest and the levels of income at which intended savings and intended investment are equal. In other words, the *IS* curve is a schedule of all income levels and interest rates at which the goods and services sector is in equilibrium.

Please note that the *IS* curve derived in panel (d) of Figure 9-2 is linear because we have assumed a linear investment function and a linear savings function and, so, a linear consumption function. We have, of course, made these assumptions earlier for simplicity. Needless to say, curvilinear functions could be used and the derivation would not change. While a linear *IS* curve would not be derived, it would be negatively sloped nevertheless.

Given a linear consumption function, and a linear investment function, we can derive the equation of the *IS* curve. Moreover, we can demonstrate that the *IS* curve is negatively sloped. All that we need to do is combine the equation of the consumption function ($C = a + by$) with that of the investment function ($I = d + ei$), and the equilibrium condition ($Y = C + I$) and solve. We proceed in the following manner:[1]

$$
\begin{aligned}
(9.1) \qquad Y &= C + I \\
&= a + bY + d + ei \\
Y - bY &= a + d + ei \\
(1-b)Y &= a + d + ei \\
Y &= \frac{1}{1-b}(a + d + ei) \\
Y &= k(a + d) + kei,
\end{aligned}
$$

where $k = \dfrac{1}{1-b}$ represents the simple multiplier. Since k, a, and d are positive, the first term of the final expression is positive. Since e is negative, the second term has a negative sign. When the rate of interest is zero, the level of national income is $k(a + d)$. As the interest rate rises above zero, the level of national income falls. Clearly, the *IS* curve has a negative slope. Just as clearly, equation (9.1) is the equation of a linear *IS* curve.

Our discussion is incomplete because it begs an essential question: Which point on the *IS* curve is the point of equilibrium for the economy as a whole? To find that point, we must know either the rate of interest or the level of national income. From Figure 6–2 of Chapter 6, we know that given the rate of interest we can find the equilibrium level of income. But how do we find the equilibrium rate of interest? For this information, we must turn to the money market.

THE *LM* CURVE

In the previous chapter, we saw that there is a relationship between the stock of money, the rate of interest, and the level of national income. We shall now examine this relationship. Let us see what happens to the rate of interest when the level of national income increases. We do so in Figure 9–3. In the figure, we have drawn three demand curves for money and one stationary supply curve of money. When the level of national income is Y_1, the equilibrium rate of interest

---

[1] We ignore the government sector.

FIGURE 9-3

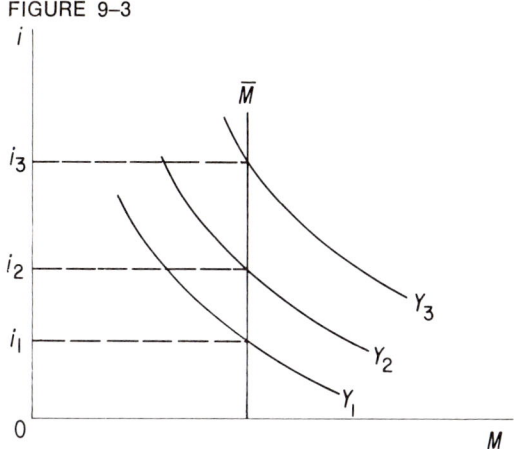

is i_1. When the level of national income increases to Y_2, the equilibrium rate of interest increases to i_2; and when the level of national income increases to Y_3, the equilibrium rate of interest increases to i_3. For the money market to stay in equilibrium when the level of national income increases, the interest rate must increase also. Thus, we may derive a curve representing the schedule of interest rates and levels of income at which the money market is in equilibrium. We call it the *LM curve*, and it is shown in Figure 9-4. Note that this curve is not linear, for it is not based on a linear demand for money curve.

Alternatively, we could have constructed the *LM* curve in a manner similar to that which was used in the derivation of the *IS* curve. This

FIGURE 9-4

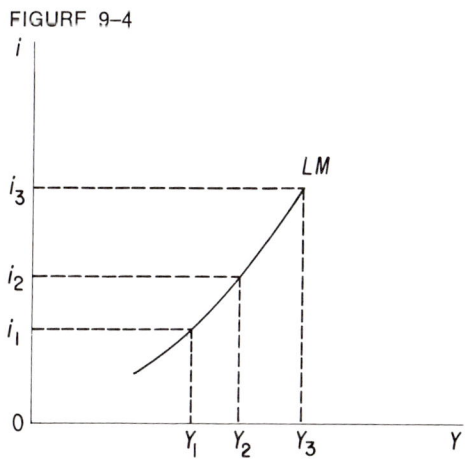

alternative method has the advantage of showing that the conditions of money market equilibrium prevail at all points along the *LM* curve. The alternative derivation is illustrated in Figure 9–5. In panel (a)

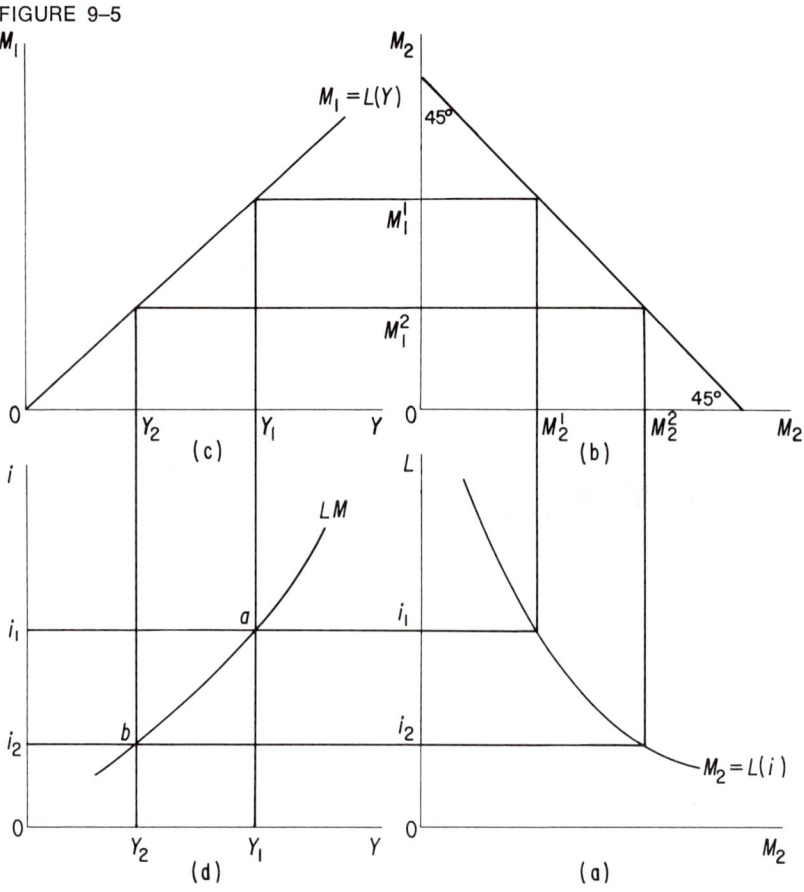

FIGURE 9–5

of the figure, we have drawn the speculative demand curve for money. In panel (b), we have drawn a line such that it intersects both the horizontal and vertical axes at an angle measuring 45°. This line represents equilibrium in the money market, and also represents the supply of money. When the supply of money is increased, the line shifts parallel to the right. When the supply of money is decreased, the line shifts parallel to the left. Given the supply of money and assuming the money market is in equilibrium, we can determine the speculative demand for money and the transactions-precautionary demand from the line drawn in panel (b). For example, suppose there is no transactions-precautionary demand. Then the entire stock of money would represent the speculative demand—assuming that the money market is in equilibrium. If, on the other hand, there is no speculative demand for money, then the entire stock of money would represent the transactions-precautionary demand for money. Hence, the line in panel (b) shows all the combinations of M_1 (transactions-precautionary demand) and M_2 (speculative demand) that can possibly exist given the stock of money. In panel (c), we have drawn the transactions-precautionary demand for money as a function of the level of national income.

Now choose any interest rate, say i_1, in panel (a). Given the speculative demand function, we note that the speculative demand for money is M_2^1. Given the stock of money and a speculative demand for M_2^1, the transactions-precautionary demand for money must equal $\bar{M} - M_2^1 = M_1^1$. This is shown in panel (b). In panel (c), we note that a transactions-precautionary demand of M_1^1 is consistent with a level of national income equal to Y_1. The relationship between i_1 and Y_1 determines point a in panel (d). Now choose another level of the interest rate, say i_2. In panel (a), the speculative demand for money is M_2^2. Given the supply of money, the transactions-precautionary demand must be M_1^2. This level of transactions-precautionary demand is consistent with income level Y_2, and so point b in panel (d) is determined. Continuing in this manner, we are able to derive the entire LM curve.

If we assume for the moment that the speculative demand for money can be represented by a negatively sloped straight line, we can determine the equation of the LM curve. Assume that the speculative demand function is given by the equation:

(9.2) $$M_2 = g + hi,$$

where g is a positive number representing the amount of money demanded for speculative purposes when the interest rate is zero, and h is a negative number representing the slope of the demand curve. Using the transactions-precautionary demand equation given in equation (8.1) of Chapter 8, and employing the equilibrium condition for the money market given in equation (8.12) of the previous chapter, we have:

(9.3) $$\bar{M} = kY + g + hi.$$

Equation (9.3) says that in equilibrium the quantity of money supplied is equal to the quantity of money demanded, and the demand function for money is the sum of the transactions-precautionary and speculative demands. Solving equation (9.3) for Y, we find:

(9.3a) $$Y = \frac{1}{k}(\bar{M} - g) - \frac{1}{k}hi.$$

The first term of equation (9.3a) may be positive or negative depending on the values of $\bar{M}$ and g. Therefore, with a zero rate of interest, the equilibrium level of national income may be positive or negative, or even zero if $\bar{M}$ and g are equal. This is not too important, however, at this point. What is important is that the sign of the slope of the LM curve is positive.

EQUILIBRIUM REVISITED

Now that we have developed both the IS and LM curves, we can turn to a more complicated model of income determination. In our simpler models, we were concerned only with the equilibrium level of national income. Now, however, we must be concerned also with the equilibrium rate of interest. To determine the rate of interest and the level of national income which simultaneously bring both the goods and services sector and the money market into equilibrium, we need only bring together the IS curve of Figure 9–1 and the LM curve of Figure 9–4, which we do in Figure 9–6.

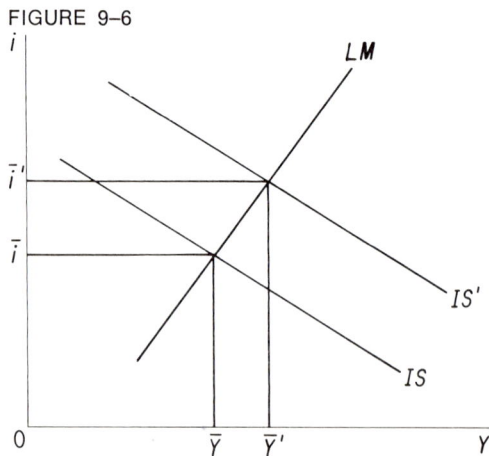

FIGURE 9–6

9 / The goods and services sector and the money market combined   143

In Figure 9–6, equilibrium is simultaneously established in the money market and the expenditure market when the interest is $\bar{i}$ and the level of national income is $\bar{Y}$, using the curves labeled *IS* and *LM*. We could obtain the same result by solving equations (9.1) and (9.3a), simultaneously. For example, we know from equation (9.1) that:

(9.4) $$Y - \frac{1}{(1-b)} ei = \frac{1}{(1-b)} (a + d),$$

and from equation (9.3a) that:

(9.5) $$Y + \frac{1}{\bar{k}} hi = \frac{1}{\bar{k}} (\bar{M} - g),$$

where $\bar{k}$ represents the Cambridge k. Therefore, solving equations (9.3) and (9.5), simultaneously for i, we find

(9.5a) $$\bar{i} = \frac{(1/\bar{k})(\bar{M} - g) - (1/(1-b))(a + d)}{(1/(1-b))e + (1/\bar{k})h}.$$

clearly, $\bar{i}$ can be either positive or negative. Let us assume $\bar{i}$ is positive. (We will look later at the case in which $\bar{i}$ is negative.) Substituting into equation (9.1) or equation (9.3a), we obtain the equilibrium value of Y, $\bar{Y}$.

(9.5b) $$\bar{Y} = \frac{1}{\bar{k}} (\bar{M} - g) - \frac{h}{\bar{k}} \left[\frac{(1/\bar{k})(\bar{M} - g) - (1/(1-b))(a + d)}{(1/(1-b))e + (1/\bar{k})h} \right].$$

CHANGES IN EQUILIBRIUM—FISCAL POLICY

Suppose that the equilibrium level of national income established in Figure 9–6 is "not high enough." Given the resources of society, the level of national income could be higher only if more resources are employed. To achieve a higher level of national income and stimulate more utilization of resources, we might resort to monetary or fiscal policy. Let us suppose that there is an increase in the level of government expenditures, $\bar{G}$, and ignore the problem of finding the finances necessary for increasing the level of $\bar{G}$. We can assume, as a simple expedient in this case, that the government has run budget surpluses in the past, and uses these surpluses to finance its additional spending.

Prior to the increase in government expenditures, the equation of the IS curve could be given as:[2]

(9.6) $$\bar{Y} = k(a + d + \bar{G}) + kei,$$

where k represents the simple multiplier, and $\bar{G}$ the level of government expenditures. When the level of government expenditures is increased to $\bar{G}'$, the equation of the IS curve changes to:

(9.7) $$\bar{Y}' = k(a + d + \bar{G}') + kei.$$

Equations (9.6) and (9.7) are quite similar except that the first term in equation (9.7) is greater than the first term in equation (9.6). This is so because $\bar{G}'$ is greater than $\bar{G}$. This means that the IS curve of Figure 9-6 has shifted to the right, in a parallel manner, to IS'. Consequently, the increase in government expenditures has caused the level of national income to increase to $\bar{Y}'$ and the interest rate increases to $\bar{i}'$.

In an earlier example, we noted that the increase in income was equal to $k\Delta G$, where ΔG represents the change in the level of government spending (for example, $\bar{G}' - \bar{G}$). Let us see if national income changes by the same amount in our present example. If we subtract equation (9.6) from equation (9.7), we obtain:

(9.8) $$\bar{Y}' - \bar{Y} = k(a + d + \bar{G}') + kei - k(a + d + \bar{G}) - kei,$$
$$\Delta Y = k\Delta G.$$

Initially, this conclusion might seem to confirm the full-multiplier effect. On closer inspection, however, we note that $k\Delta G$ is only the change in the income-axis intercept of Figure 9-6, or the change in income when the interest rate remains constant as the IS curve shifted to IS'.[3] Thus, we conclude that at any rate of interest the IS curve shifts by $k\Delta G$. However, at the new equilibrium level of income the interest rate has gone up. While the full-multiplier effect appears to be in operation, it is not—since no account has been made for the increase in the rate of interest.

When the level of government expenditures increased, there was

---

[2] The reader should by now be able to derive equation (9.6) from earlier work.

[3] Throughout this volume, it must be emphasized, we are concerned only with parallel shifts in curves. We could also speak of changes in the slopes of curves. For example, if b were to change, the slope of the IS curve would change and changes in the equilibrium values of variables would occur. We shall avoid this form of analysis.

an initial increase in the level of national income. However, the rise in the level of national income causes the demand curve for money to shift to the right. Given a fixed supply curve of money, the rate of interest rises, and so the level of investment falls. Hence, there is a "watering down" of the multiplier effect because of the increase in the rate of interest. The increase in the rate of interest is neglected in the simple multiplier analysis since the money market is ignored.

There does exist a situation in which it is possible for the full-multiplier effect to prevail when there is a change in the level of government expenditures. If the *LM* curve were horizontal, the full-multiplier effect would obtain. Under what circumstances would the *LM* curve be horizontal? It would be horizontal if we assume the existence of a liquidity trap. While we have noted the faulty logic behind the assumption of the existence of the trap, we will nevertheless see how the trap can cause the full-multiplier effect to obtain. In Figure 9–7,

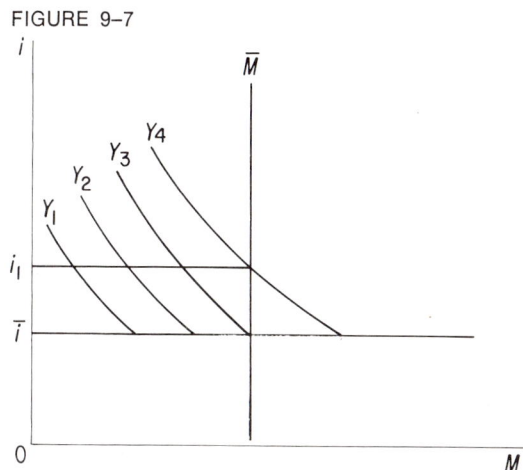

FIGURE 9–7

four money demand curves from the family of demand curves are shown. The four money demand curves come together in the liquidity trap. Thus, given the supply curve of money, when the level of income is Y_1, the interest rate will be $\bar{i}$. When the income level increases to Y_2, the interest rate will not change. It will remain at $\bar{i}$. When the level of income increases to Y_3, the equilibrium rate of interest still remains at $\bar{i}$. When the income level finally reaches the level of Y_4, however, the rate of interest increases to i_1. We are now able to trace

FIGURE 9-8

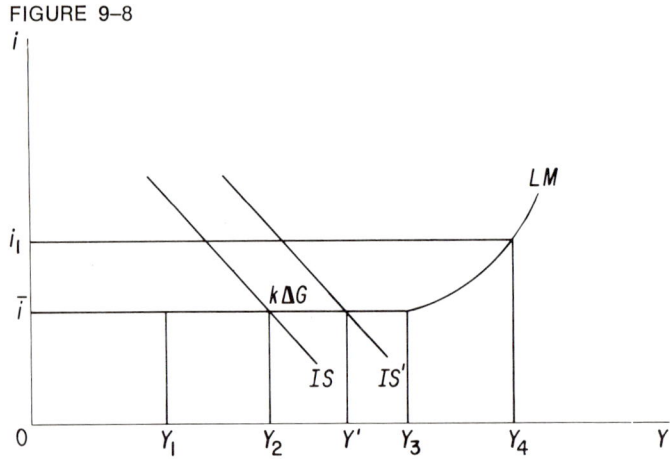

out the *LM* curve, and it appears as in Figure 9-8.[4] Suppose now that we are given the *IS* curve labeled *IS* in Figure 9-8. Equilibrium is established at income level Y_2, and interest rate i. With an increase in the level of government expenditures, the *IS* curve shifts to the right by $k\Delta G$ to the curve *IS'*. The equilibrium level of national income has risen to Y', and the interest rate has not changed. The full-multiplier effect obtains.

Of course, we may take a completely opposite point of view regarding the demand for cash balances. Above we assumed the existence of the liquidity trap. That is to say, we assumed that the demand for money was infinitely elastic. Suppose, however, that the demand

---

[4] It is important to note that a horizontal *LM* curve can be derived in another manner. So long as the demand curves come together and form a single curve, and so long as $\bar{M}$ cuts the single portion of the demand curve, as in the figure in this footnote, there will be a horizontal portion to the *LM* curve. As we shall see later, the *LM* curve derived in this manner will enable one to reach different conclusions with the use of monetary policy than with the *LM* curve of Figure 9-8.

for cash balances does not depend in any way on the rate of interest. Suppose that the demand for cash balances depends only on the level of national income. The family of demand curves would be completely interest inelastic, and the *LM* curve would be vertical. The reason for this is simple. One of the vertical demand curves would coincide with the supply curve of cash balances. Hence, equilibrium in the money market would prevail at one level of national income but at any (or many) rate(s) of interest.[5] The *LM* curve would have to be vertical. Given the usual negatively sloped *IS* curve and a vertical *LM* curve, as the *IS* curve shifts parallel to the right, there is no change in the equilibrium level of income. There is only a rise in the rate of interest. This is illustrated in Figure 9–9; the interest rate

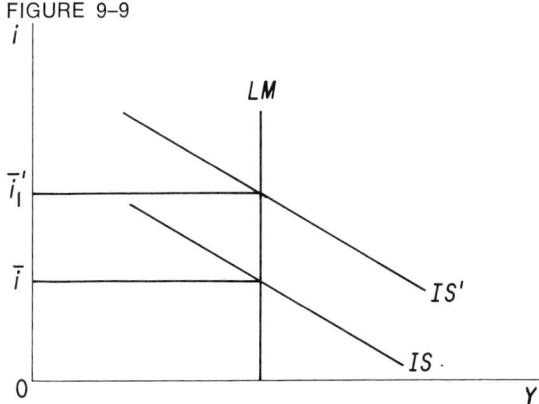

FIGURE 9–9

has increased from $\bar{\imath}$ to $\bar{\imath}'$ after the rightward shift in the *IS* curve. There is no multiplier effect whatsoever in this case. Of course, we are, in reality, considering only the transactions-precautionary demand for money, when we assume the demand curve for cash balances is completely interest inelastic.

CHANGES IN EQUILIBRIUM—MONETARY POLICY

A second possible method that can be employed to raise the level of national income is monetary policy. Suppose that the monetary

---

[5] Note that if the supply curve of cash balances was positively sloped, the *LM* curve would not be vertical. Rather as the level of income increased, so would the equilibrium rate of interest, and so the *LM* curve would possess the usual positive slope.

authority elects to increase the supply of money. This means that the supply curve of cash balances shifts to the right from $\bar{M}$ to $\bar{M}'$ as in Figure 9–10. The monetary authority might, for example, purchase

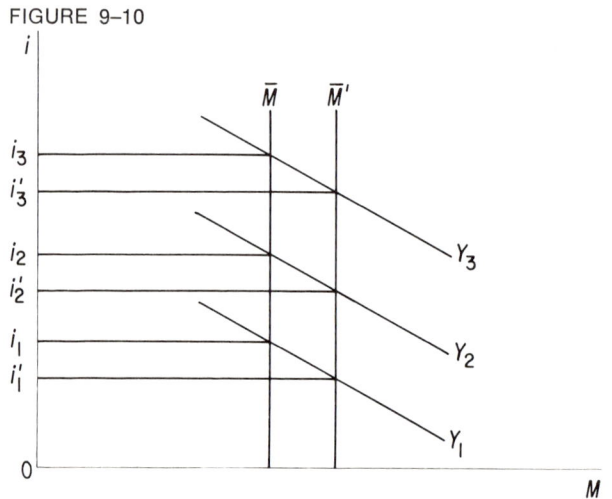

FIGURE 9–10

government securities from the banking system. Thus, given the family of money demand curves, for each level of income, the equilibrium rate of interest falls. Therefore, the *LM* curve shifts to the right, and, given a fixed *IS* curve, the level of national income increases while interest rates fall. Clearly, both monetary policy and fiscal policy can raise the level of national income. The results of the easy money policy approach are shown in Figure 9–11. We see that the rightward shift

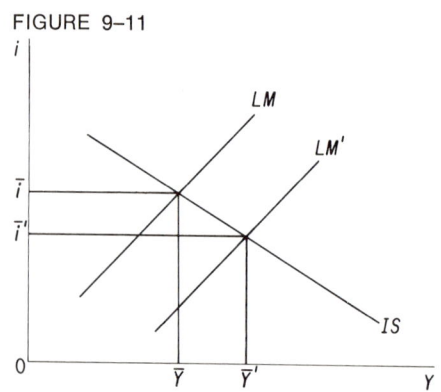

FIGURE 9–11

of the LM curve from LM to LM' has caused the level of national income to rise from $\bar{Y}$ to $\bar{Y}'$, and the rate of interest to fall from $\bar{\imath}$ to $\bar{\imath}'$. It is obvious that both monetary and fiscal policy bring about changes in the level of income. However, there is one important difference: with fiscal policy the rate of interest usually rises, whereas with monetary policy the rate of interest usually falls.[6]

If the liquidity trap exists, and if the level of national income has been determined by the intersection of the IS curve and the original LM curve in the trap, easy money policy will merely extend the trap and so have no effect on the rate of interest or the level of income. That is to say, if the supply curve of cash balances shifts to the right, and the original supply curve of cash balances intersected the trap portion of the money demand curves, the horizontal portion of the LM curve must be extended. Let us look at Figure 9–12. In panel

FIGURE 9–12

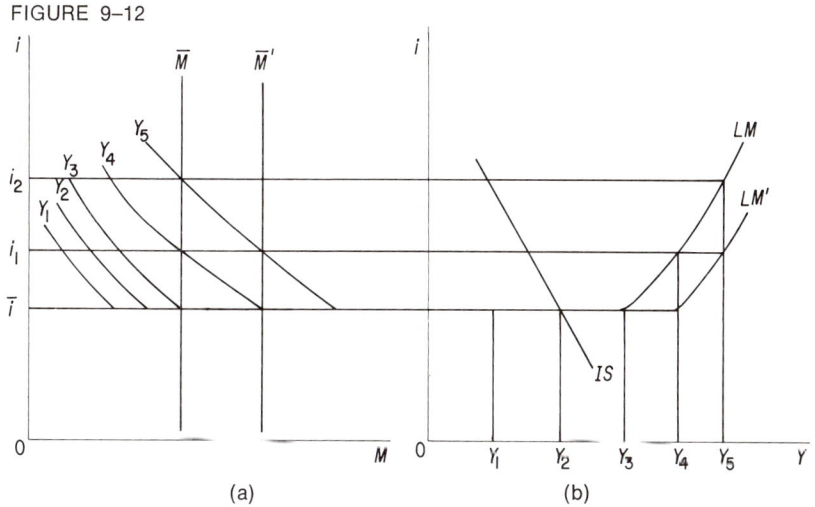

(a), given the supply curve of cash balances $\bar{M}$ and the family of demand curves, the rate of interest at which the money market is in equilibrium is $\bar{\imath}$ for income levels Y_1, Y_2, and Y_3. When the level of income increases to Y_4, the interest rate increases to i_1; and when the level of income increases to Y_5, the interest rate rises to i_2. These points trace out the curve LM in panel (b) of the figure. Now, let the supply curve of cash balances shift rightward to $\bar{M}'$. Given the

---

[6] The reader should be aware that monetary policy and fiscal policy can both be employed to lower the level of income as well as raise it.

same family of money demand curves, the LM curve labeled LM' is traced out in panel (b). Given the IS curve, there has been no change in the interest rate or the level of national income. Monetary policy has been ineffective.

Suppose, on the other hand, that the demand curves for cash balances are completely interest inelastic. In such a case, we are considering only the transactions-precautionary demand for money. An easy money policy will shift the LM curve to the right. The new supply curve of cash balances will coincide with a demand curve representing a higher level of national income. Thus, given an IS curve with a negative slope, the interest rate will fall, and the level of income will increase in proportion to the shift in the supply curve of money. That is to say, if only the transactions-precautionary demand for money exists, then:

$$\tag{9.9} M_d = \bar{k}Y,$$

where $\bar{k}$ is the Cambridge k. Assuming these transactions-precautionary demand curves are completely inelastic with respect to the interest rate, a demand curve at a particular level of income will coincide with the supply curve of cash balances. If the supply curve shifts to the right we say:[7]

$$\tag{9.10} \Delta \bar{M} = \bar{k} \Delta Y$$

$$\Delta Y = \frac{\Delta \bar{M}}{\bar{k}},$$

where $\Delta \bar{M}$ is the change in the money supply. Thus, the level of national income changes in proportion to the change in the supply of money. Monetary policy is very effective in this case.

We have shown that monetary policy is not effective when there is a liquidity trap, and that fiscal policy is not effective when only

---

[7] Since $\bar{M} = M_d$ in equilibrium, we say:

(a) $$\bar{M} = \bar{k}Y.$$

Then,

(b) $$\bar{M} + \Delta \bar{M} = \bar{k}(Y + \Delta Y)$$
$$= \bar{k}Y + \bar{k}\Delta Y$$

Subtracting (a) from (b), we obtain:

(c) $$\Delta \bar{M} = \bar{k} \Delta Y, \text{ or}$$
$$\Delta Y = \frac{\Delta \bar{M}}{\bar{k}}.$$

the transactions-precautionary demand for money is considered. We have also shown that fiscal policy is an effective tool against the trap, and that monetary policy is effective when there is no trap. Moreover, it is also true that if the *IS* curve is vertical, only fiscal policy can change the level of national income. With a vertical *IS* curve, and a positively sloped *LM* curve, not only will an increase in government expenditures raise the level of national income and the rate of interest, but the full-multiplier effect will obtain. Under these circumstances, employing monetary policy shifts the *LM* curve to the right as always; but, with a vertical *IS* curve, only the rate of interest changes (it falls). There is no effect on the level of national income.

How might a vertical *IS* curve prevail? Suppose that we assume the level of investment is independent of the rate of interest. This was the first assumption that we made with regard to the level of investment. Consequently, we say:

(9.11) $$I = d,$$

where d represents a constant level of investment regardless of the level of interest rates. Accordingly, we write the equation of the *IS* curve as (ignoring the level of government expenditures):

(9.12) $$Y = \frac{a + d}{(1 - b)}.$$

Clearly, the level of national income in the expenditure sector is now independent of the interest rate. The *IS* curve will be a vertical line.

CHANGES IN EQUILIBRIUM—OTHER POLICIES

To raise the level of income, it might also be possible to employ policies designed to shift the investment function to the right or the consumption function upward. Obviously, such policies would not be as effective as either monetary or fiscal policy. For example, government officials might try to convince individuals and businesses that good times are "just around the corner." Such "jawboning" might cause shifts in the appropriate functions. Assuming it were possible to shift the investment function to the right, or the consumption function upward, the analysis would be similar to the analysis describing an increase in government expenditures. The *IS* curve would shift to the right, and the full-multiplier effect would not prevail as long as the *LM* curve was positively sloped. As we just mentioned, we might find a completely inelastic investment function. In such a case, the full-multiplier effect would be felt even with a positively sloped LM curve. There is no "watering down" of investment due to the rising interest rate because investment does not depend upon the rate of interest.

Finally, we should note that we can also influence the level of national income by applying pressure to the demand for cash balances. If some kind of persuasion policy were applied such that the family of money demand curves were to shift leftward, we would find, given the supply curve of money, that the rate of interest would fall for every level of income. This means that at all interest rates people demand less cash. They are spending more. Hence, the LM curve shifts to the right, and, given a negatively sloped IS curve, the equilibrium level of national income rises and the interest rate falls. Such a policy, if possible, would yield results identical to an easy money policy. Naturally, this persuasion policy, coupled with easy money policy, would cause the level of national income to rise more, and the interest rate will fall more, than with either monetary or fiscal policy alone.

CONCLUDING COMMENT

In this chapter, we examined several aggregate equilibrium models of income determination. Among other things, we looked at elementary monetary and fiscal policy, and the conditions under which the simple multiplier will and will not work. One shortcoming of all of our work thus far, however, has been our lack of concern with the price level. Surely the level of economic activity influences and is influenced by the price level. It is to this variable that we turn in the next chapter.

10 The price level

IN ALL OUR PREVIOUS ANALYSIS, we have assumed that all variables—national income, consumption, investment, government spending, and the money supply—were given in nominal or money terms. We assumed, furthermore, that the price level was given and constant. This assumption was obviously incorrect and misleading. Therefore, we must relax our assumption of a constant price level. We do so in this chapter.

It is helpful to make several simplifying assumptions in our analysis. First, we assume that prices, when they do change, change proportionately. Thus relative prices will not change. Strictly speaking, this is not the case—for changes in other variables may well affect relative prices. For example, a change in the rate of interest may imply changes in the prices of capital-intensive goods relative to labor-intensive goods. We ignore, by assumption, such changes. Second, we assume away all distributional effects of a change in the price level. Thus, we assume that contracts, pensions, and other income flows, usually regarded as fixed, adjust with the price level. Without this assumption, we would be forced to consider changes in the distribution of income, and such a task is beyond the scope of this book. Finally, all changes in the price level are regarded as permanent.

The introduction of the price level into our analysis means that we will be able to consider variables in real terms rather than in nominal ones. We will be able to adjust the nominal variables for changes in the price level. Thus, we say that if the money value of national

154 The essentials of macroeconomic analysis

income doubles and the price level more than doubles, the real value of national income actually has fallen. The gains in national income have been more than offset by the rise in the price level.

THE PRICE LEVEL AND THE EXPENDITURES SECTOR

Since we must now recast the relationships of the previous chapter in real terms rather than in money terms, we must convert the definitional expression of national income into real terms. Accordingly, we have:

(10.1) $$\frac{Y}{P} = \frac{C}{P} + \frac{I}{P} + \frac{G}{P},$$

where P represents an index of the price level (recall our definition of a price index from Chapter 2), Y/P is real income, I/P is real investment, and G/P is real government expenditures. These terms are nothing more than the nominal values of the variables deflated by the price index. In other words, they are the nominal values of national income, investment, and government expenditures adjusted for changes in the price level.

Since government expenditures have been regarded as an exogenously determined constant, real government expenditures, we will assume, will also be an exogenously determined constant; so we simply ignore them in the analysis that follows. It should be noted that the analysis of Chapter 7 can be cast in real terms by simply inflating or deflating the relevant variables by the price level, P.

With regard to the consumption function, we assume that real consumption depends upon the level of real income, or:

(10.2) $$\frac{C}{P} = C(Y/P),$$

and in linear terms:[1]

(10.3) $$\frac{C}{P} = a/P + b(Y/P).$$

---

[1] In this linear consumption function, as in all the linear approximations that we use, the constant term is still a constant. That is to say, when the level of real income in equation (10.3), for example, is zero the level of real consumption is a/P. Thus, if P were to change so would a. See M. J. Bailey, *National Income and the Price Level,* 2d ed., (New York: McGraw-Hill Book Co., 1971), pp. 28–32.

Furthermore, since we have deflated the consumption function by the price index, we must do the same for the savings function. Accordingly, we have in the linear case:

(10.4) $$\frac{S}{P} = -a/P + (1-b)(Y/P),$$

where all variables are now presented in real terms.

With regard to the investment function, we write:

(10.5) $$\frac{I}{P} = f(i),$$

and

(10.6) $$\frac{I}{P} = d/P + ei/P,$$

where we assume that investment is a linear function of the rate of interest only. When investment depends upon the level of national income as well as the rate of interest, we have in linear terms:

(10.7) $$\frac{I}{P} = d/P + ei/P + f(Y/P).$$

Finally, when investment depends not only on the rate of interest and the level of national income but on the wage rate as well, we have in linear terms:

(10.8) $$\frac{I}{P} = d/P + ei/P + f(Y/P) + l(w/P),$$

where w/P represents the real wage rate—the nominal wage rate adjusted for changes in the price level. We assume that l is a negative number. Given our assumptions concerning changes in the price level, there is no reason to suppose that expected profits or the risks associated with any investment will be changed by changes in the price index. Therefore, our analysis will usually employ equation (10.6).

Combining equations (10.1), (10.3), and (10.6), we obtain the equation of the *IS* curve in real terms. We have:

(10.9) $$\frac{Y}{P} = \frac{k(a+d)}{P} + \frac{kei}{P},$$

where k represents the simple multiplier.

156 The essentials of macroeconomic analysis

It is important to note that equation (10.1) holds regardless of the interpretation of any of the other equations in this chapter. Equation (10.1) is merely a definition of real income, whereas the other equations depend upon the assumption of proportionate price changes and fully adjusted changes in contracts and pensions. Since we have assumed that all prices, pensions, and contract incomes change by the same proportion, the basket of goods that each individual can command will be completely unaffected because—following our assumption—the distribution of income has not changed. While it may appear that we simply took the equations of the previous chapters and divided them by P, certainly we have done more than that—as we will see later in this chapter.

THE PRICE LEVEL AND THE MONETARY SECTOR

Our assumption regarding the permanency of price level changes is very important in this section. We have assumed that, once the price level changes, the change is regarded as permanent. We will make this assumption regardless of whether the price level changes a little bit or a lot. At a later point, we will discuss price expectations. For the moment, then, all price changes are regarded as once and for all time changes.

Given this important assumption, we consider the demand curve for cash balances to be:

(10.10) $$\frac{M_d}{P} = L(i, Y/P),$$

and in linear terms

(10.11) $$\frac{M_d}{P} = \bar{k}(Y/P) + g/P + hi/P.$$

Our deflation of the nominal demand curves for money appears reasonable under the assumptions that we have made. Individuals and business firms should regard the quantity of goods and services that a particular money balance will purchase in the same light as any other real quantity. The various reasons for which cash is held will rise in money value in direct proportion to the price level. If the price level increases by 10 percent, for example, people will desire to hold 10 percent more cash to meet necessary contingencies. Equations (10.10) and (10.11) have the property that if the price level changes and if the real variables remain the same with the interest rate constant, M_d and Y will rise in the same proportion as the price level.[2]

With regard to the supply side of the money market, we assume that the monetary authority does not react to changes in the price level that are regarded as permanent changes. Thus, we assume that the monetary authority holds the supply curve of money constant in money terms. Hence, if the demand curve for nominal cash balances shifts to the right, the monetary authority responds in the same manner regardless of whether the shift is due to a rise in real income with the price level constant or to a rise in the price level with real income remaining constant. Thus, the money supply curve remains the same as before, or:

(10.12) $$M_s = \bar{M}.$$

Dividing both sides of equation (10.12) by P, we have:

(10.13) $$M_s/P = \frac{1}{P}\bar{M},$$

indicating that the left-hand sides of equations (10.13) and (10.10) are both given in real terms. Equilibrium in the money market, in real terms, is determined when:

(10.14) $$M_d/P = M_s/P.$$

We are now able to determine the real LM curve. For simplicity, let us employ the linear demand curve for real cash balances. Using the equilibrium condition from equation (10.14), we obtain:

(10.15) $$M_d/P = k(Y/P) + g/P + hi/P = \frac{1}{P}\bar{M} = M_s/P.$$

Solving for Y/P, the equation of the LM curve in real terms is:

(10.16) $$\frac{Y}{P} = \frac{1}{k}\left[\frac{1}{P}\bar{M} - g/P - (h/P)(i)\right].$$

It is interesting and important to note that $1/P$ appears on the right-hand side of equation (10.16). Since the price level is a variable, we now have a family of LM curves—one for each particular value

---

[2] It must be noted at this point that in equations (10.3), (10.4), (10.6), (10.7), (10.8), (10.9), and (10.11) we have deflated variables a, d, e, h, and g by the price index. This is necessary since, in the original equations of the previous chapters, these variables were given in nominal terms. Note that nowhere have we deflated the interest rate by the price level.

of P. We may examine this notion more closely, if we look at equilibrium in the money market.

In Figure 10–1, we have drawn four demand curves for real cash

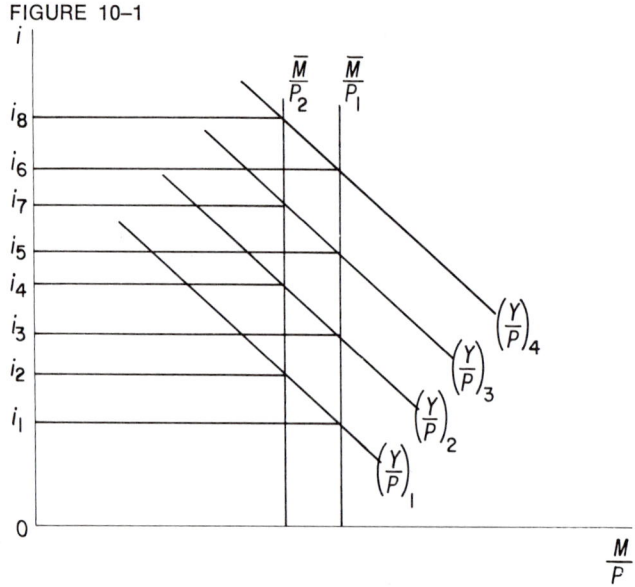

FIGURE 10–1

balances and two supply curves of real cash balances. The graph is somewhat analogous to the case in which only nominal values were considered. As the level of real national income increases, the demand curve for real cash balances shifts to the right. Suppose $(Y/P)_1$ is the given level of real income. You must recognize that there are many combinations—an infinite number—of Y and P that will yield $(Y/P)_1$. One combination might be Y_1 and P_1 so that $(Y_1/P_1) = (Y/P)_1$. Another combination might be Y_2 and P_2 such that $(Y_2/P_2) = (Y/P)_1$. Thus, there are an infinite number of price levels consistent with the level of real income $(Y/P)_1$. Given the demand curve for cash balances, it should be clear from equation (10.15) that equilibrium in the money market will depend upon the price level. In Figure 10–1, therefore, if the level of real income is $(Y/P)_1$ and the price level is P_1, the money market is in equilibrium with interest rate i_1 and the quantity of real cash balances $(\bar{M}/P_1)$. Suppose, however, that the level of real income is still $(Y/P)_1$ but the price level is P_2. (Assume that P_2 is greater than P_1). The supply curve of real cash balances shifts leftward to $(\bar{M}/P_2)$.

The money market is in equilibrium with interest rate i_2, and a level of real cash balances $(\bar{M}/P_2)$. Now suppose that the level of real income increases to $(Y/P)_2$. From above, we know that any price level will yield this level of real income provided the level of money income adjusts. Thus, we may assume that the price level is P_1. With this price level, the supply curve shifts rightward to $(\bar{M}/P_1)$ and the equilibrium rate of interest becomes i_3. With a higher price level, P_2, the equilibrium rate of interest will be i_4. We have, in effect, derived a family of LM/P curves, real LM curves.[3]

With the price level P_1, we see from Figure 10-1 that, as the level of real income increases from $(Y/P)_1$ to $(Y/P)_2$ to $(Y/P)_3$ to $(Y/P)_4$, the equilibrium rate of interest increases from i_1 to i_3 to i_5 to i_6. The corresponding LM/P_1 curve is traced out in Figure 10-2.

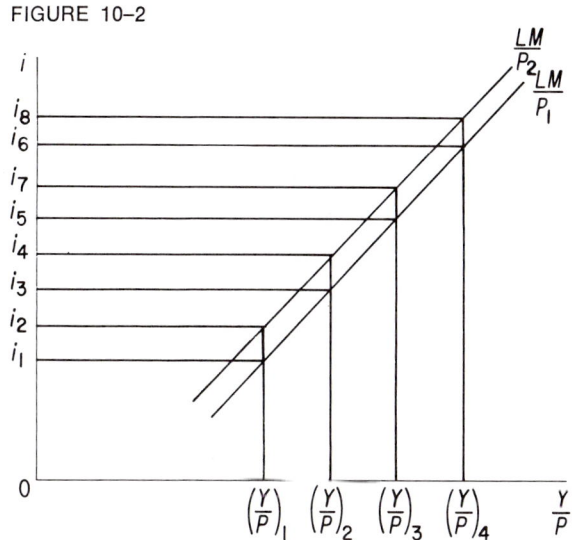

FIGURE 10-2

When the price level increases to P_2, we see from Figure 10-1 that, as the level of real national income increases from $(Y/P)_1$ to $(Y/P)_2$ to $(Y/P)_3$ to $(Y/P)_4$, the equilibrium rate of interest increases from i_2 to i_4 to i_7 to i_8. The corresponding LM/P_2 curve is traced out in Figure 10-2. Thus, we have developed a family of real LM curves—one curve for each price level.

---

[3] Note that a rise in the price level from P_1 to P_2 has the same general effect on the supply of real cash balances as would a shift to a tight money policy at a constant price level.

FIGURE 10-3

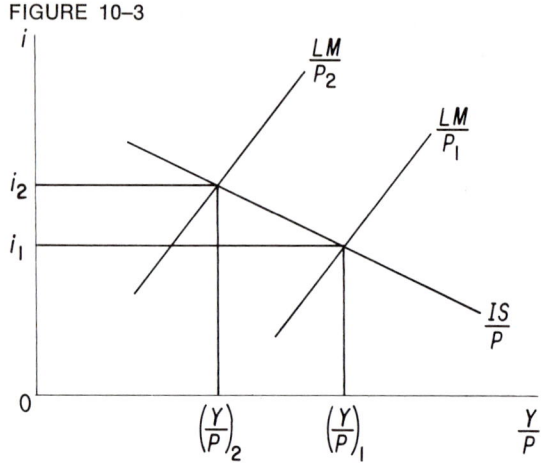

With this family of real LM curves, equilibrium for the system clearly depends upon the price level. Thus, in Figure 10-3, given the IS/P curve (the real IS curve), when the price level is P_1, the equilibrium level of income is $(Y/P)_1$ and the equilibrium rate of interest is i_1. The real income level $(Y/P)_1$ is called the level of real aggregate demand. However, when the price level increases to P_2, the equilibrium level of real national income decreases to $(Y/P)_2$ and the equilibrium rate of interest increases to i_2. We now have an indeterminate solution to our system: we must specify a price level to obtain a solution, otherwise an infinite number of equilibria exist. From equations (10.9) and (10.16) it is easy to see why we have an indeterminate solution. We have two equations but three unknowns—(Y/P), i, and P. Either one of the variables must be given, or we need another equation which introduces no new unknowns. Thus, given the value of P we can reach a determinate equilibrium. In the next chapter, we shall keep the price level as an unknown and introduce another equation into our model. This will enable us to extend our model considerably.

THE PRICE LEVEL AS A VARIABLE IN THE MONETARY SECTOR

From our analysis above, with particular reference to equation (10.15), we note that the price level is a variable in the monetary sector. Yet, the price level is not a variable in the expenditure sector where the individual product prices are determined. Since the price level is a composite of the prices of particular goods and services, should not the price level be a variable in the expenditure sector also? After all, any disequilibrium in the price level must be corrected by changes in individual product prices.

Furthermore, it must be noted that a given combination of the rate of interest and the level of real income, which yields an equilibrium in the expenditure sector, yields the same equilibrium regardless of the price level. This may be a bit difficult to understand. Nevertheless, let us try. The level of nominal income is measured by:

(10.18) $$Y = p_1 q_1 + p_2 q_2 + \cdots + p_n q_n,$$

where the p's represent product prices, and the q's represent quantities of the various products. If the quantities of the products do not change, but prices rise, then income, Y, will increase. If product prices increase proportionately, income increases and so does the price level; but these changes are proportional to the change in prices. If all prices rise by 20 percent while the quantities remain constant, income rises by 20 percent also. If all prices rose by 20 percent, the price level would increase by 20 percent too. However, if income and the price level both increased by 20 percent, the level of real income, Y/P, does not change. Thus, the interest rate on the real IS curve does not change, and the price change does not alter the expenditure sector. This occurrence leads to the following question, "If the price level does not affect the relationships in the expenditure sector, how can the expenditure sector affect the price level?"

Suppose that, in the market for each product, the quantity demanded is greater than the quantity supplied. The price in each market will rise, in the absence of price controls. If all prices rise proportionately, the excess of quantities demanded over quantities supplied will not change; for if all prices rise, then money income rises also. The demand curve and the supply curve for each commodity shift in an upward direction as prices and incomes rise. If all prices rise by 20 percent, money incomes rise by 20 percent. There has been no change in real terms. The excess demand in each commodity market must be the same after the price change as before.[4] Hence, there will be a continuing rise in individual prices, and a continuing rise in the price level, unless there is a change in the rate of interest.

---

[4] Assume no change in the rate of interest.

We know now, of course, that a change in the price level will bring about a change in the rate of interest. But it does so through the money market. When the price level increases, the supply curve of real cash balances shifts to the left. Given the demand curve for real cash balances, the rate of interest must rise. The interest rate plays a key role in the relationship between the monetary sector and the expenditure sector.

Suppose for a moment that the level of real national income is "too low." (We will see what this means in the next chapter.) Also, suppose that individual prices are such that quantities demanded in commodity markets are less than quantities supplied. Individual prices are too high, and so the price level is too high. With a price level that is too high, the monetary sector will produce an interest rate that is too high to bring about a higher level of real national income. The quantities demanded in the aggregate are less than quantities supplied in the aggregate. We say that aggregate demand is less than aggregate supply. When such a situation exists, the surpluses on the various markets cause individual prices to fall, and so the price level falls. The supply curve of real cash balances shifts rightward, and, given the demand curve for real cash balances, the interest rate falls. In other words, as the price level falls, the real LM curve shifts rightward, and the equilibrium level of real national income increases while the rate of interest falls. The level of real national income is no longer "too low."

The adjustment process is illustrated in Figure 10–4. The initial level of national income is $(Y/P)_1$, and the initial level of interest

FIGURE 10–4

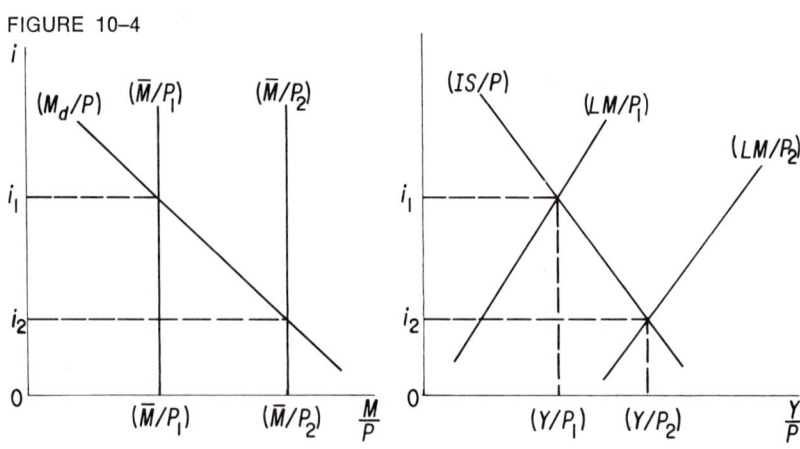

rates is i_1. Under the assumption that an excess supply of goods and services exists in the expenditure sector, the price level falls from P_1 to P_2. Consequently, the supply curve of real cash balances shifts rightward from $(\bar{M}/P_1)$ to $(\bar{M}/P_2)$, indicating that the purchasing power of the original stock of nominal balances has increased. As the real value of the money supply increases, assuming that the demand for cash balances remains constant[5], the interest rate falls. As the interest rate falls, investment expenditures increase and the level of national income begins to rise. In other words, the reduction in the price level causes the real value of the money supply to increase to $(\bar{M}/P_2)$, which—under the assumption of a constant demand for real cash balances—causes the LM curve to shift rightward from LM/P_1 to LM/P_2. As a result, the equilibrium level of real national income increases from $(Y/P)_1$ to $(Y/P)_2$, and the equilibrium level of interest rates declines from i_1 to i_2.

Please note that the expenditure sector played a key role in the transition of the price level even though the price level is not a variable in the expenditure sector. Furthermore, the monetary sector played a key role in the transition of the interest rate to the proper level even though, as we will see later, the monetary sector is not necessary to determine the rate of interest.

CONCLUDING NOTE

In this chapter, we introduced the price level into our model of income determination so that we could speak of the variables of the previous chapters in real terms. By so doing, we discovered that we may not be able to reach a unique equilibrium solution. We can overcome this problem by introducing another sector to our economy, and we do this in the next chapter.

---

[5] We will see shortly that this is a simplifying assumption. Actually, the demand curve for real cash balances will shift to the right as the level of real income increases. However, the results indicated in Figure 10-4 will prevail. The interest rate will fall and the level of real national income will rise.

11 The employment sector—Equilibrium reestablished

IN THE PREVIOUS CHAPTER, we found that the introduction of the price level into our model posed a problem. The solution to our model was indeterminate: our model, consisting of two equations, had three unknowns. In order to solve the system of equations representing the model, we must either specify one of the variables—or, we must introduce another equation without introducing another variable. In this chapter, we introduce another equation without introducing another variable, and thereby ensure that we have a model consisting of three equations and three unknowns—a model with a determinate solution.

Thus far, our economic system consists of two sectors: an expenditure sector, and a monetary sector. We shall make our system yield a determinate solution by introducing an employment sector, and thereby expand our model to three sectors.

THE EMPLOYMENT SECTOR

The employment sector is best viewed by appealing to some of the basic tools of microeconomic analysis. To begin with, we assume that physical output (real output or real income) depends upon two factors of production—labor and capital. That is to say, we assume that all final output, inflated or deflated by the price index, depends upon only these two factors of production. Since we are concerned with aggregate output, factors of production are examined in an aggregate sense. Thus, we say:

(11.1) $$\frac{Y}{P} = f(N,K),$$

where N represents the labor input, and K represents the capital input. Furthermore, we assume that the quantity of capital is fixed. Hence, our analysis is short run,[1] and we say:

(11.2) $$\frac{Y}{P} = g(N).$$

We call equation (11.2) the short-run production function for the economy. Moreover, we assume that, in the short run, real output initially increases as more and more labor is added to the fixed amount of capital, but after some point output reaches a maximum, and then, with each additional dose of labor, output begins to fall. This reflects the law of diminishing returns. An aggregate production function, characterized by the law of diminishing returns, is illustrated in Figure 11–1, with output plotted on the vertical axis and the quantity of

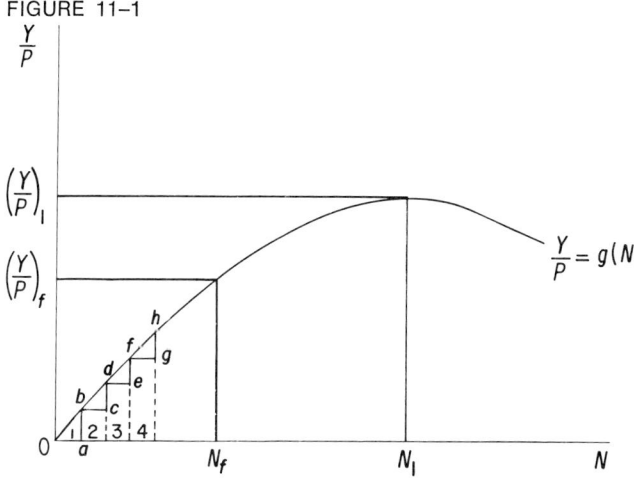

FIGURE 11–1

labor plotted on the horizontal axis. Obviously, the production function indicates that real output reaches a maximum at the level of $(Y/P)_1$, when N_1 units of labor are employed. Units of labor may

---
[1] Note that the short run as used here is different from the short run we talked about in regard to the consumption function in Chapter 5. There "run" had to do with time, while here "run" has to do with fixed versus variable factors of production.

be thought of as labor hours so that we need not make any assumptions about all workers being the same.

The demand curve for labor is derived from the production function. We assume that pure competition prevails everywhere; i.e., there are no monopoly elements in the hiring of labor, or the selling of output. Additionally, we assume that producers are in business to maximize profits. Employing these usual assumptions, the principles of microeconomic theory argue that labor is hired up to the point where the value of the marginal product of labor is equal to the wage rate, or:

(11.3) $$VMP_N = w,$$

where w represents the money, or nominal, wage rate. However, VMP_N (value of the marginal product of labor) is merely the marginal physical product of labor times the price of output. In our model, the price of output is the price level. Thus, we say:

(11.3a) $$P \cdot MP_N = w,$$

where MP_N represents the marginal product of labor, and is defined as the change in output for each unit change in labor input. From equation (11.3a) we obtain:

(11.3b) $$MP_N = \frac{w}{P},$$

where w/P represents the real wage rate. According to the profit-maximizing rule, labor is hired up to the point where the marginal physical product of labor is equal to the real wage rate—w/P. In essence, equation (11.3b) is the demand function for labor.

Since the production function is characterized by diminishing returns, the marginal physical product of labor falls—in Figure 11-1, from *ab* to *cd* to *ef*—as additional doses of labor are added to the fixed quantity of capital. Consequently, the demand curve for labor must be negatively sloped. After all, if each additional unit of labor is less productive than the unit that preceeded it, each additional unit of labor will only be hired at a lower real wage. Thus, the demand for labor increases only as the real wage rate decreases—assuming that the quantity of capital is constant. Thus, the quantity of labor demanded is a function of the real wage rate; that is precisely what equation (11.3b) says. In the case of the production function drawn

FIGURE 11–2

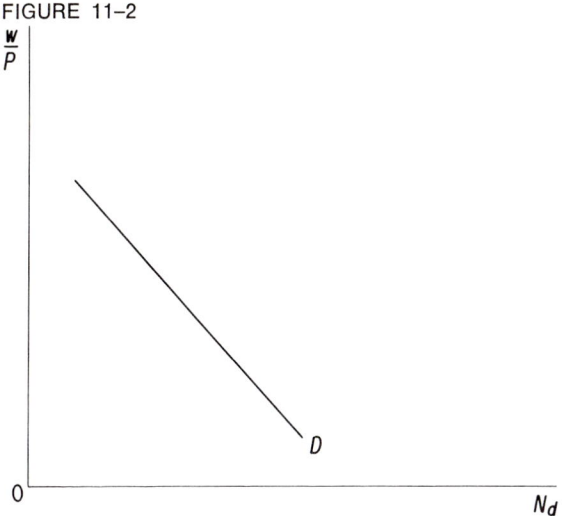

in Figure 11–1, the derived demand curve for labor is a negatively sloped, straight line. It is illustrated in Figure 11–2.

On the supply side of the labor market, we assume that the quantity of labor supplied is a function of the real wage rate also. As the real wage rate increases, the quantity of labor supplied increases. This assumption is typically Classical in nature, and will be examined more closely in a later chapter. For simplicity, we assume that a linear relationship exists between the real wage rate and the quantity of labor supplied. Also, note that the labor supply curve of Figure 11–3 cuts the vertical axis at a positive real wage rate. This means that the quantity of labor supplied will be zero even at some positive real wage rate, probably the rate associated with the subsistence level of income. Our equation for the labor supply function is given as:

(11.4) $$N_s = h(w/P).$$

We can now view the entire labor market. In order to do so, we bring together, in Figure 11–4, the demand curve for labor and the supply curve of labor. They intersect at labor level N_f, and real wage rate $(w/P)_f$. At this real wage rate, the labor market is cleared. All the people who wish to be employed are employed. Full employment prevails. Given the production function of Figure 11–1, and the full-employment level of labor utilization—N_f, the full-employment level

FIGURE 11-3

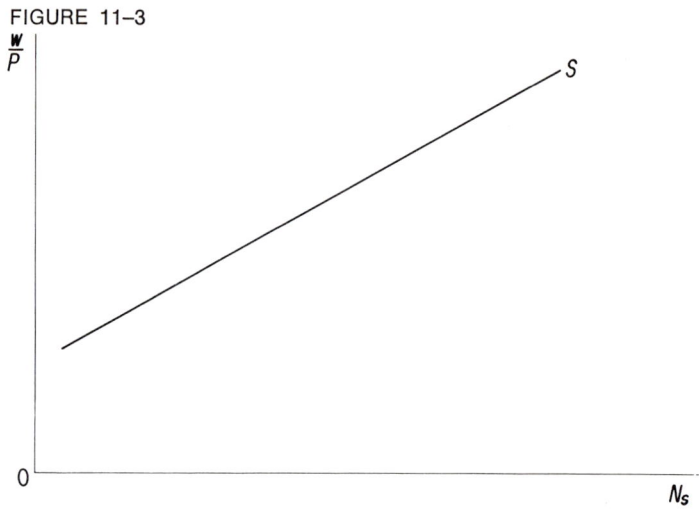

of real output is shown in Figure 11–1 as $(Y/P)_f$. There is no reason to believe that this level of output is the maximum quantity of output that the economy can produce (i.e., the level of output associated with N_1). The level of output $(Y/P)_f$ is that level of output associated with full employment, and full employment depends upon the real wage rate.

FIGURE 11-4

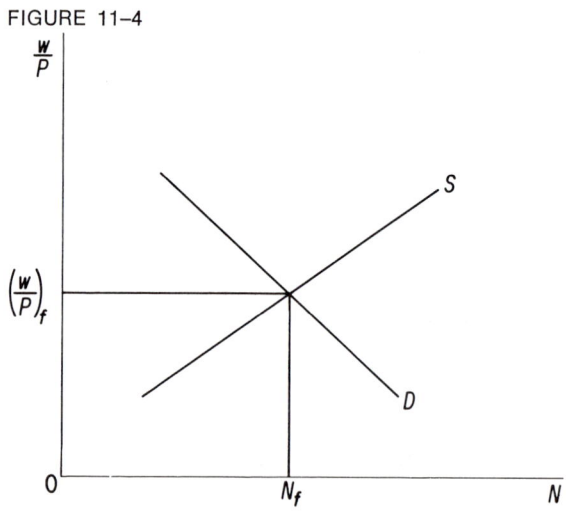

11 / The employment sector—Equilibrium reestablished   169

The level of real output, $(Y/P)_f$, is called the level of aggregate supply, or simply aggregate supply. This is the amount of real output actually produced by society. Clearly, the amount of output actually produced can be less than the level associated with the full employment of labor. Just as clearly, it can be equal to the level of real output associated with the full employment of labor. It is not quite so clear whether aggregate supply can exceed the level of real output associated with the full-employment level of labor—whether labor can be overfully employed? We will look at these questions in a later chapter.

The level of real output associated with the full-employment level of labor utilization is independent of the rate of interest. Thus, if we plot the full-employment level of output and the interest rate on the same graph, we would obtain the relationship drawn in Figure 11–5. At all rates of interest, the level of aggregate supply

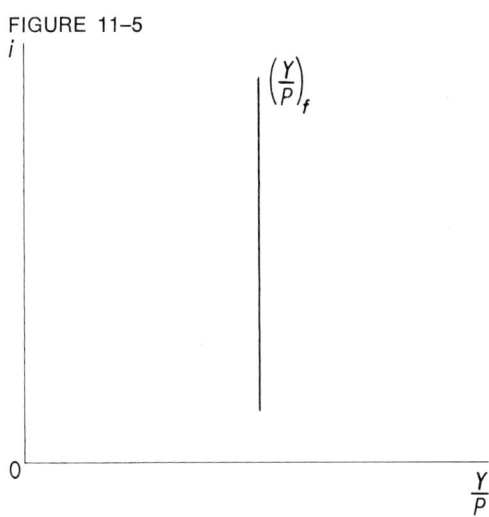

FIGURE 11–5

remains at $(Y/P)_f$—provided that the real wage remains at $\left(\dfrac{w}{P}\right)_f$. We have now added the third equation to our system of equations. We now say:

(11.5) $$\frac{Y}{P} = g(N_f) = (Y/P)_f,$$

where N_f represents the full-employment level of labor usage. The three equations in our system are:

(11.6) $$(Y/P) = \frac{k(a+d)}{P} + \frac{kei}{P},$$

where k is the simple multiplier,

(11.7) $$(Y/P) = \frac{1}{\bar{k}}\left[\frac{1}{P}\bar{M} - g/P - (h/P)(i)\right],$$

where $\bar{k}$ is the Cambridge k, and,

(11.8) $$(Y/P) = (Y/P)_f,$$

where we employ linear functions throughout. Equations (11.6), (11.7), and (11.8) now represent a system of three equations in three unknowns, (Y/P), i, and P. In general, such a system can be solved.[2] We view the simultaneous solution graphically, in Figure 11–6, by

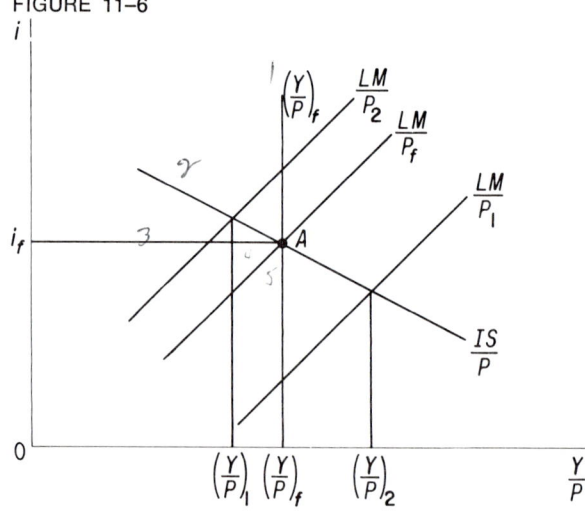

FIGURE 11–6

piecing together the three equations just given. The only point in the figure at which all three curves intersect is point A. At that point, the level of real income is $(Y/P)_f$, the interest rate is i_f, and the price level is P_f. These are the equilibrium values of the three variables, and the economy is said to be in *full-employment equilibrium*.

---

[2] The equations must be consistent and independent. In our case, both conditions are satisfied.

11 / The employment sector—Equilibrium reestablished

Suppose that the price level is P_2. With this price level, the real LM curve is LM/P_2 in the figure. The level of aggregate demand, given by the intersection of the real IS and the real LM curves, is $(Y/P)_1$. However, the level of aggregate supply, in real terms, is $(Y/P)_f$. Since aggregate supply is greater than aggregate demand, we have a surplus in the aggregate. Thus, the price level declines. It continues to fall to P_f, and causes the real LM curve to shift rightward to the point where aggregate supply and aggregate demand are again equal. The economy returns to equilibrium, assuming price flexibility in the downward direction. If the price level were P_1, just the opposite would be true. That is to say, the level of aggregate demand would be $(Y/P)_2$. Aggregate demand would exceed aggregate supply. This means that inflationary tendencies exist, and prices are bid up. The real LM curve shifts to the left until equilibrium is established at the full-employment level of real output.

Go back for a moment to the case in which aggregate demand was less than aggregate supply. Ask yourself the question: How is the level of real income increased? Earlier, we would have resorted to fiscal or monetary policy. Now, however, market forces induce the increase in the level of real output, assuming prices are sufficiently flexible. Thus, we might not have to increase the level of government expenditures, or resort to an easy money policy. The market may well increase the level of real output.

WALRAS' LAW AND EQUILIBRIUM

We have now expanded our economic system to three sectors. However, an economy can be divided into four sectors: namely, the expenditure sector, the monetary sector, the employment sector, and the bonds sector. Thus, we could also talk of the bonds market. Indeed, we referred to the bonds market when we discussed equilibrium in the money market. However, because of the equilibrium characteristics of our model, we need not consider the bonds market explicitly. We can ignore an explicit examination of the bonds market because we know that when three markets in a four-market economy are in equilibrium, the fourth market is in equilibrium too. If three markets are stable and well-behaved, the fourth market is stable and well-behaved also. Let us see why this is so.

Walras' law states that the value of all goods demanded on the market is equal to the value of all goods supplied on the market, given the prices of the goods. We may develop a corollary to Walras' law. Consider a simple exchange economy with no production. Suppose that there are m commodities, n individuals, and the quantity of each commodity initially possessed by each individual is known. Furthermore, assume that tastes are given, and that one commodity is designated as the *numéraire*. The numéraire is the commodity which is used to price all other commodities—if you like, the numéraire is the unit of account. By definition, the price of the numéraire commodity is one: one unit of numéraire will always purchase another unit of numéraire. Hence, there are $m - 1$ unknown equilibrium prices—the prices of all commodities except the numéraire. Moreover, there are mn additional unknowns—the final quantities of the m commodities held by the n individuals. Therefore, we have a total of $m + mn - 1$ unknowns. Accordingly, we assume that we need that many equations to solve for the equilibrium values of all the unknowns.

Let us count the equations of this system. We must appeal again to microeconomic concepts. To begin with, for each of the n individuals, there are $m - 1$ equations expressing the equality of marginal utility to price ratios. For an individual to be in equilibrium, the following must be true:

(11.9) $\quad MU_1/P_1 = MU_2/P_2 = MU_3/P_3 = \cdots = MU_m/P_m,$

where the Ps represent the prices of the m commodities, and the MUs represent the marginal utilities of these same m commodities. Equation (11.9) is really $m - 1$ separate equations, and since this must be true for all n individuals we have $mn - n$ equations. For each individual, his initial income must equal his final income. There is budget balance. Since there are n individuals, we have another n equations. Finally, for each of the m commodities, the total amount initially possessed by various individuals must equal the amount finally possessed, since there has been no production and since we assume no losses of commodities. Here are another m equations. We have a grand total of $mn + m$ equations. Since we have $m + mn - 1$ unknowns, it may seem as if we have an overdeterminate system of equations. We do not, however.

If we sum up all the budget equations, we note:

(11.10) The total value of all final quantities
$\qquad\qquad$ = The total value of all initial quantities.

Now, summing up the equations for $m - 1$ goods, according to statement (11.10), we have:

(11.11) The total value of $m - 1$ final quantities
= The total value of $m - 1$ initial quantities.

Subtracting statement (11.11) from statement (11.10), we obtain:

(11.12) The total final value of the mth good
= The total initial value of the mth good.

Hence, since the mth commodity is already implied, we can subtract one equation from the $m + mn$ equations, by employing Walras' law and get $m + mn - 1$ equations. We may now solve the system of equations. The implication, of course, is that if we have equilibrium in $m - 1$ markets, we must have equilibrium in the mth market as well. Thus, if we have equilibrium in the expenditure, monetary, and employment sectors, we have equilibrium in the bonds market as well. We can, therefore, ignore the bonds market. We shall do so, and we note that point A in Figure 11-6 represents the unique equilibrium for the four-sector economy.

Be certain that you do not misunderstand the meaning of the previous paragraph. When we say that our analysis will ignore—for the most part—the bonds market, we do not mean that the bonds market is unimportant. To the contrary, all markets—all the sectors—are equally important in aggregate equilibrium analysis. Our statement about ignoring the bonds market simply means that we need not write an equation to describe equilibrium in that market. Nevertheless, it remains an integral market in our economic system.[3]

DISTURBANCES TO EQUILIBRIUM

Now that we have developed a three-sector model which represents a four-sector economy, we shall look a bit closer at the workings of the model, and investigate how the relevant variables change when full-employment equilibrium is disturbed and a new equilibrium established. We will examine three cases. First, we will examine a disturbance in the expenditure sector. Second, we will examine a dis-

---

[3] As we will note in Chapter 18, Walras' Law need not apply to all four markets (labor, commodities, money, and bonds). In that chapter we view a system in which the money, bonds, and commodities markets are in equilibrium but the labor market is not.

174 The essentials of macroeconomic analysis

turbance in the monetary sector. Third, we will examine a disturbance in the employment sector.

Suppose that the economy is in equilibrium with a level of real national income equal to $(Y/P)_f$, an interest rate equal to i_f, and a price level equal to P_f. Point A in Figure 11-7 is the equilibrium

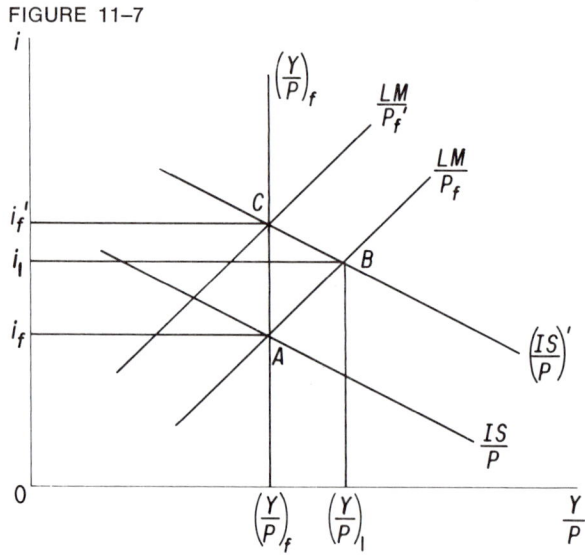

FIGURE 11-7

point. The economy is fully employed—everyone seeking employment at the prevailing real wage rate is employed. Suppose that real investment spending increases at all rates of interest, causing the investment function to shift rightward. Such a shift may come about due to some kind of a psychological change causing businessmen to invest more at all prevailing rates of interest. (We assume a parallel shift in the real investment function to the right.) Thus, the equation of the new real IS curve is:

(11.13) $$(Y/P) = \frac{k(a + d')}{P} + \frac{kei}{P}.$$

The difference between equation (11.13) and equation (11.6) is the constant term from the investment function. Since d/P represents the level of investment when the interest rate is zero, we note that, since the real investment function has shifted to the right, d/P must have increased. Indeed, we have assumed that it has increased to $\frac{d'}{P}$.

Comparing equation (11.13) to equation (11.6), we see that the real *IS* curve has shifted parallel to the right by $d'/P - d/P$, or $\Delta\left(\dfrac{d}{P}\right)$ at every rate of interest. In Figure 11–7, the new real *IS*, or expenditure sector equilibrium curve, is given by $(IS/P)'$. The new expenditure sector equilibrium curve and the real *LM* curve (the monetary sector equilibrium curve) intersect at point *B*. The level of aggregate demand has risen to $(Y/P)_1$, and the rate of interest has increased to i_1. The economy is not in equilibrium: aggregate demand, $(Y/P)_1$, is greater than aggregate supply, $(Y/P)_f$. When aggregate demand exceeds aggregate supply, inflationary pressures exist in the economy and the price level begins to increase. As the price level increases, the monetary sector equilibrium curve shifts leftward—reflecting a decline in the supply of real cash balances. The price level continues to rise, and the *LM* curve continues to shift leftward, until prices have risen by enough to restore the equality between aggregate supply and aggregate demand. When that occurs, the real *LM* curve will have shifted leftward to (LM/P'_f) in Figure 11–7. Hence, the equilibrium level of real national income given by $(Y/P)_f$ is reestablished.

The new equilibrium point in the figure is point *C*. While the level of real output is the same at *C* as at *A*, the level of the interest rate has increased. The outward shift in the real investment function has set in motion market forces which cause the level of real output to remain the same but the interest rate to rise. Furthermore, the price level has increased from P_f to P'_f. Thus, while the level of real income has remained unchanged, the level of nominal income must have increased.

In the preceding chapter, we noted that real consumption was a function of real income. Therefore, in our present example, the level of real consumption remains the same since the level of real income is unchanged. However, since the price level has gone up, the level of nominal consumption has increased also. Ignoring the level of real government expenditures (assuming that they either remain constant at some positive amount, or are zero),[4] the level of real investment must be unchanged since real investment plus real consumption equals the level of real income. Consequently, the initial increase in real in-

---

[4] We continue to ignore the role of real government expenditures by assuming that it remains constant in real terms. The reader is referred back to Chapter 7 where all the government multipliers can be now converted to real terms.

vestment at each rate of interest, brought about by the shift in the investment function, has been completely negated by the rise in the interest rate. Thus, in Figure 11–8, the level of real investment remains

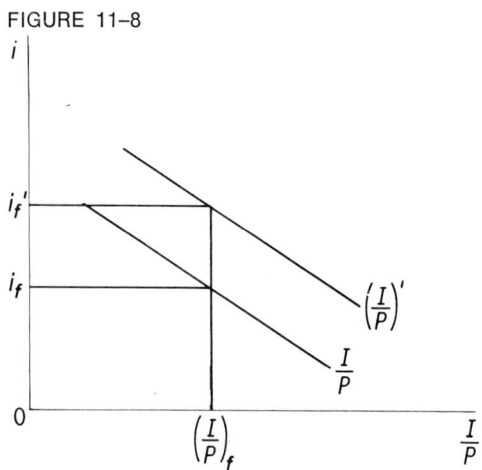

FIGURE 11–8

constant at $(I/P)_f$ despite the fact that the investment function has shifted rightward from I/P to $(I/P)'$. This occurs because the interest rate has risen from i_f to i'_f. Of course, since the price level has risen, the nominal level of investment must have increased.

Since the full-employment level of real output is still being produced and consumed after the shift in the real investment function, the same quantity of labor must still be employed. Thus, the labor market must still be in equilibrium. Consequently, the real wage rate must not have changed. However, since the price level has gone up, the nominal wage rate must have increased also.

The result is illustrated in Figure 11–9. In panel A, we have shown equilibrium in the labor market. In panel B, we have drawn a ray, extending from the origin, whose slope represents the equilibrium real wage rate, $(w/P)_f$. Prior to the shift in the investment function, the price level was P_f, and, according to Figure 11–9B, the nominal wage rate was w_1. Consequently, $(w_1/P_f) = (w/P)_f$. After the shift in the investment function, the equilibrium price level rose to P'_f. According to Figure 11–9B, the nominal wage rate rose to w_2. However, since $(w_2/P'_f) = (w_1/P_f)$, it is clear that $(w_2/P'_f) = (w/P)_f$ also. The real wage rate remains unchanged, but the nominal wage rate has increased.

FIGURE 11-9

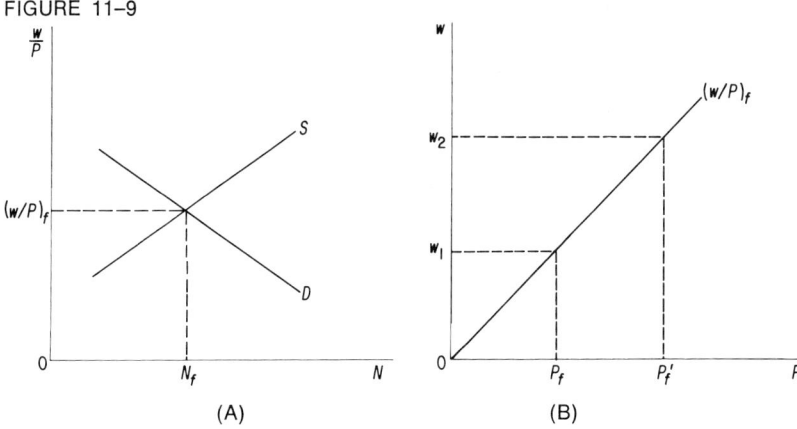

In the monetary sector, some changes must have occurred. Since the price level has gone up, the real supply of money must have gone down, assuming that no change is made by the monetary authority. Thus, the supply curve of real cash balances has shifted leftward in Figure 11-10 from $\dfrac{\bar{M}}{P_f}$ to $\dfrac{\bar{M}}{P'_f}$. Given that the level of real income does not change, the interest rate rises to i'_f from i_f. The equilibrium level of real cash balances falls. Finally, given the inelastic supply curve of nominal cash balances, and the increase in the level of nominal income, the demand curve for nominal

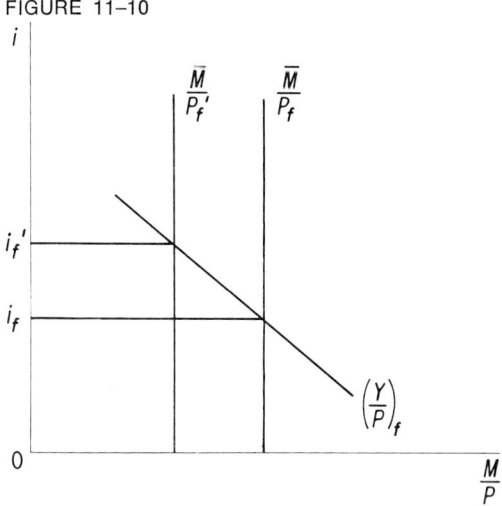

FIGURE 11-10

balances shifts rightward. The equilibrium level of nominal cash balances is unaffected by the shift in the real investment function, but, as we already know, the interest rate rises.

Let us now look at a disturbance in the monetary sector, and trace the changes in the key variables. Suppose, for some reason, that the monetary authority desires to pursue an easy money policy, and so increases the nominal supply of money. Such a policy causes the real supply of cash balances to increase, and, given the family of demand curves for real cash balances, at all levels of real income, the interest rate falls. This point is demonstrated in Figure 11–11.

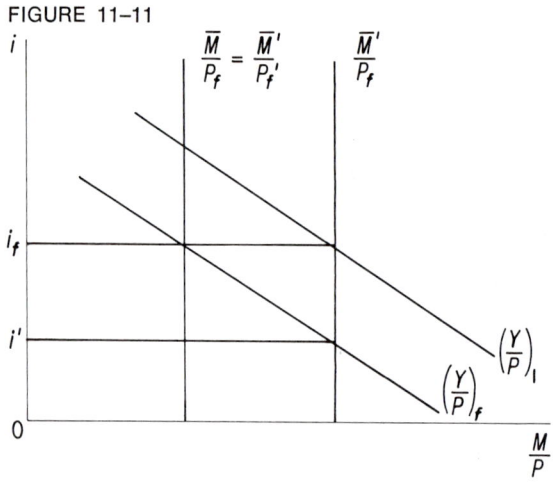

FIGURE 11–11

Prior to the increase in the nominal supply of money, the money market is in equilibrium at an interest rate of i_f, a price level of P_f, a nominal supply of cash balances of $\bar{M}$ and at the real income level $(Y/P)_f$. When the nominal supply of money increases from $\bar{M}$ to $\bar{M}'$ at the real income level $(Y/P)_f$ the interest rate will fall to i'. (For interest rate i_f to remain as the equilibrium rate in the money market, the level of real income must increase to $(Y/P)_1$.) In other words, the increase in the nominal supply of money has caused the real LM curve to shift rightward from LM/P_f, in Figure 11–12 to LM'/P_f. (The same conclusion can be reached from equation (11.7). Since the first term inside the brackets goes up when the nominal supply of money is increased, the Y/P axis intercept increases.) The real LM curve has shifted to the right. Equilibrium of

FIGURE 11-12

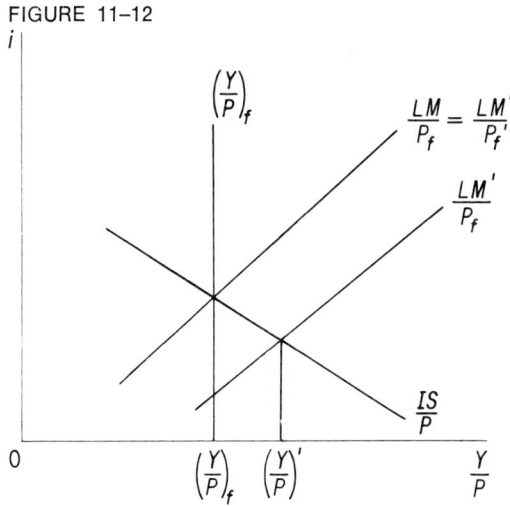

the economy has been disturbed. Aggregate demand is now greater than aggregate supply, since aggregate demand has increased to $(Y/P)'$.

Inflationary tendencies now exist, so the price level increases. As the price level increases, the real LM curve shifts back to the left. In fact, it will shift just far enough to equate aggregate demand and aggregate supply. The real LM curve shifts leftward back to the curve given by (LM'/P'_f). The full-employment level of output is reestablished; the equilibrium level of real output and the interest rate return to their original levels. The price level rose by the same proportionate amount as the nominal increase in the money supply.

Since the price level rose while the level of real output did not change, it follows that the level of money income must have risen too. Real consumption did not change (since the level of real income did not change), but nominal consumption must have risen. Since the interest rate did not change from one equilibrium position to the other, the level of real investment did not change; but the level of nominal investment must have gone up. The level of real cash balances remains the same, see Figure 11–11, since the interest rate and the level of real income do not change. Finally, since the price level has gone up, so too must the nominal wage rate. However, the equilibrium level of employment did not change.

Finally, we look at a change in the employment sector. Let us assume that the supply curve of labor shifts to the right. Given the demand curve, full employment requires that the real wage rate fall. In addition, the level of employment increases. With a higher level of employment, given the production function, the level of real output increases, assuming that the maximum level of output on the production function has not yet been reached. In Figure 11-13, the in-

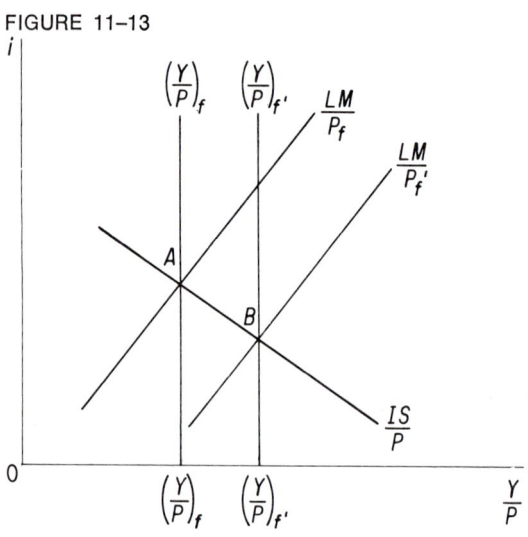

FIGURE 11-13

crease in real output, caused by the shift in the labor supply curve, is shown by the rightward shift in the employment sector equilibrium curve from $(Y/P)_f$ to $(Y/P)_{f'}$. Equilibrium has been disturbed. The economy is out of equilibrium. The level of aggregate supply now exceeds the level of aggregate demand. The level of aggregate supply is given by $(Y/P)_{f'}$ while the level of aggregate demand is given by $(Y/P)_f$. Prices are too high for full-employment equilibrium. Thus, assuming that prices are flexible downward, they fall. The falling price level shifts the real LM curve to the right until aggregate demand and aggregate supply are equal. Thus, the real LM curve shifts to LM/P'_f in the figure. Equilibrium is again attained, but now the level of real output has increased and the interest rate has fallen. The new equilibrium point is given by B.

Since the rate of interest has fallen, the level of real investment must have risen—assuming that real investment depends only on the rate of interest. Since the level of real income has gone up, we know that the level of real consumption has gone up also. Furthermore, since the supply curve of real cash balances has shifted to the right (due to the fall in the price level), we know that the equilibrium level of real cash balances has increased. Finally, with the real wage rate down, and the price level down, the money wage rate must also go down. Moreover, the money wage rate must fall by a greater percentage than the fall in the price level.

A very important assumption has been made in this example. We have assumed that prices are flexible in the downward direction. The assumption of price flexibility in the downward direction made it possible for full-employment equilibrium to be attained without reliance on either monetary or fiscal policy. Suppose, instead, that prices are assumed to be inflexible in the downward direction and that neither monetary nor fiscal policy was suggested. Then, the level of aggregate demand would be less than that level of output that would be produced, given the new full-employment level in the employment sector of the economy. With aggregate demand less than aggregate supply, the economy would be operating at less than full employment. This is not costless. Indeed the cost can be quite high, since there is unemployment. In fact, the cost of this unemployment is the difference between the full-employment level of output and the level of aggregate demand. In a later chapter, we will attempt to assess the dollar loss in output (and hence the dollar cost of operating an economy at less than full employment) in the United States during the recent past.

CONCLUDING NOTE

In this chapter, we introduced the employment sector in an attempt to reestablish a determinate solution to our model. We examined the adjustment process for changes in the various sectors assuming that the economy was in full-employment equilibrium. In the process of viewing the adjustment process, we attempted to compare the new and old real variables as well as the new and old nominal variables. The analysis presented here lays the foundation for the more complete analysis that follows, and also lays the foundation for the analysis of disequilibria. We have attempted in this chapter to note the direction of change in the many variables when other variables first change. The analysis here can be useful in viewing equilibrium situations as well as disequilibria.

12 The rate of interest: Real or monetary?

IN CHAPTER 8, we reached the conclusion that the interest rate was determined in the money market; i.e., that the supply of and demand for money determined the equilibrium rate of interest. However, in the last chapter, we noted that the equilibrium rate of interest was also determined by the simultaneous equilibrium of the expenditure, monetary and employment sectors; i.e., by the intersection of the *IS*, *LM*, and employment sector curves. Therefore, we must ask the question: Is the interest rate a real or a monetary phenomenon? It is the purpose of this chapter to see what determines the rate of interest.

THE EMPLOYMENT AND EXPENDITURE SECTORS ARE SELF-CONTAINED

Equations (11.6), (11.7), and (11.8) of the previous chapter represent a system of three equations in three unknowns. However, if we focus our attention on equations (11.6) and (11.8) alone—repeated here as equations (12.1) and (12.2)—we have two equations:

(12.1) $$(Y/P) = \frac{k(a+d)}{P} + \frac{kei}{P},$$

(12.2) $$(Y/P) = (Y/P)_f,$$

in two unknowns. The unknowns are the level of real national income, and the rate of interest. The employment and expenditure sectors are self-contained; they are all that is needed to determine the level of real national income and the interest rate. Since the employment and expenditure sectors may be considered the real sectors, as opposed to the monetary sector in our model, we can call the rate of interest a real phenomenon. Indeed, our models in the previous chapter implied that the rate of interest was determined by real factors. The real *LM* curve always shifted, and the equilibrium interest rate, already determined by the intersection of the real *IS* curve and the employment sector equilibrium curve, was maintained. This result was true in each of our examples in the previous chapter. Does this make the interest rate a real phenomenon?

The Classical economists would answer in the affirmative. They felt that the rate of interest was truly a real phenomenon. According to Classical theory, the interest rate was determined by productivity and thrift. The level of investment was a function of the rate of interest, as was the level of savings. As the interest rate fell, the level of investment would increase, but the level of savings would fall. Thus, in Figure 12–1, the equilibrium rate of interest would be determined

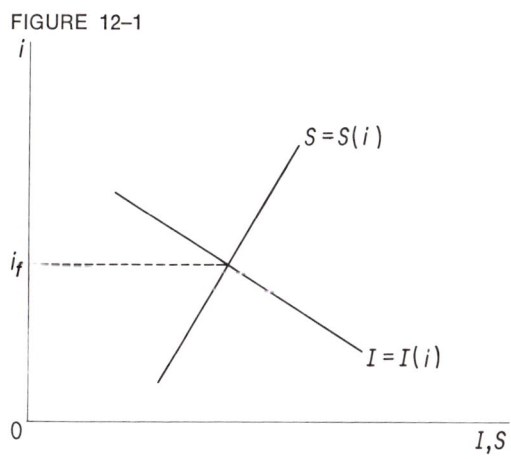

FIGURE 12–1

by the intersection of the investment function and the savings function. The equilibrium rate of interest would be i_f. Our models, like the Classical model, determine the equilibrium rate of interest by considering only real variables. Does this render our previous analysis of the interest rate invalid? Just what does determine the rate of interest?

THE INTEREST RATE AS A REAL PHENOMENON

To better understand the factors determining the rate of interest, we shall examine an equilibrium system which contains greater detail than the models in the previous chapter. Such an equilibrium system is illustrated in Figure 12-2.

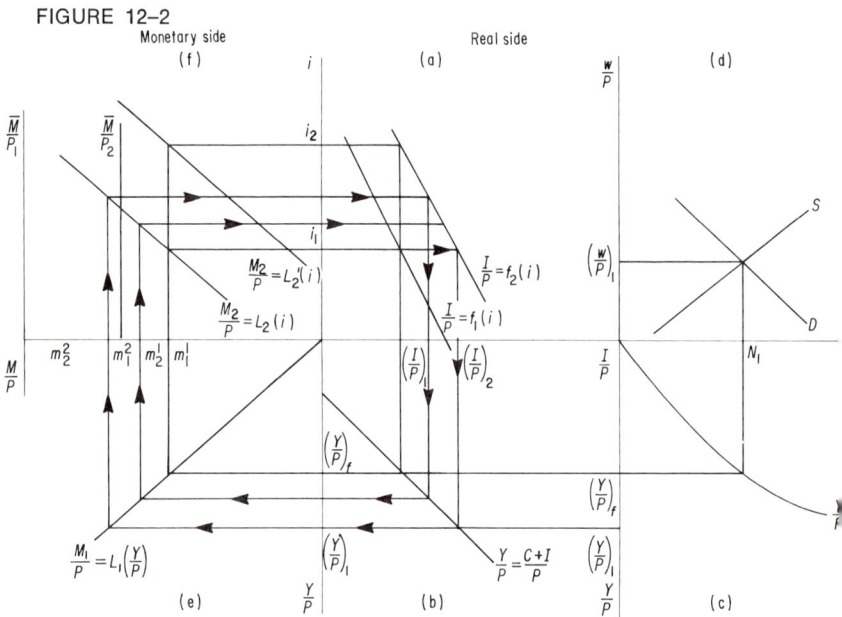

FIGURE 12-2

In panel (a), two investment functions are drawn. Let us look at one of these functions, say $I/P = f_1(i)$. This investment function is identical to the investment function of the previous chapter. It says that real investment depends only on the rate of interest. In panel (b), we have indicated the relationship between the equilibrium level of real investment and the equilibrium level of real income. Given the real consumption function, as the level of real investment increases, the level of real income increases too. Furthermore, when the level of real investment is zero, the level of real income is equal to the level of real consumption—as indicated in the panel. Again, our analysis ignores the government sector. Note that as the interest rate falls, the level of real investment increases. Given the consumption function, the level of real aggregate demand increases also (i.e., the new aggregate demand function intersects the 45° line of Chapter 4 at a higher level of real national income). Panel (b) depicts these new, potential equilibrium levels of real national income. Panels (a) and (b) represent the expenditure sector of the economy. In panel (c), we have drawn a production function. In panel (d), we have drawn the demand curve for and the supply curve of labor. Panels (c) and (d) represent the employment sector of the economy. Panels (a), (b), (c), and (d) together summarize the real side of the economy.

In panel (e), we have drawn the transactions-precautionary demand for money. Finally, in panel (f), we have drawn the relationship between the interest rate and the speculative demand for money. Panel (f) also indicates the level of the real stock of money. The numbers on the horizontal axis of panel (f) increase as a movement is made from right to left. The initial stock of real balances is given as $\bar{M}/P_1$. The mechanics of panel (f) together with panel (e) should become more clear as the analysis proceeds. Panels (e) and (f) depict the money side of the economy.

Suppose that the economy is in full-employment equilibrium. The economy is in equilibrium when: the interest rate is i_1, the level of real investment is $(I/P)_1$, the level of real national income is $(Y/P)_f$, the level of employment is N_1, the real wage rate is $(w/P)_1$, transactions-precautionary demand is m_1^1, speculative demand is m_2^1 (i.e., $\bar{M}/P_1 - m_1^1$), and price level is P_1. Suppose that there is an outward shift in the investment function—as assumed in the previous chapter. The new investment function is $I/P = f_2(i)$. At the prevailing rate of interest, the level of real investment increases to $(I/P)_2$. Consequently, the level of aggregate demand increases to $(Y/P)_1$, which is greater than the level of aggregate supply, $(Y/P)_f$. We know from our previous analysis that this causes the price level to rise. Other changes also occur in the economy. As the level of real aggregate demand increases, the demand for real transactions-precautionary balances increases from m_1^1 to m_1^2. Given the real money supply, the increase in the transactions-precautionary balances causes the quantity of real speculative balances demanded $(\bar{M}/P_1 - m_1^2 = m_2^2)$ to fall. Hence, the interest rate rises, and the level of real investment tends to fall. The movements in the variables can be traced in the figure by following the arrows. Unfortunately, the movement indicated by the arrows ignores the rise in the price level. Since aggregate demand is greater than aggregate supply, it must be remembered that the price level increases, and that this causes the real value of the money supply to fall.

In panel (f), the reduction in the real money supply causes the left-hand axis to shift to the right. The shift is illustrated by the axis moving from $\bar{M}/P_1$ to $\bar{M}/P_2$. Of course, the speculative demand curve must shift to the right also. That is to say, if the speculative demand curve is so many units of measurement away from the line $\bar{M}/P_1$ at a particular level of the interest rate, it must be that far from the line $\bar{M}/P_2$. But how far must the real money supply line, and the speculative demand curve, shift to the right? The answer is simple. From the last chapter, we know that prices will rise just enough to bring aggregate supply and aggregate demand into balance. Thus, $(Y/P)_f$ must be reestablished as the equilibrium level of real income. This can only be accomplished if the interest rate rises to i_2, and the level of real investment falls back to the original level $(I/P)_1$. The real investment level of $(I/P)_1$ is reestablished when the real money supply line and the speculative demand function shift rightward to $\bar{M}/P_2$ and $L'_2(i)$, respectively. The equilibrium rate of interest has gone up, and the real quantity of money demanded for speculative reasons has fallen. It falls to $(\bar{M}/P_2 - m_1^1)$ from the original level $(\bar{M}/P_1 - m_1^1)$. However, our point is that the interest rate has increased, and the immediate cause of the increase in the interest rate was a change on the real side of the economy—the outward shift in the real investment function. The interest rate is a real phenomenon.

THE INTEREST RATE AS A MONETARY PHENOMENON

Instead of Figure 12–2, refer to Figure 12–3, and assume that the economy is once again in equilibrium. The initial equilibrium values are given as: i_1 for the rate of interest, $(I/P)_1$ for the level of real investment, $(Y/P)_f$ for the level of real national income, N_1 for the level of employment, $(w/P)_1$ for the real wage rate, m_1^1 for the quantity of transactions-precautionary balances demanded, $m_2^1 = \bar{M}/P_1 - m_1^1$ for the real quantity of speculative balances demanded, and P_1 for the price level.

Now, let us suppose that there is a change on the monetary side of the economy. Suppose that the proportion of real national income over which individuals wish to keep command in money form in-

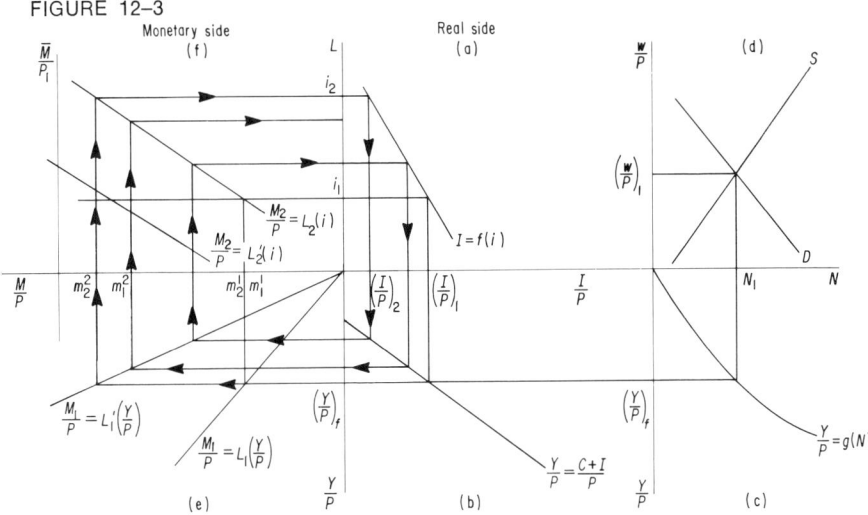

FIGURE 12-3

creases. In other words, at all levels of real income, individuals demand more money for transactions-precautionary purposes. Hence, the transactions-precautionary demand function in panel (e) rotates from $L_1(Y/P)$ to $L'_1(Y/P)$. Immediately the quantity of transactions-precautionary balances demanded increases to m_1^2, and the quantity of real balances demanded for speculative purposes falls to $m_2^2 = \bar{M}/P_1 - m_1^2$—given the real supply of cash balances.

With the demand curve for real speculative balances given as $L_2(i)$, the interest rate rises, causing the level of real investment to fall. Consequently, the level of real aggregate demand declines. Hence, aggregate demand is less than aggregate supply. Assuming flexible prices (we will look at some causes of inflexible prices later), the price level falls. With the price level falling, the real value of the money supply increases, and the real money supply line of panel (f) shifts to the left. The demand curve for speculative balances must, of course, shift along with the real supply line. Since the aggregate supply of output has not changed, full-employment equilibrium can only be restored at that level of real income. Thus, real investment must fall back to its original level. As the money supply line shifts to the left, the demand curve for speculative balances also must shift leftward by enough to ensure that the interest rate i_1 is reestablished. The quantity of real speculative balances and the quantity of real transactions-precautionary balances demanded have changed, but nothing else has changed. The quantity of real transactions-precautionary balances demanded is now $m_1{}^2$, while the quantity of real speculative balances demanded is $m_2{}^2 = \bar{M}/P_2 - m_1{}^2$. The interest rate has not changed. A change in the monetary side of the economy has occurred, and there has been no change in the interest rate. How can we say that the interest rate is a monetary phenomenon?

THE INTEREST RATE AS A REAL AND A MONETARY PHENOMENON

From the previous discussion, it appears that the interest rate is a real variable, or at least influenced more by real factors than by monetary factors. However, the conclusion is not correct. Indeed, we will see in a later chapter that a change in the rate of interest can be observed when there is a change in the monetary sector. This will be demonstrated when we discuss the *real balance effect*. To deny that the monetary sector has any influence on the interest rate would deny any interrelationship between the monetary sector and the real sector of the economy. Clearly, in the analysis of the preceeding sections, the interrelationship between the several sectors was obvious. In the first section, there was a shift in the investment function which induced changes in the monetary sector and the interest rate. If you follow the arrows around Figure 12–2, you should note that the interest rate rises and then falls, and then rises again. There were fluctuations in the interest rate in the transition from one equilibrium to another. The general trend was simply for the interest rate to rise, but monetary and real factors caused the rate to move up as well as down.

In the second case, the interest rate did not change. However, once again following the arrows around Figure 12–3, you should note that the interest rate initially rose and then fell and then rose again. This continuous change in the rate of interest was caused by both monetary and real factors. Obviously, the monetary sector and the real sector of the economy are interrelated, and so the interest rate is both a real and a monetary phenomenon. It is not solely a monetary variable as Keynes felt, nor is it solely a real variable as the Classical economists felt. It is both!

CONCLUDING COMMENT

In this chapter, we saw that the interest rate cannot be viewed as a real variable alone, nor can it be viewed as a monetary variable alone. It is both. The interest rate is determined by the interdependence of the real and monetary sectors of the economy.

In the next chapter, we look more closely at the mechanism by which a change in a monetary variable changes the rate of interest. We will examine the *real balance effect*.

13 Additions to the model— The real balance effect[1]

WHEN THE PRICE LEVEL changes, the supply of real cash balances changes. A change in the level of real cash balances, in turn, causes consumption expenditures and production decisions to change. The demand for real cash balances changes also. These changes—resulting from the change in the supply of real cash balances—are called the *real balance effect,* or the *Pigou effect.*

THE REAL BALANCE EFFECT AND THE LEVEL OF CONSUMPTION

Let us suppose that real consumption expenditures, in addition to depending upon the level of real national income, also depend upon the level of real cash balances. The rationale underlying this supposition is simply that as the level of real cash balances increases, people—feeling wealthier in real terms—tend to consume more goods and services. Conversely, as the level of real cash balances decreases, people—feeling poorer in real terms—tend to consume fewer goods and services. In effect, the assertion that real consumption expenditures depend on the level of real cash balances, as well as the level of real national income, assumes that real consumption depends on both an

---
[1] This chapter may be omitted without seriously affecting a basic understanding of macroeconomic principles. However, the real balance effect is essential to a complete understanding of the Classical system and material in later chapters does draw occasionally on the concept of real cash balances.

income flow and a cash stock. Ask yourself the question: Is it not likely that individuals spend on consumer goods and services according to their level of income and available stock of cash?

Consequently, we can expand our old linear consumption function to include the *real balance* effect. The expanded consumption function is:

(13.1) $$C/P = a/P + bY/P + q(\bar{M}/P),$$

where q is a positive number, and $\bar{M}/P$ represents the level of real cash balances. Ignoring government expenditures, the equation of the real *IS* curve becomes:

(13.2) $$Y/P = \frac{k(a+d)}{P} + \frac{kei}{P} + \frac{kq\bar{M}}{P},$$

where k represents the simple multiplier.

Equation (13.2) is a single equation in three unknowns; i.e., it contains three variables: real income, the interest rate, and real cash balances. Therefore, before we can graph equation (13.2), we must assume that one of the variables is given to us. In other words, we can graph the real *IS* curve of equation (13.2) by assuming that we know the level of real cash balances. Moreover, for every level of cash balances given to us, we must draw a different real *IS* curve. If we make the additional assumption that the quantity of money is constant also, then each price level yields a different level of real balances, and a different real *IS* curve. For example, from equation (13.2), we see that as the price level increases, the level of real national income falls at every level of the interest rate. Consequently, as the price level rises, the real *IS* curve must shift to the left. As the price level falls, the real *IS* curve must shift to the right. Thus, in Figure 13-1, when the price level rises from P_1 to P_2, the real *IS* curve shifts from IS/P_1 to IS/P_2. When the price level falls from P_1 to P_3, the real *IS* curve shifts from IS/P_1 to IS/P_3. Each price level is associated with its own level of real cash balances, and its own real *IS* curve.

Our model now contains a family of real *LM* curves and a family of real *IS* curves. However, it contains only one employment sector equilibrium curve. Our model now reveals that the equilibrium values of the variables in the employment and expenditure sectors are no longer independent of shifts occurring in the monetary sector. After all, a change in the supply of nominal cash balances (i.e., the supply

FIGURE 13-1

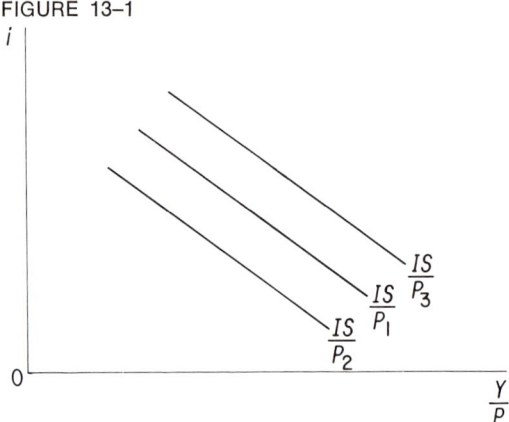

or quantity of money) induces a real balance effect. The employment and expenditure sectors are no longer self-contained.

Let us examine Figure 13-2, and study the interaction of the three sectors in our economic system. Suppose that equilibrium is attained at point A, a point of full-employment, with the interest rate equal to i_f, the price level equal to P_f, the full-employment level of real national income equal to $(Y/P)_f$, and the level of real cash balances equal to $\bar{M}/P_f$. Now suppose that the money supply increases from $\bar{M}$ to $\bar{M}'$, causing the real LM curve to shift to the

FIGURE 13-2

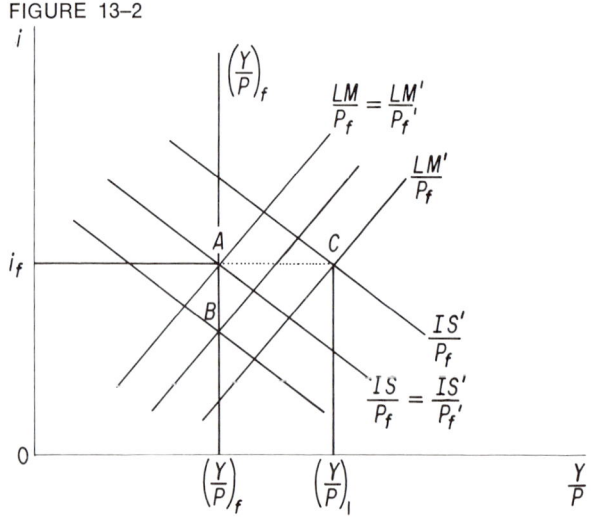

right from LM/P_f to $LM'/P_{f'}$. Since the nominal supply of cash balances has increased, due to the increase in the money supply, the level of real balances has increased also. From equations (13.1) and (13.2), we know that an increase in real balances forces aggregate demand to increase also—it is the real balance effect. Hence, the real IS curve shifts to the right from IS/P_f to IS'/P_f, indicating that the level of aggregate demand has increased from $(Y/P)_f$ to $(Y/P)_1$. However, since the level of aggregate supply is constant at the full-employment level $(Y/P)_f$, excess demand and inflationary pressures force the price level to rise. Our earlier analysis told us that increases in the price level cause the real supply of cash balances to fall, and the real LM curve to shift to the left. Since the level of real balances falls as the price level increases, the real balance effect reduces the amount of excess aggregate demand, and the real IS curve shifts to the left. The inflationary pressures continue—the price level continues to rise—until equilibrium is reestablished at point A.

If we look more closely at the money market, illustrated in Figure 13-3, we can see why full-employment equilibrium can be

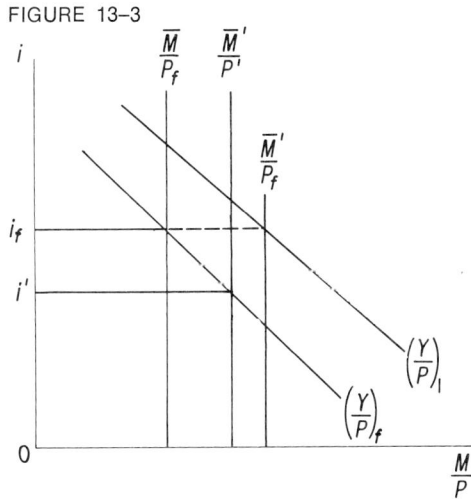

FIGURE 13-3

restored only at a point like A in Figure 13-2. We can see why full-employment equilibrium cannot be restored at a point like B in Figure 13-2. Let us assume that the money market is in equilibrium with the interest rate equal to i_f, and the level of real national income equal to $(Y/P)_f$—when the supply of real cash balances is given as $\bar{M}/P_f$. If we disturb the money market equilibrium by increasing the supply of nominal cash balances to $\bar{M}'$, the supply curve of real cash balances is forced to shift to $\bar{M}'/P_f$. Consequently, the real balance effect stimulates an increase in aggregate demand, and pushes the demand curve for real cash balances to the right also.[2] Moreover, we have just argued that a stimulatory real balance effect—from a position of full-employment equilibrium—causes the price level to rise. The increase in the price level, in turn, forces the supply curve of real cash balances to shift back to the left. Furthermore, since the level of real income cannot exceed the full-employment level of aggregate supply, $(Y/P)_f$, the demand curve for real cash balances must return to its initial position in Figure 13-3. Therefore, if the supply curve of real balances shifts leftward to $\bar{M}'/P'$, and the demand curve for real balances returns to its initial position, it appears that an interest rate equal to i' might be established in the money market. The interest rate i' would be consistent with general equilibrium at a point like B in Figure 13-2.

However, this cannot happen. With the interest rate equal to i', there still exists some excess demand (aggregate demand must still be greater than aggregate supply). With the level of real income at $(Y/P)_f$, the level of real consumption is the same regardless of whether the interest rate is i' or i_f. However, real investment is higher at the lower interest rate of i'. Aggregate demand must be greater than aggregate supply. Therefore, the interest rate is too low for full equilibrium. Since the interest rate is too low, the level of real balances is too high. Consequently, the price level must be too low also; and it must, therefore, continue to increase. i' cannot be the equilibrium interest rate, and point B cannot be the point of aggregate equilibrium.

From our previous analysis, we know that the increase in the price level will be proportionate to the increase in the supply of nominal balances—if the money supply is increased when the economy is in full-employment equilibrium. As a result, the equilibrium value of real cash balances remains unchanged. Therefore, the price level must continue to rise until the supply curve of real cash balances, in Figure

---

[2] Note that we have not assumed any change in the rate of interest in our analysis. At point C in Figure 13-2, the interest rate is still i_f. Clearly, the interest rate can go up, down, or remain the same. The analysis is exactly the same in all cases.

13-3, has shifted leftward to its initial position at $\bar{M}/P_f$, and the interest rate has returned to its original level at i_f. The net result is that there has been no change in the equilibrium values of the variables in the monetary sector. Moreover, since the interest rate and real balances return to their original levels, there has been no change—in spite of our assertion to the contrary at the end of the last chapter—in the equilibrium values of the variables in the nonmonetary sector as well. Nevertheless, our analysis shows once again that an increase in nominal balances will lead to a proportionate rise in the price level, with no change in the equilibrium rate of interest or equilibrium level of national income, if the economy is fully employed.[3]

But what of our assertion that changes in the monetary sector cause changes to occur in the equilibrium values of the variables in the nonmonetary sectors? The assertion is correct. We can prove it by examining the results of a change on the demand side of the money market. Suppose that there is an increase in demand for real cash balances; i.e., at every level of the interest rate, the quantity of real cash balances demanded increases. The family of money demand curves (one curve for each level of real income) shifts to the right, and, given the supply curve of real cash balances, the real LM curve will shift to the left as indicated by the movement of the real LM curve from LM/P_f to LM'/P_f in Figure 13-4. The reason for the leftward shift in the real LM curve is not difficult to understand. When the family of demand curves for real cash balances shifts to the right in the face of a constant supply of real cash balances, the equilibrium rate of interest rises. Hence, at all levels of real income, the equilibrium rates of interest are higher, and the real LM curve must have shifted to the left. Point A is no longer a point of equilibrium. It cannot be maintained. Indeed, since the level of aggregate demand has fallen to $(Y/P)_1$, while the level of aggregate supply remains at $(Y/P)_f$, excess aggregate supply and deflationary pressures force the price level to fall. Consequently, the real value of the money supply increases and the real LM curve shifts back to the right. At

---

[3] It is important to note that this proportionate relationship between the nominal supply of money and the price level exists only when an injection of new money occurs at the full-employment level of real national income. With less than the full-employment level of real output, the relationship between the supply of nominal balances and the price level is not so strong. While the level of nominal balances and the price level can be expected to move in the same direction, a proportionate relationship will not exist.

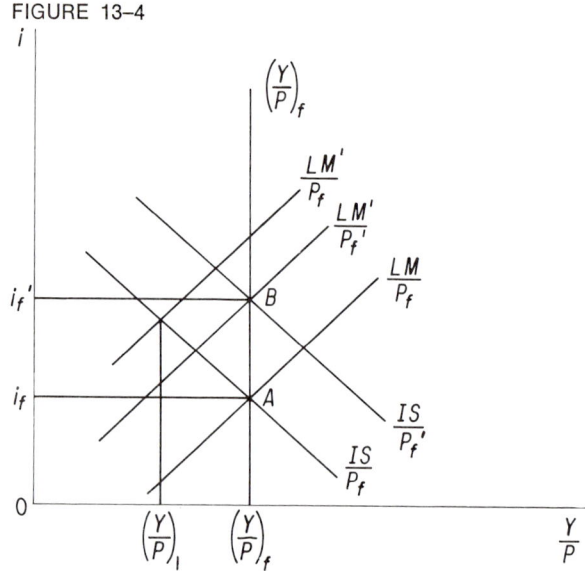

FIGURE 13-4

the same time, the real *IS* curve also shifts to the right—due to the increase in real cash balances. Since the full-employment equilibrium output is $(Y/P)_f$, it follows that the interest rate will rise to i'_f as the price level increases to P'_f. The real balance effect, in the expenditure sector, has produced a change in the rate of interest as the result of an initial change in the monetary sector. The rate of interest is both a monetary and a real phenomenon. All the sectors of the economy are interrelated.

The importance of the real balance effect cannot be underestimated in this context. Suppose that real cash balances were not a variable in the expenditure sector. The expenditure sector equilibrium curve would not have shifted when the price level fell. Equilibrium would have been reestablished at the original interest rate, as well as the original level of real national income. The real balance effect offers a direct link between the monetary sector and the real sector of the economy.

Additionally, the real balance effect offers a possible solution to a situation in which full employment cannot be reached at a positive rate of interest. Consider the case presented in Figure 13-5. Given the real *IS* curve IS/P_1, and the real *LM* curve LM/P_1, aggregate demand is less than aggregate supply. The economy is below the full-

FIGURE 13-5

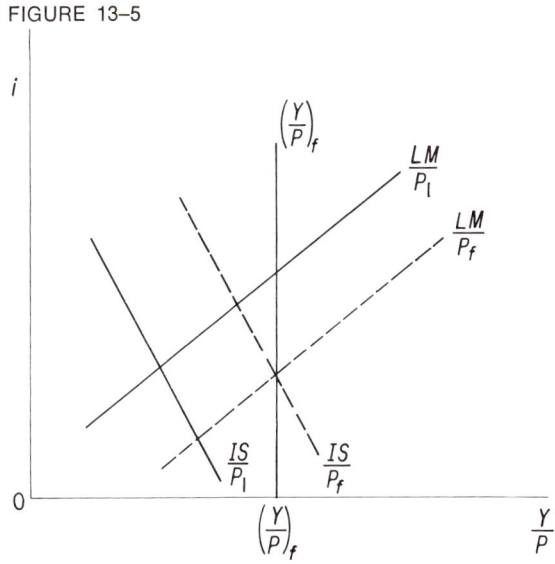

employment level of real national income. Prices will fall, and the real LM curve will shift to the right as the real value of the money supply increases. However, if the real IS curve does not shift also, the full-employment level of real output cannot be attained—at least not at a positive interest rate. Ignoring the real balance effect, the investment function would have to shift outward, or the consumption function would have to shift upward, or the level of real government expenditures would have to increase in order to achieve full employment. The logical solution would be to increase the level of real government expenditures. The increase in government spending would cause the real IS curve to shift to the right, and the full-employment level of real output would be reached. However, with the inclusion of the real balance effect, as the price level falls and real cash balances increase, the real IS curve will shift to the right increasing the possibility that full-employment equilibrium will occur at a positive rate of interest. Additional government spending would be unnecessary.

You might argue that the theoretical existence of a real balance effect in consumption is undeniable, but that the practical significance of the effect is minimal. It is not powerful enough to move the economy to full employment. To be sure, much empirical work needs to be done in this area, but the mere existence of the real balance effect as a theoretical tool opens up an interesting variable for the establishment of equilibrium.

THE REAL BALANCE EFFECT AND THE EMPLOYMENT SECTOR

The real balance effect is not limited to the expenditure sector of the economy. Indeed, real balances also enter into the production function. They facilitate factor payments, and reduce the levels of other resources required to produce a given level of output. Accordingly, as the level of real cash balances increases, the employment sector equilibrium curve shifts to the right; and as the level of real cash balances decreases, the employment sector equilibrium curve shifts to the left. Therefore, when we consider real cash balances as a factor of production, an entire family of employment sector equilibrium curves is generated. Each sector of the economy now consists of a family of curves, and the determination of equilibrium becomes quite difficult.

Suppose that we view an economy in equilibrium, as given by point A in Figure 13-6. Let us disturb this equilibrium by forcing the real investment function to shift to the right. As a result, the real IS curve shifts to the right also (from IS/P_f to IS'/P_f), and aggregate demand exceeds aggregate supply. The price level is bid up, and the level of real balances decreases. Hence, the real LM curve shifts to the

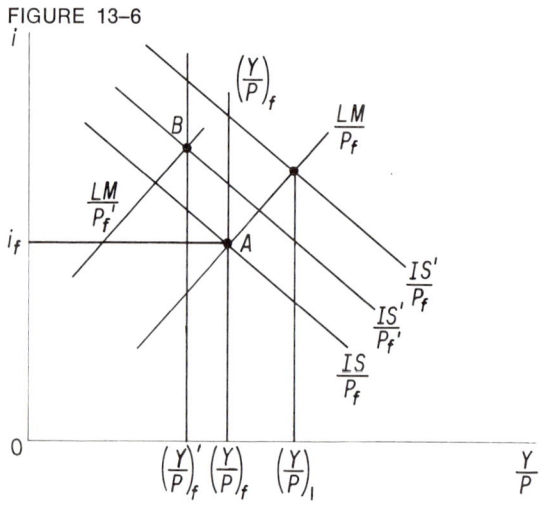

FIGURE 13-6

left, the real *IS* curve shifts to the left, and the employment sector equilibrium curve shifts to the left too. Equilibrium is eventually reestablished, but it lies at a lower level of real output. In Figure 13–6, equilibrium is reestablished at point B, with real output declining to $(Y/P)'_f$.

Please note that it is very difficult to predict the new level of the interest rate. It may be higher, lower, or even remain the same as the old interest rate. It depends upon the magnitude of the shifts in the three-sector equilibrium curves. All that we can actually predict is that there will be some price level at which the three-sector equilibrium curves will intersect, and that a lower level of real output will be produced.

REAL BALANCES AND THE MONETARY SECTOR

The real balance effect exists in the money market as well as in the other markets. Since money is used to buy goods and, in a sense, goods are used to buy money, the existence of the real balance effect in the expenditure sector suggests a real balance effect in the monetary sector as well.

The demand for money function can be expanded to include the real balance effect. The expanded demand function is:

(13.3) $\qquad M_d/P = L(i, Y/P, \bar{M}/P)$,

or in linear form:

(13.4) $\qquad M_d/P = g/P + \bar{k}(Y/P) + hi/P + z\bar{M}/P$,

where z is a positive number.

Combining equation (13.4) with the real money supply function, the equation of the real *LM* curve becomes:

(13.5) $\qquad Y/P = 1/\bar{k}(\bar{M}/P - hi/P - z\bar{M}/P - g/P)$,

or

(13.6) $\qquad Y/P = 1/\bar{k}(x\bar{M}/P - hi/P - g/P)$,

where $x = (1 - z)$.

Let us consider an example in which there is a real balance effect in the expenditure sector and the monetary sector, but not in the employment sector. Suppose that the economic system is in equilibrium, and that the equilibrium is disturbed by an increase in the supply of money. We know that the real *IS* and real *LM* curves both shift to the right, since the level of cash balances has increased. Aggregate demand exceeds aggregate supply, and the price level is bid up. Since there has been no change in the employment sector equilibrium curve, the new full-employment equilibrium level of output and the old full-employment equilibrium level of output must be the same. The result is identical to the ones discussed earlier in this chapter. Therefore, the real balance effect has always been included—implicitly or explicitly—in the real *LM* curve. To prove the point, refer back to equation (10.16) of Chapter 10 and note that the first term on the right-hand side of the equation is the level of real cash balances.

However, there is still an interesting question to ask: Which sector is more sensitive to the real balance effect? Which curve shifts farther to the right as the level of real cash balances increases? From equation (13.6), we can determine that, as the supply of money increases, the change in the level of real income at any given level of the interest rate is given by:

(13.7) $$\Delta(Y/P) = \frac{x}{k} \Delta(\bar{M}/P).$$

Furthermore, from equation (13.2), the change in the level of real income for any interest rate is:

(13.8) $$\Delta(Y/P) = kq\Delta(\bar{M}/P).$$

If the coefficient of the term on the right-hand side of equation (13.7) is greater than the coefficient of the term of the right-hand side of equation (13.8), the real *LM* curve shifts farther to the right than the real *IS* curve at any interest rate, and vice versa. Regardless, of the shift, however, real cash balances will be the same before and after the increase in the supply of nominal balances, so there will be no change in the equilibrium level of real income or the equilibrium interest rate.

A DIGRESSION ON SAY'S LAW

Most people do not work simply for the sake of working, but rather to obtain goods and services that yield satisfaction. The very act of production, therefore, constitutes a demand for other goods, or it may be said that supply creates its own demand. There can be no general glut or shortage. If one places more value on a little more leisure than on more goods gained from a little more work, there will be voluntary unemployment. This general concept is known as Say's law. The law differs markedly from the simple identity that expenditures equal the value of output. Say's law implies that any increment of output will generate an equivalent increase in income and total spending. Thus, the full-employment level of output will always be maintained.

Originally the law was couched in terms of a barter economy, and acknowledged that there could be some temporary maladjustments; i.e., temporary shortages or gluts. A man might, for example, produce too many shoes, so the price of shoes would fall. Hence, he might not be able to purchase all the beer he wanted. He would, therefore, produce a different product in the future or, acquire more leisure by producing fewer shoes. Furthermore, since money is merely a medium of exchange, it was thought Say's law would prevail in a money economy as well as in a barter economy. If goods are to be sold for money, the supply schedule of each good can be thought of as constituting a demand schedule for money. Similarly, a demand schedule for goods amounts to a supply schedule of money. At each possible (relative) price for each good, there is either excess demand (excess supply of money), or excess supply (excess demand for money), or neither excess demand nor excess supply (equilibrium). Consequently, there exists an aggregate net demand schedule for money. However, Say's law depends upon the proposition that goods are exchanged for goods. The demand for goods depends upon relative prices—the amount that each good will buy of each other good. If Say's law holds, the demand and supply schedules would be independent of absolute prices. Thus, the excess demand or supply of each good is independent of absolute prices and so is the excess demand and excess supply of money. The aggregate net demand for money depends *only* on relative prices!

A possible inconsistency has arisen. We have seen that an increase in the supply of money will increase the price level. Thus, there appears to be a second demand schedule for money—one based on absolute prices. Suppose that all markets are in equilibrium; i.e., that relative prices are such that excess demand is zero in each market. There would appear to be an infinite number of absolute prices that can produce the same relative prices. However, such is not the case. All sectors are related through the real balance effect. The various sectors of the economy are highly interrelated. Any notion that relative prices are determined in the real sector while the absolute price level is determined in the monetary sector should be dismissed. Relative prices and the absolute price level are simultaneously determined in the interdependent system.

To assume that the absolute price level is determined in the monetary sector while relative prices are determined in the real sector implies that there are two distinct economic processes. This implies that the equations describing the real framework of the economic system have nothing in them that relates to the monetary framework. This is not true. After all, the equations of the real side of the economy now contain real cash balances. Since real cash balances also appear in the equation of the real LM curve, we can no longer view the two sides of the economy as distinct. Rather, we must now recognize the interdependence of the two sides of the economy through the real balance effect.

CONCLUDING NOTE

In this chapter, we introduced the notion of the real balance effect. While the magnitude of the real balance effect may not be too great, we cannot deny the existence of the effect.[4] Furthermore, the real balance effect demonstrates the high degree of interdependence between the monetary sector and the real sector. Finally, the introduction of the real balance effect clearly points out that the interest rate is both a real and a monetary phenomenon.

---

[4] A considerable amount of empirical work has been done in an attempt to measure the effectiveness of the real balance effect. The results seem to be mixed. See for example L. E. Gallaway and P. E. Smith, "Real Balances and the Permanent Income Hypothesis," *Quarterly Journal of Economics*, Vol. 75 (1961), pp. 302–313; and J. G. Gurley, "Excess Liquidity and European Monetary Reforms, 1944–1952," *American Economic Review*, Vol. 43 (1953), pp. 76–100.

14 Some further additions to the model[1]

IN THIS CHAPTER, we shall discuss a few additional modifications to our model. In most cases, these additions simply clear up some of the details that have been referred to earlier but have not yet been explained. Although these additions add a great deal of indeterminancy to our models, they also demonstrate more clearly the highly interdependent nature of the various sectors of the economic system.

CONSUMPTION AND THE RATE OF INTEREST

We noted, in Chapter 5, that the Classical economists regarded consumption as a function of the rate of interest. If you recall, the Classical economists argued that the level of real savings increases as the rate of interest increases. Since real consumption expenditures are equal to the portion of real income that is not saved, and since savings increases with the interest rate, the level of real consumption must fall as the interest rate rises. Thus, if we accept the Classical argument that real consumption depends upon the rate of interest as well as the level of real income, we must expand our linear consumption function to include the *interest rate effect*. The new linear consumption function is:

(14.1) $$C/P = a/P + bY/P + ci/P,$$

---
[1] This chapter like the previous one may be omitted without seriously affecting the understanding of the principles of macroeconomic theory. However, the additions to the model indicated in this chapter demonstrate the high interdependence of an economic system.

where c is a negative number indicating that the level of real consumption falls as the interest rate rises. It is possible that c could be a positive number, thereby reversing the consumption-interest rate relationship. More about the "sign" of c in a moment. Given equation (14.1), the equation of the real IS curve becomes:

(14.2) $\qquad Y/P = k(a + d)/P + k(e + c)i/P.$

Fortunately, equation (14.2) is a single equation in two variables, Y/P and i. Therefore, we have a single real IS curve—not a family of curves. If the interest rate and real consumption vary inversely (i.e., if c is a negative number), as the Classical economists argue, the real IS curve will have the usual negative slope. However, if the interest rate and real consumption vary directly (i.e., if c is a positive number), and the relationship between the interest rate and the level of real consumption is a strong one, the real IS curve may have a positive slope. More precisely, in equation (14.2), if c is a positive number and is greater in absolute value than e, the real IS curve will have a positive slope.

Unfortunately, the argument over the direction of the consumption-interest rate relationship, and the slope of the real IS curve, is not easily settled. There are valid economic reasons supporting both cases. The economic explanation of the inverse relationship between real consumption expenditures and the interest rate (i.e., the explanation of the negatively sloped real IS curve) is very traditional. It argues that interest income is a reward for postponing present consumption. The higher is the level of interest rates, the greater is the interest income, and the larger is the inducement to postpone consumption in order to save. Consequently, as the interest rate rises, the level of real consumption expenditures declines while the level of savings rises. In economic jargon, the consumption function given in equation (14.1) shifts downward, and the savings function shifts upward, because real consumption expenditures have been reduced at every level of real national income. Consequently, if all other things remain equal, the level of real national income falls. In this case, the interest rate effect implies that the real IS curve, given by equation (14.2), is negatively sloped. There is much empirical evidence to support this case.[2]

---

[2] Lester D. Taylor, "Savings out of Different Types of Income," *Brookings Papers*, Vol. 2 (1971).

The economic explanation of the direct relationship between real consumption expenditures and the interest rate (i.e., the explanation of the positively sloped real *IS* curve) is less traditional, and has less empirical support.[3] It argues that most individuals, and households, formulate consumption and savings plans. Specifically, it hypothesizes that households establish and maintain a target level of savings: for example, $3,000 to be accumulated over the next five years. At any existing interest rate, the household knows the amount it must save in each year to achieve its goal. Suppose that the interest rate equals 5 percent per annum. If the household saves $520 each year for the next five years, the principal plus interest income will yield slightly more than $3,000 ($3,017 to be exact) at the end of the five-year period. In the process, the household will have postponed $2,600 of consumption ($520 × 5 = $2,600). Now let the interest rate increase to 10 percent per annum. Accordingly, the household must save only $450 in each of the next five years to achieve its goal (to be exact, if the household saves $450 per year at 10 percent interest, the principal plus interest income will equal $3,022 after five years). In the process, the household will have postponed $2,250 of consumption ($450 × 5 = $2,250). The point to note is that the value of consumption which was postponed fell by $350. The $350 became available for additional consumption. Thus, as the interest rate rose, the level of consumption rose also. In this case, the interest rate effect implies that the real *IS* curve, given by equation (14.2), may be positively sloped.

In either case, we will assume that the introduction of the interest rate effect into the consumption function causes no trouble for our equilibrium analysis. We will utilize both negatively and positively sloped real *IS* curves.

REAL INVESTMENT AS A FUNCTION OF THE LEVEL OF REAL INCOME

When we discussed the level of investment in Chapter 6, we mentioned that investment might well depend upon the level of national income. We can now examine this relationship in real terms. As the level of real income increases, investment opportunities become more

---

[3] W. E. Weber, "The Effect of Interest Rates on Aggregate Consumption," *American Economic Review*, Vol. LX, No. 4 (September, 1970).

plentiful, and the level of real investment expenditures increases. Thus, the investment function becomes:

(14.3) $\qquad I/P = f(i, Y/P)$,

or in the linear case:

(14.4) $\qquad I/P = d/P + ei/P + fY/P$,

where f is a positive number. The investment function now becomes a family of curves, as illustrated in Figure 14–1. In the figure, the level of real investment increases, at every rate of interest as the level of real income increases. This, as income increases from $(Y/P)_1$ to $(Y/P)_2$ to $(Y/P)_3$, the real investment curve shifts to the right.

We can now derive the equation of the real *IS* curve when the level of real investment is a function of real income. Let us assume that consumption is a function of real income only (this is a simplifying assumption, and in no way biases our results), while real investment is a function of both the interest rate and real income. The equation of the real *IS* curve becomes:

(14.5) $\qquad Y/P = \dfrac{1}{(1 - b - f)} (a/P + d/P + ei/P)$.

Given equation (14.5), we are not able to predict the slope of the real *IS* curve. We know that $(1 - b)$ is a positive number, since b is positive and less than unity in value. However, since f is a positive number also, it may be that f is greater than $(1 - b)$. If this is the case, the slope of the real *IS* curve will be positive.

Another look at Figure 14–1 demonstrates the difficulty in predicting the slope of the expenditure sector equilibrium curve. Suppose that the level of real income is $(Y/P)_2$ and the rate of interest is such that equilibrium is achieved at point *a*. At point *a*, the level of real investment is $(I/P)_1$. For the level of real investment to increase to $(I/P)_2$, the interest rate must fall. That much is clear. However, the level of real income can rise (if path *ab* is followed), fall (if path *ac* is followed), or stay the same (if path *ad* is followed). Moreover, the real *IS* curve could have a positive slope if the path *ac* is followed, or a negative slope if the path *ab* is followed. Therefore, we conclude that the real *IS* curve will be positively sloped when the marginal propensity to invest (f) is greater than the marginal propensity to save $(1 - b)$.

The possibility of a positively sloped real *IS* curve raises an impor-

FIGURE 14-1

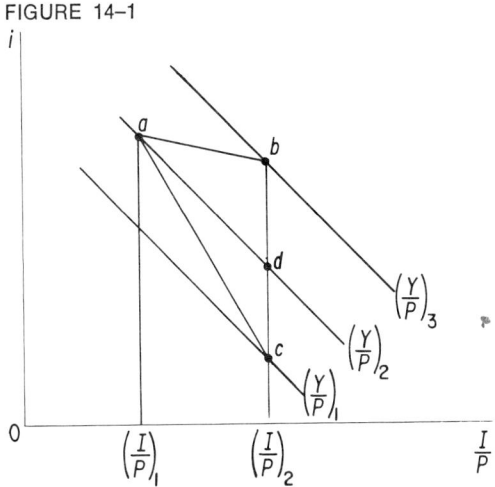

tant new problem. It forces us to distinguish between stable and unstable equilibria. To demonstrate the point, let us examine a case in which the real IS curve is negatively sloped and the real LM curve is positively sloped. Assume that the economy is in full-employment equilibrium. Such a situation is illustrated in Figure 14–2. Now suppose that the employment sector equilibrium curve shifts to the right, causing the level of aggregate supply to increase. (We will examine some of the reasons for such a shift later. For now we need only assume

FIGURE 14-2

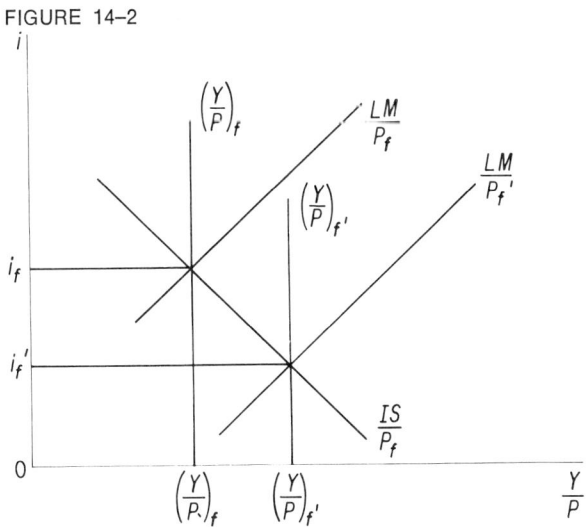

that the shift occurs.) Since aggregate demand is less than aggregate supply, the price level should fall (assuming that prices are sufficiently flexible), and the real LM curve should shift to the right. A new equilibrium would be established at a higher level of real national income, and at a lower rate of interest. The adjustment process is simple and stable.

However, the adjustment process is more complicated when we examine a positive sloped real IS curve. One positively sloped real IS curve is illustrated in Figure 14–3. When the employment sector

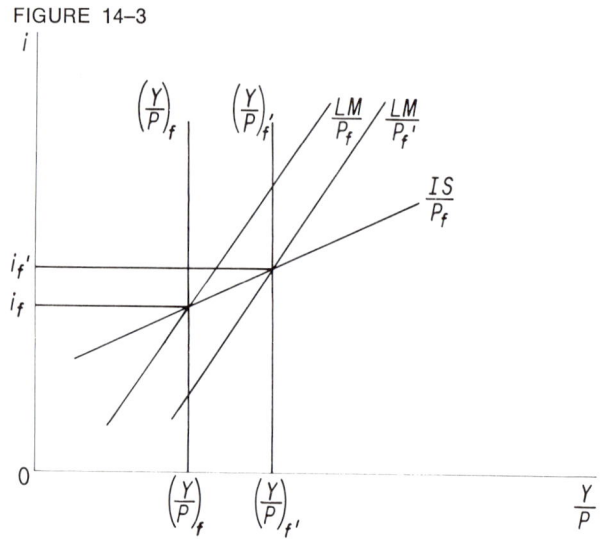

FIGURE 14–3

equilibrium curve shifts to the right, prices fall and the real LM curve shifts to the right. Equilibrium is reestablished at a higher level of real national income, and—in this case—a higher rate of interest. Since equilibrium was reestablished, the adjustment process is stable. However, let us examine the case of the positively sloped real IS curve illustrated in Figure 14–4. When the employment sector equilibrium curve shifts to the right and the price level falls, the gap between the level of aggregate supply and aggregate demand increases rather than decreases. With a fall in the price level, the real LM curve shifts to LM/P'_f, and the level of aggregate demand (given by the intersection of the real LM and IS curves) falls. The disequilibrium is worsened rather than improved. It is an example of an *unstable equi-*

FIGURE 14-4

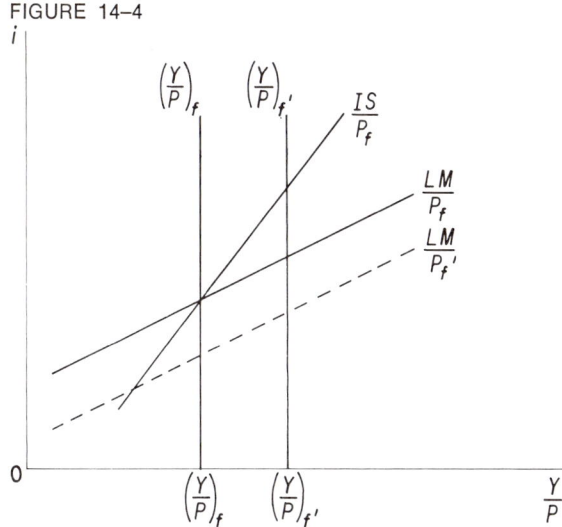

librium. When equilibrium is disturbed, economic forces are thrown into operation which move the economy farther away from equilibrium, and an equilibrium is never reestablished. The examples illustrated in Figures 14-2 and 14-3 were cases of stable equilibria: once disturbed, equilibrium was reestablished. The example illustrated in Figure 14-4 is a case of an unstable equilibrium: once disturbed, equilibrium was not reestablished.

There is an important point in this stability analysis. The analysis implies that the market equilibrium curves must intersect in certain ways. If they do not, the equilibrium will be unstable. For a stable equilibrium to exist, the real *IS* curve must cut the real *LM* curve from above; i.e., at the point of intersection between the real *IS* and *LM* curves, the slope of the real *IS* curve must be less than the slope of the real *LM* curve. Since market forces generally tend to close the gap between aggregate supply and aggregate demand, we can rule out the unstable intersections. We will ignore the unstable cases.

REAL INVESTMENT AND THE REAL WAGE RATE

In Chapter 6, we noted that the level of nominal investment may be a function of the nominal wage rate. Now we can examine this relationship in real terms. We assume that changes in the real wage rate are the result of changes in the demand for labor only. In other words, we assume that the supply curve of labor remains constant. We make this assumption in order to be certain that the total wage bill will increase. Accordingly, the linear real investment function becomes:

(14.6) $\qquad I/P = d/P + ei/P + f(Y/P) + 1(w/P),$

where w represents the nominal wage rate, and 1 is a negative number indicating that the level of real investment falls as the real wage rate rises (i.e., as the total wage bill increases).[4] The equation of the real IS curve becomes:

(14.7) $\qquad Y/P = k(a + d)/P + kei/P + klw/P,$

where we have ignored the real balance effect in the consumption function. Even though we have ignored the real balance effect in the consumption function, equation (14.7) still yields a family of real IS curves because of the presence of the real wage rate. Thus, as the price level rises and the real wage rate falls, the level of real investment increases, and so does the level of real national income, if we assume no other changes in the economy.

Suppose that there is an upward shift in the production function such that the new demand curve for labor lies everywhere above the old demand curve for labor. Given a positively sloped supply curve of labor, the real wage rate must rise, and the level of employment must rise also. The higher level of employment causes the level of real output to increase. More importantly, when the level of employment increases as a result of an increase in the real wage rate, the total real wage bill increases. Consequently, some producers might begin to cut down on the level of investment expenditures, since investments are now less profitable as a result of the rising labor costs.

In Figure 14-5, a shift in the production function and the corresponding shift in the demand curve for labor are illustrated. When the production function shifts upward, the demand curve for labor shifts to the right causing a higher real wage rate, a higher level of employment, a higher level of real national output, and a higher total

---

[4] Again, it must be mentioned that this is only a working assumption. It does not necessarily follow that an increase in the total real wage bill will cause the level of real investment to fall. Profitability of investments depends upon the total cost of all factors of production as well as revenues and potential revenues from the investment.

14 / Some further additions to the model   211

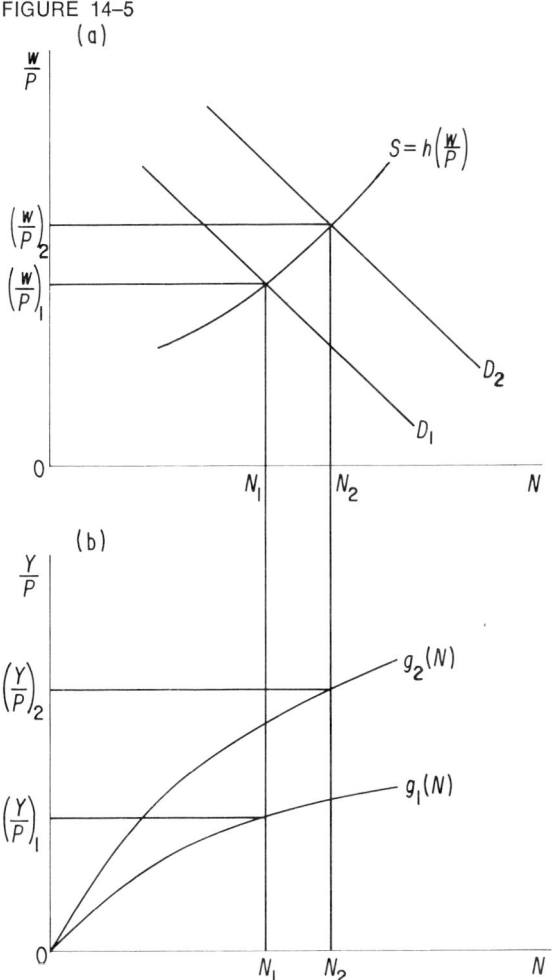

FIGURE 14–5

real wage bill. In the figure, the subscripts 1 refer to the original functions, and the original equilibrium values; while the subscripts 2 refer to the new functions, and the new equilibrium values.

When the production function shifts upward—as we have assumed—the investment function is subjected to two opposing influences. On the one hand, the increase in the level of real income means that the level of real investment expenditures will increase at every interest rate. On the other hand, the increase in the real wage rate means that the level of real investment expenditures will fall at every interest rate. Thus, the increase in the level of real income causes the real investment function to shift to the right, while the increase in the real wage rate causes the real investment function to shift to the left. If we assume that the rightward shift in the real investment function prevails, and if we assume that the real IS curve is not positively sloped, the real IS curve will shift to the right with the employment sector equilibrium curve.

In Figure 14–6, the shift in the expenditure sector equilibrium curve

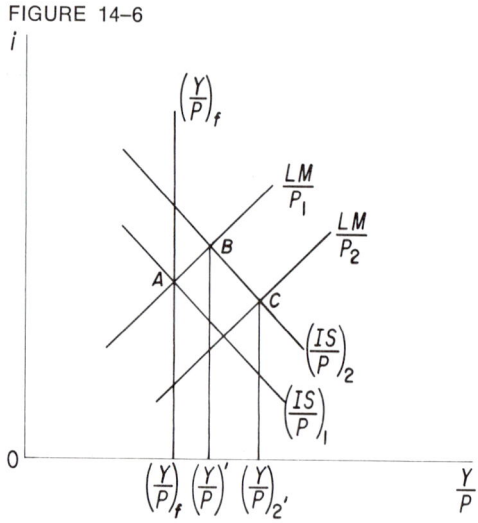

FIGURE 14–6

is given by the movement from $(IS/P)_1$ to $(IS/P)_2$, while the shift in the employment sector equilibrium curve is given by the shift from $(Y/P)_1$ to $(Y/P)_2$. The level of aggregate demand is given as $(Y/P)'$ (the intersection of $(IS/P)_2$ and LM/P_1), while the level of aggregate supply (after the shift in the employment sector equilibrium curve) is $(Y/P)_2$. Since the level of aggregate demand is less than the level of aggregate supply, the price level should fall and the real LM curve should shift to the right.[5] Equilibrium should be reestablished at point C.

It is important to note the degree of indeterminancy involved in this analysis. For example, if we had introduced a real balance effect into the production function, the employment sector equilibrium curve would shift to the right as the price level fell. Point C would not

---

[5] Assuming a real balance effect in the expenditure sector, the real IS curve will shift to the right too. We shall ignore such an effect.

be a point of equilibrium. Furthermore, even with point C as the equilibrium point, we can only guess at the direction of change in many of the variables. Try it. As long as the supply curve of labor is positively sloped, the level of real income will go up. If the supply curve of labor were backward bending, the level of labor utilization would fall and it would be possible for the level of real output to fall. In our example, the level of labor utilization went up, so the level of real output had to go up also. The total real wage bill and the real wage rate rose also. The level of real consumption could rise because the level of real income rose; or, real consumption could fall because the rate of interest fell—depending upon the assumption made regarding the relationship between the rate of interest and the level of real consumption, and the strength of this relationship. Moreover, the rate of interest could have risen (depending on the magnitude of the rightward shift in the employment sector equilibrium curve), and could have undone the impact of the rightward shift in the real investment function. Finally, the price level in our example fell, but it could have risen. If the employment sector equilibrium curve shifted to the right such that the new level of aggregate supply was something less than $(Y/P)'$, point C would lie to the left of point B, and the price level would rise. The real value of cash balances would decrease instead of increasing. Indeed, our system is now quite indeterminate.

Obviously, as we add more variables to the system, we are less able to make meaningful predictions. Nevertheless, we do benefit from the exercise: we get a better understanding of how interdependent our economic system really is, and how difficult it is to predict the impact of policy measures on real economic variables.

THE BONDS MARKET

By employing a corollary of Walras' law (see Chapter 11), we were able to ignore one of the markets in a four-market economic system. We have, in previous chapters, ignored the bonds market. Therefore, it is now time to examine the bonds market directly.

We begin our analysis by assuming that households and individuals are the sole demanders of bonds, while business firms are the sole suppliers. Clearly, both assumptions are unrealistic. Households do borrow (i.e., supply bonds) and business firms do lend (i.e., demand bonds). Nevertheless, the assumptions are useful because they greatly simplify our analysis without biasing our conclusions.

Moreover, we assume that the demand for real bonds varies directly

214 The essentials of macroeconomic analysis

with the level of real income, the level of real cash balances, and the rate of interest. In other words, as the level of real income increases, and as the level of real cash balances increases, the quantity of real bonds demanded increases. In both cases, individuals demand more bonds because they are wealthier. As the rate of interest rises, the quantity of real bonds demanded rises also. In this case, individuals demand more bonds—according to our theory of the demand for money—because they are moving out of money in order to capture capital gains.

We assume that the supply of real bonds varies directly with the level of real national income, and inversely with the rate of interest and the level of real cash balances. In other words, as the level of real income increases, the quantity of real bonds supplied increases at all rates of interest. The higher level of real national income and the larger volume of real output dictate that business firms have greater requirements for capital to finance plant and equipment expansions, and to finance inventories. As the interest rate rises, the quantity of real bonds supplied decreases. The higher level of interest rates means that the interest obligation on the bonds has increased, making borrowing more expensive. Finally, as the level of real cash balances increases, the quantity of real bonds supplied decreases at every rate of interest. The higher level of real cash balances means that less borrowing is required to cover the daily operations of firms. Indeed, we have already argued that, as real cash balances increase, more factors are freed to take part in productive activity, and the level of output of the firms is increased.

Consequently, we can write the demand for real bonds—in linear form—as:

(14.8) $\qquad B^d/P = a_1(Y/P) + a_2 i/P + a_3(M^H/P)$,

where a_1 represents the proportion of any increment to real income which is used to purchase bonds, a_2 represents the increment in the demand for bonds due to an incremental change in the interest rate, and a_3 represents the proportion of any increment to real cash balances in the hands of households which is used to purchase bonds. a_1, a_2 and a_3 are positive numbers.

The supply of real bonds—in linear form—is written as:

(14.9) $\qquad B^s/P = b_1(Y/P) + b_2 i/P + b_3(M^F/P)$,

where b_1 represents the proportion of any increment in real income which the firm chooses to borrow to finance plant expansion and inventories, b_2 represents the increment in the supply of bonds due to an incremental change in the interest rate, and b_3 represents the proportion of any increment to real cash balances in the hands of business firms which is used to reduce the supply of bonds. b_1 is a positive number. b_2 and b_3 are negative numbers.

The bonds market is illustrated in Figure 14–7, assuming given

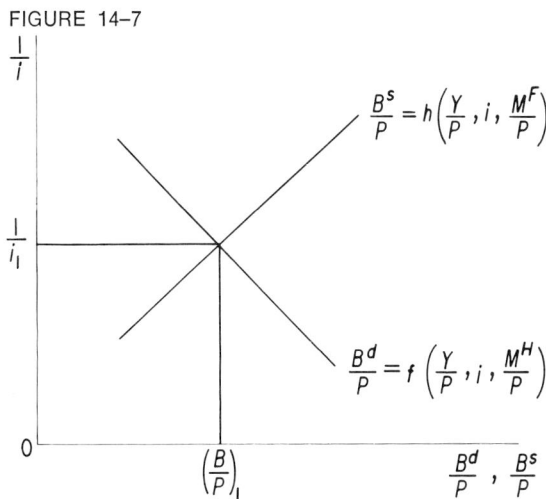
FIGURE 14–7

levels of real income and real balances. In Figure 14–7, we have plotted $1/i$ on the vertical axis, and the quantity of real bonds on the horizontal axis. We have plotted $1/i$ on the vertical axis in order to ensure that the demand and supply curves have their "normal" shapes. If we had plotted the interest rate on the vertical axis, we would have had to draw a positively sloped demand curve and a negatively sloped supply curve. By using the variable $1/i$, we are able to invert the curves and draw them with their customary slopes.

In Figure 14–7, the bonds market is in equilibrium when the interest rate is i_1, and the level of real bonds supplied and demanded is $(B/P)_1$. Of course, the money market will also be in equilibrium at interest rate i_1.

In order to obtain a bonds market equilibrium curve, all we need do is set equation (14.8) equal to equation (14.9) and solve for Y/P. This is the same procedure used in developing the equations of the real *IS* curve and the real *LM* curve. The bonds market equilibrium curve is:

$$(14.10) \quad Y/P = \frac{1}{(a_1 - b_1)} \left[\frac{(b_2 - a_2)}{P} i + b_3(M^F/P) - a_3(M^H/P) \right].$$

Since households spend increments in real income not only on bonds but on goods, services, and money as well, we expect b_1 to be larger than a_1, and $(a_1 - b_1)$ to be a negative number. For similar reasons, we expect $(b_2 - a_2)$ to be a negative number. Therefore, the coefficient of i, after removing the brackets in equation (14.10), is a positive number. Accordingly, the equilibrium curve for the bonds market is positively sloped. Two bonds market equilibrium curves are illustrated in Figure 14–8.

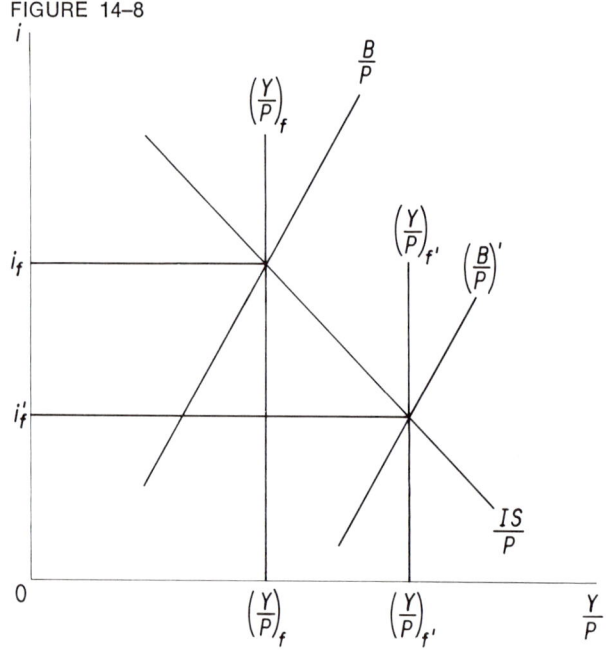

FIGURE 14–8

A closer examination of equation (14.10) reveals two points worth remembering. First, as the level of real output increases, the interest rate must also increase for equilibrium to be maintained in the bonds market. Second, since the quantity

$$\frac{1}{(a_1 - b_1)} [b_3(M^F/P) - a_3(M^H/P)]$$

is a positive number, the bonds market is always in equilibrium at a positive level of real national income—even when the rate of interest is zero.

Now we are able to examine the characteristics of an economic system, in full-employment equilibrium, which contains an expenditure sector, an employment sector, and a bonds market sector. We have omitted the monetary sector. The economic system is illustrated in Figure 14–8. The economy is in equilibrium at an interest rate of i_f, and a level of real national income equal to $(Y/P)_f$.

Suppose that the employment sector curve shifts to the right, causing the level of aggregate supply to increase to $(Y/P)'_f$. Since aggregate demand is less than aggregate supply, the price level will fall, and the bonds market equilibrium curve will shift rightward as a result of the increase in real cash balances.[6] Thus, the level of real output increases, and the interest rate falls to i'_f. Of course, with a real balance effect in the expenditure sector, the interest rate could rise rather than fall. Furthermore, whatever the three sectors we choose to view (or whatever sector we choose to omit), we know from Walras' law that the equilibrium values of the variables must be the same. We now have an alternative approach to the equilibrium analysis of the previous chapters.

Let us now examine an economic system which contains a monetary sector, a bonds market sector, and an employment sector. We have omitted the expenditure sector. Since the bonds market equilibrium curve and the real LM curve are both positively sloped, it is necessary to determine whether the bonds market curve cuts the real LM curve from above or below in order to determine whether the economic system is stable. Examine Figure 14–9. Ignore the real LM curve for a moment, and concentrate on the real IS curve and the bonds market equilibrium curve. Equilibrium is established at point A with the real IS curve and the bonds market equilibrium curve cutting the figure into four sections. In section I, there is an excess supply of goods and services (XSG), and an excess supply of bonds (XSB). See point B. The level of real output, or aggregate supply, is too great for equilibrium in the expenditure sector; while the rate of interest is too low for equilibrium in the bonds market. In section II, there is an excess supply of goods and services (XSG), and an excess demand for bonds (XDB). The level of real output, or aggregate supply, is too great for equilibrium in the expenditure sector; while the rate of interest is too high for equilibrium in the bonds market. In section III, there is an excess demand for goods and services (XDG), and

---
[6] We ignore any real balance effect in the expenditure sector.

218   The essentials of macroeconomic analysis

FIGURE 14-9

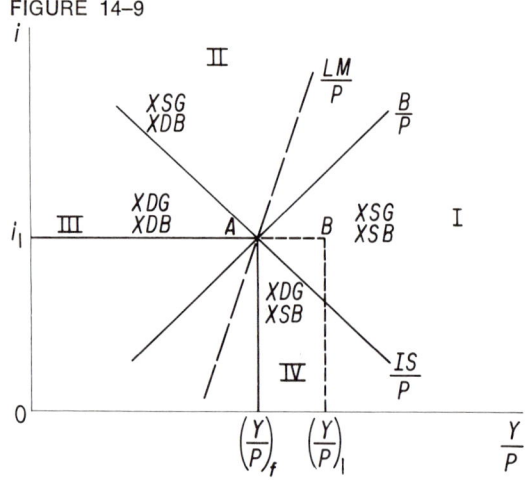

an excess demand for bonds (XDB). The level of real output, or aggregate supply, is too low for equilibrium in the expenditure sector; while the rate of interest is too high for equilibrium in the bonds market. Finally in section IV, there is an excess demand for goods and services (XDG), and an excess supply of bonds (XSB). The level of real output, or aggregate supply, is too low for equilibrium in, the expenditure sector; while the rate of interest is too low for equilibrium in the bonds market. Therefore, there is an excess demand (supply) for goods and services at all points to the left (right) of the real IS curve, and an excess demand (supply) for bonds at all points to the left (right) of the bonds market equilibrium curve.

Now draw the real LM curve into Figure 14–9. Clearly, in a section in which there is both an excess demand for goods and services and an excess demand for bonds (section III), there must be an excess supply of money. On the other hand, in a section in which there is both an excess supply of goods and services and an excess supply of bonds (section I), there must be an excess demand for money. However, in the sections in which there is an excess demand for bonds and an excess supply of goods and services (section II), or an excess supply of bonds and an excess demand for goods and services (section IV), there may be either an excess demand or an excess supply of money. These conclusions follow from the fact that money is spent for both goods and services and bonds. There can never be an excess demand for or an excess supply of all three. Therefore, when the expenditure sector and the bonds market are in equilibrium simultaneously (i.e., when there is no excess supply or demand in either sector), the monetary sector—or money market—must be in equilibrium also. Consequently, since the real *IS* curve and the bonds market equilibrium curve intersect at point *A*, the real *LM* curve must pass through point *A* also. Clearly, the bonds market equilibrium curve cuts the real *LM* curve from above, and the economic system is stable. We should note that there is an excess demand (supply) for money at all points to the right (left) of the real *LM* curve.

We are now prepared to view the interaction of the labor market, the bonds market, and the money market. In Figure 14–10, the econ-

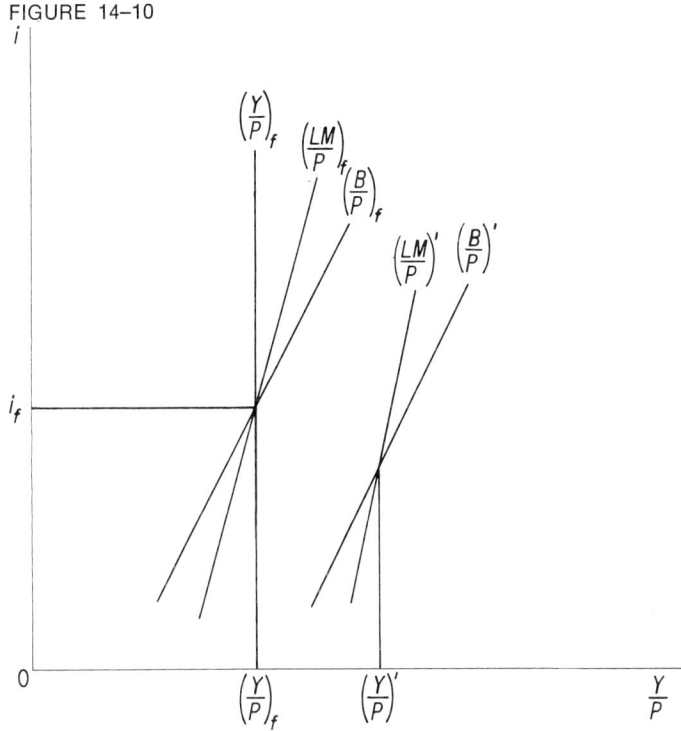

FIGURE 14–10

omy is in equilibrium at a level of real income equal to $(Y/P)_f$, and an interest rate of i_f. Suppose that the nominal supply of money were to increase. The real LM curve would shift rightward to $(LM/P)'$, and the bonds market equilibrium curve would shift rightward to $(B/P)'$. The bonds market equilibrium curve shifts because of the increase in real cash balances in the hands of firms and households. The level of aggregate demand would increase, and the price level should rise. The price level rises, the real *LM* curve and the bonds market equilibrium curve shift back to the left, until the excess aggregate demand disappears. The level of real national output remains at the full-employment level, and the interest rate remains at i_f. Since the price level increases, the nominal values of the variables increase also, but the real values remain the same before and after the increase in the nominal supply of money. Once again, we find that the rise in the price level is proportional to the increase in the nominal supply of money—when measured at the equilibrium rate of interest. Consequently, for purposes of analysis, it does not matter which model we employ. The results regarding proportionality between the nominal supply of money and the price level always obtain, given our initial assumption of full-employment equilibrium.

A NOTE ON MONEY CREATION

In Chapter 7, we mentioned the possibility of money creation as a way of financing government expenditures. The notion of money creation creates a possibility that the supply of real bonds influences the demand function for cash balances. Suppose that money is raised by the public sector through the sale of bonds. If the private sector does not evaluate equally the change in its holdings of bonds and the corresponding opposite change in its future tax liabilities to service the debt created by the sale of the bonds, then real bonds must enter the demand function for real cash balances. Under such conditions a change in the price level will change the real value of government bonds, and will change the real nonmonetary wealth of households. And this may cause a change in the demand for real cash balances. Thus, we must expand the demand function for real cash balances to include the stock of real bonds. The expanded demand function for real cash balances, in linear form, is:

(14.11) $\quad M^d/P = g/P + \bar{k}(Y/P) + hi/P + t(B/P).$

As the price level rises, the level of real bond holdings will fall, and—since individuals feel less wealthy—the demand for real cash balances will fall also. However, since people are less wealthy in real terms they may demand more real cash balances to offset this loss. The situation is not readily predictable.

The sale of bonds by the government directly changes the nominal and real amount of bonds, since the monetary authority is simply exchanging bonds for money. However, there will be a further change in the level of real bonds, since there is also a change in the price level. When the supply of nominal bonds increases, the nominal supply of money falls. As the nominal supply of money falls, assuming full employment, the price level will fall proportionately. As the price level falls and the nominal supply of bonds increases, the level of real bonds (B/P) must increase. Thus, we conclude that the change in nominal bondholdings and in real bondholdings will be in the same direction. Unfortunately, we are no longer able to say that a change in the stock of money will bring about a proportionate change in the price level. The way in which the stock of money is changed may well affect the change in the price level. Clearly, currency confiscation or creation will change the price level, and have an effect on the level of real bonds. Consequently, with real bonds in the demand function for real balances, we are no longer able to predict that a change in the supply of money induces a proportionate change in the price level—even at full employment!

CONCLUDING COMMENT

In this chapter we added some refinements to our model, expanded the equations describing our economic system, and noted the large degree of indeterminancy which we created. It might be helpful to summarize our expanded model. The expenditure sector equilibrium curve, in general terms, is:

(14.12) $\qquad Y/P = f(i, \bar{M}/P, G/P, w/P)$.

The employment sector equilibrium curve is:

(14.13) $\qquad (Y/P)_f = g(N_f, \bar{M}/P)$.

Finally, the monetary sector equilibrium curve is:

(14.14) $\qquad L(i, Y/P, B/P, \bar{M}/P) = \frac{1}{P} \bar{M}$.

In addition to these equations, we introduced the bonds market. Please note that we have three equations in seven unknowns. It is no wonder that we do not have a determinate solution to our system.

In the next chapter, we will complicate our model even more. We will add an international sector.

15 The international sector

WE HAVE scarcely mentioned the international sector, and its influence on the determination of the level of real national income. The major reason for neglecting the international sector is that it plays a relatively minor role in the determination of the level of real national income in this country. To be sure, international entanglements have increased, and we are concerned with the international repercussions of policy decisions. For these reasons, we will take a brief look at the international sector.

Furthermore, a general knowledge of macroeconomics does require some understanding of the international sector. For some economies, the international sector has a significant effect on the level of aggregate demand. Indeed, many less developed countries rely on the international sector as a stimulus to growth in the level of economic activity.

THE IMPORT FUNCTION

The level of real aggregate demand in an economy depends upon the level of real consumption, the level of real investment, the level of real government expenditures, and the level of real net foreign investment. Real net foreign investment, in the simplest sense, is determined by the difference between real exports (X/P) and real imports (M^*/P). Thus, the level of aggregate real income is:

(15.1) $\quad Y/P = C/P + I/P + G/P + (X/P - M^*/P)$.

Let us examine the real net foreign investment component of equation (15.1). In general, we assume that the real value of exports is determined abroad. A country has little control over its exports since export sales, in general, depend upon the economic conditions of the countries which buy products from the country in question. Hence, we assume that X/P is an exogenously determined constant. On the other hand, we assume, for simplicity, that the level of real imports depends directly upon the level of real national income. In linear form, we write the import function as:

(15.2) $$M^*/P = j/P + m(Y/P),$$

where m represents the marginal propensity to spend on imported goods. The quantity j/P may be either positive or zero, for it is simply the real quantity of goods and services imported when the level of real income is zero.

The marginal propensity to spend on imported goods, m, is positive but less than one in value. That is to say, when the level of real national income rises, the amount of the increase in real income which is spent on imported goods and services is less than the increase in income itself. Thus, the real net foreign investment function can be written as:

(15.3) $$N/P = (\bar{X}/P) - j/P - m(Y/P),$$

where $(\bar{X}/P)$ represents the exogenously determined level of exports, and N/P represents real net foreign investment. From equation (15.3), it is clear that the level of real net foreign investment falls as the level of national income increases—given a level of real exports. Assuming that $(\bar{X}/P) - j/P$ is a positive number, the real net foreign investment function is illustrated in Figure 15-1.

Under the conditions that real consumption and real investment both depend upon real income, and that real investment depends upon the rate of interest also, we can draw an aggregate demand function which includes the international sector. See Figure 15–2. The bottom curve is the consumption function. The next curve, in ascending order, represents the consumption plus investment functions, and its slope is greater than the slope of the consumption function because investment is a positive function of real income. The next curve simply adds a constant level of real government expenditures to the consumption and investment functions. Finally, the uppermost curve in Figure 15–2 adds real net foreign investment to real consumption, investment

FIGURE 15-1

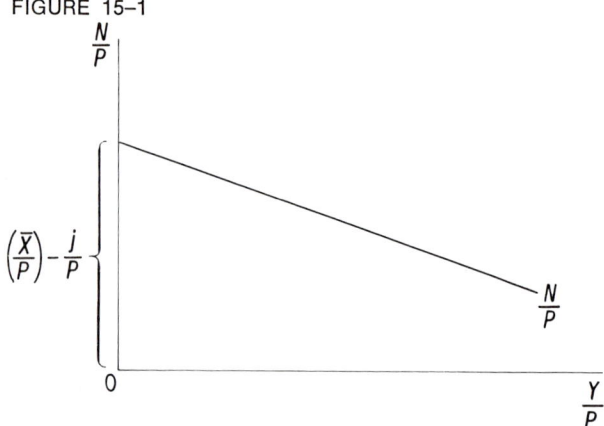

and government expenditures. It represents the expanded aggregate demand function. The slope of the aggregate demand function is less than the slope of the curve just below it because the real net foreign investment function (illustrated in Figure 15–1) is negatively sloped. Indeed, for this reason, it is possible for the new aggregate demand function to be negatively sloped. The equation of the expanded aggregate demand, or aggregate expenditure, function is:

(15.4) $\quad E/P = [(a + d)/P + e\bar{i}/P + (\bar{X}/P) - j/P + (\bar{G}/P)]$
$\qquad\qquad + (b + f - m)(Y/P),$

where $\bar{i}$ is the given rate of interest, and E/P represents real aggregate demand or real aggregate expenditures. The bracketed term is positive

FIGURE 15-2

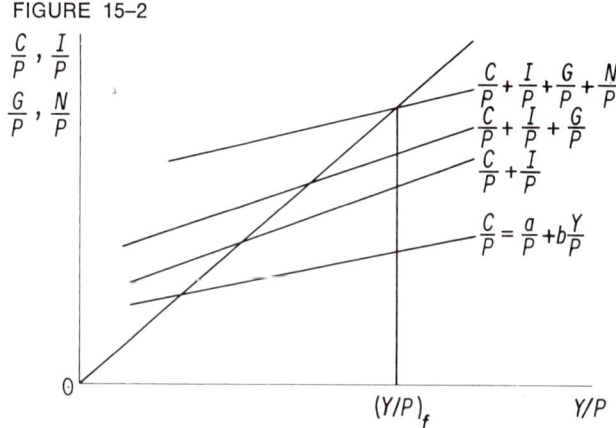

provided that $[(a+d)/P + (\bar{X}/P) + (\bar{G}/P)]$ is greater than $(e\bar{\imath}/P - j/P)$. Under these conditions, there will be positive real expenditures even when the level of real income is zero. Furthermore, if $(b+f)$ is greater than m, the new aggregate expenditure function will have a positive slope. This condition is likely to hold true—particularly for an economy that is not a large importer of foreign goods and services. Therefore, with the level of real aggregate expenditures given by equation (15.4), the equilibrium level of real national income is $(Y/P)_f$ in Figure 15–2.

We must now expand the equation of the real IS curve to include real net foreign investment. The equation of the new real IS curve is:

$$(15.5) \quad Y/P = m'\left[\frac{(a+d+\bar{G}+\bar{X}-j)}{P}\right] + m'(ei/P),$$

where $m' = 1/(1-b-f+m)$. Assuming that m' is positive, the real IS curve will have the usual negative slope. Provided that j is less than $(a+d+\bar{G}+\bar{X})$, the level of real income will be positive even when the interest rate is zero.

Analytically an increase in real exports will cause the level of real net foreign investment to increase, and cause the real IS curve to shift to the right. Indeed, at every level of the interest rate, the real IS curve will shift to the right by an amount equal to:

$$(15.6) \quad \Delta(Y/P) = m'\Delta(X/P).$$

However, the rightward shift in the real IS curve is not the only impact of an increase in exports on the economic system. Suppose that the economy is at full-employment equilibrium, as in Figure 15–3. An increase in exports will increase aggregate demand and shift the real IS curve to the right. Since the economy is fully employed, no further employment can be created, and the level of real output cannot increase. However, there will probably be a movement of resources from the production of import-competing, and nontrade-related, industries to export industries. Consequently, even though total real output does not increase, the composition of the constant level of real output is changed—the quantity of export goods and services has increased relative to the quantity of all other goods and services. Since the increase in exports causes the level of aggregate demand to exceed the level of aggregate supply, the price level increases, and the interest rate increases also. Examine Figure 15–3. With the outward shift in

FIGURE 15-3

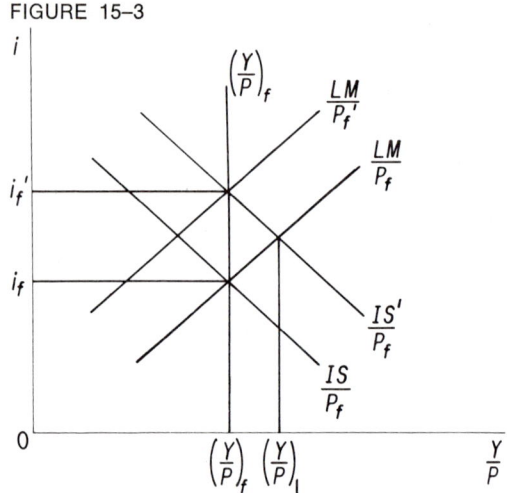

the real IS curve, the level of aggregate demand increases to (Y/P_1). As prices increase, the real LM curve shifts leftward to LM/P'_f. Consequently, the original level of real output prevails, but the interest rate rises to i'_f. Since the level of real output is unchanged, the level of real consumption remains unchanged also. However, the increase in the rate of interest must cause the level of real investment to fall. Given a constant level of real imports (since real imports depend upon real income), it follows that the increase in real exports has been offset by an equal decrease in the level of real investment. Moreover, as we saw earlier, the interest rate and the price level have increased.

Unfortunately, the adjustment process does not stop at this point. The *exchange rate* must change also. Since the exchange rate is defined as the price of domestic currency in terms of foreign currency (i.e., the foreign currency price of domestic currency), and since an increase in the foreign demand for domestically produced goods causes an increase in the demand for domestic currency, the exchange rate should rise. Whether it does will depend upon the type of exchange rate mechanism in operation. In any case, the pressure for the exchange rate to change creates further adjustments in the economy.

FIXED AND FLEXIBLE EXCHANGE RATES

A *fixed exchange rate* is not allowed to change. It is maintained at a constant level (called the official exchange rate) through the actions of a governmental or quasi-governmental agency. Conversely, a *flexible exchange rate* is allowed to change. Its value (called the equilibrium exchange rate) is determined by the market forces of supply and demand. As supply and demand conditions in the exchange market change, the equilibrium value of the flexible exchange rate changes also. Each of these two exchange rate mechanisms—fixed and flexible exchange rates—implies a different adjustment process.

The difference in the two exchange rate mechanisms is easily demonstrated. Imagine a world consisting of two countries, Inland and Outland. Inland's currency is called the peso, and Outland's currency is called the dollar. We have illustrated the supply (S) and demand (D) curves for the peso in Figure 15–4. The market price of the

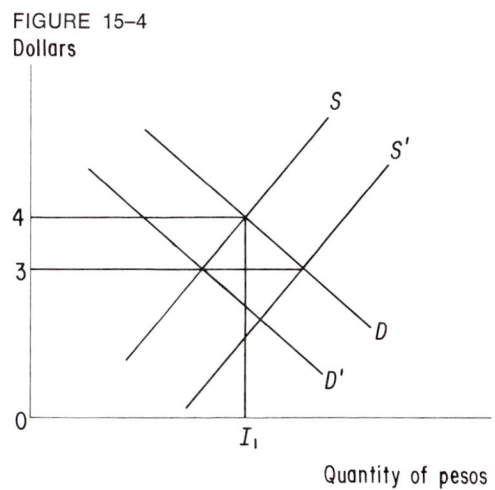

FIGURE 15–4

peso in terms of the dollar is indicated on the vertical axis, while the quantity of pesos exchanged is given on the horizontal axis. Thus, the equilibrium price of the peso is $4 per unit (i.e., the dollar price of the peso), and the quantity exchanged at that price is I_1. The market is in equilibrium.

Now suppose that the equilibrium rate is not the official rate. Rather, let the official rate be less than $4, say $3 per peso. Clearly, for the official rate to be an equilibrium rate there must be some interference with the market mechanism. With no interference, there will be an excess demand for the peso, since it is underpriced in terms of the dollar. Market forces would cause the price of the peso to be bid up in terms of the dollar. In order for the $3 price to be the equilibrium price, either the demand curve for the peso must shift to the left to D', or the supply curve of the peso must shift to the right to S'.

One method of increasing the supply of pesos is to have the monetary authority in Outland sell pesos at the official rate of $3. However, it could not do so indefinitely. Eventually, Outland's monetary authority is bound to run out of pesos. At that point, the official rate would have to change. Indeed, as the monetary authority began to run out of pesos, people would suspect that the official rate would soon rise to the market rate. They would buy pesos at the official rate of $3 hoping to sell them at $4 per peso as soon as the rates were changed. They would earn a handsome profit. They would have profited from a dollar *devaluation* (i.e., as the price of the peso rises, the value of the dollar falls—for each peso now buys more dollars, and the dollar has been devalued). The point is that the action by Outland's monetary authority cannot shift the supply curve of pesos to S' indefinitely. Another policy must be found.

An alternative policy is to have the government of Outland pursue a program designed to reduce the excess demand for pesos by Outlanders, causing the demand curve for pesos to shift leftward to D'. How could this be accomplished? Since the demand for pesos by Outlanders is derived from their demand for Inland's exports, and since the demand for imports (Inland's exports) depends on the level of real income, the government of Outland could reduce the demand for pesos by reducing the demand for imports by deflating Outland's level of real income, perhaps through increased taxes. As the level of real income falls in Outland, expenditures on real imports fall, and the demand curve for pesos shifts to the left to D'.

However, the decrease in the level of real output and economic activity in Outland will bring about a fall in the price level, assuming prices are flexible downward. Outland's goods will become relatively less expensive than Inland's. This will reduce the desire to import from Inland, and induce a further decrease in the demand for pesos. Furthermore, there will be an increase in the demand for Outland's goods on the part of Inlanders—since they are now cheaper—which increases the supply of pesos, further alleviating the exchange rate problems.

As another alternative, the government of Outland could pursue a restrictive monetary policy. A decrease in the money supply in Outland would raise interest rates, making investment returns in Outland relatively attractive. There would be an increased demand for dollars, or an increased supply of pesos, as Inlanders attempt to invest in Outland, and the exchange rate pressures will be relieved. Whichever policy is followed, the general result is that the level of income in Outland begins to fall or, at least, to rise less rapidly. Outland must sacrifice its domestic levels of income and employment in order to maintain a fixed exchange rate.

There is a third alternative. Controls such as tariffs and quotas could be designed to cut down on imports, and reduce the demand for pesos. These controls, of course, are discriminatory and are, in fact, nothing more than a disguised exchange rate devaluation. Generally, controls cause resources to be inefficiently allocated, and create severe domestic economic problems.

As an alternative to fixed exchange rates and their disruptive effects on the domestic economy, the two countries could establish a system of flexible exchange rates. The market would determine the price of the peso and, in our example, it would be $4. The market would be cleared, and the equilibrium quantity would be I_1. Any departure from this equilibrium would throw forces into operation which would return the system to equilibrium. Government interference would not be required, and domestic levels of income and employment would not be sacrificed for the sake of keeping the exchange rate fixed. No set of policies would have to be followed. The market for the peso and, hence, the dollar would always be in equilibrium.

ADJUSTMENT WITH A FIXED EXCHANGE RATE

Let us now view the domestic adjustment process under a fixed exchange rate system. Figure 15–5 will aid our analysis. Suppose that Inland has a current level of real national income equal to $(Y/P)_1$, and a current interest rate equal to i_1. Furthermore, suppose that the rate of interest is also the world rate of interest.[1] If Inland desires to raise its level of national income, it can use two alternative policies: monetary policy or fiscal policy. (At this point we are not concerned about whether the level of income $(Y/P)_1$ is the full-employment level of real income.)

---

[1] A world rate of interest may be difficult to imagine. We use the concept only for purposes of analysis.

FIGURE 15-5

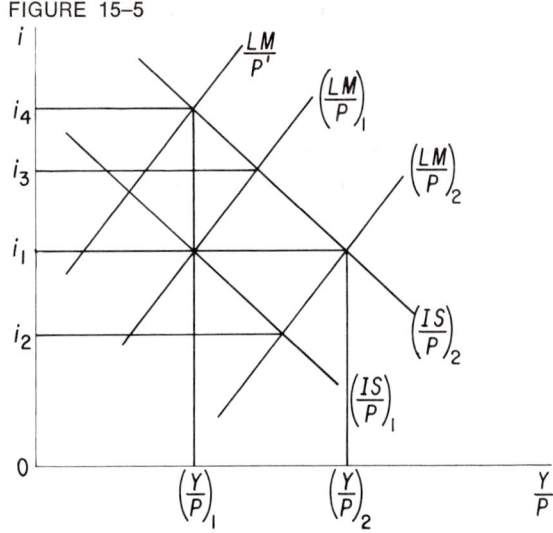

Suppose that an easy money policy is employed in an attempt to raise the level of real national income. When the nominal stock of money is increased in Inland, the rate of interest falls. Given the real IS curve $(IS/P)_1$ in Figure 15–5, as the nominal supply of money increases, the real LM curve shifts to $(LM/P)_2$, and the interest rate in Inland falls to i_2. Since the world interest rate is still i_1, higher than the rate in Inland, we presume that investment funds flow from Inland to the rest of the world—Outland. This outflow of funds from Inland decreases the price of Inland's currency—the peso—in terms of Outland's currency—the dollar. In other words, the price of the dollar is bid up in terms of the peso. This must happen because there is an excess supply of pesos seeking to be converted into dollars. In order to maintain the fixed exchange rate, the monetary authority of Inland will have to sell dollars for pesos, lowering the price of the dollar in terms of pesos.

However, selling dollars for pesos in Inland takes pesos out of circulation and lowers the money supply in Inland. Hence, the real LM curve shifts back to the left forcing the rate of interest in Inland to rise. In fact, the rate of interest will eventually rise back into equality with the world rate. As long as the interest rate in Inland is lower than the world rate, pesos will be exchanged for dollars and the price of the dollar in terms of the peso will be bid up. The monetary authority in Inland will continue to be forced to sell dollars and, thus, to reduce the money supply which they had originally increased in order to raise the level of real national income. The net result is that there is no shift in the real LM curve, no change in the rate of interest (i_1), and no change in the level of real income $(Y/P)_1$. Monetary policy has not increased the level of real national income.

Since an easy monetary policy has not raised the level of real national income, Inland policy makers might employ fiscal policy. Assume that there is an increase in real government expenditures, financed out of a prior surplus. Consequently, there will be a rightward shift in the real IS curve. The interest rate in Inland rises to i_3 in Figure 15–5. Investment funds flow into Inland. The price of the peso is bid up in terms of the dollar, or the price of the dollar falls in terms of the peso. In order to maintain the exchange rate, the monetary authority in Inland must raise the price of the dollar in terms of the peso. To do this, the monetary authority is forced to increase the domestic money supply. Thus, the real LM curve will shift to the right. As long as the interest rate in Inland exceeds the world interest rate, funds flow in and the monetary authority is forced to continue to buy dollars. The money supply continues to increase until the interest rates in Inland and Outland are equalized. This occurs when the money supply in Inland has increased sufficiently to shift the real LM curve to $(LM/P)_2$. The level of real national income has gone up, but the interest rate has fallen back to its original level. The increase in real government expenditures has caused an inflow of funds from Outland and has forced the level of real income upward.

Now suppose that Inland was producing at the full-employment level of national income. Consequently, the level of real national income cannot go up. $(Y/P)_1$ is the full-employment level of output. The increase in real government expenditures, coupled with the required increase in the money supply, forces the level of aggregate demand to increase to $(Y/P)_2$. Since aggregate demand is greater than aggregate supply, the price level rises. The real LM curve shifts back to the left to (LM/P'), and the original level of real income is reestablished. In the process, the interest rate rises to i_4. This interest rate is well above the world interest rate, requiring the monetary authority in Inland to continue to increase the money supply. Hence, the real LM curve shifts to the right, creating more inflationary pressure. In an attempt to maintain the exchange rate, the price level must continue to increase.[2]

Moreover, if the original level of real income is at less than full employment, it is possible for the real income level $(Y/P)_2$ to be established as the new equilibrium. However, if the original level of real income is not at full employment, it is not necessary to rely on the foreign trade sector of the economy to bring about full-employment equilibrium. We will see in a later chapter that this problem can be solved domestically. Nevertheless, the level of real national income can be raised, with a fixed exchange rate, when fiscal policy is employed—if we begin from a less than full-employment level of real output.

ADJUSTMENT WITH A FLEXIBLE EXCHANGE RATE

We know that with a system of flexible exchange rates, it is not necessary for the monetary authority to work to stabilize exchange rates. Suppose that Inland institutes a fiscal policy program which seems to work well under a fixed exchange rate system. An increase in the level of real government expenditures shifts the real IS curve to the right, in Figure 15–6, from $(IS/P)_1$ to $(IS/P)_2$. The rate of interest increases, resulting in an immediate inflow of investment funds into Inland. There is an increased demand for pesos, causing the price of the peso in terms of the dollar to rise. The price of Inland's exports rises, and Inland's level of exports falls. On the other hand, the prices of Outland's goods become relatively less expensive to Inlanders, since dollars are now cheaper, Inland's imports increase. Assuming that no change in the price level occurs as a result of changes in the foreign trade sector of the Inland economy, the level of net foreign investment falls and the real IS curve shifts back to the left. Hence, the interest rate begins to fall back toward its original level. The real IS curve continues to shift back to the left as long as there is an interest rate differential—for this differential keeps the price of Inland's goods low relative to the price of Outland's goods. Finally, the rate of interest falls back to its original level as the real IS curve shifts to the left.

---

[2] Of course, if there is a real balance effect in the expenditure sector, the real IS curve will shift to the left as the price level rises, and the equilibrium rate of interest will fall back to the original level, and the pressure on the price level will disappear.

FIGURE 15–6

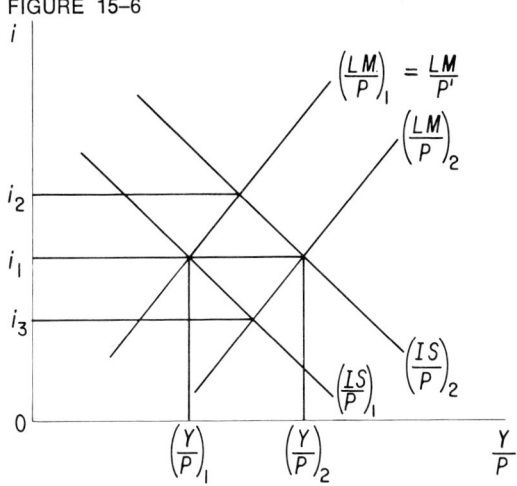

In equilibrium, the level of real national output does not change. It remains at $(Y/P)_1$. Fiscal policy, in the face of flexible exchange rates, has not worked. Even if the level of real output was below the full-employment level, fiscal policy would be a failure. Reliance on the foreign trade sector will not work.

Instead, Inland may try an easy monetary policy in order to raise the level of real national income. An increase in the nominal money supply causes the real LM curve in Figure 15–6 to shift to the right to $(LM/P)_2$. The interest rate in Inland falls to i_3, and investment funds flow to Outland in order to take advantage of the higher rate of return. The price of dollars in terms of the peso is bid up, and the price of the peso in terms of the dollar falls. Since the peso is now cheaper, goods from Inland appear relatively cheap to Outlanders. As a result, there is an increase in demand for Inland's goods, and exports rise. At the same time, there is a decrease in the demand for goods from Outland—since these goods are relatively more expensive to Inlanders. Thus, the real IS curve shifts to the right. Equilibrium is established when the interest rate in Inland and Outland are equal. This occurs when the level of real output in Inland has reached $(Y/P)_2$. Clearly, the easy monetary policy has raised the level of real national output.

However, it must be mentioned that the level of real national income can only be raised if the original level of real income was at less than full employment. If the original level of real income was at the full-employment level, we would simply have an increase in the price level which causes the real LM curve to shift back to the left to (LM/P'), reestablishing the original equilibrium. Nevertheless, with less than full employment, and a flexible exchange rate, the level of real national income may be increased by employing monetary policy.

With full employment already established, the implementation of fiscal policy with a fixed exchange rate and monetary policy with a flexible exchange rate will bring about a shift in society's resources, but no change in the level of real output. During intermediate stages, the price level will rise. In the fixed exchange rate case, the shift of resources is accomplished by the monetary authority through its buying of dollars. In the case of the flexible exchange rate, the shift of resources is accomplished through the market mechanism brought about by the supply and demand conditions for the dollar and the peso. In this latter case, equilibrium is automatically established without the interference of the monetary authority.

CONCLUDING COMMENT

In this chapter, we viewed the foreign exchange mechanism and its relationship to the level of economic activity. To be sure, we have only touched on the importance of the international sector in determining the level of economic activity. Nevertheless, we have seen that there is a significant difference in the adjustment mechanism between a fixed exchange rate system and a flexible exchange rate system. Depending upon the type of exchange rate mechanism, we may employ either fiscal or monetary policy to raise the level of real national income. Fiscal policy can be used to raise the level of national income under a fixed exchange rate system, and monetary policy can be used to raise the level of national income under a flexible exchange rate system. However, you must interpret these conclusions cautiously. When the international sector is insignificant relative to the rest of the domestic economy, as in the United States, both monetary and fiscal policy can be used to raise the level of real national income regardless of the form of the exchange rate system. Our conclusions are simple generalizations which become increasingly true as the importance of the international sector increases relative to the rest of the domestic economy.

APPENDIX

The impact of the international sector on the domestic economy can be illustrated in a more precise manner. From equations (15.5) and (15.6), we know that the impact of an increase in real export sales to the rest of the world shifts the real *IS* curve to the right by an amount equal to:

(15.7) $$\Delta(Y/P) = m'\Delta(X/P),$$

where $m' = 1/(1 - b - f + m)$. Moreover, from equation (15.5), we know also that any increase in real government expenditures, real investment expenditures, or real consumption expenditures (all other variables remaining constant), shifts the real *IS* curve rightward by an amount equal to:

(15.8) $$\Delta(Y/P) = m'\Delta(Z/P),$$

where Z represents C, I, or G. Therefore, each dollar increment to real aggregate demand—regardless of whether it originates in the international sector or the domestic sector—produces an identical incremental shift in the real *IS* curve; i.e., each dollar increase produces the same increment to excess aggregate demand, m'.

Now suppose that the marginal propensity to spend on imported goods and services, m, equals zero. In other words, suppose that there is no demand for foreign goods in the domestic economy; no portion of any increase in real national income is spent on imported commodities. Under this assumption, an increase in real aggregate demand shifts the real *IS* curve to the right by an amount equal to:

(15.9) $$\Delta(Y/P) = \bar{m}'\Delta(Z/P),$$

where $\bar{m}' = 1/(1 - b - f)$. On careful inspection, you will see that m' is less than $\bar{m}'$. If m is greater than zero, $m' = 1/(1 - b - f + m)$ must be less than $\bar{m}' = 1/(1 - b - f)$.

Therefore, we can conclude that the increases in real aggregate demand in the domestic economy, resulting from an increase in real income, becomes smaller as the marginal propensity to import becomes larger. In other words, the propensity to import dampens the stimulatory impact of an increase in real aggregate demand on the economy. If the propensity to import is sufficiently large, the international sector will have a significant impact on the domestic economy.

16 Aggregate supply

FOR THE MOST PART, our analysis has been aggregate demand oriented. We built an income-expenditure model of the economy—income changes only as aggregate demand changes, an increase in expenditures induces an increase in real or nominal income. Clearly, the level of expenditures, or aggregate demand, is the moving force. To be sure, we have not ignored aggregate supply completely. Our analysis of the employment sector equilibrium curve was aggregate supply oriented. Nevertheless, most of our analysis has been aggregate demand oriented.

Yet, we know from our analysis that aggregate supply is important. At full employment, aggregate supply represents the maximum level of output that society is *able* to produce given its resource endowment. At less than full employment, aggregate supply represents the maximum level of output that society is *willing* to produce given prices, wages, and technology. Obviously, we need to know more about aggregate supply, and that is the purpose of this chapter.

THE RELATIONSHIP BETWEEN REAL OUTPUT AND THE PRICE LEVEL

There are several methods of describing aggregate supply. In the market sector analysis, we used the employment equilibrium curve to describe aggregate supply. In the income-expenditure approach, we used the 45° line to describe aggregate supply. However, those are not the only alternatives. It is also possible to define the aggregate supply function as a price-quantity relationship—just as the supply function is defined in microeconomic theory. Therefore, let us define the *aggregate supply function* as a relationship between the quantity of real output produced and the price level necessary to make that level of output profitable.

We can derive the aggregate supply function with the aid of Figure 16-1. In panel (a), we have drawn the aggregate production function

FIGURE 16-1

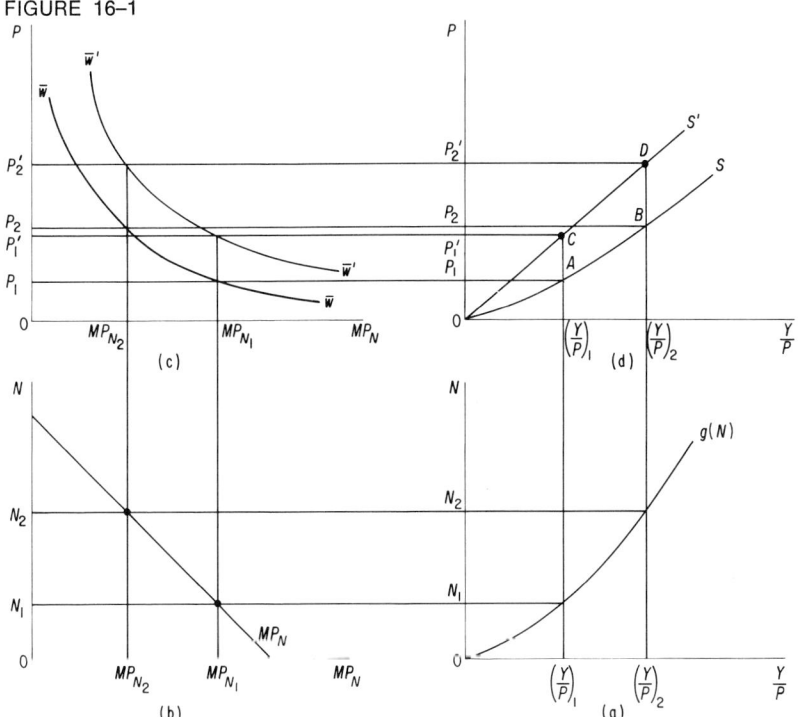

for the economy as a whole. It is the same production function that was used in Chapter 11, except that the axes have been reversed. The quantity of real output is plotted on the horizontal axis, and the level of employment on the vertical axis. The aggregate production function has its usual shape, reflecting the law of *diminishing returns*. As the level of employment increases, the quantity of real output produced increases also, but at an ever diminishing rate, assuming that the other factors of production remain constant.

In panel (b), we have drawn the *marginal physical product of labor curve* for the economy as a whole. It indicates the addition to aggregate real output that results from the addition of each unit of labor to the production process (see Chapter 11). Because of diminishing returns in the production process, the marginal physical product of labor falls as the quantity of labor employed increases. Once again, the axes have been reversed from the usual presentation.

Recall, from Chapter 11, that profit-maximizing behavior requires that business firms hire labor up to the point where the marginal physical product of labor equals the real wage rate. Therefore, as the level of employment increases and the marginal product of labor decreases, the real wage rate must decrease also. This result is illustrated in panel (c). In panel (c), we have drawn a constant money wage rate contour. These contours are derived from equations (11.3), (11.3a), and (11.3b) of Chapter 11. Each contour shows all the possible combinations of the price level and the marginal product of labor that yield a given money wage rate. Thus, as the level of employment increases and the aggregate marginal product of labor falls, the price level must rise in order to force the real wage rate ($\bar{w}/P$) downward as is required by the constant money wage rate $\bar{w}$. For example, suppose that the money wage rate is \$5. A marginal product of labor equal to 2½, and a price level of \$2, are consistent with the money wage rate of \$5 (i.e., $P \times MP_N = \bar{w}$). However, if the marginal product increased to 5, the price level would have to fall to \$1 in order to be consistent with the money wage rate of \$5. Instead, if the marginal product of labor decreased to 2, the price level would have to rise to \$2.5 in order to remain consistent with the given money wage rate. In other words, the contours in panel (c) are rectangular hyperbolas.

In panel (d), we have drawn the aggregate supply curve. Suppose that the quantity of labor employed is N_1. Given the production function, the level of real output is $(Y/P)_1$, and the marginal product of labor is MP_{N1}. The marginal product is indicated in panel (b), while the level of real output is given in panel (a). In order to establish the money wage rate w, given a marginal product of labor equal to MP_{N1}, the price level must be P_1—as shown in panel (c). The combination of a price level equal to P_1 and a level of real output equal to $(Y/P)_1$ is given by point A in panel (d). Point A is one point on the aggregate supply curve. Now suppose that the level of employment increases to N_2. Given the production function, the level of real output rises to $(Y/P)_2$, and the marginal product of labor falls to MP_{N2}. Given a money wage rate equal to $\bar{w}$, the price level must equal P_2. A level of real output equal to $(Y/P)_2$ and a price level equal to P_2 determine point B in panel (d). Proceeding in this manner, we locate all the combinations of real output and the price level which are consistent with the money wage rate $\bar{w}$. These combinations represent the aggregate supply function, S. In other words, the aggregate supply function summarizes those combinations of the level of real national output and the price level which are necessary to maintain a particular money wage rate, when the level of employment is changing.

If the money wage rate increased, the contour in panel (c) would shift rightward to $\bar{w}'$. That is to say, for a given price level, the marginal product of labor would have to increase (or, for a given marginal product of labor, the price level would have to increase) in order to maintain the new higher money wage rate. Under the circumstances, given the employment level N_1, and the level of real output $(Y/P)_1$, the price level necessary to maintain the new money wage rate, $\bar{w}'$, is P'_1. Thus, point C in panel (d) is determined. When the level of employment increases to N_2, the price level must increase to P'_2, and the real output rises to $(Y/P)_2$. Thus, point D in panel (d) is determined. We now have a new aggregate supply curve given by S'.

It is important to note at this point that the aggregate supply curve does not determine the price level, nor does it determine the level of real output. In order to determine the values of these variables, we must look at both aggregate demand and aggregate supply.

Our method of constructing the aggregate supply function illustrates another difference between Keynesian and Classical macroeconomic theory. The aggregate supply functions drawn in panel (d) of Figure 16–1 were derived on the assumption of a fixed (i.e., constant and rigid) money wage rate. It is a Keynesian assumption, and they are Keynesian aggregate supply functions. Contrary to the Keynesian assumption of a fixed money wage rate, the Classical economists assumed the existence of a perfectly flexible money wage rate; i.e., the money wage rate could fluctuate freely upward as well as downward. Furthermore, they assumed (as we did in Chapter 11) that the real wage rate would be determined by the intersection of the marginal product of labor curve (the demand for labor curve) and the supply of labor curve. These Classical assumptions drastically alter the shape of the aggregate supply function. Given a freely fluctuating money wage rate, equilibrium in the labor market determines the level of employment. Given the production function, the equilibrium level of employment determines the level of real national output. A shift in either the demand or supply curve of labor alters the real wage rate and, in most cases, the level of employment.[1] Consequently, the level of real output changes too, at least up to the full-employment point. At full employment a change in the price level cannot induce a change in the level of real national output, but—provided there is perfect money wage flexibility—does force the money wage rate to rise. Moreover, if the price level doubles, the level of employment—full employment or less than full employment—will remain unchanged provided that the money wage rate doubles also. If the level of employment remains the same, it follows that the level of real output does not change as the price level changes. Thus, the aggregate supply curve would be completely price-inelastic as shown in Figure 16–2.

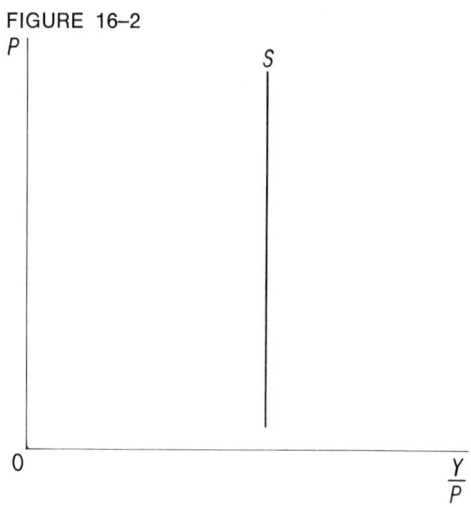

FIGURE 16–2

Whether the Keynesian or Classical assumptions are more realistic is a matter of debate. Often the aggregate supply curve is drawn to include both, as in Figure 16–3, where the money wage rate is assumed to be fixed until the full-employment level of real output is reached.

---

[1] It is, of course, possible for the demand and supply curves both to shift so that the level of employment does not change. We shall ignore such a case.

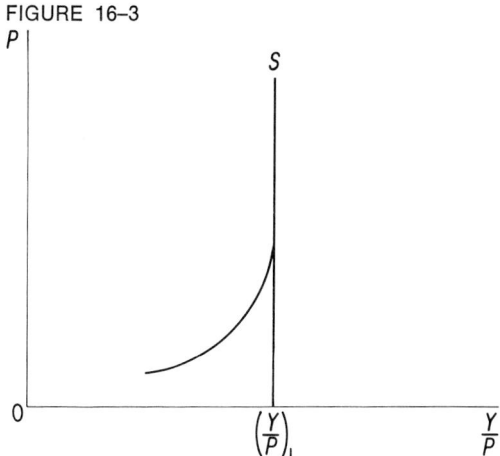

FIGURE 16-3

Beyond the full-employment level of real output, the aggregate supply curve becomes vertical due to complete wage flexibility.

Whereas the Classical economists assumed a continuously fully-employed economy, the Keynesians did not. It is quite possible in the Keynesian system, as we will see, for the level of real national output to be less than $(Y/P)_1$. Furthermore, this lower than full-employment level of real output will be an equilibrium level of real national output. We will see precisely what the Keynesians mean by "less than full-employment equilibrium" shortly.

AN ALTERNATIVE APPROACH TO AGGREGATE DEMAND

We have examined aggregate demand in two ways. On the one hand, we viewed aggregate demand as the aggregate expenditure function in the income-expenditure approach; while, on the other hand, we viewed (real) aggregate demand as being determined by the intersection of the (real) IS and (real) LM curves. Now, we must look at aggregate demand as a function of the price level. To do so, we assume that the demand for real balances depends upon the level of real national income only. Accordingly, we say:

(16.1) $$M^d/P = \bar{k}(Y/P)$$

which is nothing more than the transactions-precautionary demand for real cash balances that we discussed in Chapter 8. If we multiply both sides of equation (16.1) by P, we obtain:

(16.2) $$M^d = P\bar{k}(Y/P).$$

In equilibrium, we know that:

(16.3) $$\bar{M} = P\bar{k}(Y/P).$$

Dividing both sides of equation (16.3) by $\bar{k}$, we have

(16.4) $$\bar{M}/\bar{k} = P(Y/P),$$

or

(16.5) $$\bar{M}V = P(Y/P),$$

where $1/\bar{k} = V$, and V represents the *income velocity of money;* i.e. the number of times the average dollar turns over during a given period of time. The notion that $1/\bar{k} = V$ is not difficult to understand. Suppose that we assume that all individuals are identical, and select one representative from this group. Assume that he receives an income of $600, 12 times a year. For our purposes, let us assume that a year is 360 days long. Suppose that this individual spends his $600 income over a 30-day month at a rate of $20 per day. Over the 30-day period, he has an average balance of $300—one half of his monthly income; or, in other words, the percentage of income over which he chooses to keep command in money form is approximately 4.2. Thus, $\bar{k}$ is $\frac{1}{24}$ or 4.2 percent. Alternatively, the average dollar turns over every 15 days. Since 15 days is one-half the income period, and since there are 12 income periods per year, we say that the average dollar is turned over 24 times per year. Hence, we conclude that V is 24, or $V = 1/\bar{k}$, or $\bar{k} = 1/V$.

Equation (16.1) represents the quantity theory of money. It represents the demand for real cash balances. The quantity theory is a theory of the demand for money. It states that the demand for real balances is proportionate to the level of real output. Therefore, it follows that there is a direct relationship between the money supply and the price level. Given the maximum level of real output (the full-employment level), an increase in the nominal supply of money must be accompanied by a proportionate increase in the price level in order to maintain equilibrium in the money market.

The quantity theory of money should not be confused with equation (16.5). Equation (16.5) is the *equation of exchange*. Equation

(16.5) is always true *ex post*. That is to say, given $\bar{M}$, we can always determine the level of V if the level of nominal income, $P(Y/P)$, is known. Thus, if $\bar{M}$ is $5 billion, and nominal income is $10 billion, velocity must be 2. Hence, given the supply of money and the level of nominal income, the velocity can always be calculated. However, this says nothing about the demand for real cash balances. On the other hand, the quantity theory of money is the transactions-precautionary demand for money. It is a theory, not just an *ex post* accounting relationship.

Since velocity is said to be fairly constant, we will consider it to be a constant. Given a nominal supply of money, the left-hand side of equation (16.5) is a constant. Thus, P times (Y/P) must always equal the constant value $\bar{M}V$. Accordingly, the relationship between P and (Y/P) may be plotted as a rectangular hyperbola, as in Figure 16–4, along which P times (Y/P) always equals $\bar{M}V$. This

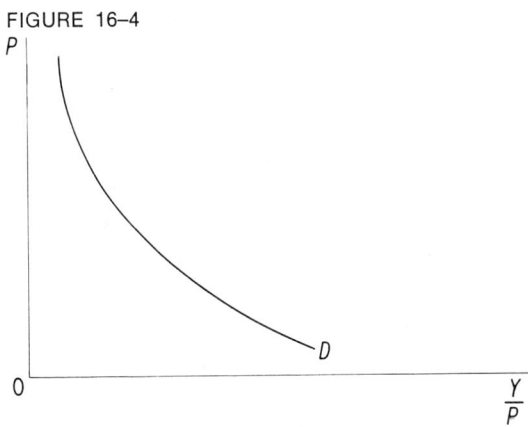

FIGURE 16–4

curve is the *aggregate demand function*. The aggregate demand function is defined as a relationship between the quantity of real output demanded and the price level. When the money supply increases, the aggregate demand curve shifts to the right; when the money supply decreases, the aggregate demand curve shifts to the left.

Since, in the construction of Figure 16–4, we assumed that the demand for real balances depends on the level of real national income only, and since we considered the transactions-precautionary demand for money only, we have constructed a Classical aggregate demand function. Alternatively, if we assume that the demand for real cash balances depends on the interest rate as well as the level of real income, we can construct a Keynesian aggregate demand function. Because of the speculative demand for money function, the Keynesian aggregate demand function will not be a rectangular hyperbola. This is easily demonstrated. A linear demand curve for money, in which both the transactions-precautionary demand and the speculative demand for money are considered, is:

(16.6) $\qquad M^d/P = \bar{k}(Y/P) + g/P + hi/P.$

Assuming equilibrium in the money market, we can solve equation (16.6) for (Y/P):

(16.7) $\qquad Y/P = 1/\bar{k}[\bar{M}/P - g/P - (h/P) \cdot i],$

which is the equation of the real LM curve.

We know that this real LM curve has a positive slope. Using Figure 16–5AB, we can illustrate why the Keynesian aggregate demand curve is not a rectangular hyperbola. In Figure 16–5A, with the price level at P_2, the level of real aggregate demand would be $(Y/P)_2$. When the price level rises to P_1 (assuming that there is no real balance effect in the expenditure sector), the level of aggregate demand would fall to $(Y/P)_1$. Note that, at the interest rate i_2, the price level increase caused the real LM curve to shift by the amount ab. Since the money supply is assumed to be constant, the distance ab measures the change in the price level. However, at the same rate of interest, the level of real income fell, but only by $(Y/P)_2 - (Y/P)_1$, and this amount is less than the change in the price level. If we assume that nominal income is constant, we conclude that, for a rise in the price level, of 10 percent, the level of real aggregate demand will fall by less than 10 percent. However, if the real LM curve were completely inelastic (as suggested by considering only the transactions-precautionary demand for money), as in Figure 16–5B, the percentage rise in the price level would be matched by an equal percentage fall in the level of real aggregate demand. Hence, given the initial real LM curve $(LM/P_2)'$, and a leftward shift to $(LM/P_1)'$, the distance cd and the distance $(Y/P)_2 - (Y/P)_1$ are equal. The result is that the relationship between the price level and the level of real aggregate demand traces out a rectangular hyperbola. However, such is definitely not the case when the real LM curve has a positive slope due to the de-

FIGURE 16-5

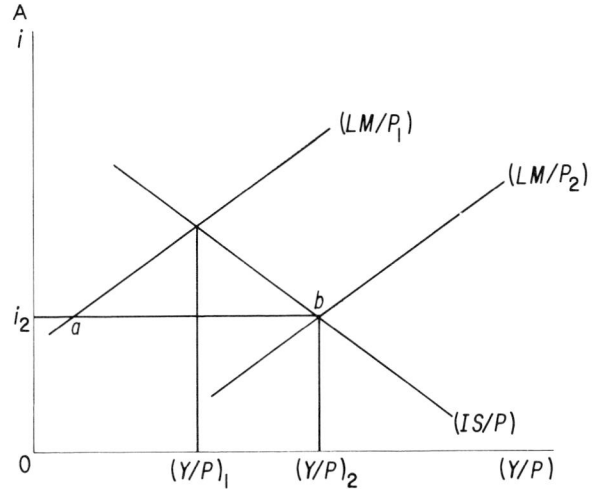

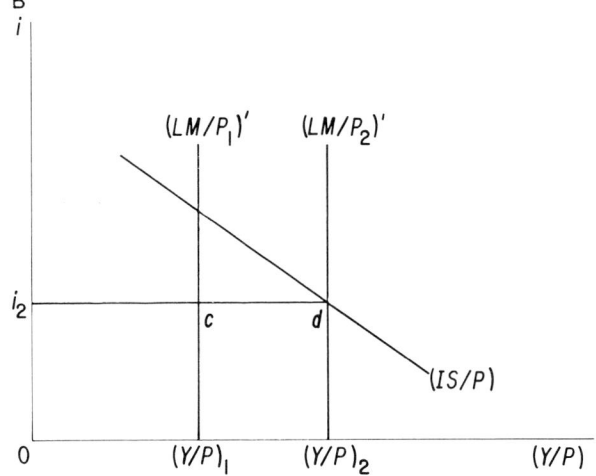

mand for speculative balances. In such a case, the percentage increase in the price level will be greater than the percentage fall in the level of real aggregate demand. As a result, the aggregate demand curve will be negatively sloped, but it will not be a rectangular hyperbola. However, in either case—Keynesian or Classical—the aggregate demand curve is still the schedule of intersection points between the real *IS* curve and a family of real *LM* curves.

The Keynesian speculative demand for money concept raises the possibility of the existence of the liquidity trap. We have already dismissed the "trap" as a curiosity; nevertheless, it may be interesting to consider what the existence of the trap would mean to the aggregate demand function. Consider Figure 16–6. We know from our earlier

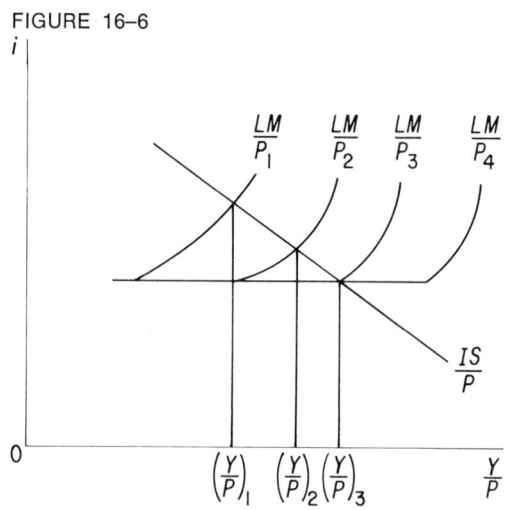

FIGURE 16–6

analysis that the presence of a liquidity trap means that the real LM curve possesses a horizontal section. Furthermore, as the price level falls, the horizontal section of the real LM curve is merely extended. The level of real national income rises, while the interest rate remains constant, and equilibrium is maintained in the money market. Hence, given the real IS curve as the price level falls from P_1 to P_2 to P_3, and the real LM curve is extended rightward, the interest rate will fall and the level of real aggregate demand will increase. However, when the price level falls from P_3 to P_4, the level of real aggregate demand does not increase nor does the interest rate fall. For present purposes, the important point is the fact that the level of real aggregate demand will initially increase as the price level falls; but, after some point, as the price level falls, the level of real aggregate demand will not continue to increase. Hence, we trace out the aggregate demand function of Figure 16–7. After price level P_3 is reached, further decreases in the price level do not cause the level of real aggregate demand to increase. Given the liquidity trap, the level of real aggregate demand can never rise above $(Y/P)_3$.

FIGURE 16-7

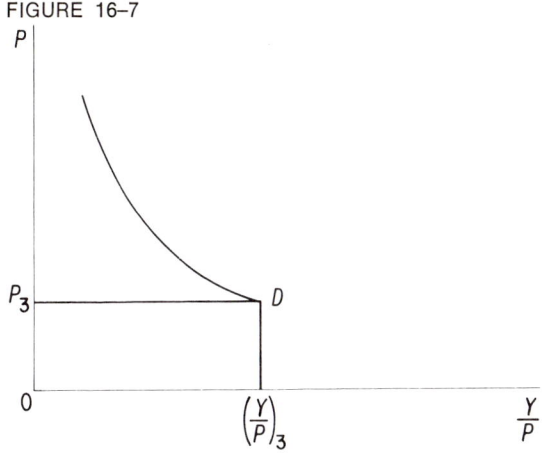

AGGREGATE DEMAND AND AGGREGATE SUPPLY COMBINED

We now bring together the aggregate demand curve and the aggregate supply curve. By so doing, we are able to revisit macroeconomic equilibrium. However, rather than noting the equilibrium levels of real national income and the rate of interest, or the level of real output and real expenditures, we are able to directly determine the equilibrium level of real national output and the equilibrium price level.

While there are several shapes possible for both the aggregate demand and aggregate supply curve, let us assume initially that the shape of the supply curve is described by Figure 16-3, and the demand curve is described by Figure 16-4. In this manner, we can to some extent satisfy both Keynesians and Classicals viewpoints. It should be clear that if the demand curve is negatively sloped throughout, there will always be a determinate equilibrium level of real national income and an equilibrium price level, since the aggregate supply curve begins at the origin. In fact, an equilibrium will be established even in the extreme Keynesian case of the liquidity trap. Of course, equilibrium might not be at the level of real national output consistent with full employment. In Figure 16-8, equilibrium is established at a real output level of $(Y/P)_1$ and a price level of P_1, while the full-employment equilibrium is achieved at a real output level of $(Y/P)_f$. The equilibrium at $(Y/P)_1$ represents a Keynesian *less-than-full-employment-equilibrium*.

FIGURE 16-8

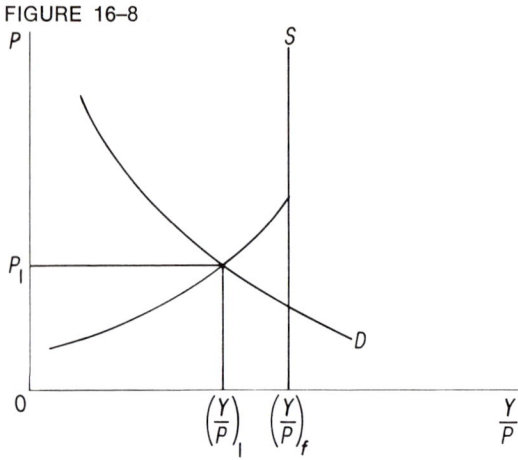

Note that equilibrium is established in the portion of the aggregate supply curve in which money wages are assumed to be inflexible. Since aggregate supply at full employment is greater than the equilibrium level of real output, we say that the economy is not attaining its full potential level of output. Thus, there must be some unemployed resources. Hence, the equilibrium established in Figure 16–8 is described as a "less-than-full-employment equilibrium." The unemployment in the labor market is the result of a money wage rate which has been pegged too high. At the prevailing money wage rate, the quantity of labor demanded is less than the quantity of labor supplied. Consequently, the level of real output will be less than full potential output. Society has incurred a cost by operating at less than full employment. The cost, of course, is the difference between $(Y/P)_f$ and $(Y/P)_1$. However, this cost of unemployed resources would disappear if the money wage rate were permitted to fall. The labor market would be cleared and the full-employment level of real output could be attained. Under these circumstances, the level of real output produced would be $(Y/P)_f$.

It is interesting to note that the real balance effect in the expenditure sector need not push the economy to full employment when money wages are rigid.[2] The presence of the real balance effect in the expenditure sector causes the real IS curve to shift to the right as the price level falls. All this will do, however, is flatten the slope

---

[2] This paragraph should be omitted by those who have not read Chapter 13.

of the aggregate demand curve, but not necessarily push aggregate demand to the full-employment level. Suppose, for example, that we deal with the case of the liquidity trap. In Figure 16-9, as the price

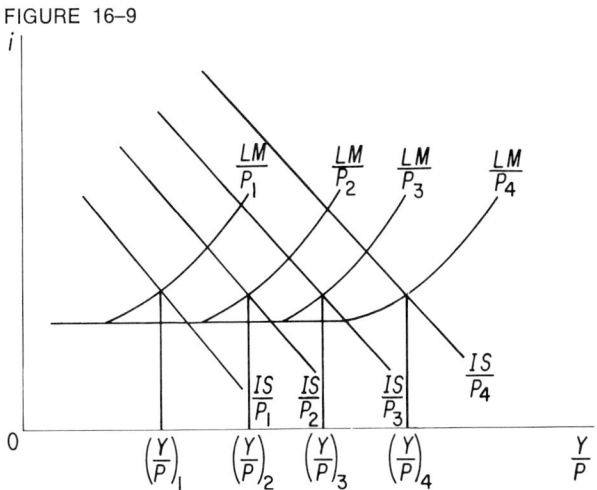

FIGURE 16-9

level falls, the real *LM* curve shifts to the right, and the real *IS* curve shifts to the right also. Despite the existence of the liquidity trap, the level of real output will increase as the price level falls.[3] Thus, in the figure, as the price level falls from P_1 to P_2 to P_3 to P_4, the level of aggregate demand increases from $(Y/P)_1$ to $(Y/P)_2$ to $(Y/P)_3$ to $(Y/P)_4$. This, however, is no guarantee that the full-employment level of real output will be produced. Full-employment can only be guaranteed if the money wage rate is flexible downward, with one possible exception—the existence of the liquidity trap. If the liquidity trap exists, even with flexible money wage rates, it may not be possible to reach any kind of equilibrium, as demonstrated in Figure 16-10. The aggregate demand and aggregate supply curves never intersect. However, with the liquidity trap, an exceptionally strong real balance effect in the expenditure sector could save the day. The aggregate demand curve will be negatively sloped throughout, and will intersect the supply curve, at some price level, at the full-employment

---

[3] We will ignore the rate of interest in this analysis. Even if we employ a real *LM* curve that is horizontal throughout, as the price level falls, the real *IS* curve will shift to the right. Hence, as the price level falls, the level of real aggregate demand will increase.

FIGURE 16-10

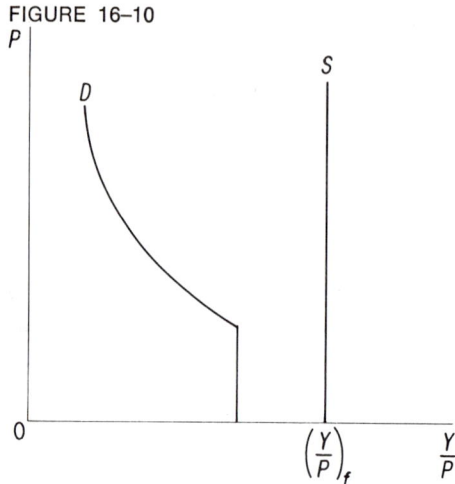

level of real output. This latter point follows from Figure 16-9, which indicates that as the price level falls toward zero, the level of real national output will increase toward infinity. Thus, the aggregate demand curve characterized by the real balance effect ensures full-employment equilibrium given the Classical aggregate supply curve.

We conclude that equilibrium at less than full employment exists only if money wages are rigid in the downward direction, causing the labor market to be out of equilibrium. Hence, less than full-employment equilibrium is not overall equilibrium. It is not overall equilibrium because the labor market is not in equilibrium. We will look more closely at the labor market in a later chapter, since this market appears to be the key to the Keynesian notion of equilibrium.

THE EMPLOYMENT FUNCTION

In defining aggregate supply, J. M. Keynes once suggested that it is a relationship between the level of employment and the level of aggregate demand.[4] Let us try to derive this Keynesian-inspired aggregate supply function.

In Figure 16-11, we have plotted the level of aggregate demand in money terms on the vertical axis, and the nominal level of national income on the horizontal axis. Nominal income is merely the price

---

[4] See J. M. Keynes, *The General Theory of Employment, Interest, and Money* (London: Macmillan and Co., 1960), p. 280.

FIGURE 16-11
$D = C + I$

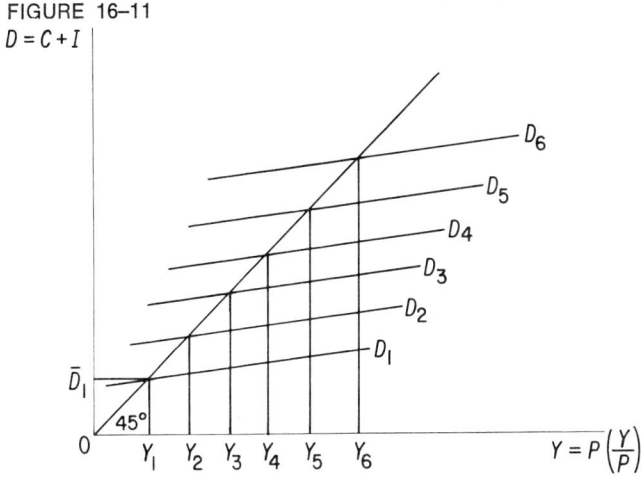

level times the level of real output. The 45° line summarizes the points at which aggregate demand and aggregate income are equal. Six aggregate demand functions are drawn, and six levels of aggregate income are indicated.

Clearly, for each level of nominal income, there are many possible combinations of the price level and the level of real income. For each level of nominal income indicated in Figure 16–11, we are able to trace out a rectangular hyperbola to show those combinations of price level and real output which are consistent with the given level of nominal income, as shown in Figure 16–12. The method employed is identically the same as that used to derive the aggregate demand curve above. Indeed, recall that as the level of the nominal supply of money changed, we would have traced out different aggregate demand curves. Similarly, as the level of the nominal supply of money increases, the level of nominal income increases also. The method is identical to that used above. Therefore, we assume that the greater is the supply of nominal balances, the greater will be the level of nominal national income.

In addition to the various levels of aggregate demand illustrated in Figure 16–12, we have drawn in the aggregate supply curve. We have used a Keynesian aggregate supply curve, but could have used the Classical curve as well. The reason for drawing in the aggregate supply curve is simple. We wish to determine the equilibrium levels of real national output: $(Y/P)_1$ through $(Y/P)_6$. These represent

FIGURE 16-12

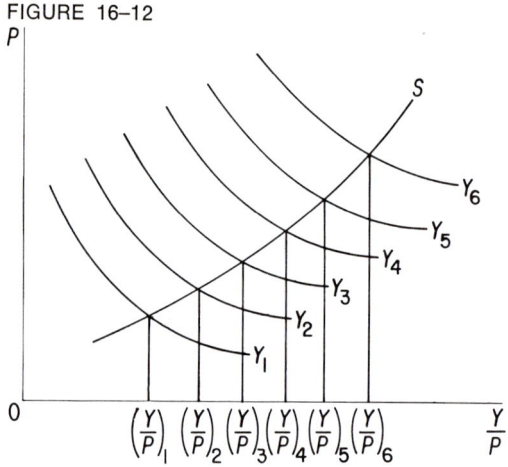

equilibrium levels of aggregate demand in the special Keynesian sense. These equilibrium levels of real output indicate the levels of employment necessary to attain a given level of nominal aggregate demand. For example, if the aggregate demand function is D_1 in Figure 16–11, then the equilibrium level of nominal income is Y_1, and the equilibrium level of nominal aggregate demand is D_1. Given the aggregate supply function, the level of real output, from Figure 16–12, is $(Y/P)_1$; and given the production function, we are able to determine the level of employment required to produce $(Y/P)_1$. Thus, we are able to match up the equilibrium level of aggregate demand, given the aggregate demand function D_1, with the appropriate level of employment.[5] Indeed, we can trace out the entire set of points relating the level of employment to the equilibrium level of nominal aggregate demand. This is the Keynesian aggregate supply function. It is called the employment function, and it appears in Figure 16–13.

The precise shape of the employment function is important. With the aid of Figure 16–14, we can demonstrate that the employment function will have the shape shown in Figure 16–13.

The aggregate supply function is drawn in panel (a) of Figure 16–14. Three constant nominal national income contours are also drawn in that panel. The intersections of the supply function and the income contours determine various levels of price and real output. Let us take contour Y_1. It intersects the aggregate supply curve at

---

[5] The equilibrium level of nominal aggregate demand is sometimes referred to as effective demand.

16 / Aggregate supply 253

FIGURE 16-13

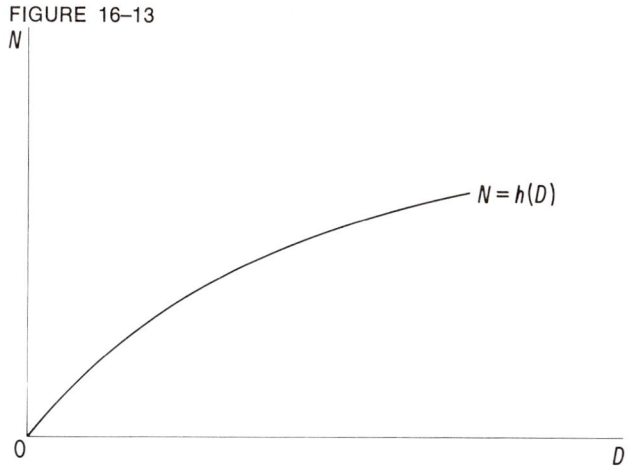

FIGURE 16-14

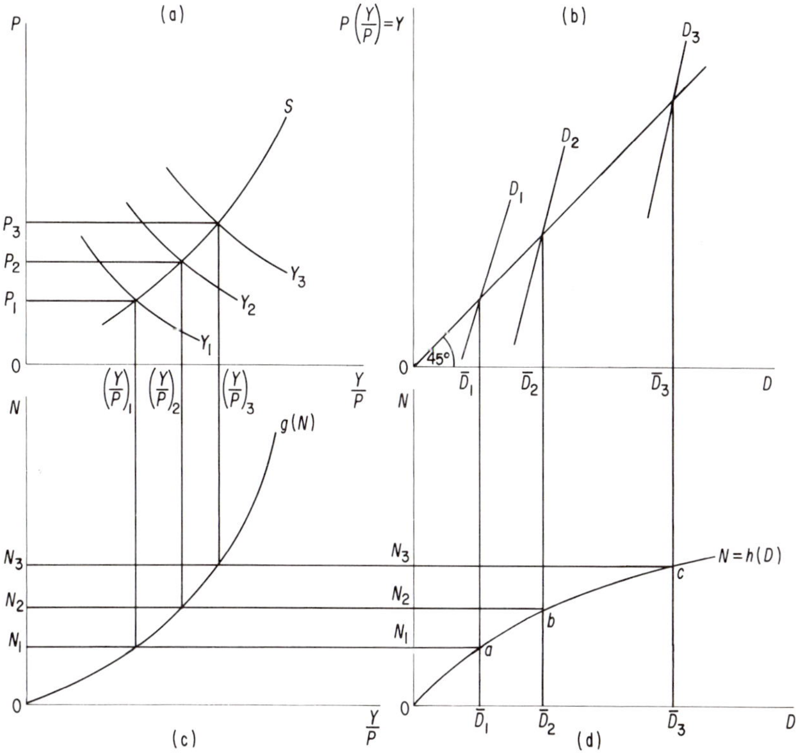

254 The essentials of macroeconomic analysis

price level P_1, and level of real output $(Y/P)_1$. Hence, given the production function in panel (c), the level of employment must be N_1. The aggregate demand function D_1, in panel (b), yields the equilibrium level of nominal aggregate demand $\bar{D}_1$. (Note that, in panel [b], since the axes have been reversed from Figure 16–11, the aggregate demand curves cut the 45° line from below rather than from above.) Finally, in panel (d), the relationship between the level of aggregate demand $\bar{D}_1$ and its employment level N_1 determines point a. Now look at contour Y_2 in panel (a). The price level will be P_2, and the level of real output $(Y/P)_2$. Hence, the level of employment must be N_2. Please note, in panel (a), that $P_2 \times (Y/P)_2$ is exactly twice $P_1 \times (Y/P)_1$. That is to say, the second area is exactly two times the first, or the second equilibrium yields a level of nominal aggregate demand exactly twice as large as the first equilibrium level of nominal aggregate demand. Thus, in panel (b), $\bar{D}_2$ on the horizontal axis must be twice the measure of $\bar{D}_1$. Consequently, we can draw the aggregate demand function D_2.[6] The level of aggregate demand $\bar{D}_2$ and its level of employment determine point b in panel (d). Similarly, point c in panel (d) is determined. However, please note that the area $P_3 \times (Y/P)_3$ (in panel [a]) is exactly two times the area $P_2(Y/P)_2$, so that $\bar{D}_3$ on the horizontal axis of panel (b) is exactly two times $\bar{D}_2$.

It is important to note that as the level of aggregate demand in nominal terms rises, so does the level of employment.[7] However, the level of employment increases at a decreasing rate. Suppose that output was below the full potential level, indicating a relatively low level of employment. As a policy matter, the level of aggregate demand must go up. As it goes up, the level of real output, employment, and the price level all go up.

THE RELATIONSHIP BETWEEN REAL OUTPUT, THE PRICE LEVEL, AND AGGREGATE DEMAND

From Figure 16–14, it is easy to sketch the relationship between aggregate demand, the price level, and the level of real output. In

---

[6] Note that the aggregate demand function in panel (b) may only be drawn after the results in panel (a) are known. The geometry in this analysis is crucial to the precise determination of the shape of the employment function.

[7] Had we used a Classical aggregate supply curve, the level of employment would have remained the same for all levels of aggregate demand. This would have been the full-employment level of labor utilization.

FIGURE 16-15

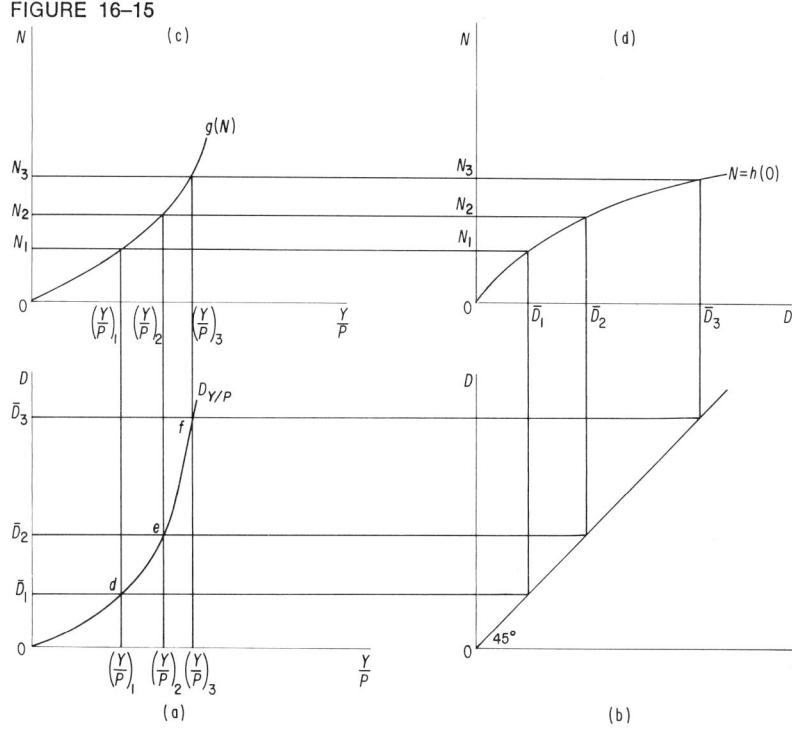

Figure 16–15, we have redrawn the (c) and (d) panels of Figure 16–14. However, in panel (b) of Figure 16–15, we have drawn a 45° line which transfers aggregate demand from the horizontal axis to the vertical axis, and allows us to derive the relationship between aggregate demand and the level of real national output in panel (a).

We know from panel (d) that when the level of aggregate demand is $\bar{D}_1$, there is an employment level of N_1, and from panel (c) a level of real output equal to $(Y/P)_1$. Thus, in panel (a), we obtain point d. With the level of aggregate demand $\bar{D}_2$, the employment level is N_2, and from the production function the level of real output is $(Y/P)_2$. Consequently, point e in panel (a) is obtained. Finally, given aggregate demand level $\bar{D}_3$, and employment level N_3, the level of real output is $(Y/P)_3$, and we obtain point f in panel (a). As the level of aggregate demand goes up, so does the level of real output; however, real output increases at a decreasing rate. Thus, as aggregate demand increases, both real output and employment increase, but at decreasing rates.

Since the equilibrium level of aggregate demand may be defined as the price level times the level of real output, and if the rate of increase in real output falls as the level of aggregate demand increases, it follows that the rate of increase of the price level must be increasing as the level of aggregate demand increases. Thus, we conclude that as long as unemployed labor is available, employment, output, and the price level will rise as aggregate demand increases; however, the increase in employment and real output is smaller and the rise in the price level is larger, the higher is the initial level of employment. Once full-employment is reached, we expect the price level and the money wage rate to increase proportionately in this Keynesian system.

If less than full employment prevails, we may no longer conclude that an increase in the nominal supply of money will cause a proportionate increase in the price level. An easy monetary policy designed to raise the level of aggregate demand will not only increase the price level but also the level of employment and the level of real output. However, the price level will increase at a faster rate as the level of aggregate demand increases; but the increase will still be less than proportionate. Only at full employment will an increase in the nominal supply of money bring about a proportionate increase in the price level.

CONCLUDING NOTE

In this chapter, we looked at the concept of aggregate supply more closely than in previous chapters. We now have several ways of looking at the concept of macroeconomic equilibrium. The later approach is aggregate supply oriented; while the former methods are, for the most part, aggregate demand oriented. The aggregate supply approach allowed us to gain a closer view of the employment sector and, indeed, enabled us to develop an employment function. With this function, we were able to relate the level of employment to the level of aggregate demand, to the price level, and to the level of real national output.

17 Inflation

HERETOFORE, our analysis has treated the price level either as a constant, or as a variable capable of discrete, predictable and stable changes. Our analysis completely ignored expectations of changes in the future price level. In order to include price expectations in our analysis, we must examine the concept of price inflation.

Inflation is usually defined as an economic condition in which there is a rising trend in the price level of output over time. This is not the same as saying that the price level will rise to a new level and remain stable. Instead, inflation means that there is a general, and continuous, upward trend in the price level. In this chapter, we will examine the economic implications of inflation.

DEMAND-PULL INFLATION

One traditional argument used to explain the presence of inflation in the economy is to say that the level of aggregate demand is too high (i.e., exceeds the level of aggregate supply), and so causes prices to rise. If aggregate demand could be reduced, the price level would stabilize and inflation would disappear. In this sense, inflation is the result of excess aggregate demand—it is *demand-pull inflation.*

Since—according to this argument—the only necessary prerequisite for inflation is excess aggregate demand, it is clear that inflation pressures may exist even if the economy is at a less-than-full-employment level of output. In the last chapter, we saw that, from a less-than-full-employment position, the level of real output, employment, and the price level would all increase when aggregate demand increased. However, once full employment was attained, only the price level would continue to increase when aggregate demand increased. Although full employment is not a necessary prerequisite to inflation, we will analyze the full-employment case in detail. Let us assume that the economy is in a position of full employment, as shown in Figure 17–1. The

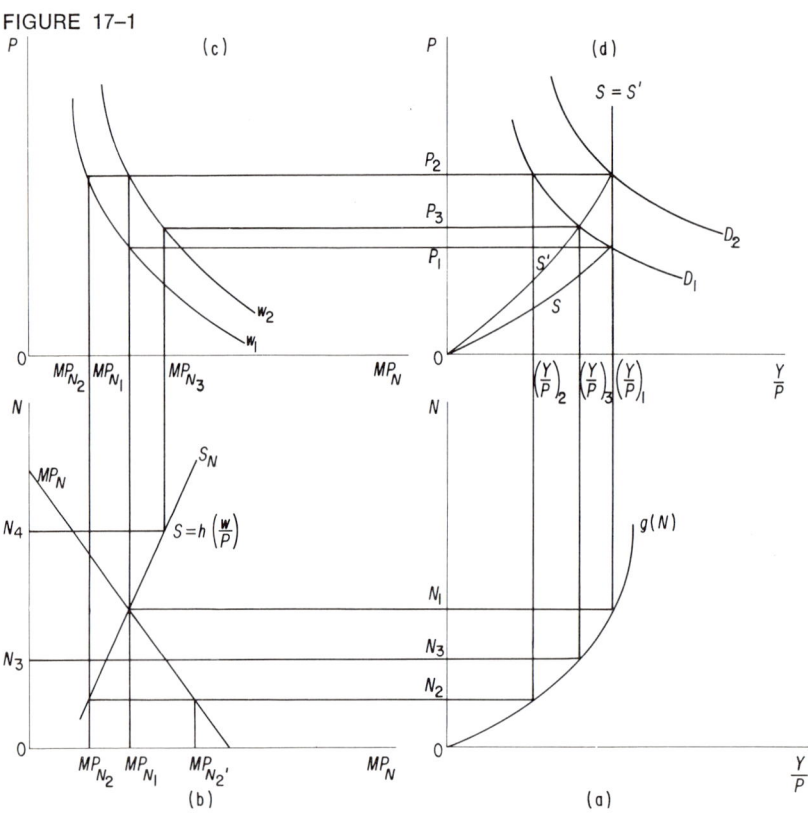

FIGURE 17-1

aggregate supply curves in panel (d) have been drawn to reflect both Keynesian and Classical assumptions, but since we are only concerned with the portion of the supply curve consistent with full employment, we examine the vertical or Classical portion of the curves only. Now suppose that there is an outward shift in the aggregate demand curve to D_2. Clearly, the level of real output cannot increase beyond the full-employment point. However, the price level does increase from P_1 to P_2 given supply curve S. As the price level increases, given a stationary demand for labor curve (the marginal product of labor curve in panel [b]), the money wage rate must increase too. Since the production function has not shifted, the demand curve for labor cannot shift. Hence, the initial money wage rate is too low. The money wage rate must increase from w_1 to w_2, as shown in panel (c). Consequently, the aggregate supply curve shifts to the left. Since the level of labor utilization remains at N_1, the marginal product of labor remains at MP_{N_1}. Thus, the increase in the money wage rate must be proportional to the increase in the price level.

The increase in the level of aggregate demand induced an increase in the price level, and a proportionate increase in the nominal wage rate. However, a new equilibrium has been attained, and unless there is another outward shift in the aggregate demand function, the economy will continue to operate at a stable price level of P_2. There has been a once and for all increase in the price level, nothing more. There is no upward trend. In order for the price level to continue rising, there must be a continual increase in the level of aggregate demand. Ask yourself the question: How might such a phenomenon occur?

Alternatively, you might ask the question: How did the aggregate demand curve shift to the right in the first place? One method of forcing a rightward shift in aggregate demand would have been to increase the money supply. From the previous chapter, you should recall that each aggregate demand function is consistent with a different stock of nominal balances. Hence, as the nominal supply of money increases, the aggregate demand curve shifts to the right. If the nominal supply of money were to continually increase, the aggregate demand curve would continually shift to the right, and the price level would increase continually also. The point is that without the increase in the supply of money, there can only be a one-shot increase in the price level, and therefore, inflation cannot persist.

Do not be fooled. Easy monetary policy is not the only source of price inflation. Another method of forcing a rightward shift in aggregate demand would have been to increase the level of government expenditures, assuming that the increase occurs without an injection of additional money. If the nominal money supply increased to finance the new government expenditures, the situation would be identical to that in the previous paragraph. Under the assumption that the nominal money supply remains constant, if the level of government expenditures were to increase continually, the aggregate demand curve would continually shift to the right, and the price level would rise continually. Without a continuous increase in government expenditures, price inflation cannot persist. Thus, we conclude that an expansionary monetary or fiscal policy—or both—are necessary prerequisites to demand-pull price inflation.

An interesting problem arises when inflationary pressures exist, but prices and wages are not permitted to rise. In such a case, viewing Figure 17–1, with the price level equal to P_1 after the shift of the aggregate demand curve from D_1 to D_2, aggregate demand will exceed aggregate supply and producers will attempt to produce more output because of the apparent shortages. Since more output cannot be produced for the economy as a whole (since it is fully employed), these shortages will persist, and goods and services will not be allocated according to market criteria. Secondary distribution criteria, such as rationing, will have to be employed in the sale of goods and services.

Now let us examine the case of a decrease in aggregate demand. The analysis is somewhat complicated, for there are several different possibilities depending upon the assumptions which are made. In the simplest case, a decrease in aggregate demand causes the reverse of the case just described. For example, viewing Figure 17–1, if the economy is at full-employment equilibrium with price level P_2 and real output level $(Y/P)_1$, when the level of aggregate demand falls from D_2 to D_1, the price level must fall to P_1, and the nominal wage rate must fall to w_1. The aggregate supply curve must shift to the right. Full employment is maintained, but the price level and the nominal wage rate have fallen proportionately. A once and for all fall in the price level occurs, just as described in earlier chapters. However, this is not deflation. It is not a continuous fall in the price level. In order for this to occur, the monetary authority must continuously decrease the nominal supply of money; or the fiscal authority must continuously contract the level of government expenditures (assuming the nominal money supply remains constant).

Now suppose that prices are not flexible downward. Suppose that the price level stays at P_2, and suppose that the money wage rate stays at w_2, despite deflationary pressures. Fewer goods and services will be purchased. In our case, $(Y/P)_2$ is the level of real aggregate demand. If prices cannot fall, producers are only willing to produce this amount—unless for some reason they choose to accumulate inventories. Thus, the level of employment must fall to N_2. Sticky prices and wages have caused the level of employment to decrease. On the other hand, suppose that the price level does not fall, but that the money wage rate does. Unemployment will not be created. The falling money wage rate will cause the real wage rate to fall, and the quantity of labor required to produce the real output level $(Y/P)_2$, namely N_2, will just be supplied. While there is no unemployment, the real wage rate is only MP_{N_2}, while the marginal product of N_2 units of labor is $MP_{N'_2}$ (see panel [b]). Labor is being paid less than it adds to total output, and is being exploited. Labor exploitation has taken the place of unemployment.

In order to illustrate the point about labor exploitation more clearly, we have drawn a labor supply curve into panel (b) of Figure 17–1. Recall from Chapter 11 that the quantity of labor supplied depends upon the real wage rate, and, from equation (11.3b), that the real wage rate equals the marginal product of labor. Furthermore, we know that as the real wage rate increases, the quantity of labor supplied will increase too. The labor supply curve of panel (b) reflects all these points. Thus, the money wage rate falls just enough, from w_2 to w_1, so that the real wage rate falls from MP_{N_1} to MP_{N_2}. The decrease in aggregate demand has not brought with it involuntary unemployment, since the quantity of labor supplied and demanded at real wage rate MP_{N_2} is N_2, although the level of labor utilization in the economy has fallen and exploitation prevails.

It is also possible that the price level is flexible in the downward direction, but that the money wage rate is not. In such a case, we speak of the *wage stop*. Once again refer to Figure 17–1. When aggregate demand falls from D_2 to D_1, given the aggregate supply curve S', the level of real output will fall below the full-employment level. The level of real output falls to $(Y/P)_3$. The level of employment required to supply this level of real national output is N_3. Furthermore, with the money wage rate fixed at w_2, and the lower price level P_3, the real wage rate has increased to MP_{N_3} (see panel [c]). Consequently, the quantity of labor supplied will increase to N_4, while the quantity of labor demanded will fall to N_3. Again, unemployment has been created. However, in all cases where unemployment has been created, it has been caused by the rigidity of the money wage rate. In all cases where the money wage rate was flexible, no unemployment was created.

COST-PUSH INFLATION

In the previous section, we examined the effects of a shift in the aggregate demand function on the price level. Another traditional argument used to explain the presence of price inflation in the economy says that wage rates—as well as the costs of other factors of production—are rising too rapidly. If wages and other factor costs could be reduced, the price level would stabilize, and inflation would disappear. In this sense, inflation is the result of excessively high costs of production—it is *cost-push inflation*.

When there are changes in the costs of production, the aggregate supply curve will shift.[1] When the costs of production increase, the aggregate supply curve shifts to the left; when the costs of production fall, the aggregate supply curve shifts to the right. One cause of a shift in the aggregate supply curve is an increase in the nominal wage, caused either by government action or union pressures.

In Figure 17-2, we have drawn a fully employed economy with the price level at P_1, real output $(Y/P)_1$, a nominal wage rate of w_1, a real wage rate of MP_{N_1}, and a level of employment of N_1. The aggregate supply curve is given by S, while the aggregate demand curve is given by D_1. Suppose that the nominal wage rate is increased to w_2. The aggregate supply curve will shift to S'. Hence, the price level must increase to P_2, given the aggregate demand curve D_1, while the level of real output falls to $(Y/P)_2$. The declining level of real output decreases the quantity of labor demanded from N_1 to N_2. Thus, some unemployment is created. When the nominal wage rate increases to w_2, and the price level rises to P_2, the real wage rate increases to MP_{N_2}, and—at that real wage rate—there is unemployed labor in the amount $N_3 - N_2$. The increase in the nominal wage rate has caused the level of real output to fall, the price level to increase, and unemployment to occur.

Once again, we have had a once and for all increase in the price level. There is no continuous rise in prices. There is no price inflation. However, prices would continue to rise if the nominal wage rate continued to increase. If there is continuing pressure on the part of labor unions, for example, to bid up the nominal wage rate as the price level increases (e.g., cost of living clauses in labor contracts), then there can be continuing upward pressure on the price level.

Since unemployment has been created by the increase in the nominal wage rate, government policy could be directed toward counteracting the rise in unemployment. To accomplish this goal, it is necessary to shift the aggregate demand curve of Figure 17-2 far enough to

---

[1] Indeed we noted in the previous section that a change in the nominal wage rate from w_1 to w_2 shifted the aggregate supply curve from S to S'.

FIGURE 17-2

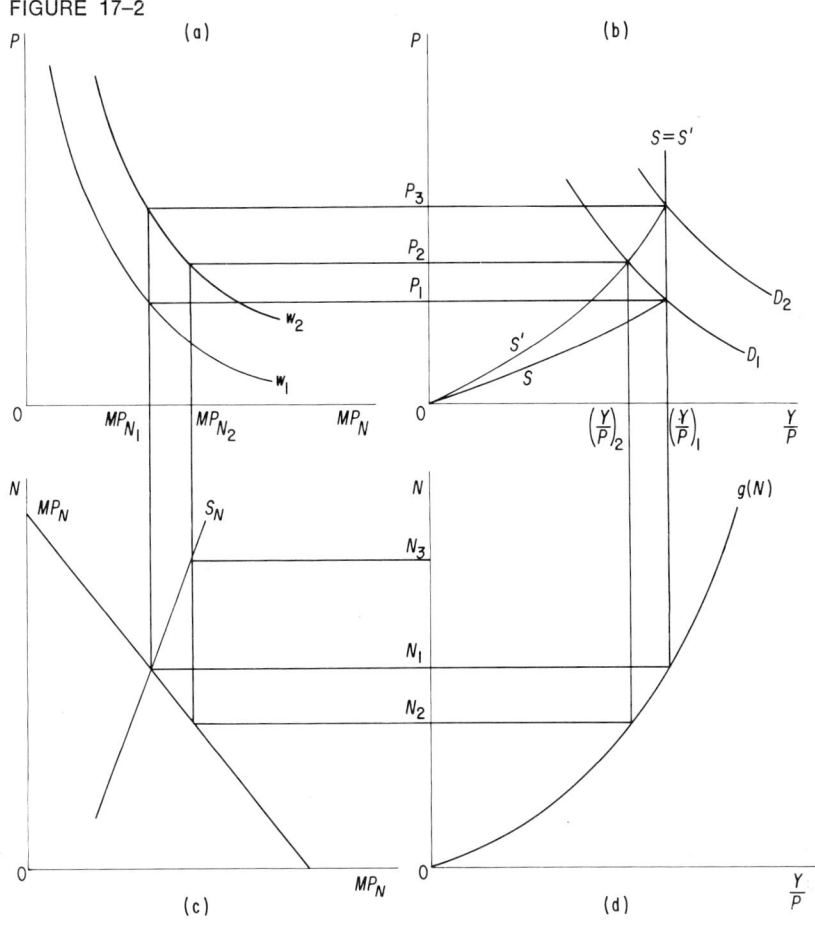

the right so that it intersects the aggregate supply curve at the real income level $(Y/P)_1$. An appropriately large increase in the nominal money supply would shift the aggregate demand curve to the right to D_2, and so the full-employment level of real output would again be reached. The level of employment would rise, and the real wage rate would fall, since the price level would increase to P_3. The increase in the nominal supply of money, together with the rise in the nominal wage rate, has caused the price level to increase to P_3. If this increase in the price level caused another increase in the nominal wage rate, and a corresponding drop in the level of employment, and if fiscal policy was employed to raise the level of employment, the price level would increase still further. In this sense, it is possible for the price level to continue to rise again, but the monetary and fiscal authorities must feed the inflation fires.

EMPLOYMENT AND THE PRICE LEVEL

Our analysis seems to imply that there is a tradeoff between the price level and the level of unemployment. Indeed, we have just seen that both the theory of demand-pull and the theory of cost-push inflation argue that reduced rates of unemployment (higher rates of employment) can be achieved only at the expense of increased rates of price inflation. Thus, as the unemployment rate falls, the rate of price inflation increases. The relationship between unemployment and price inflation is illustrated in Figure 17–3. The relationship is summarized by a function called the *modified Phillips curve*,[2] and has been constructed for our economy over the period 1955 through 1970.

A close examination of the Phillips curve reveals an interesting point. It says that when more than 7.5 percent of the labor force is unemployed, the annual rate of price inflation is zero; i.e., the price level is stable at an unemployment rate of 7.5 percent or larger. When the unemployment rate falls to 5.5 percent, the annual rate of price inflation increases to 1.2 percent. When the unemployment rate falls to 4 percent, the annual rate of price inflation increases to 3.4 percent. Finally, when the unemployment rate falls below 3 percent, the annual rate of price inflation becomes infinitely large. If the Phillips curve is stationary (i.e., if it does not shift), it represents the menu of choices available to society. Society can choose any level of unemployment provided that it is willing to endure the associated rate of price inflation; or society can choose any rate of price inflation provided that it is willing to endure the associated level of unemployment. The options are clear.

The reason for the strong negative relationship between the unemployment rate and the rate of price inflation is not difficult to under-

---

[2] In this contex, see A. W. Phillips, "The Relationship between Unemployment and the Rate of Change of Money Wage Rates in the United Kingdom, 1861–1957," *Economica,* Vol. 25 (November, 1958), pp. 283–99. In this article the curves were empirically derived and were convex. We shall see that they need not be convex. Further discussion of the Phillips curve can be found in P. A. Samuelson and R. M. Solow, "Problems of Achieving and Maintaining a Stable Price Level; Analytical Aspects of Anti-Inflationary Policy," *American Economic Review,* Vol. 50 (May 1960).

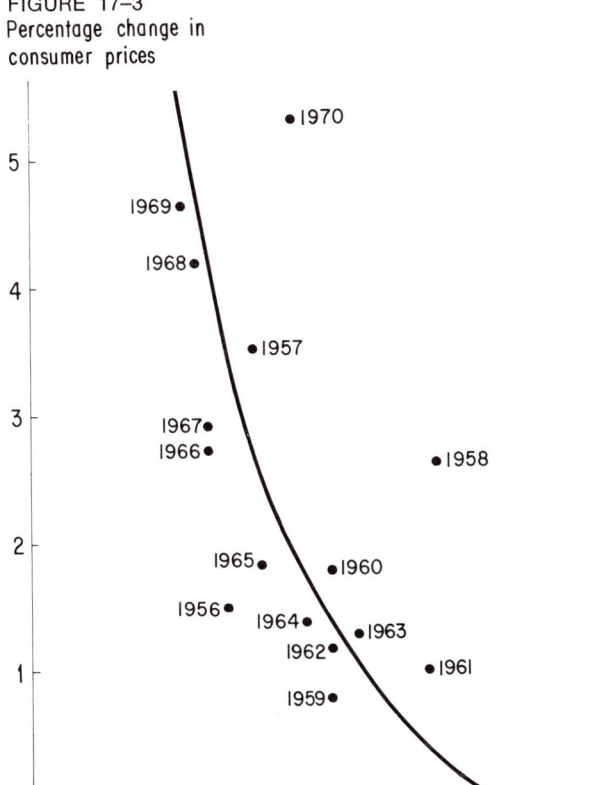

FIGURE 17-3
Percentage change in consumer prices

Source: Calculated by the authors from data reported in *The Economic Report of the President*, January 1972.

stand. Examine Figure 17-4. Figure 17-4 restates a conclusion that we reached in Chapter 16. It says that as the level of aggregate demand increases, the price level increases at an increasing rate; while the level of employment increases at a diminishing rate. It implies that the rate of price inflation increases at an increasing rate as the unemployment rate falls. (Why?) Consequently, the Phillips curve should be convex to the origin, as drawn in Figure 17-3.[3]

---

[3] Note that in Figures 17-1 and 17-2, when the aggregate supply curve shifted from S to S', the slope of the curve increased. This means the rate of change of price with respect to real output increased. The rate of change of price with respect to employment too will increase, when the function of Figure 17-4 shifts to the left.

FIGURE 17-4

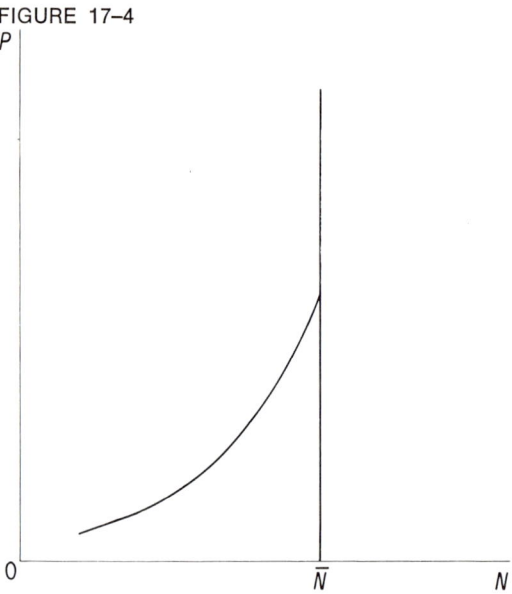

However, there is an important discrepancy between Figures 17-3 and 17-4. The Phillips curve in Figure 17-3 indicates that the rate of price inflation becomes infinitely large at less than the full-employment level; while the aggregate supply curve in Figure 17-4 indicates that the rate of price inflation becomes infinitely large at full employment only. Ask yourself the question: How can one explain the apparent inconsistency? The answer rests with the characteristics of the labor market. At every moment in time, regardless of the wage rate or rate of price inflation, some members of the labor force are *structurally unemployed*. They cannot find employment, even though they are searching, because they do not have adequate job skills; or, as the recent experience of the aerospace industry suggests, they cannot find suitable jobs because they are overskilled. Moreover, at every moment in time, regardless of the wage rate or the rate of price inflation, some members of the labor force are *frictionally unemployed*. They are in the process of changing jobs. Consequently, at some positive unemployment rate, the economy behaves as if it were fully employed.

In an earlier paragraph we alluded to the stability of the Phillips curve. Now we must acknowledge that there is no reason for the Phillips curve to remain stationary forever.[4] Indeed, if actual price inflation leads people to expect more price inflation, the Phillips curve could shift to the right. For example, suppose that labor unions expect the annual rate of price inflation to increase from 2 percent to 3 percent. If the price level rises while labor's nominal wage remains constant, the real purchasing power of labor income would decline. To avoid the decline in real income, labor may bargain for and receive a wage increase sufficient to cover current and all expected future increases in the rate of price inflation (e.g., cost of living escalator clauses in labor contracts). Now recall our discussion of Figure 17–2. As the nominal wage rate rises, the aggregate supply curve shifts to the left causing the price level to increase. The price level increases at every level of output and every level of employment. Therefore, the current unemployment rate is now associated with a higher price level and a faster annual rate of price inflation. In fact, the rate of price inflation increases at every unemployment rate. The Phillips curve shifts to the right as illustrated in Figure 17–5A. Expectations of price inflation have worsened society's choices.

If there is a different Phillips curve for every expected level of price inflation, the Phillips curve cannot portray the long-run tradeoff between unemployment and price inflation. Every time that the economy moves up and along a Phillips curve (i.e., moves toward a lower unemployment rate and a faster rate of price increase), the expectations of future price increases may cause the economy to move vertically onto a higher Phillips curve. See points a, b, and c in Figure 17–5A. In fact, if the expected increase in price inflation is completely anticipated and effectively offset by increases in nominal wages, neither the real wage rate nor the level of unemployment will change. Consequently, the economy will move vertically up the family of Phillips curves from point a to b to c. The line connecting points a through c is usually called the *long-run Phillips curve*. The point at which it cuts the horizontal axis, U^*, is the *natural rate of unemployment*. No price increase—however large—can move the economy to an unemployment rate which is less than the natural rate. In this sense, the long-run Phillips curve suggests the existence of an inflationary equilibrium.

---

[4] For a more detailed discussion of this point, see R. W. Spencer, "The Relationship between Prices and Employment: Two Views," *Monthly Review*, Federal Reserve Bank of St. Louis, March 1969; and G. L. Perry, "Changing Labor Markets and Inflation," *Brookings Papers on Economic Activity*, Vol. 3 (1970).

268 The essentials of macroeconomic analysis

FIGURE 17-5

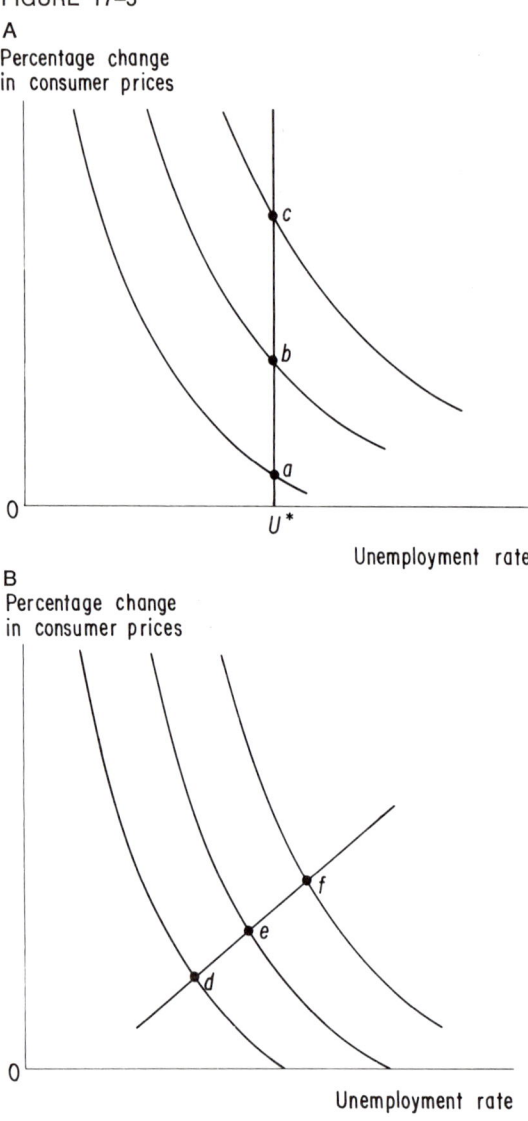

A
Percentage change
in consumer prices

Unemployment rate

B
Percentage change
in consumer prices

Unemployment rate

It is even possible for the long-run Phillips curve to have a positive slope, as illustrated in Figure 17-5B. Suppose that an increase in the supply of money causes the price level to increase. According to Figures 17-1 and 17-2, the increase in the price level causes the nominal wage rate to be bid up, which causes the price level to increase even more. According to Figure 17-2, unemployment is created. Suppose that, in order to reduce the unemployment rate, the money supply is increased once again. The price level must increase again. The nominal wage rate is bid up again, and the price level increases once again. More unemployment is created. More money is created, and the price level continues to rise. The cycle is repeated over and over again. The economy is experiencing a rising rate of unemployment, and an increasing rate of price inflation. In Figure 17-5B, the economy is moving from point d to point e to point f. Once again, the long-run Phillips curve suggests the existence of an inflationary equilibrium.

INFLATIONARY EQUILIBRIUM

When people expect a constant price level, the interest rate i represents both the nominal rate of interest and the real rate of return. However, when there are expectations of price level changes, the equality between the nominal rate of interest and the real rate of return disappears. Consequently, we say:

(17.1) $$i = r + E,$$

where E represents the expected rate of change in the price level, and r is the real rate of return.

From equation (17.1), it is clear that the *real rate of return* is the difference between the nominal interest rate and the expected rate of price change. Since business decisions are generally based on the real rate of return, real investment may be said to depend upon the real rate of interest, or:

(17.2) $$I/P = d/P + er/P,$$

where the level of real investment depends only on the real rate of interest. Now, given the real consumption function and assuming that real consumption depends only on the level of real income, we obtain a real *IS* curve given by:

(17.3) $$Y/P = k(a + d)/P + ker/P.$$

From the point of view of the holder of cash balances, the money rate of interest is most important. Generally, and mistakenly, he is concerned with the nominal return on his cash only, neglecting the real return. Thus, we have the usual real *LM* curve, or:

(17.4) $$Y/P = \frac{1}{k}\left[\frac{1}{P} \cdot \bar{M} - g/P - (h/P)(i)\right].$$

In Figure 17–6, let us assume that full-employment equilibrium is established at point A, if the expected rate of change in the price level is zero ($E = 0$). However, if E is positive (note that the nominal rate of interest is plotted on the vertical axis of Figure 17–6), the

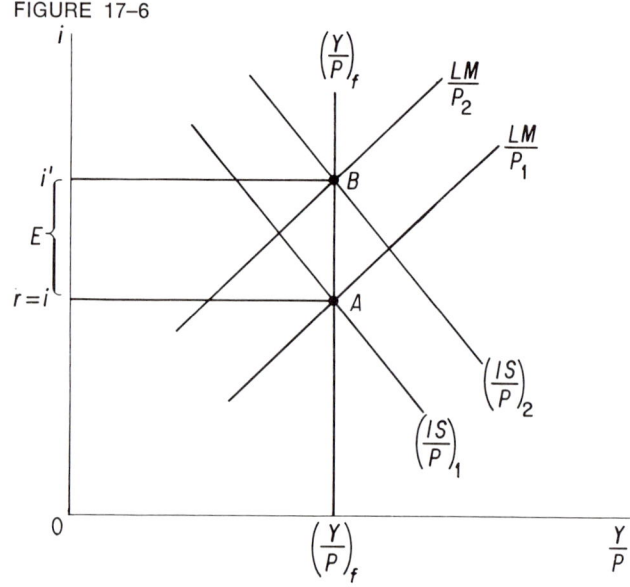

FIGURE 17–6

real IS curve must shift upward from $(IS/P)_1$ to $(IS/P)_2$. The shift occurs because the real IS curve is given in terms of the real rate of interest. For example, if the real rate of interest is 4 percent per annum, and the expected rate of change in the price level is 3 percent per annum, the nominal rate of interest must be 7 percent per annum. The real IS curve will shift up. Given the real LM curve, the level of aggregate demand now exceeds the level of aggregate supply, forcing the price level to increase. Consequently, the real LM curve shifts to the left, and a new equilibrium is established at point B. The equilibrium level of real national output has not changed, but the nominal rate of interest has gone up. In fact, the nominal rate of interest has gone up by an amount equal to E. Furthermore, the mere expectation of a price increase has actually caused the price level to rise. However, this is a once and for all increase in the price level. The price level will not rise continuously. In order to have the price level continue to increase, there must be a continuous increase in the nominal supply of money. It follows, therefore, that with an expected rate of increase in the price level greater than zero and an increase in the stock of money, the price level will increase. However, the overall increase in the price level will be greater than the increase in the level of nominal balances. In our analysis the economy began at a position of full-employment equilibrium, and returned to a position of full-employment equilibrium. It is a case of *inflationary equilibrium*.

THE EFFECTS OF INFLATION

Clearly there is some value in trying to stabilize the price level. The cost of inflation is high. This is not to say that inflation necessarily is costly. For example, if all prices in the economy including the value of all assets, debts, and pensions were to move together in the same proportion and there was no uncertainty about the exact rate of increase in prices, it would follow that the general price level would, in fact, be of no significance at all. Unfortunately, such is not likely to be the case. Prices usually vary in their rates of increase, pensions rarely carry with them cost of living clauses, and it is usually not possible to predict the rate of price increase with certainty.

Since differential price movements exist, it is probable that inflation will produce significant changes in the distribution of income. To a great extent, inflation will represent a tax on many individuals. Salaried workers, for example, are likely to have their real purchasing power fall since their salaries are likely to adjust very slowly to price changes. Those individuals on fixed incomes will surely have some of their real purchasing power "taxed" away. Individuals who receive fixed rent or interest payments will be hurt since renegotiation of contracts, if at all possible, will probably be very costly. Finally, those who hold wealth in the form of currency or bank deposits will be hurt since these claims are fixed in nominal value.

To be sure, some individuals benefit from inflation. Those individuals who earn profits are likely to benefit from price inflation, since costs usually lag behind selling prices in terms of speed of adjustment. Wage earners may gain or lose according to how fast their wages adjust to changes in prices. Conceivably, unions may speed up the rise in wages and thereby protect workers. However, because unions often engage in contracts, it could also be that wage adjustments may not come along rapidly enough, and the position of some workers may be worsened. Finally, those holding wealth in the form of stocks and land may benefit if the prices of these goods rise faster than the general price level. Whatever the case, there will in all likelihood be a redistribution of income because of inflation.

Furthermore, price inflation may have serious affects in the international sector of the economy. If prices rise more rapidly in the United States than in the rest of the world, our products become more expensive when compared with those of foreign competitors. As a result, it is likely that our level of imports will rise and our level of exports will fall. Hence, balance-of-payments problems could arise. Finally, it may be argued that inflation could have a negative affect on economic growth. As we will see in Chapter 19, for growth to occur there must be capital accumulation. With inflation, it could be argued that expectations of continuing inflation causes the marginal propensity to save to fall. Hence, one of the major sources of capital accumulation is weakened. There is really no solid empirical evidence to support this last point, however. Growth in countries has taken place with stable prices, falling prices, and also rising prices.[5]

CONCLUDING COMMENT

In this chapter we have examined the concept and economic impact of price inflation. We defined price inflation as a continuous upward trend in the price level of output. We noted that, under ordinary circumstances, the rate of price inflation and the unemployment rate are inversely related—that is what the modified Phillips curve told us. However, we also concluded that, under circumstances of fully anticipated price inflation, the unemployment rate and the rate of price inflation could move together. In this sense, we noted the possibility of an inflationary equilibrium. Most important of all, we concluded that, although there are several initial causes of price inflation, the inflationary process cannot continue without continuous injections of nominal balances or governmental expenditures.

---

[5] Additional comments on the costs of inflation can be found in Gardner Ackley, "Stemming World Inflation," *The Atlantic Papers,* Vol. 2 (1971), pp. 20–26.

18 Keynesian and Classical economics: The fundamental difference

THROUGHOUT our entire analysis we have used models which have combined elements of Keynesian and Classical economic theories. In the process, we have noted the different assumptions underlying each theoretical point of view. Nevertheless, it is still necessary to analyze—in a formal manner—the fundamental distinction between Keynesian and Classical economic theories. Therefore, in this chapter, we will analyze the concept of money illusion, and the role that it plays in forcing the economic system into a less-than-full-employment equilibrium.

THE WAGE STOP

One fundamental difference between Keynesian and Classical economic models lies in the labor market. Classical economic theory assumes—as we have throughout most of our analysis—that the supply of labor depends upon the real wage rate. Keynesian theory assumes that the supply of labor depends upon the money wage rate. Furthermore, Classical economists assume that the money wage rate is perfectly flexible, while Keynesians assume that the money wage rate is downwardly rigid. We have used both assumptions. Nevertheless, let us examine a Keynesian labor market more closely. It is illustrated in Figure 18–1.

Suppose that there exists a real wage rate $\bar{w}/P_1$, where $\bar{w}$ is defined as a downwardly rigid money wage rate; i.e., it cannot fall. The downward rigidity in the money wage can occur because of a

274   The essentials of macroeconomic analysis

FIGURE 18-1

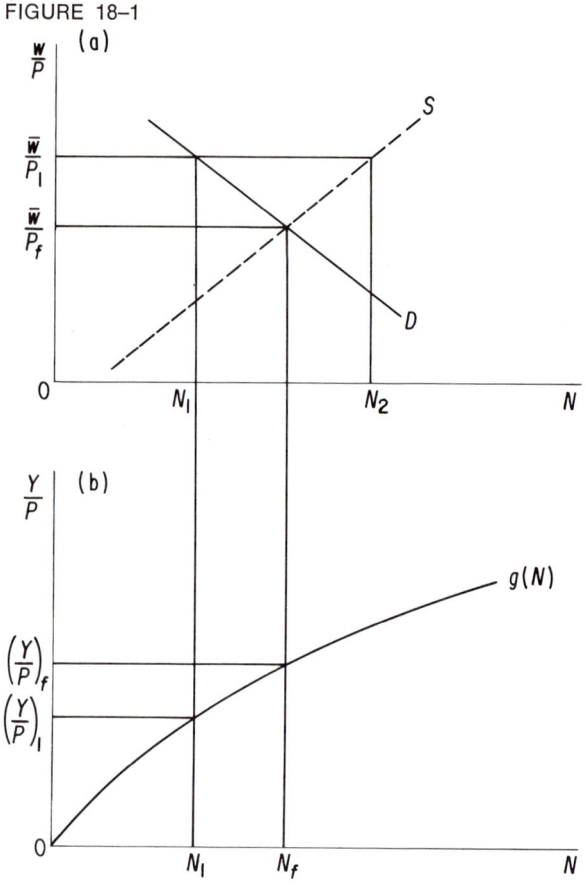

government-imposed minimum money wage rate, or because labor is so well organized and powerful that the wage rate cannot be bid any lower. The condition is called a *wage stop*. In panel a, when the real wage rate is w/P_1, N_1 units of labor are employed. However, N_1 units of labor represents the quantity of labor demanded only; therefore, at the real wage rate w/P_1 there is unemployed labor in the amount $N_2 - N_1$. Furthermore, with N_1 units of labor employed, real output is $(Y/P)_1$—as shown in panel (b). Regardless of the fact that there is unemployment in the labor market, the economy is in equilibrium. In Figure 18-2, when the real output level is $(Y/P)_1$, the real *IS* curve and the real *LM* curve and the employment sector equilibrium curve all come together. Clearly,

FIGURE 18–2

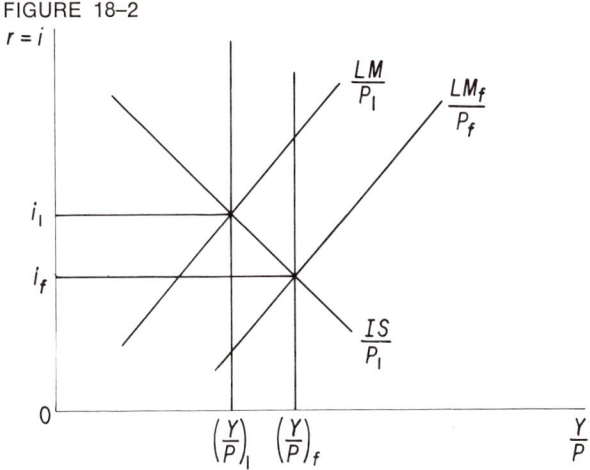

the economy is in equilibrium in spite of the unemployment in the labor market. As we demonstrated in Chapter 17, aggregate demand and aggregate supply can be equal at a level of real output less than the full-employment level.

However, you might ask the question: Is there not some mechanism by which we can induce more employment? There is. Suppose that an easy money policy were to be employed. (See Figures 18–1 and 18–2.) The real LM curve would shift to the right, and the price level should begin to increase. In addition, the level of real output should increase, and continue to increase until the full-employment level, $(Y/P)_f$, is reached. Moreover, the level of employment will reach N_f as the real wage rate falls to $\bar{w}/P_f$.[1] Furthermore, the equilibrium rate of interest falls. Finally, please note that the money supply has increased and the price level has risen, but the increase in the price level must be less than proportionate to the increase in the nominal supply of money. If this were not the case, the real LM curve would shift back to the original curve. Thus, we conclude that, at less than full employment, an increase in the nominal supply of money, followed by a less-than-proportionate increase in the price level, will move the economy to a full-employment equilibrium. The problem of the downwardly rigid money wage rate has been solved. However, the solution required two conditions: the nominal money supply must increase

---

[1] We ignore shifts in the real IS curve caused by the real balance effect.

more than proportionately to the price level, and the supply of labor must be a function of the real wage rate.

The Keynesian assumption, or recognition, of the wage stop implies that the supply of labor is a function of the money wage rate alone. If the money wage rate is frozen by law or institutional forces, the labor supply curve becomes a horizontal line reaching from the vertical axis to the full-employment level of labor utilization—as shown by the labor supply curves in Figure 18–3. Given labor supply curve S_1,

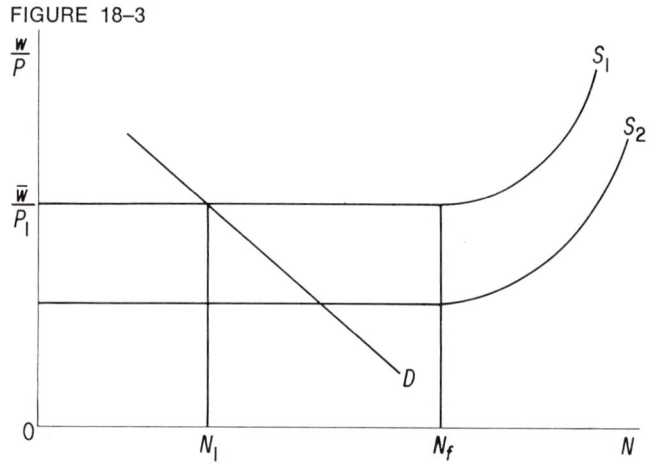

FIGURE 18–3

as the demand curve for labor shifts to the right, the nominal wage rate does not change until the full-employment point is reached. Thus, only after N_f units of labor have been hired does the money wage rate increase. If the price level rises, the supply curve shifts down to S_2. Even though the real wage rate has fallen, the amount of labor supplied at the lower real wage rate is the same as at the higher real wage rate. There is *money illusion* in the labor market. Individuals react to the nominal variables rather than to the real variables. Hence, we may conclude that the Keynesian labor market suffers from money illusion.

At first glance, it might appear that we have now offered a somewhat different definition of full employment than we have used in our analysis. However, the definition is the same. At real wage rate $\bar{w}/P_1$, anywhere from zero to N_f units of labor will be offered. Given a demand for labor curve D and a supply curve S_1, N_f units of labor will be offered. Given the demand for labor curve D with supply curve S_1, N_1 units of labor will be demanded. Thus, there will be unemployment in the amount of $N_f - N_1$. It is *involuntary unemployment*. It represents the number of workers willing to work at the existing level of the real wage rate who are not able to find employment. It is the same definition that we have used.

Since they assume different supply of labor functions, it is interesting to note the difference between the Keynesian and Classical adjustment processes in the labor market. It underscores the importance of money illusion to the Keynesian less-than-full-employment equilibrium. Classical economists argue that if the real wage rate were too high there would be an oversupply of labor. As a result the money wage rate would fall, and so the real wage rate would fall also. By assuming competitive conditions, if the money wage rate fell, the marginal cost curve of output would shift to the right, as shown in Figure 18-4

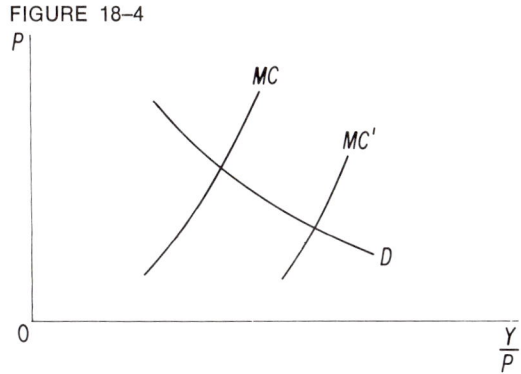

FIGURE 18-4

(the shift from MC to MC'). Consequently, given the demand curve for output, the level of output would increase. Furthermore, the price level would fall. Since the level of output increases, the quantity of labor demanded would increase, and full-employment equilibrium in the market would be established. In Figure 18-5, the adjustment process would ensure that the quantity of labor demanded and supplied would eventually reach N_f; and the initial unemployment $(N_1 - N_2)$ created by the excessively high money wage rate would be removed.

However, Keynesians argue that such an adjustment process could not take place. The Classical argument presumes that all of the new output produced would be purchased; and, the Keynesians believe that this might not happen. Since the marginal propensity to consume

FIGURE 18–5

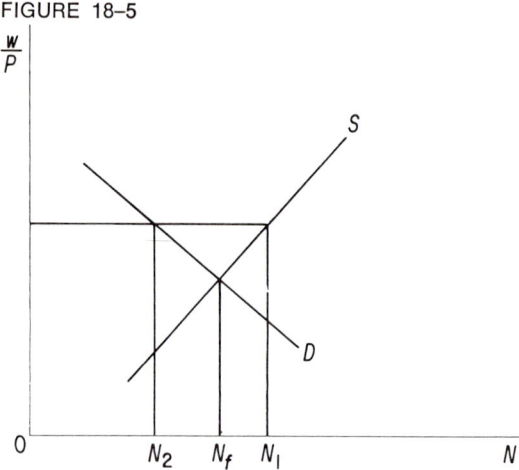

is less than one, all the new output could not be taken off the market as consumption goods. Since all the newly produced output would not be consumed, the level of intended investment would have to increase to guarantee that the higher levels of real output and employment could be sustained. If intended investment does not increase, unintended inventories will accumulate. Thus, prices will fall, and so will the levels of output and employment. Consequently, the economy returns to the original situation. In Figure 18–6, when the money wage rate falls, the level of real output increases by $\Delta(Y/P)$. However, when real output increases, real consumption increases by $\Delta(C/P)$ only, assuming that real consumption depends on real income only. Unintended inventories accumulate in the amount I_v. These inventories must be eliminated for the higher level of real output to be sustained. Otherwise, the level of real output will fall back to its original level. The level of employment will fall back to its original level, and the real wage rate will adjust to its original level. Clearly, if the higher level of real output is to be maintained, the level of real investment will have to increase. That is to say, the aggregate expenditure curve must shift upward and cut the 45° line at point m.

According to Classical theory, the unintended inventories would be eliminated because the price level would fall as the marginal cost curve of output shifts to the right. Hence, the real value of the money supply increases, and, given the demand curve for real cash balances,

FIGURE 18-6

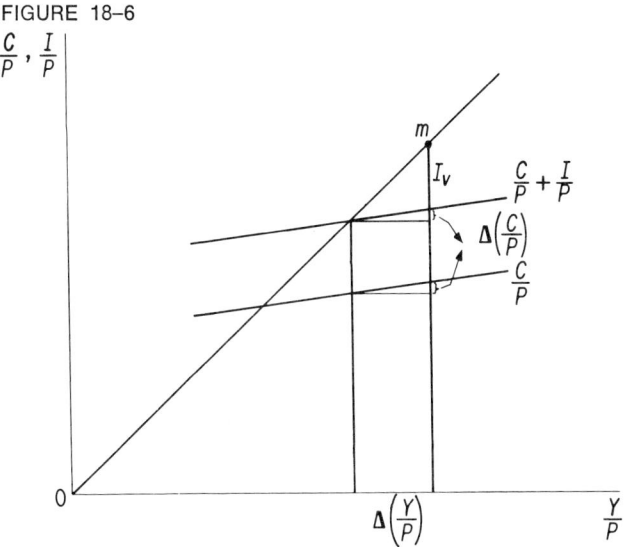

the interest rate falls. The lower interest rate brings forth a higher level of real investment, and so the new level of real output can be sustained.

However, Keynesian theory counters with the argument that the interest rate might not fall because of the existence of the liquidity trap. If the liquidity trap does not exist, the Keynesians would argue that there might not be an increase in the level of investment because the falling interest rate may have little or no effect on the level of investment. The investment function may be *interest inelastic*. Finally, Keynesian theory might be forced to argue that, even if the investment function is not interest inelastic, the new higher levels of real output might not be maintained because wages and prices will not be able to fall sufficiently. There is a wage stop. Thus, even if the price level does fall indefinitely, the existence of the wage stop raises the possibility that the demand for labor curve may never intersect the supply curve of labor at the full-employment level. In Figure 18-3, given the wage stop, it may be that the demand curve for labor will cut the horizontal axis at some point short of N_f. Full employment could not exist, and so the level of real output would have to fall back toward its original level. While the level of real output would certainly be less than the full-employment level, we can only obtain this result by assuming that there exists money illusion in the labor market. Therefore, we conclude that, in the final analysis, it is money illusion in the labor market that forces the economy into a less-than-full-employment equilibrium.

THE QUANTITY THEORY OF MONEY[2]

A second fundamental difference between Keynesian and Classical economic models lies in the money market.[3] Classical economic theory argues—as we have in most of our analysis—that there is a strong positive, and predictable, relationship between the quantity of money (i.e., the supply of nominal cash balances) and the price level. The relationship is called the *quantity theory of money*, and was discussed in detail in Chapter 16. The quantity theory of money predicts two results. From a position of less-than-full-employment, an increase in the supply of money (i.e., nominal cash balances) induces a less-than-proportionate increase in the price level, and forces some increase in the level of real output and employment. However, from a position of full employment, an increase in the quantity of money induces a proportionate increase in the price level, with no increase in the levels of real output and employment.

Keynesian economic theory rejects the quantity theory of money. It argues that even at full employment the quantity theory cannot work unless several conditions are fulfilled. For the quantity theory of money to be valid, Keynesian theory argues that the speculative demand for money must be zero, and that the equilibrium level of aggregate demand must increase in the same proportion as the nominal supply of money. However, we shall see that the Keynesian argument is incorrect, and that the quantity theory of money is invalid only when there is money illusion in the money market.

Let us use a Keynesian framework (e.g., the income-expenditure approach) to analyze the quantity theory of money. Invoking Walras' law, we will ignore the bonds market. Suppose that the level of real expenditures, E/P, depends upon the level of real output, the interest rate, and the level of real cash balances, or:

(18.1) $$E/P = f(Y/P, r, \bar{M}/P).$$

---

[2] In this section we draw on the material developed in Chapter 13. If that chapter has been omitted it is suggested that this section be omitted also.

[3] The section draws heavily upon the work of D. Patinkin. See his "Keynesian Economics and the Quantity Theory," in K. K. Kurihara (Ed.), *Post Keynesian Economics* (Rutgers, N.J.: Rutgers University Press, 1954); and *Money, Interest, and Prices* (2d Ed.; New York: Harper and Row, 1965), especially Chaps. 9–12.

Also, suppose that the full-employment level of real income is given by:

(18.2) $\quad\quad\quad\quad Y/P = (Y/P)_f.$

Therefore, the equilibrium condition requires that:

(18.3) $\quad\quad\quad\quad E/P = Y/P.$

In Figure 18–7, equilibrium occurs at $(E/P)_f$ and $(Y/P)_f$. Obvi-

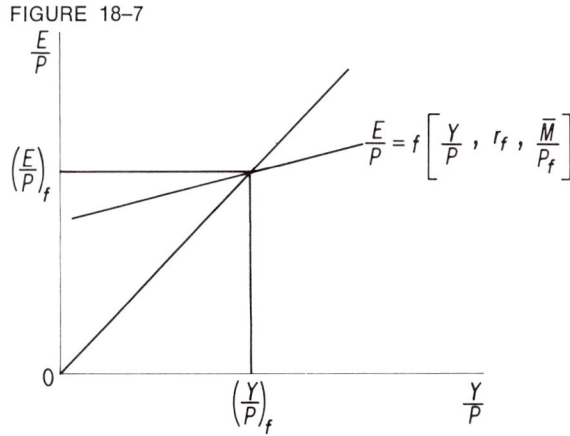

FIGURE 18–7

ously, we have assumed that the interest rate and the price level take their equilibrium values. Otherwise, we could not properly position the real expenditure function. Furthermore, we have assumed that real consumption depends upon the level of real income and the level of real cash balances, while real investment depends upon the real rate of interest (return) and the level of real income.[4]

Moreover, the labor market is characterized by a Classical supply of labor function. Thus, in Figure 18–8, the labor market is in equilibrium at a level of employment equal to N_f, and real wage rate of w_f/P_f. Since full employment exists, the full-employment level of real output must be $(Y/P)_f$.

Finally, the demand for real cash balances is given by:

(18.4) $\quad\quad\quad\quad M^d/P = L_1(Y/P) + L_2(r),$

---

[4] We assume that the real rate of interest return and the nominal rate of interest are equal.

FIGURE 18-8

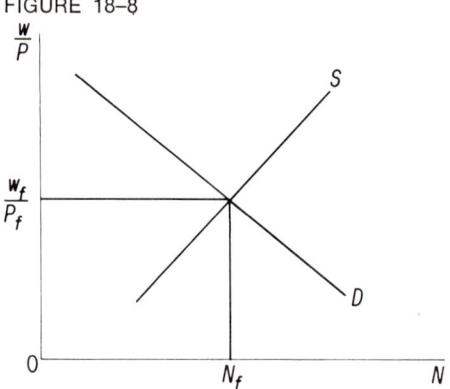

while the demand for nominal balances is given by:

(18.5) $M^d = PL_1(Y/P) + PL_2(r) = PL(Y/P, r)$.

Equilibrium in the money market is illustrated in Figure 18–9,

FIGURE 18-9

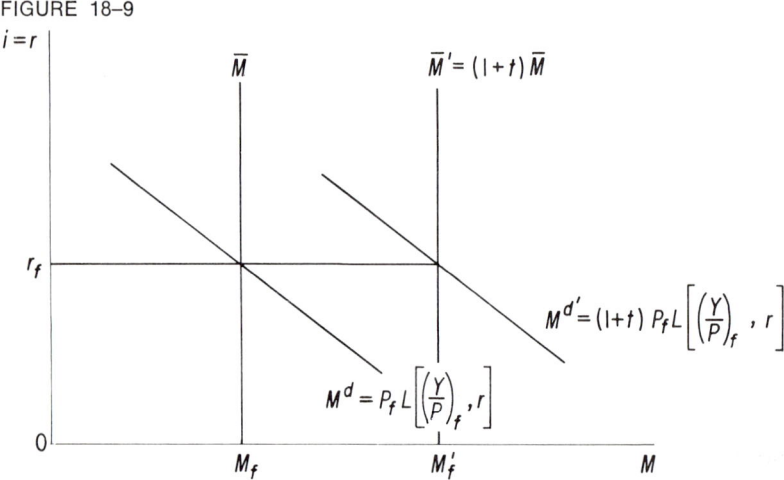

where the nominal supply of money is $\bar{M}$ and the demand for money function is M^d. Equilibrium in the money market requires:

(18.6) $M^d = P_f L[(Y/P)_f, r] = \bar{M}$.

Substituting equations (18.1) and (18.2) into equation (18.3), we obtain:

(18.7) $$(Y/P)_f = f[(Y/P)_f, r, \bar{M}/P_f].$$

Equation (18.7) is the equilibrium equation for the expenditure sector. Labor market equilibrium is given by:

(18.8) $$MP_N = h(w/P),$$

where MP_N represents the demand for labor function and $h(w/P)$ represent the supply of labor function.

Now suppose that the nominal supply of money is increased to $\bar{M}' = \bar{M} + t\bar{M}$, where t is some positive number. Inspecting equations (18.6), (18.7), and (18.8), it can be seen that the equilibrium conditions are satisfied at the values r_f, $(1 + t)w_f$, and $(1 + t)P_f$. In other words, if the right-hand side of equation (18.6) is multiplied by the quantity $(1 + t)$, the left-hand side must be multiplied by the same quantity, and so the new equilibrium price level must be $(1 + t)P_f$. Thus, the new money wage rate must be $(1 + t)w_f$. Consequently, the aggregate expenditure function is the same before and after the injection of the additional money into the system. It is true that the aggregate expenditure function, E/P, will initially shift up due to the increase in real cash balances; however, since the upward shift means that aggregate demand is greater than aggregate supply, the price level must rise, real balances must fall, and the real expenditure function must shift down to its original position. (Additionally, the demand and supply functions in the labor market will not shift. Why?)

However, the results are somewhat different in the money market. The supply curve of nominal balances, shown in Figure 18-9, shifts rightward to $\bar{M}' = (1 + t)\bar{M}$. Ignoring the liquidity trap, the demand curve for nominal balances must shift to the right if the equilibrium rate of interest is to remain at r_f. We know that the demand curve for nominal balances depends upon the price level, and the equilibrium equations indicate that the price level will increase to $(1 + t)P_f$. Thus, the demand curve for nominal balances will shift to the right to $M^{d'} = (1 + t)P_f L[(Y/P)_f, r]$. Thus, the equilibrium level of nominal cash balances is $\bar{M}'_f$. Clearly, the price level has increased in the same proportion as the nominal supply of cash balances.

The quantity theory of money has worked. What of the Keynesian criticisms? Clearly, our analysis has included a nonzero speculative demand for money. After all, equation (18.4) does include the speculative demand for money. Furthermore, aggregate money expenditures are initially $P_f(E/P)_f$. After the increase in the money supply, aggregate money expenditures increase to $(1+t)P_f(E/P)_f$. The level of aggregate money expenditures has increased in proportion to the increase in the nominal supply of money. We did not have to assume this latter point, however. It is an outcome of our model. Therefore, both criticisms are satisfied.

Interestingly, we need not assume a real balance effect in order to have the quantity theory hold. Suppose that we remove the real balance effect from the real expenditure function. Equations (18.6) and (18.8) ensure that the price level rises proportionately with the nominal supply of money, and that the rate of interest does not change.

It must be emphasized that we have chosen a system free of money illusion. If the expenditure function, for example, was influenced by nominal rather than real cash balances, the rigid quantity theory would not hold. A larger portion of the adjustment burden would be placed on the interest rate (it would have to rise), and so an increase in the quantity of money would cause a proportionately greater increase in the price level and the nominal wage rate. Once again, these results occur because of the presence of money illusion in the expenditure sector.

Earlier in this chapter, we saw that the presence of money illusion in the labor market raises the possibility of a less-than-full-employment equilibrium. Now we know the reason. The quantity theory of money cannot work when money illusion is present in the labor market. At first glance it may appear that it is the presence of a rigid money wage rate which hinders the quantity theory of money. However, it is money illusion. From equations (18.6), (18.7), and (18.8) we can see that, if the real wage rate were rigid, the quantity theory would work and the nominal values of the variables would adjust as necessary.

Finally, let us assume that money illusion exists in the money market. Suppose that the equilibrium equation for the money market is given by:

(18.9) $\qquad L_1[P(Y/P)_f] + L_2(r) = \bar{M}.$

In real terms,

(18.10) $\qquad L_1[P(Y/P)_f]/P + L_2(r)/P = \bar{M}/P.$

Please note that the transactions-precautionary demand is consistent with the form $PL_1\,[(Y/P)_f]/P$. Consequently, if the nominal supply of money and the price level increase proportionately, the transactions-precautionary demand for money is free from money illusion. However, when the nominal supply of money and the price level increase proportionately, the real amount of money people choose to hold for speculative purposes changes. It changes because there is money illusion in the speculative demand for money. In other words, the second term on the left-hand side of equation (18.10) displays money illusion, while the first term on the left-hand side of the equation does not.

Suppose that there is an increase in the nominal supply of money. Aggregate demand now exceeds aggregate supply. The price level will increase. From equation (18.9), we see that the quantity of nominal balances demanded for transactions-precautionary purposes increases and, given our form of the transactions-precautionary demand function, the increase in the transactions-precautionary demand is proportional to the increase in the quantity of money. Even so, the total demand for money does not increase in the same proportion as the quantity of money. There has been no change in the speculative demand for money. There is an excess supply of money which will be diverted to the bonds market. The price of bonds will be bid up, and the interest rate will fall. There will be an increase in the quantity of money demanded for speculative purposes as the rate of interest falls. The excess supply of money will be absorbed by the increased transactions-precautionary demand caused by the higher price level, and by the increased quantity of speculative balances demanded caused by the lower interest rate. A new equilibrium is reached with a lower interest rate and a higher price level. Most important, the price level has increased more than proportionately with the quantity of money. Of course, if the speculative demand for money were equal to zero, there would be no excess supply of money, and so the quantity theory of money would work.[5]

Clearly, the quantity theory does not work when money illusion exists. Thus, it appears that the major distinction between the Keynesian and Classical theories is the existence of money illusion in the Keynesian theory. If this phenomenon exists in the money market, the quantity theory will not work. If it exists in the labor market,

---

[5] Also, one of Keynes's criticisms of the quantity theory would have been removed. However, the criticism it seems is borne out of money illusion, and not a weakness in the quantity theory.

the quantity theory will not work. If it exists in the expenditure sector, the quantity theory will not work. In the final analysis, it is money illusion which forces the economy into a less-than-full-employment equilibrium. It is the fundamental difference between Keynesian and Classical macroeconomic theory.

THE MONETARIST—NEO-KEYNESIAN CONTROVERSY

Throughout this book we have emphasized the importance of money in the determination of the level of economic activity. By emphasizing the importance of money, we implicitly suggest that monetary policy also plays an important role in the determination of the level of economic activity. However, fiscal policy is employed to effect the level of economic activity also. This suggests that the government sector, and its effect on aggregate demand, is important in influencing the level of real national output.

In the previous section, we compared the Classical version of the determination of the level of economic activity with the Keynesian version by employing the Keynesian income-expenditure approach. We saw that the quantity theory of money could survive the Keynesian attack in a purely theoretical setting. Still, a debate exists between one group which places major emphasis on fiscal policy as the primary economic stabilizer and a second group which feels that money and, therefore, monetary policy is most important as the primary economic stabilizer. The former group, the present-day followers of J. M. Keynes, is referred to as the Neo-Keynesians or the "New Economists." The latter group, led by the persuasive Milton Friedman of the University of Chicago, is referred to as the Monetarists.

The Neo-Keynesians feel that both fiscal and monetary policy are significant determinants of the level of real output. However, primary emphasis is placed on the influence of fiscal policy on the components of aggregate demand—consumption, investment, and government expenditures. Monetary policy, though important, plays a secondary role in that its primary function is to influence interest rates and, thereby, affect the level of aggregate demand through the investment component. Expansionary fiscal policy will have, for example, a substantial impact on the level of real output and employment provided monetary policy cooperates with fiscal policy. Thus, as the level of output increases, the demand for money will increase causing the rate of interest to rise. This tends to reduce the level of investment and to partially offset the expansionary fiscal policy. Neo-Keynesians would, therefore, ask for an easy money policy to avoid the rise in interest rates. However, they do not feel that the lack of monetary cooperation will totally offset the effects of expansionary fiscal policy.

On the other hand, the Monetarists contend that changes in the money supply are the single most important factor in the determination of the level of real output, employment, and prices. Essentially, they argue that there is a direct link between money and the level of economic activity.

According to the Monetarists, emphasis should be shifted from the various Keynesian components of aggregate demand to the demand for money. They argue that there is a stable and predictable relationship between the amount of money people wish to hold and the level of national output. Monetarists hold that the proportion of national output over which people wish to keep command in money form is constant. They feel that $\bar{k}$ is stable or that V (velocity) is stable. Thus, for example, if the level of money national income $(P(Y/P))$ is $600 billion and $\bar{k}$ is $1/6$, then society wishes to hold money balances in the amount of $100 billion. Suppose further that the actual supply of money is $100 billion. Equilibrium prevails because

(18.11) $$M^d = \bar{k}(P(Y/P)) = \bar{M}$$
$$100 = 1/6(600) = 100.$$

Let the money supply increase by $50 billion. People are now forced to hold $150 billion even though, due to the fact that the level of national income is $600 billion, they wish to hold only $100 billion. Since society is now forced to hold $150 billion and they wish this to be $1/6$ of national income, then it follows that national income must rise to $900 billion—since $1/6$ of $900 billion is $150 billion. Equilibrium can only be reestablished when the amount of money held is $1/6$ of national income. Note that it is the level of money national income that increases to $900 billion. Either P or Y/P or both will change. Naturally, if society is fully employed, it is only P that will increase.

Furthermore, the Monetarists are critical of the adjustment process mechanism of fiscal policy as suggested by the "New Economists." For example, if a deficit is created in an attempt to stimulate the economy, the Monetarists argue that the policy will not be effective unless it is accompanied by an increase in the supply of money. An increase in government spending will initially cause the level of national income to increase. However, the increase in the level of national income, given $\bar{k}$, will cause people to choose to hold higher levels of cash balances. In order to acquire these higher levels of cash balances, individuals will decrease their consumption expenditures. As a result, the decrease in private spending will just balance the increase in government spending. The equilibrium level of national output will not change. Fiscal policy, as a result, is rendered useless.

Consequently, Monetarists argue that only monetary policy should be employed to stabilize the economy. However, they do not necessarily argue for discretionary monetary policy on the part of the monetary authority. Rather, many of them argue that a monetary rule is preferred to discretionary power. Because the time lag between the point at which the need for a policy change occurs and the time at which a policy change is felt is fairly long, it is often the case that the current economic situation has changed and, by the time the new policy is felt, it is the exact opposite of the policy then needed.[6] Friedman, therefore, concludes that the money supply should increase annually at a rate equal to the long-run growth in real productivity.

The Neo-Keynesians, of course, refute the arguments of the Monetarists by arguing that the economy is more complex than the Monetarists seem to believe. Some changes in aggregate demand, for example, come about because of strikes and changing expectations about future events. Furthermore, the Neo-Keynesians argue that it is possible that changes in aggregate demand will cause changes in the demand for money which require that the monetary authority respond to the "needs of trade" and so increase the supply of money.

The final argument against the Monetarist position is one that has occupied much of the attention of economists in recent years. Neo-Keynesians argue that $\bar{k}$ and, therefore, V is not stable. Consequently, they argue that the Monetarist model is subject to much error in prediction. On the other hand, Neo-Keynesians argue that aggregate demand is much more stable than velocity. That is to say, they argue that the multiplier is more stable than the velocity of money. As a result a Keynesian model is a better predictor of the level of economic activity than is a Monetarist model. This argument is, of course, one that can be, and has been, subjected to empirical verification.

We accept, or reject, an economic model on the basis of its ability to predict more, or less, accurately than some alternative economic model. If the Monetarist model predicts a level of gross national prod-

---

[6] The subject of lags is discussed in Chapter 20.

uct, a rate of price inflation, and a level of unemployment which more closely approximates the actual levels than the Keynesian model, then the Monetarist model provides a more appropriate description of aggregate economic activity. If the Keynesian model has more predictive reliability, then it provides the better description of aggregate economic activity. Thus, the crux of the argument between the Keynesians and the Monetarists is simply which theory best approximates (i.e., explains and predicts) the actual behavior of gross national product, prices and unemployment.

The economic forecasts of a Keynesian model and a Monetarist model are summarized in Table 18-1. The table compares the values

TABLE 18-1

		Monetarist	Keynesian	Actual
1969	GNP*	$ 957.2	$ 940.0	$ 948.0
	Price inflation	4.1%	3.5%	5.1%
	Unemployment	3.5%	4.1%	3.6%
1970	GNP*	$ 997.2	$1,007.0	$ 988.4
	Price inflation	4.6%	4.0%	5.7%
	Unemployment	5.4%	4.6%	5.9%
1971	GNP*	$1,076.9	$1,066.0	$1,072.9
	Price inflation	4.0%	4.0%	3.4%
	Unemployment	5.7%	5.6%	5.9%

* In billions of dollars.
Source: *Monthly Report of the Federal Reserve Bank of St. Louis*, March 1972, p. 35.

of current-dollar gross national product, the rate of price inflation and the level of unemployment as predicted by each model with the actual values of the same variables for the years 1968 through 1971. The predictions of the Monetarist model were consistently closer to the actual figures, except for the 1969 forecast for gross national product where the Keynesian model performed slightly better, and the 1971 prices forecast where the two models performed equally. Conclusions as to the comparative merits of each model, based on the data Table 18-1 must be drawn with care. There are only three years of comparative data, and the evidence is somewhat mixed. Nevertheless, the evidence does suggest (but not prove) that there is a reasonably strong link between the money supply and economic activity. Consequently, the Monetarist hypothesis that monetary policy is the most appropriate tool for controlling aggregate economic activity cannot be cast aside. The evidence suggests that the Monetarist model is just as good, if not better, as a predictive tool than the Keynesian model.

CONCLUDING COMMENT

In this chapter, we have argued that the fundamental difference between Keynesian and Classical macroeconomic theories is the concept of money illusion. A Keynesian economic system is characterized by money illusion in both the labor market and the money market (and the bonds market, when it is included in the analysis), whereas a Classical economic system is not. Most important, you should realize that it is the presence of money illusion which prevents the Keynesian economy from reaching its full-employment potential. Also, you should realize that, in the absence of money illusion, the quantity of money is a primary determinant of the level of economic activity.

Finally, we noted that the Classical and Keynesian debate still exists today in the form of the controversy between the Monetarists and the New Economists. This debate is basically the same as that which existed for many years over the use of the Keynesian theory of the determination of the level of economic activity and the quantity theory of money as a theory of the determination of the level of economic activity.

19 Some growth economics

OUR AGGREGATE equilibrium models of the preceding chapters have demonstrated many of the difficulties in attaining and maintaining full employment. We also noted in Chapter 17 that there exists a tradeoff between a high level of employment and a stable price level. Usually a stable price level and a high level of employment are two objectives of any society.

A third objective of society is economic growth—growth in the levels of real national output. Generally, *economic growth* is defined to mean growth in the level of real national output per capita. Presumably, such a measure indicates the per capita share of the national output. If this share is increasing, growth is occurring; if not, growth is not taking place. In this chapter, we will examine the factors necessary for real national output to increase. Obviously, if real national output per capita is increasing, the growth in real national output must be greater than the growth in the size of the population. In much of our analysis, we will assume that population is not growing, and therefore, we can speak of growth in real national output and real national output per capita simultaneously.

There is no reason to assume that a rise in the level of real national output per capita necessarily increases the welfare of society. If everyone's share of national output were to increase, the welfare of society might increase. However, this is not what real national output per capita tells us. It tells us nothing of the distribution of real national output. Real national output per capita could increase with most of

292   The essentials of macroeconomic analysis

the gains accruing to a few people, while many people are experiencing a decline in their share of national output. In such cases, it would be extremely difficult to say that the welfare of society has increased. In fact, the change in society's welfare can never be known until the distribution of output is known, and until subjective values can be placed on the utility or satisfaction each individual receives from his share of the real national output. Nevertheless, in this chapter, we shall examine the concept of economic growth.

THE REQUIRED RATE OF INVESTMENT

Our models have looked at gross investment only. That is to say, in our models, the term real investment included the portion of total investment used to replace old and worn-out real investment as well as the portion of investment used to increase the capital stock. Ignoring technical progress, if gross investment does not exceed replacement requirements, the full-employment level of output cannot change. However, when there is net investment, the size of the capital stock will increase. With a larger capital stock, the productive capacity of society increases, and so we have a potentially higher level of real national output.

Clearly, during periods of economic prosperity, there will be a great deal of net investment, and the productive capacity of society will increase. In order for the increase in productive capacity to be utilized, the level of aggregate demand must increase. However, ask yourself the question: How much must aggregate demand increase in order to keep pace with the increase in productive capacity? The answer is important. If full employment prevails, and the productive capacity of society increases, aggregate demand must increase also. If it does not increase, there will be unused capacity, and the level of employment will fall. We must know the size of the required increase in aggregate demand.

Interestingly, the level of investment serves a dual purpose. Investment increases the level of the capital stock, and so raises the level of productive capacity. In addition, investment is a component of aggregate demand. Accordingly, increases in investment raise aggregate demand as well as increasing the level of the capital stock. Thus, to answer the question as to how much aggregate demand must rise to ensure that the additional capital stock is utilized, we must focus on the level of investment and understand its dual role in the process of economic growth.

We can determine the increase in investment expenditures required to raise the level of aggregate demand to the productive capacity of society in Figure 19–1. Suppose that, in the current time period, busi-

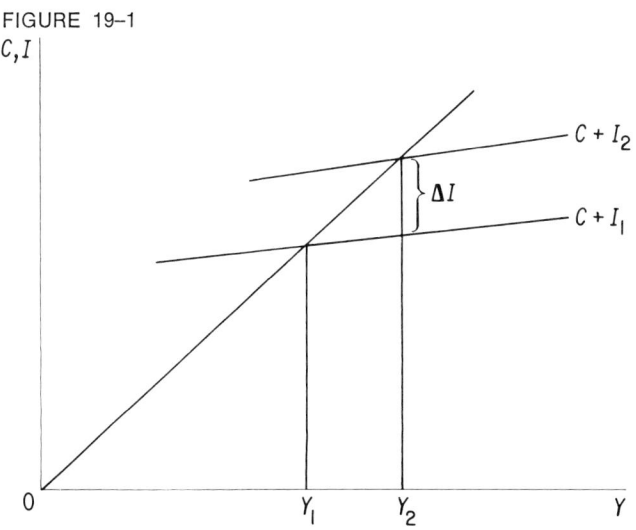

FIGURE 19–1

ness firms have sufficient capital to produce the current level of output Y_1. (We have for simplicity assumed a constant price level, so that our variables are given in both real and nominal terms.) Suppose that investment expenditures equal I_1 when the level of income equals Y_1. Now suppose that entrepreneurs expect output to increase to Y_2 next year. In order to justify these expectations, however, the level of aggregate demand must increase by enough so that the output level Y_2 is consumed. The aggregate demand function must shift upward by ΔI to $C + I_2$.

However, we have not really answered the question: How much must the level of investment increase so that the additional productive capacity is utilized? A more complete answer is illustrated in Figure 19–2. To begin, the increase in national income required to employ the current year's investment is:

(19.1) $$(Y_{t+1} - Y_t) = \sigma I_t,$$

where σ represents the output-capital ratio. For example, if it takes

294 The essentials of macroeconomic analysis

FIGURE 19-2

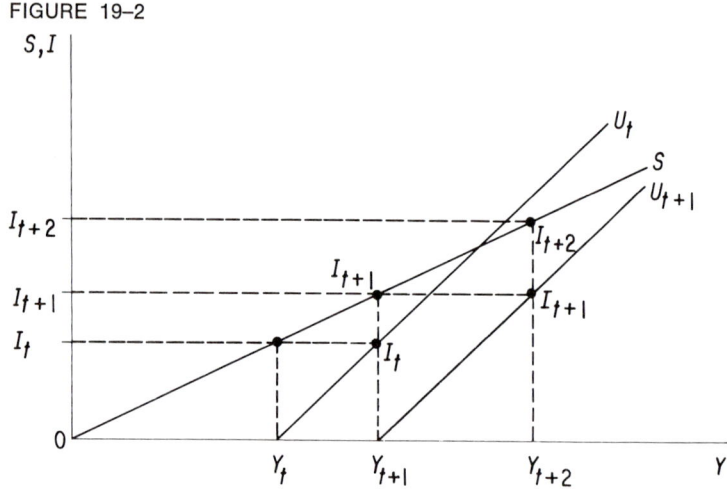

$3 billion of investment to produce $1 billion of output, the output-capital ratio is 1:3. In other words, if σ equals $\frac{1}{3}$, each additional $3 billion of investment increases the productive capacity of the economy by $1 billion. The relationship between investment and productive capacity, summarized in equation (19.1), is illustrated in Figure 19-2 by the curves labeled U_t and U_{t+1}. The curve U_t indicates that a level of investment equal to I_t raises society's productive capacity to Y_{t+1}. The slope of the U curves equals $(1/\sigma)$.

Furthermore, the level of savings available to finance investment expenditures is:

(19.2) $$S_t = (1 - b)Y_t,$$

where $(1 - b)$ represents the marginal and average propensities to save. Equation (19.2) is the long-run savings function from Chapter 5. It is illustrated in Figure 19-2 by the curve labeled S. Its slope equals $(1 - b)$.

Now suppose that the economy is at an initial level of income equal to Y_t, an initial level of savings equal to S_t, and an initial level of investment equal to I_t. From equation (19.1), given I_t, we know that the productive capacity of the economy will increase to Y_{t+1}. (Move along the U_t curve.) However, if aggregate demand and income are to expand by amounts sufficient to utilize the new productive capacity, investment must increase to I_{t+1}—at I_{t+1} investment exactly offsets the level of savings S_{t+1}. Investment must increase by an amount equal to $(I_{t+1} - I_t)$, or $I_t I_{t+1}$, or:

(19.3) $\quad (I_{t+1} - I_t) = 1/k(Y_{t+1} - Y_t),$

where k is the multiplier.

Equating equation (19.1) and (19.3), the growth rate of investment required to maintain full-capacity equilibrium is:

(19.4) $\quad k(I_{t+1} - I_t) = \sigma I_t,$

$$\frac{(I_{t+1} - I_t)}{I_t} = \sigma/k.$$

Thus, we conclude that the proportional increase in investment required to raise the level of aggregate demand as much as the level of productive capacity is σ/k, or the output-capital ratio times the marginal propensity to save.[1] If full-employment equilibrium is to be maintained over time, the *required rate of growth* of investment is directly proportional to the output-capital ratio and the marginal propensity to save.[2]

It is interesting to note that the equilibrium growth rate of investment requires that the absolute level of investment expenditures increase by a continually increasing amount. Society must invest larger and larger amounts, if it is to utilize all its productive capacity—even though capacity grows at the constant rate σ/k. Again, the point is easily seen in Figure 19-2. As the economy's capacity increases from Y_t to Y_{t+1} to Y_{t+2}, the required increase in investment increases from $I_t I_{t+1}$ to $I_{t+1} I_{t+2}$. A constant rate of growth in productive capacity requires an ever increasing amount of investment. The conclusion is interesting because it says that today's investment must always be greater than yesterday's savings for a full-employment equilibrium to be maintained in a growing economy. Our static equilibrium condition merely stated that intended savings and intended investment must be equal for equilibrium to prevail—in the absence of growth. The difference is fundamental.

Furthermore, it is interesting to note that our analysis implies that the level of investment and the level of output grow at the same rate. We will demonstrate this shortly.

Finally, please note the nature of the importance of investment.

---

[1] Recall from Chapter 4 that the multiplier is simply 1/MPS.

[2] For a more complete discussion, see E. Domar, "Expansion and Employment," *American Economic Review*, Vol. 37 (March 1947), pp. 34–55.

First, an increase in the level of aggregate demand depends upon the rate of increase in investment. The absolute level of investment is of no importance. Second, the increase in productive capacity depends upon the amount of investment as well as the rate of increase in investment. Also, note that our earlier models looked only at the level of investment in determining the level of aggregate demand; while this model stresses the importance of the growth of national income to maintain full employment. The former is called *static* economic analysis, the latter is called *dynamic* economic analysis.

THE WARRANTED RATE OF GROWTH

Alternatively, we could ask the question: How much increase in national income is required to generate sufficient demand, using the acceleration principle, to absorb the increased national output? In our model of the accelerator effect, from Chapter 6, we noted that the level of induced investment depended upon the change in income between time periods multiplied by the capital-output ratio, or:

(19.5) $$I_t = v(Y_t - Y_{t-1}).$$

Assuming that intended investment equals intended savings (from equation [19.5] in equilibrium, we have:

(19.6) $$v(Y_t - Y_{t-1}) = (1 - b)Y_t,$$
$$(Y_t - Y_{t-1})/Y_t = (1 - b)\sigma,$$

where σ, the output-capital ratio, is equal to the reciprocal of the capital-output ratio v. Furthermore, we note that the multiplier k is equal to $1/(1-b)$. Therefore:

(19.7) $$(Y_t - Y_{t-1})/Y_t = \sigma/k.$$

The term on the left-hand side of equation (19.7) is called the *warranted rate of growth*. It is the rate of growth of national output required to keep the economy in equilibrium, over the long run, when induced investment depends upon the change in the levels of national income over several periods of time.[3]

We can now see the sense of our conclusion that, in equilibrium, the level of investment and the level of national output grow at the

---

[3] For a more detailed analysis, see R. Harrod, *Towards a Dynamic Economics* (London: Macmillan and Co., 1951).

same percentage rate. If we equate equations (19.7) and (19.4), we find:

(19.8) $$\frac{Y_t - Y_{t-1}}{Y_t} = \frac{I_t - I_{t-1}}{I_t} = \sigma/k.$$

The required rate of growth in induced investment is equal to the warranted rate of growth in national income.

These alternative approaches differ. In the first case, we noted that investment created excess capacity, and an increase in aggregate demand was necessary to justify the increased capacity. In the second case, we assumed that business firms possess the desired amount of capital, and an increase in national output is required to induce firms to continue investing. In the first case, excess capacity precedes a change in aggregate demand. In the second case, an increase in aggregate demand calls for greater productive capacity. Neither approach is superior, both processes probably occur together.

SOME GENERAL COMMENTS ON GROWTH MODELS

From a logical viewpoint, both models are airtight. However, the assumptions of the models are questionable. For example, the models assume a constant capital-output ratio and a constant marginal propensity to save. These assumptions are satisfactory if you believe that aggregate demand is based on the multiplier analysis alone. However, we have seen in past chapters that money plays an important role in the determination of the levels of aggregate demand and economic activity. Yet the monetary sector does not appear in these growth models. If the rate of growth of output does not reach σ/k, there could be unemployment. However, appropriate monetary action could alter σ and k, and thereby set equilibrating adjustments toward full employment into motion.

Suppose that there is unemployment, and the monetary authority reacts by increasing the supply of nominal balances. With increased money balances, the marginal propensity to consume may increase, and so the marginal propensity to save may fall. Consequently, the growth rate falls. Furthermore, as the rate of interest falls, the level of investment should increase. At the margin, therefore, more capital per unit of output is used, since capital is substituted for labor as the price of capital falls. Thus, the output-capital ratio falls, and the growth rate falls, but aggregate demand and output increase. Note that both the required rate of growth and the warranted rate of growth fall as the marginal propensity to save and the output-capital ratio fall. Since the growth rate falls, it follows that full employment will be maintained with a lower rate of growth.

The declining rate of growth (both required and warranted) is not reflected in the growth models we have viewed, since the monetary sector is ignored. Sustained growth at a high rate requires that the money stock increase as aggregate demand increases. If it does not, as the demand for money increases, the interest rate will increase, causing the level of investment to fall, which in turn, reduces the level of aggregate demand. In addition, sustained growth requires that resources be sufficiently mobile so that they will shift from one industry to another as the composition of aggregate demand changes. Labor in particular must be mobile. As capital expands in one industry, at the expense of another industry, the labor force which is complimentary to capital must move also. Finally, there must be changes in the level of technology in order to sustain a high rate of growth.

Our concept of a high rate of growth has implied that the rate of growth of national output is greater than the rate of growth of population. Accordingly, per capita national output increases. If it does not, we will observe economic stagnation and a *stationary state*. In theory, stagnation and a stationary state result from the law of diminishing returns.

It is clear from our previous analysis that increased investment expenditures are necessary to sustain economic growth. However, as more net investment occurs, more capital becomes available and its productivity declines. Consequently, the returns to capital tend to fall. Since capital is less productive, the output-capital ratio declines, and so capacity increases by a smaller amount than was previously expected. Given the consumption function, less investment would then be needed for the level of aggregate demand to increase by enough to sustain the full-employment equilibrium. Moreover, with the falling productivity of capital, profits probably fall, and so business savings will fall. Hence, the marginal propensity to consume is likely to increase. The consumption function becomes more steeply sloped, and the level of investment required for full employment falls even more. All this is illustrated in Figure 19–3, where C_1 represents the original consumption function, and C_2 represents the new consumption function with the greater marginal propensity to consume. With the original consumption function, it is necessary for investment to increase

FIGURE 19-3

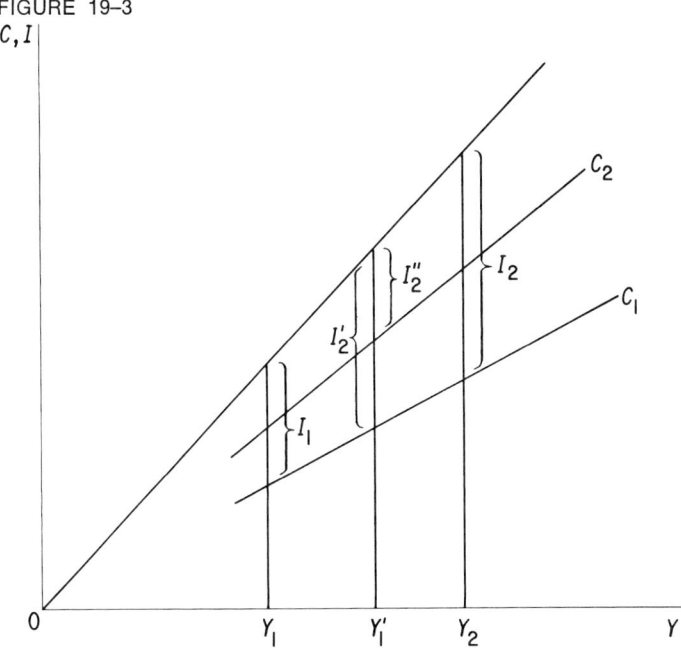

to I_2 to avoid excess capacity. However, with the productivity of capital falling, the level of investment need only reach I'_2. With diminishing returns, capacity can only increase to Y'_1. With consumption function C_2, however, the level of investment must only be I''_2 for the level of output Y'_1 to be a full-employment level to output.

However, diminishing returns are still consistent with growth, even though the rate of growth of national output is less than it would be in the absence of diminishing returns. Of course, as the rate of growth of national output declines, the possibility of declining per capita output increases. Furthermore, as the returns to capital fall, net investment will fall too. Eventually net investment will reach zero, at which time the stationary state is reached. Diminishing returns to capital, therefore, will eventually induce a stationary state of economic stagnation.

However, technological change can and does prevent stagnation from occurring. Technological change shifts society's production function upward, and thereby increases the productivity of capital. In viewing the rising costs of labor, it is altogether probable that technological innovations which are labor saving will come forward and prevent the stationary state from occurring. We will present more on technical progress shortly.

NEOCLASSICAL GROWTH THEORY

To overcome some of the weaknesses of the growth models just discussed, we must look at neoclassical growth theory.[4] In our previous discussion, if both labor and capital were to increase by 1 percent, the level of output would increase by 1 percent also. In neoclassical growth theory, the same result holds. It means that the aggregate production function is homogeneous of the first degree.[5] Furthermore, in our previous discussion, if labor were to increase by 1 percent, but capital remained constant, there would be no increase in the level of output. The additional labor would remain unemployed. The analysis required a simultaneous increase of 1 percent in capital for output to increase by 1 percent. It is a conclusion derived from equation (19.8). With neoclassical theory, on the other hand, a 1 percent increase in the utilization of one factor of production, while the other factor of production is held constant, does lead to an increase in output. Hence, if labor were to increase, while capital remained constant, output would increase. Also, in our previous analysis, technology was assumed to be constant. In neoclassical growth theory, technology is allowed to change.

If output depends upon capital and labor, the aggregate production function is:

(19.9) $$Y = f(K, L),$$

where K represents the stock of capital, and L represents the supply of labor (we assume that all labor is employed). The aggregate production function is characterized by diminishing returns. The change in output is given by:

(19.10) $$\Delta Y = MP_L \Delta L + MP_K \Delta K,$$

where MP_L represents the marginal product of labor, and MP_K repre-

---

[4] For a more detailed analysis, see R. M. Solow, "A Contribution to the Theory of Economic Growth," *Quarterly Journal of Economics,* Vol. 70 (February 1956), pp. 65–94.

[5] A production function is homogeneous of the first degree when an equiproportionate change in all inputs leads to a similar change in output. Thus, if all inputs double, output will double also.

sents the marginal product of capital. Dividing both sides of equation (19.10) by Y, we find:

(19.11) $\quad \Delta Y/Y = MP_L(\Delta L/Y) + MP_K(\Delta K/Y),$

where $\Delta Y/Y$ represents the growth rate of national output. We can rewrite equation (19.11) as:

(19.11a) $\quad \Delta Y/Y = MP_L(L/Y)(\Delta L/L) + MP_K(K/Y)(\Delta K/K),$

where $\Delta L/L$ and $\Delta K/K$ represent the growth rates of the labor force and the capital stock, respectively.

If the production function is homogeneous of the first degree, and if each factor of production (capital and labor) is paid according to its marginal contribution to output, the total output of the economy will be distributed to labor and capital.[6] In other words,

(19.12) $\quad\quad\quad\quad Y = MP_L L + MP_K K,$

or,

(19.12a) $\quad\quad\quad 1 = MP_L(L/Y) + MP_K(K/Y).$

If we set MP_K (K/Y) equal to r, we know from equation (19.12a) that MP_L (L/Y) must equal $(1-r)$. In other words, if capital and labor are the only factors of production, the portion of total output not paid to the capital stock must be paid to the labor force—assuming that all output is distributed. Substituting these values into equation (19.11a), we find:

(19.13) $\quad\quad\quad \Delta Y/Y = (1-r)(\Delta L/L) + r(\Delta K/K).$

Equation (19.13) summarizes a fundamental relationship in neoclassical growth theory. The implications of equation (19.13) for economic growth differ significantly from those obtained from our earlier growth models. According to equation (19.13), there will be a change in output when either capital or labor changes. In the earlier models, growth in the level of national output required an increase in the capital stock. If only the labor force grows, there would be no change in the level of output. Not so in the present case. For example, if $\Delta L/L$ equals 5 percent and $\Delta K/K$ equals zero, output will increase by a percentage amount equal to $(1-r)0.05$. If $\Delta L/L$ equals 5 percent and $\Delta K/K$ equals 3 percent, output will grow at a percentage

---

[6] A detailed discussion of this point can be found in R. D. G. Allen, *Macro-Economic Theory: A Mathematical Treatment* (London: Macmillian and Co., 1968), pp. 44–48.

rate equal to $(1-r)0.05 + (r)0.03$. If r equals 0.20, total output will increase by 4.6 percent. In our earlier analysis, total output would have increased only by 3 percent; i.e., the growth rate of output could not exceed the rate of increase in investment.

The neoclassical growth process, summarized in equation (19.13), is illustrated in Figure 19–4. The vertical axis measures the growth

FIGURE 19–4

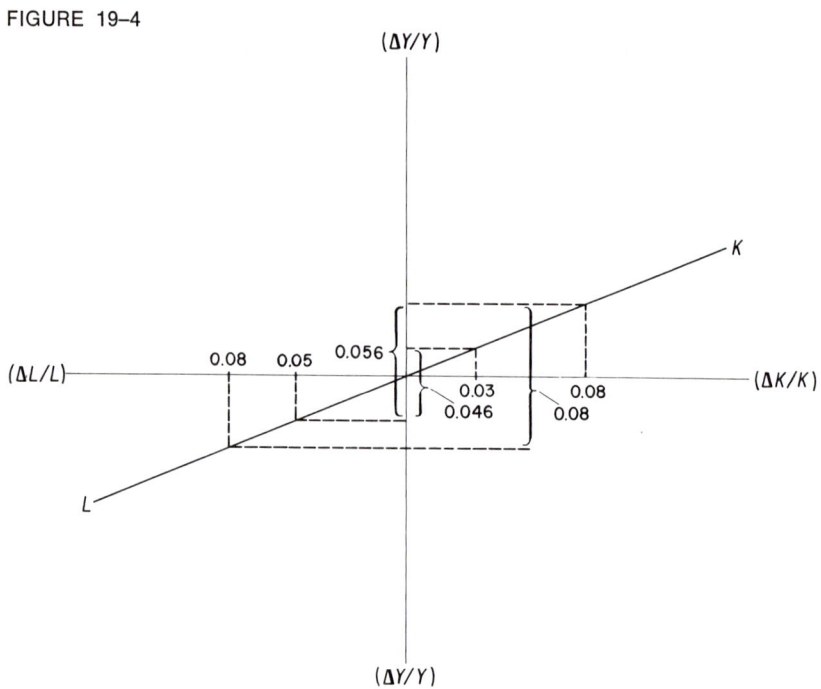

rate of national output, and the horizontal axis measures the growth rate of labor and capital. The curve labeled K represents the growth contribution of the capital stock, assuming that r remains constant. Its slope equals r. Similarly, the curve labeled L represents the growth contribution of the labor force, assuming that r remains constant. Its slope equals $(1-r)$. If the labor force grows at 5 percent per annum and the capital stock grows at 3 percent per annum, national output will grow at 4.6 percent per annum. If the labor force continues to grow at the 5 percent annual rate, but the capital stock grows at an annual rate of 8 percent, national output will grow at an annual rate of 5.6 percent. If both factors of production grow at an 8 percent rate, national output will grow by 8 percent also.

It is interesting to note that, in the first example, ($\Delta L/L = 0.05$ and $\Delta K/K = 0.03$), total output grows at a rate faster than the capital stock, but slower than the labor force. In the second example, ($\Delta L/L = 0.05$ and $\Delta K/K = 0.08$), total output grows at a rate faster than the labor force, but slower than the capital stock. The growth rate of national output lies between the growth rates of the factors of production. In the third example, ($\Delta L/L = 0.08$ and $\Delta K/K = 0.08$), total output grows at the same rate as labor and capital. Clearly and more precisely, in all three examples, the growth rate of national output is a weighted average of the growth rates of the factors of production; and the growth contribution of each factor of production is determined by its marginal physical productivity.

It is also interesting to note that, depending on the relative growth rates of capital and labor, the level of output per capita and the output-capital ratio may change. In the first example, output per capita falls, while the output-capital ratio rises. In the second example, output per capita rises, while the output-capital ratio falls. In the third example, output per capita and the output-capital ratio are constant. These conclusions are easily demonstrated.

Common sense indicates that the growth rate of per capita output equals the growth rate of total output minus the growth rate of the population (in our example, the labor force), or:

(19.14) $\quad \Delta(Y/L)/(Y/L) = (\Delta Y/Y) - (\Delta L/L),$
$\qquad\qquad\qquad\quad = (1 - r)(\Delta L/L) - (\Delta L/L) + r(\Delta K/K),$
$\qquad\qquad\qquad\quad = -r(\Delta L/L) + r(\Delta K/K),$

where $\Delta(Y/L)/(Y/L)$ represents the rate of growth of per capita output. Therefore, if $(\Delta K/K)$ is greater than $(\Delta L/L)$, (Y/L) must be increasing. Similarly, the growth rate of the output-capital ratio equals the growth rate of total output minus the growth rate of the capital stock, or:

(19.15) $\quad \Delta(Y/K)/(Y/K) = (\Delta Y/Y) - (\Delta K/K),$
$\qquad\qquad\qquad\quad = (1 - r)(\Delta L/L) + r(\Delta K/K) - (\Delta K/K),$
$\qquad\qquad\qquad\quad = (1 - r)(\Delta L/L) - (1 - r)(\Delta K/K),$

where $\Delta(Y/K)/(Y/K)$ represents the rate of growth of the output-capital ratio. Therefore, if $(\Delta L/L)$ is greater than $(\Delta K/K)$, (Y/K) must be increasing. Finally, if $(\Delta L/L)$ equals $(\Delta K/K)$, equations (19.14) and (19.15) indicate that (Y/L) and (Y/K) are constant.

However, there is an important qualification to the conclusions based on equations (19.14) and (19.15). Since the aggregate production function is subject to diminishing returns, neither output per capita nor the output-capital ratio can rise indefinitely. Indeed, neoclassical growth theory predicts that, in the absence of technical progress, output per capita and the output-capital ratio eventually become constant. In other words, labor, capital, and output eventually grow at the same percentage rate.

In order to understand the last point, let us reexamine equation (19.13). We know, from our previous analyses, that the absolute increase in the capital stock (ΔK) is equal to the level of investment expenditures. We also know that the level of investment expenditures, since it must equal the level of savings in equilibrium, is a constant proportion of income; i.e., the increase in the capital stock, or the level of investment expenditures, equals $(1 - b)Y$. If we substitute the quantity $(1 - b)Y$ into equation (19.13) as a replacement for (ΔK), we find:

(19.16) $\qquad \Delta Y/Y = (1 - r)(\Delta L/L) + r(1 - b)(Y/K).$

The components of equation (19.16) are illustrated in Figure 19-5.

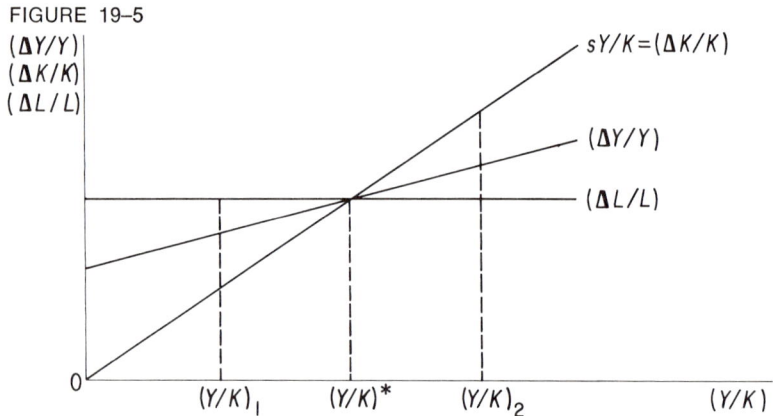

FIGURE 19-5

All of the growth rates—$(\Delta Y/Y)$, $(\Delta K/K)$ and $(\Delta L/L)$—are measured on the vertical axis, and the output-capital ratio is measured on the horizontal axis. The diagram is drawn under two assumptions: the growth rate of the labor force is assumed to be constant at some exogenously determined level, and the growth rate of the capital stock is proportional to the output-capital ratio. Therefore, the height of the line labeled $(\Delta L/L)$ measures the constant rate of growth in the labor force, while the height of the positively sloped line labeled sY/K measures the growth rate of the capital stock. We know from our previous analysis that the growth rate of total output lies intermediate between the growth rates of the two factors of production, when the factors are growing at different rates. When the growth rate of the labor force $(\Delta L/L)$ exceeds the growth rate of the capital stock $(\Delta K/K)$, we know that the growth rate of labor force $(\Delta L/L)$ exceeds the growth rate of output $(\Delta Y/Y)$, which exceeds the growth rate of the capital stock $(\Delta K/K)$. When the growth rate of the labor force $(\Delta L/L)$ is less than the growth rate of the capital stock $(\Delta K/K)$, we know that the growth rate of the labor force $(\Delta L/L)$ is less than the growth rate of output $(\Delta Y/Y)$ which is less than the growth of the capital stock $(\Delta K/K)$. Accordingly, the height of the positively sloped curve labeled $(\Delta Y/Y)$ measures the growth rate of total output.

In Figure 19-5, suppose that the economy begins at an initial output-capital ratio $(Y/K)_1$. Clearly, $(\Delta L/L)$ is greater than $(\Delta Y/Y)$ which is greater than $(\Delta K/K)$. The level of per capita output is falling. However, the output-capital ratio is rising, and it is rising toward $(Y/K)^*$. At $(Y/K)^*$, all the growth rates are equal, and the level of per capita output as well as the output-capital ratio are constant. Instead, suppose that the economy begins at $(Y/K)_2$. Clearly, $(\Delta K/K)$ is greater than $(\Delta Y/Y)$ which is greater than $(\Delta L/L)$. The level of per capita output is rising. However, the output-capital ratio is falling, and it is falling toward $(Y/K)^*$. Once again, at $(Y/K)^*$, all the growth rates are equal, and the level of per capita output as well as the output-capital ratio are constant. Therefore, we conclude that labor, capital, and output eventually grow at the same percentage rate.

Suppose that the level of per capita output, associated with the equilibrium growth rate, is "too low." Suppose that society wishes to increase its level of per capita output. Ask yourself the question: How can it be accomplished? A partial answer lies in Figure 19-6AB. The rate of growth of the population (i.e., in our analysis, the labor force) could be reduced from $(\Delta L/L)$ to $(\Delta L/L)'$, as shown in part A of Figure 19-6. At the old output-capital ratio $(Y/K)^*$, the growth rate of the capital stock $(\Delta K/K)$ is now greater than the growth rate of output $(\Delta Y/Y)'$ which is now greater than the growth rate of the labor force $(\Delta L/L)'$. Obviously, per capita output must increase. However, it cannot increase forever. It can only increase until a new

FIGURE 19-6

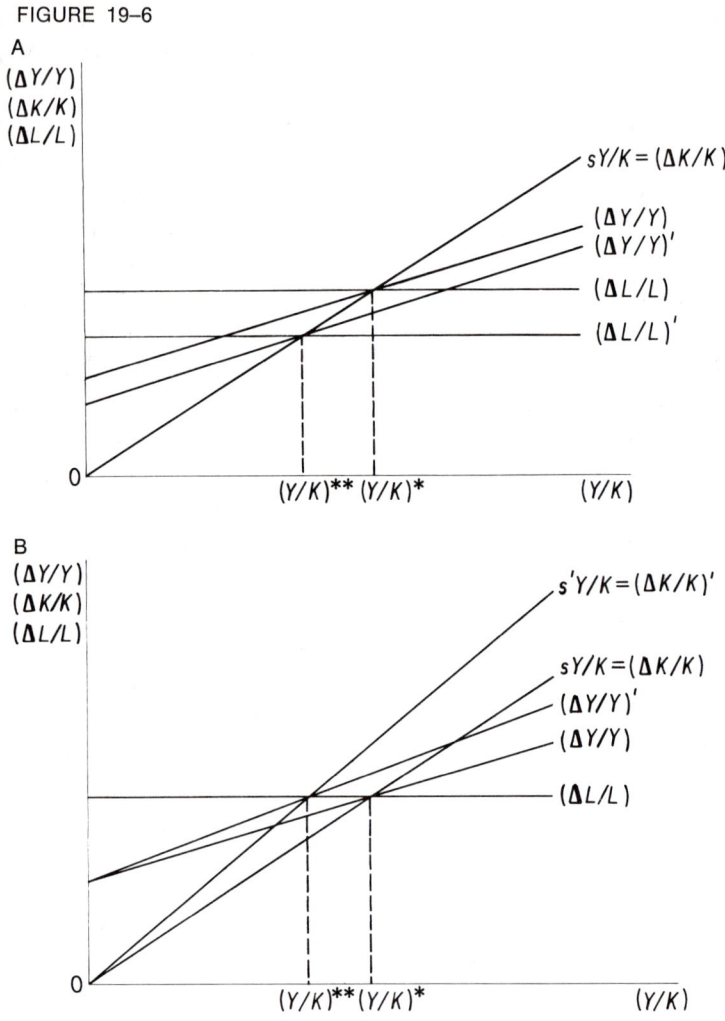

equilibrium is established at $(Y/K)^{**}$; and, from that point on, per capita output remains constant at its new higher level. (A further increase in per capita income would require a further reduction in the population's growth rate.) Also, note that the new growth rate of total output is less than it was previously. Why?

Since population control raises the possibility of a reduced rate of growth of total output, it may be an unacceptable method of raising per capita output. Another method is to increase the rate of capital formation from sY/K to $s'Y/K$, as shown in part B of Figure 19-6. At the old output-capital ratio $(Y/K)^*$, the growth rate of the capital stock $(\Delta K/K)'$ is now greater than the growth rate of output $(\Delta Y/Y)'$ which is now greater than the growth rate of the labor force $(\Delta L/L)$. Once again, per capita output must increase. Once again, it cannot increase forever. It can only increase until a new equilibrium is established at $(Y/K)^{**}$; remaining constant thereafter. However, please note that, in this case, the growth rate of total output has not been reduced. In fact, the growth rate of total output is the same as it was previously. Why?

These are not society's only choices. It can experience a permanently rising level of per capita output. All that it must do is generate continuous increases in productivity. It must experience technological improvements. It must experience technical progress.

ECONOMIC GROWTH AND TECHNICAL PROGRESS

We alluded to the importance of technical progress in sustaining economic growth when we talked about the stationary state. Now we must see the importance of technical progress in raising a society's standard of living, or level of per capita output.[7] The impact of technical progress on economic growth is illustrated in Figure 19-7. If we

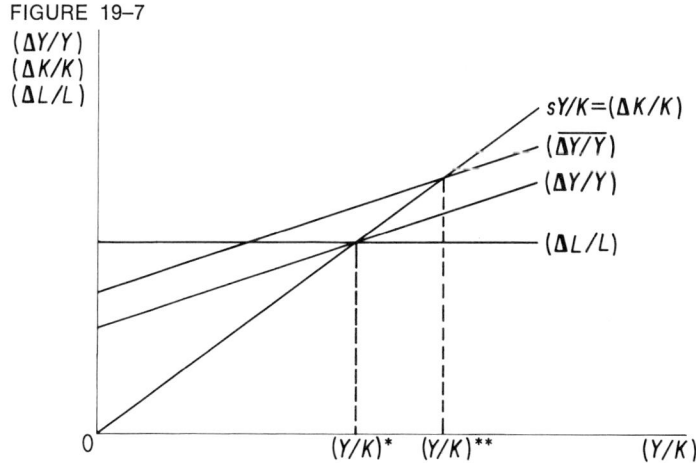

FIGURE 19-7

---

[7] For a detailed analysis, see T. W. Swan, "Economic Growth and Capital Accumulation," *Economic Record,* Vol. 32 (November 1956), pp. 334-361.

assume that technical progress adds to the growth of output independently of capital and labor (this concept is called *neutral technical progress*), the vertical distance between the positively sloped lines $(\overline{\Delta Y/Y})$ and $(\Delta Y/Y)$ represents the growth contribution of technical progress. Accordingly, the height of the curve labeled $(\overline{\Delta Y/Y})$ measures the new growth rate of total output at each output-capital ratio and at the existing growth rate of the labor force.

At the old output-capital ratio $(Y/K)^*$, the growth rate of total output $(\overline{\Delta Y/Y})$ is now greater than the growth rate of the capital stock $(\Delta K/K)$ which is greater than the growth rate of the labor force $(\Delta L/L)$. Obviously, per capita output must increase. Furthermore, the output-capital ratio is rising, and continues to rise until it reaches the new equilibrium level $(Y/K)^{**}$. However, at $(Y/K)^{**}$, output is still growing at a faster rate than the labor force. Thus, the level of per capita output increases continually at a percentage rate equal to $((\Delta Y/Y) - (\Delta L/L))$.

According to our assumptions, the new growth rate of total output can be found by altering equation (19.13) to account for technical progress. That is:

(19.17) $\qquad (\overline{\Delta Y/Y}) = (1 - r)(\Delta L/L) + r(\Delta K/K) + m,$

where m represents the rate of technical progress. At the equilibrium point $(Y/K)^{**}$, we know that $(\overline{\Delta Y/Y}) = (\Delta K/K)$. Therefore, equation (19.17) can be written as:

(19.18) $\qquad (1 - r)(\overline{\Delta Y/Y}) = (1 - r)(\Delta L/L) + m,$
$\qquad\qquad (\overline{\Delta Y/Y}) = (\Delta L/L) + m/(1 - r).$

Therefore, the new growth rate of per capita output is:

(19.19) $\qquad \Delta(\overline{Y/L})/(Y/L) = (\overline{\Delta Y/Y}) - (\Delta L/L)$
$\qquad\qquad\qquad\qquad = m/(1 - r).$

Clearly, per capita output increases as long as technical progress continues.

CONCLUDING NOTE

In this chapter, we have examined several growth models. In so doing, we took a short dynamic look at the static macroeconomic models of the previous chapters. Indeed, growth is a dynamic process.

The models are a bit oversimplified in that they do not accurately reflect all sectors of the economy, and so tend to overstate the necessary rates of growth in investment and national income for full employment to prevail. Nevertheless, they clearly demonstrate the importance of a growing labor force and capital stock as well as continuous technical progress to the process of economic growth.

20 A view of macroeconomic policy

THROUGHOUT THIS BOOK, we have examined, for the most part, macroeconomic theory. Of course, we did refer to policy problems and programs, but clearly emphasis was on the theoretical foundations of macroeconomic analysis.

In this chapter, we shall take a closer look at macroeconomic policy. We will attempt to look, as objectively as possible, at recent macroeconomic policy in this country. However, please realize that this is no simple task. For example, if fiscal policy is employed to raise the level of national income, it might be desirable to reduce the level of taxation in order to keep more purchasing in the hands of the private sector. Hence, there is a "fiscal effect." However, if at the same time the level of government expenditures is to remain constant, we are faced with a problem. Ask the question: Where will the necessary funds come from? One solution is for the U.S. Treasury to sell bonds. Selling bonds causes the rate of interest to rise, and so there is a "monetary effect." This monetary effect is, of course nothing more than an effect on the price of credit, but that is what monetary policy is all about, although in this particular setting the selling of bonds should not be considered as monetary policy. Therefore, it is often most difficult to separate fiscal from monetary policy. Nevertheless, we shall try.

In the first section, we will look at fiscal policy; while in the second section we will look at monetary policy. However, do not forget that the two policies affect each other. Finally, we will examine wage and price controls.

FISCAL POLICY

We know from our theoretical analysis that a budgetary deficit will have an expansionary effect on the economy, while a budgetary surplus will have a contractionary effect on the economy. Thus, we could determine whether recent fiscal policy has had an expansionary or a contractionary effect on the economy by examining the size of the federal deficit or surplus. If the federal budget shows a deficit in the current period, but the size of the deficit is smaller than that of the preceding period, we might conclude that, while the budget still has an expansionary effect on the economy, it is less expansionary currently than it was in the previous period. Although this is a convenient rule to implement, it is much too simple, and is—as we shall see—misleading. Therefore, in order to analyze the expansionary or contractionary effect of fiscal policy, we must understand the concept of the *full-employment surplus*.

The concept of the full-employment budget surplus was developed by President Kennedy's Council of Economic Advisors, and is currently being employed by the Nixon administration. The concept is explained with the aid of Figure 20–1. In Figure 20–1, we have mea-

FIGURE 20–1

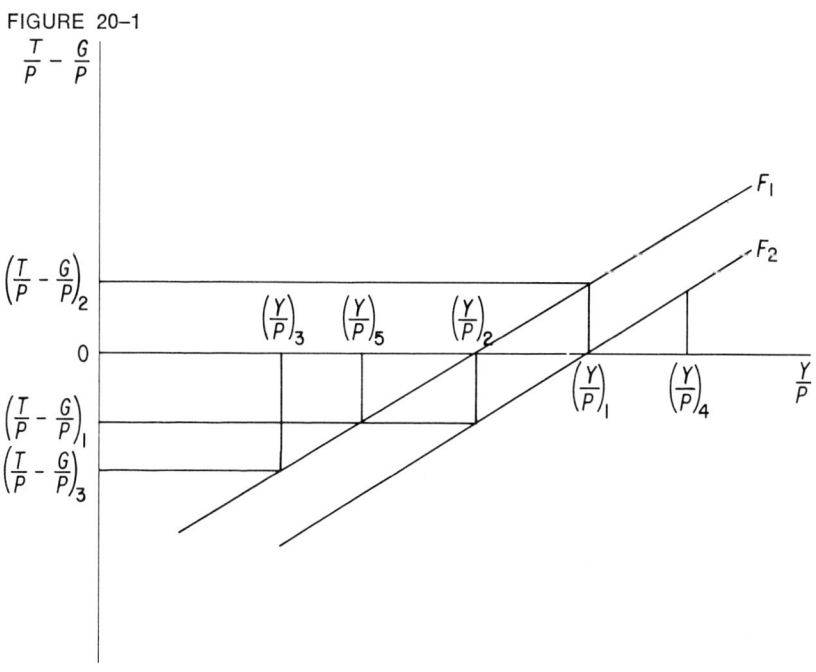

sured real income on the horizontal axis, and the real value of the budget surplus on the vertical axis. Let us assume that $(Y/P)_1$ is the full-employment level of real income.[1] Line F_1 represents one possible fiscal program. For example, at a level of real national income that is low, like $(Y/P)_5$, tax revenues are low, and so there is a deficit. The real value of this deficit is $(T/P - G/P)_1$. With this fiscal program (budget), an increase in the level of real national income to $(Y/P)_2$ would increase the size of tax revenues so that the budget deficit would fall to zero. On the other hand, if the level of real national income were to increase to the full-employment level, there would be a budgetary surplus in the amount $(T/P - G/P)_2$. This surplus would come about, of course, from the increase in tax revenues as well as a decrease in government transfer payments as the economy nears the full-employment level of real output. $(T/P - G/P)_2$ is a full-employment budget surplus.

From earlier analysis, we know that, in the absence of a government sector, equilibrium would be established when:

(20.1) $\qquad Y/P = C/P + I/P = C/P + S/P,$

or:

(20.1a) $\qquad I/P = S/P.$

With the addition of a government sector, the equilibrium expression must be expanded to:

(20.2) $\quad Y/P = C/P + I/P + G/P = C/P + S/P + T/P,$

or:

(20.2a) $\qquad I/P + G/P = S/P + T/P,$
$\qquad\qquad I/P - S/P = T/P - G/P.$

Hence, from equation (20.2a), if the economy were in equilibrium at level of real output $(Y/P)_5$, the deficit of $(T/P - G/P)_1$ associated with budget program F_1 must be matched by an excess of real savings over real investment. However, this is precisely what we would expect with less than full employment. With less than full employment, the level of real investment is too low. Nevertheless, from equation (20.2a) the deficit makes it appear as if the budget is stimulating the economy. However, it is not. The economy is in a less-than-full-

---

[1] Throughout the analysis we will assume that the price level remains constant. Such an assumption, of course, is truly a simplifying one.

employment equilibrium. The budgetary deficit is being offset by an excess of real savings over real investment. Furthermore, it should be noted that at the full-employment level of real income there must be a surplus of real investment over real savings for equilibrium to be maintained. The excess of real investment over real savings is required to offset the budgetary surplus. Thus, the knowledge that the federal budget is in deficit or surplus is insufficient to indicate whether the economy is expanding or contracting. We must also know whether real investment is greater than, or less than, real savings.

Let us assume that an expansionary fiscal policy is pursued. Accordingly, there would be a cut in taxes (or tax rates), and an increase in government expenditures. Consequently, there would be a rightward shift of line F_1 to F_2. Please note that the new fiscal policy line intersects the horizontal axis at the full-employment level of real output. Expansionary fiscal policy has eliminated the budget surplus at full employment. Unfortunately, there is absolutely no guarantee that the full-employment level of real output can ever be reached. The equilibrium condition of equation (20.2a) tells us that equilibrium can only be attained, with a balanced federal budget, if *ex ante* real investment and *ex ante* real savings are equal. If real savings exceeds real investment, there must be a budgetary deficit if the full-employment level of real output is to be maintained. Without a budgetary deficit there will be deflation. If real investment exceeds real savings, we know that there must be a budgetary surplus for the full-employment level of real output to be an equilibrium one. Without a budgetary surplus, there will be inflation.

Something of a problem has arisen. Reduction of the full-employment surplus to zero is no guarantee that a full-employment equilibrium will be established. Suppose that the level of real national income is below the full-employment level; i.e., there is a deflationary gap. Real aggregate demand falls short of real aggregate output. In other words, we find that:

(20.3) $Y/P + S/P + T/P > Y/P + I/P + G/P,$
$S/P + T/P > I/P + G/P,$
$\text{Gap} = S/P + T/P - I/P - G/P,$
$\text{Gap} = (T/P - G/P) + S/P - I/P.$

The first term on the right-hand side of the last line of equation (20.3) is the full-employment surplus. If this full-employment surplus is equal to zero, the deflationary gap is eliminated if and only if real investment and real savings are equal. At best the full-employment surplus will only serve to point out the direction in which fiscal policy should move. For example, if there is a budgetary deficit and the level of real savings exceeds the level of real investment, the economy must be at a less-than-full-employment equilibrium, and the deficit should be increased in order to move the economy toward full employment.

However, there is no guarantee that the expansionary fiscal policy will be successful. Indeed, an increase in the budgetary deficit may be contractionary rather than expansionary. Consider the income level $(Y/P)_2$, and budget program F_2 in Figure 20–1. There is a deficit of $(T/P - G/P)_1$. Suppose that the budget program line were to shift to F_1, indicating a more restrictive budget. At first glance it might appear that the budget deficit would disappear. However, such would only be the case if there were no change in the level of economic activity. However, the increase in taxes (or tax rates), or the decrease in government expenditures that causes the budget program line to shift from F_2 to F_1, is likely to cause the level of real national income to fall. Suppose that this shift in the budget program line causes the level of real national income to fall all the way to $(Y/P)_3$. In such a case, the size of the deficit increases from $(T/P - G/P)_1$ to $(T/P - G/P)_3$. If we judge the impact of the budget in terms of the size of the deficit only, we must conclude that the budget has become more expansionary. However, using all the relevant economic information, we come to the opposite conclusion. Thus, we must conclude that the size of the surplus or deficit is an unreliable guide in assessing the impact of the budget.

We must adjust our budgetary information for possible changes in the level of economic activity. To accomplish this, we use the notion of the full-employment budget surplus or deficit. This is a measure that reflects only changes in the budget program, but not the changes in the level of economic activity created by changes in the budget program. The full-employment budget surplus is simply the difference between revenues and expenditures given existing expenditure programs and tax rates, with government transfer payments adjusted to what they would be at full employment, and with revenues adjusted to what they would be at full employment.

One more point is in order. Again, look at Figure 20–1. Assume that the budget program is given by line F_2, and that full employment prevails with the level of real income given by $(Y/P)_1$. Suppose that economic growth takes place so that the full-employment level of real income increases to $(Y/P)_4$. The current budget now becomes restrictive, since there is a budget surplus at full employment. In order for full employment to prevail, there must be an excess of real investment over real savings. *Fiscal drag* occurs. The budget program line has to be shifted to the right through appropriate action. If it does not, the level of real output will fall. In fact, the budget program line must be shifted to the right at a rate equal to the long-run rate of growth of potential real national income.

The reference to potential real national income may require a slight digression. Ask this question: How can one measure potential real national output? It was noted in Chapter 17 that, at some positive unemployment rate, the economy seemed to behave as if there was full employment. Stated another way, full employment is taken to exist at some positive rate of unemployment. In recent times full employment was considered to prevail when the unemployment rate fell to 3.5 percent. Now the target is closer to 5 percent.

In 1961, Arthur Okun, a member of the staff of the Council of Economic Advisors and later Chairman of the Council, devised a formula for estimating the economy's real potential output when the unemployment rate was 4 percent.[2] Based upon an observed relationship between changes in real GNP and the unemployment rate, Okun arrived at the following equation:

$$(20.4) \qquad P = A(1 + 0.032\,(U - 4)),$$

where P is potential real GNP (corresponding to an unemployment rate of 4 percent), A is actual GNP, and U the actual unemployment rate. The 4 in the equation is the 4 percent unemployment rate. Thus, when $U = 4$ potential and actual real GNP are equal.

We now have a measure of the cost of operating the economy at less than full employment (meaning more than a 4 percent unemployment rate), based on equation (20.4). Table 20–1 summarizes the cost of operating at less than full employment. We note that in four years (1966 through 1969) full employment prevailed, and so there existed no gap between potential real GNP and actual real GNP. It should be noted that over the period 1960–70 the loss of output due to unemployment varied a great deal. However, it is fairly clear, from viewing the data, that it seems desirable to cut the unemployment

---

[2] See A. M. Okun, "Potential GNP: Its Measurement and Significance," *Proceedings of the Business and Economic Statistics Section of the American Statistical Association,* 1962.

316   The essentials of macroeconomic analysis

TABLE 20-1

Year	GNP (billions of 1958 dollars)	Unemployment rate	Gap (P-A) (billions of 1958 dollars)
1960	$488	5.6	$25
1961	497	6.7	43
1962	530	5.5	25
1963	551	5.7	30
1964	581	5.2	22
1965	618	4.5	10
1966*	658	3.8	–
1967*	675	3.8	–
1968*	707	3.6	–
1969*	727	3.5	–
1970	724	4.9	21

* Full employment based on 4 percent unemployment rate.
Source: *Federal Reserve Bulletin*.

rate—provided, of course, that the rate of inflation does not increase significantly.

Now, let us look briefly at the period from 1960 to 1970, and use the concept of the full-employment budget to assess the impact of fiscal policy on the U.S. economy. Please examine Table 20–2 and Figure 20–2.

The data in Table 20–2 represent the actual surplus or deficit for a particular calendar year compared with the full-employment budget data for the same year. These data are given in billions of dollars which have not been adjusted for price changes. It is interesting to note

TABLE 20-2

Year	Actual budget surplus (billions of dollars)	Full-employment budget surplus (billions of dollars)
1960	$ 3.5	$ 13.0
1961	– 3.8	8.8
1962	– 3.8	4.4
1963	0.7	9.0
1964	– 3.0	1.8
1965	1.2	1.0
1966	– 0.2	– 3.6
1967	–12.4	–10.5
1968	– 6.2	– 6.0
1969	9.3	11.7
1970	–10.8	6.7

Source: *Economic Report of the President* (Washington, D.C.: U.S. Government Printing Office, February, 1971), pp. 73 and 275.

FIGURE 20-2
Budget surplus or deficit

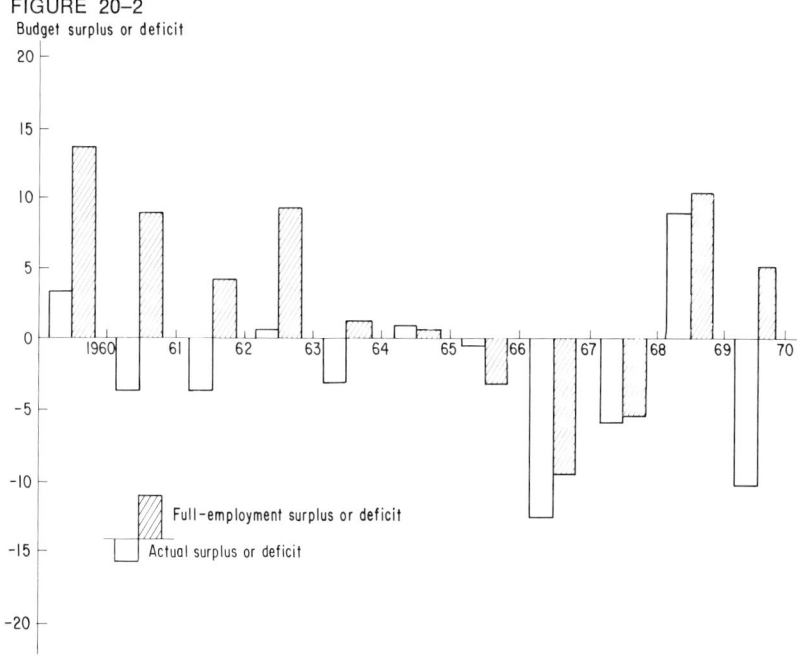

that the full-employment budget showed a surplus for 8 of the 11 years, while the actual budget reflected deficits in 7 of the 11 years.

During President Kennedy's first year in office, the actual budgetary deficit reached $3.8 billion. Early in 1961, the unemployment rate reached 6.8 percent per annum. Apparently, an expansionary fiscal policy was being used to rid the economy of recessionary ills. However, if we look at the full-employment budget, we see that there was a surplus in 1961 in the amount of $8.8 billion. Actually, the federal budget and fiscal policy were quite contractionary. In fact, by 1963 the full-employment surplus increased to $9 billion. A tax reduction was enacted in 1964, and the full-employment surplus fell, indicating an expansionary budget. By 1967, the full-employment budget reflected a deficit of $10.5 billion, and the unemployment rate fell to 3.8 percent per annum by the end of the year.

Inflationary pressures were felt by the end of the 1960s with the consumer price index rising by 5.4 percent during the year 1969. Consequently, the Nixon administration moved toward a policy of fiscal restraint, and contractionary fiscal policy prevailed. Obviously, monetary policy too changed during the 1960s, and it is to this that we now turn our attention.

MONETARY POLICY

The Federal Reserve System (the Fed) was established in 1913 to function as the independent monetary authority in the United States. More specifically, the Fed was established to satisfy two goals: It was to prevent the periodic bank failures and financial panics of past years, and it was to manage the money supply in a manner consistent with the economic needs of the country. To accomplish these goals, the Fed was given the power to engage in open-market operations (i.e., the purchase and sale of government securities), to regulate commercial banks, and to set discount rates (i.e., the basic cost of credit) so as to control the money supply.[3] Since it controls the money supply and can, therefore, alter the quantity of nominal balances, the Federal Reserve System formulates monetary policy.

The first major test of the Federal Reserve System came during the Great Depression. During the depression of the 1930s, real output and employment fell to their lowest levels in modern U.S. economic history. Thus, according to our theoretical analysis, the monetary authority should follow a policy of monetary ease, and increase the money supply. However, from 1929 through 1934, the money supply declined by nearly 23 percent.[4] Obviously, the Fed failed its first test.

The second major test of the Federal Reserve System came as the economy began to recover from the depression. The annual unemployment rate rose from 3.2 percent in 1929 to 24.9 percent in 1933, but had declined to 14.3 percent by the end of 1937. Similarly, real gross national product fell from $203.6 billion (measured in 1958 dollars) in 1929 to $141.5 billion in 1933, but had increased to $209.4 billion by the end of 1939. Clearly, an economic recovery was under way. According to our theoretical analysis, the monetary authority should have followed a policy of monetary ease, and hasten the recovery. The Fed did not. Instead, it began to fear—without just cause—

---

[3] Clearly, this is not a complete list of the powers and duties of the Federal Reserve System. For a more complete discussion, see *The Federal Reserve System: Purposes and Functions* (Washington, D.C.: The Board of Governors of the Federal Reserve System, 1963).

[4] See Milton Friedman and Anna J. Schwartz, *A Monetary History of The United States, 1867–1960* (New York: National Bureau of Economic Research, Inc., 1963), pp. 712–14.

inflationary pressures, and pursued a tight monetary policy. Obviously, the Federal Reserve System failed its second test.

By the end of the year 1941, the United States was involved in World War II. Shortly after the United States entered the war, the Federal Reserve System announced that it intended to purchase all government securities offered for sale on the open market. In this way, the Fed could guarantee that the interest rates paid on short-term government securities would not rise above 1 percent per annum, and the interest rates paid on longer term government securities would not rise above 2.5 percent per annum. The purpose of the Fed's policy was to ensure that the government would have sufficient funds to finance the war, and to guarantee that the cost of borrowing to support the war effort would be minimized. However, the policy forced the Fed to buy large quantities of government securities. As a result, the money supply grew very rapidly, and, in fact, the monetary authority had abdicated its control over the quantity of nominal balances.

This policy ended in 1951. In 1951, the Federal Reserve System reached an accord with the U.S. Treasury which terminated the Fed's commitment to keep low the cost of government borrowing. The Fed regained control over the money supply, and, once again, became an independent monetary authority. The stage was set for the Fed's third major test. It would come in the 1960s.

Before examining the 1960s, we must digress for a moment and examine the effects of the alternative Federal Reserve policies: stabilizing the rate of interest, or stabilizing the stock of money. Recall from our earlier analysis that the equation of exchange is written as:

(20.5) $\qquad MV = P(Y/P).$

If we write this expression in logarithmic form, we have:

(20.6) $\qquad \log_e M + \log_e V = \log_e P + \log_e(Y/P).$

The rate of change in equation (20.6) with respect to time is given by[5]:

(20.7) $\quad (1/M)dM/dt + (1/V)dV/dt = (1/P)dP/dt + (1/Y/P)d(Y/P)/dt$

Now, if we let $dt = 1$, we may rewrite equation (20.7) as:

(20.8) $\qquad \Delta M/M + \Delta V/V = \Delta P/P + \Delta(Y/P)/(Y/P).$

---

[5] The derivation of this equation is relatively unimportant. It involves the use of the differential calculus. What is important is the interpretation of equation (20.7).

Equation (20.8) says that the percentage change in the stock of money plus the percentage change in income velocity will be equal to the percentage change in the price level plus the percentage change in the level of real national income.

If we assume that velocity is a constant, then $\Delta V/V$ will be zero. Thus, if the rate of growth of real output is 5 percent per annum, equation (20.8) can be satisfied—without inflation—if the stock of money were to be increased at the rate of 5 percent per annum. Suppose that as the level of real national income approaches the full-employment level, its rate of growth decreases. Suppose, in fact, that the rate of growth of real national income falls to 3 percent per annum. If the monetary authority continues to increase the stock of money at the rate of 5 percent per annum, equation (20.8) says that there must be a rate of change in the price level equal to 2 percent per annum. When the growth rate of the money supply exceeds the growth rate of real output, inflation must occur.

Now suppose that the monetary authority chooses to stabilize the rate of interest. Specifically, they choose to stabilize the money rate of interest. With the money stock increasing at the rate of 5 percent per annum, it is doubtful that the authority will be able to keep the interest rate stable. We know that there will be a tendency for the price level to increase. Such a situation should cause bond prices to fall, since the real interest return on bonds is less due to the inflation. Hence, the rate of interest will increase. Suppose that the rate of interest increases from 7 percent per annum to 9 percent per annum. According to equation (17.1) of Chapter 17, this difference of two percentage points is the expected change in the price level. If we now assume that the expected change in the price level and actual change in the price level are equal, we see that for the monetary authority to stabilize the rate of interest at 7 percent per annum, it will be necessary to increase the stock of money at a rate greater than 5 percent per annum. Assume that the monetary authority has to increase the money stock at the rate of 7 percent per annum. Unfortunately, equation (20.8) is very much out of balance. If velocity is to remain constant and if the rate of increase in real national income cannot exceed 3 percent per annum, with the money stock increasing at 7 percent per annum, it is necessary for the price level to increase at the rate of 4 percent per annum. However, the price inflation will cause the rate of interest to rise even more and so, the rate of inflation will have to increase.

On the other hand, if the monetary authority had opted to control the rate of growth of the stock of money rather than controlling the rate of interest, we would not have had inflationary conditions created. Had the monetary authority chosen to do nothing when the rate of growth of real national income fell to 3 percent per annum, the worst that would have happened would have been a 2 percent per annum increase in the price level. Furthermore, if the Federal Reserve reacts to the inflationary tendencies by reducing the rate of growth of the money stock, there would have been no inflation at all. It is important to note that when there is a positive rate of growth in real national income, but its rate of growth is slowing, control of the money stock rather than control of interest rates is necessary if the price level is to remain stable. With this in mind, let us examine the happenings of the 1960s.

The period of the 1960s offers an interesting insight into Federal Reserve attempts at stabilization policy. In Table 20–3, we note the

TABLE 20–3

Year	Money stock* (billions of dollars)	Change	Unemployment	Consumer price change	Real GNP change
1960	$141.1	–	5.6%	–	–
1961	145.5	3.1%	6.7	1.1%	1.9%
1962	147.5	1.4	5.5	1.2	6.5
1963	153.1	3.8	5.7	1.2	4.0
1964	159.7	4.3	5.2	1.3	5.3
1965	167.2	4.7	4.5	1.7	5.9
1966	170.4	1.9	3.8	2.9	5.4
1967	181.7	6.6	3.8	2.8	4.2
1968	194.8	7.2	3.6	4.0	4.9
1969	198.3	1.8	3.5	5.4	2.8
1970	209.3	5.5	4.9	5.9	–0.6

* Currency plus demand deposits.
Source: *Federal Reserve Bulletin*.

relationship between the money stock, the unemployment rate, the rate of change of real GNP, and the price level. From the table, it can be seen that the unemployment rate fell and real GNP rose. However, the declining unemployment rate coupled with an increasing defense budget, and budget deficits in general, intensified the existing inflationary pressures around 1966. The increase in the rate of inflation should have signaled the monetary authority to lower the rate of increase in the money supply. However, this did not happen until 1969. By 1970, the unemployment rate had started rising, and the consumer price index continued to rise. The former was undoubtedly due to the fact that the federal budget showed a full-employment surplus and was, therefore, actually contractionary; while the latter was due for the most part to the past increases in the stock of money.

By the end of the 1960s, then, something of a dilemma had appeared on the economic scene. Prices were rising, and so was the unemployment rate. Real output began to fall. The rising prices signaled inflation, and a need for a tight money policy. On the other hand, the rising unemployment rate and the falling level of real output called for expansionary policy—either fiscal or monetary. Unfortunately, any expansionary policy would bring forth another round of inflation. The Phillips curve was shifting to the right. It appears that the Federal Reserve System had failed its third test.

WAGE AND PRICE CONTROLS

As a reaction to the apparent failure of the monetary authority, the President of the United States announced, in August of 1971, that he was imposing a wage and price freeze designed to combat rising prices and a rising unemployment rate. The imposition of these wage and price controls raises two important questions. On the one hand, we must ask whether wage and price controls were necessary to combat the economic problem of 1970–71. On the other hand, we must ask whether wage and price controls can actually control inflation and end recession.

At the outset, it is important to emphasize that we will not look at the administrative details of the wage and price controls imposed by the Nixon administration; rather, we will take as a given the existence of the controls, and merely view them from a nonpolitical, economic point of view.

Throughout this book, we have emphasized the importance of the money supply and its effect on the price level. Therefore, as you might suspect, a clue as to whether wage and price controls were necessary can be gained by looking once again at the actions of the monetary authority. However, we must now recognize that the effect of a change in the stock of money is not immediately felt. Rather, there is some unpredictable time lag—possibly as long as 18 months. Nevertheless, our theory tells us that, unless there is an offsetting change somewhere else in the economy, changes in the money supply eventually manifest themselves as changes in the price level.

Let us recall from Table 20-3 that the money supply fell relatively during the year 1969. That is to say, the rate of increase in the money stock, while positive, was significantly lower than that of the previous year. Indeed, the rate of increase of the money stock was also significantly lower than that of the following year as well. As expected, the rate of increase in the price level exhibited a downward trend during the year 1970; beginning in October, the rate of increase in the price level fell from 5.8 percent per annum to 4.3 percent per annum over the next six months. The rate of inflation fell by 1.5 percentage points.[6] It seems probable that the 26 percent drop in the rate of increase in the price level was due to the relative cutback in the money supply over the year 1969. It appears that much progress was being made against inflation over a period of time prior to the announcement of the wage and price freeze. Moreover, during the six-month period following the imposition of wage and price controls, there was an additional reduction in the rate of increase of the price level. This time, however, the fall equaled 0.7 percentage points (from 4.4 percent per annum to 3.7 percent per annum).[7] It can be argued that even the postcontrols fall in the rate of inflation is the result of the relatively restrictive monetary policy of 1969 and the mini-recession of 1970.

Do not misunderstand the point. Wage and price controls do have effects on the economy. However, these effects are probably not seen in the control of inflation; rather the effects of the controls are seen in the measures of output and productivity. It is necessarily the case that when prices and wages are rising, controls will cause prices and wages in general to remain at levels below equilibrium levels. In such cases, the quantities demanded will be greater than the quantities supplied, in both goods and services markets and in labor markets. Hence, artificial shortages are created. When artificial shortages exist, markets cannot efficiently allocate resources. Thus, secondary criteria for allocating resources must be adopted. Whatever they may be, the cost is a loss of individual freedom. Ask yourself the question: How will sellers allocate housing or automobiles when prices are frozen below

---

[6] See Milton Friedman, "Controls: An Exercise in Futility," *Newsweek,* May 22, 1972, p. 86.
[7] Ibid.

the equilibrium levels? Secondary criteria, such as quotas and "qualification" rules, will be employed. Moreover, if wage rates are prevented from rising, workers have less incentive to work their hardest. Output and the quality of output fall. Furthermore, it seems that wage and price controls misallocate resources away from the private sector and to the public sector of the economy.[8] Surely, this is not a method of curing inflation and unemployment. Wage and price controls work on the symptoms of inflation—the rising price level—only. The controls, however, do not get at the cause of the inflation. What does? Appropriate control of the money supply.

During the months just preceding May 1972, the rate of inflation was roughly constant. Prices were rising, but at a steady rate. However, additional inflationary pressures were building. The monetary and fiscal facts indicate that the inflationary pressures were building. During the year 1971, the money stock increased by about 6.2 percent. Over the first three months of 1972, the money stock increased at an average annual rate of 9.5 percent, while over the first nine months the average annual rate had fallen a bit to 7.2 percent. Moreover, fiscal policy became expansionary also. In fiscal year 1971, there was a full-employment surplus of $2.7 billion. However, there was a projected full-employment deficit of $6.5 billion in fiscal year 1972.[9] The actual budget deficit estimated from preliminary data for fiscal 1972 amounted to $22 billion and the projected actual deficit for calendar 1972 amounts to $35 billion.[10] Clearly, the prediction of continued inflation implies that the wage and price controls have not been successful. Inflation has not been cured.

Better control of the money stock is the key to curing inflation. With control of inflation, and hence, no expectations of inflation or uncertainty caused by wage and price controls, the unemployment rate will fall. If we couple monetary control with the fact that technology improves over time, there is no doubt that both recession (a rising unemployment rate) and inflation can be controlled through proper monetary policy. Naturally, the fiscal authorities must also cooperate by not producing large budget deficits which require the monetary authority to abandon appropriate monetary control. Cer-

---

[8] This happens if for no other reason than for the large quantity of resources required to implement wage and price controls.

[9] See *Economic Report of the President* (Washington, D.C.: U.S. Government Printing Office, January 1972), p. 65.

[10] See *Survey of Current Business* (Washington, D.C.: U.S. Department of Commerce, August 1972), p. 5.

tainly this is not happening. However, you must ask the question: What is appropriate monetary control?

With the aid of Figure 20-3, it can be seen how recession and infla-

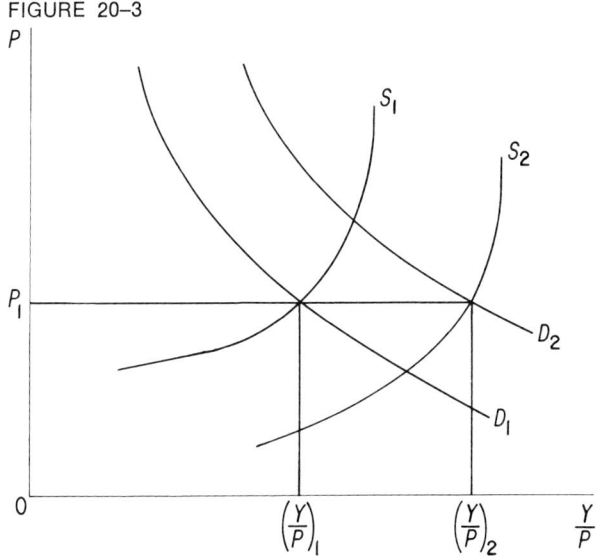

FIGURE 20-3

tion can be controlled simultaneously, and how an appropriate monetary control program can be defined. Given the aggregate demand curve D_1 and the aggregate supply curve S_1, we note that the price level is P_1, and the level of real output is (Y/P_1). If this level of output is too low, the monetary authority can increase the supply of money. This pushes the aggregate demand curve to the right to D_2. Hence the price level will increase. This may well cause unions to ask for higher wages, causing the aggregate supply curve to shift to the left and raising the price level still higher. However, if we allow for an improvement in technology, the aggregate supply curve will shift to the right to S_2. The level of real output has increased, while the price level remained the same. Importantly, if the level of real output increases, the level of employment will also increase. Hence, if the money supply increases in line with the long-run increase in real productivity, the price level will remain constant, while the level of real output and employment increase. Assuming that the labor supply does not increase too rapidly, the unemployment rate is bound to fall. The current economic problem in the United States can be solved through appropriate monetary control. Thus, we conclude that if an inappropriate monetary policy is pursued, wage and price controls cannot cure price inflation; if an appropriate monetary policy is pursued, wage and price controls are not necessary.

FISCAL LAGS, MONETARY LAGS, AND FINE TUNING

Throughout most of this book we have discussed the use of fiscal and monetary policy as if changes in these policies would be felt immediately, except earlier in this chapter when we discussed briefly the recent history of monetary policy in this country. From the standpoint of policy making, it is unfortunate (but true) that the effects of changes in either monetary or fiscal policy are not felt immediately. In fact, quite the opposite is true. Monetary and fiscal policy changes are subject to substantial time lags.

The time pattern involved in making changes in fiscal or monetary policy may be broken down into two timing lags: the *inside lag* and the *outside lag*. The inside lag refers to the time between a change in economic conditions and the actual enactment of a new policy designed to offset the change. The outside lag, on the other hand, refers to the time between the policy change and the point at which the new policy has an impact on the economy.

The inside lag may be thought of as two separate lags. On the one hand, there is the *recognition lag;* while, on the other hand, there is the *action lag*. It is clear that when an equilibrium is disturbed it will take some time to recognize that this has in fact happened. Economic statistics are not published daily. The fact of the matter is that most economic statistics are available on a quarterly or a monthly basis. As a result, it may take up to three months to recognize the need for action. Furthermore, policy makers may not make a change until such time as they are convinced of the need for action. Thus, it is conceivable that before any action takes place six months or more may elapse. This estimate may, of course, be somewhat overstated since there are *leading economic indicators* which anticipate changes in economic variables. These leading indicators include such statistics as hiring rates, new orders, and stock market prices. Nevertheless, it must be recognized that there is a lag of some indeterminate length from the time that a need for action arises and the time at which the need is recognized.

The action lag differs understandably for monetary action as compared with fiscal action. The seven-man Board of Governors of the Federal Reserve System have full authority to change the discount rate and the reserve requirement. They also represent a majority of the 12-man Open Market Committee which makes decisions regarding the buying and selling of securities. The Open Market Committee meets every three weeks so that the action lag could be quite short for monetary policy changes. Of course, this assumes that at least a majority of the members of this powerful Open Market Committee will all be convinced of the need for change at about the same time. If not, it may be quite some time before even this relatively small committee can agree on a policy change.

With regard to the action lag in fiscal policy, it would seem that the lag is considerably longer than with monetary policy. Both the administrative and the legislative branch of government must first coordinate their views. The need for legislative action may come at a time when Congress is not in session. The point in time when the need for action arises may be at the time of an election. All kinds of possibilities exist which tend to make the action lag in fiscal policy quite long. It would not be uncommon, for example, to see as much as an 18-month lag in fiscal policy.

While the inside lag in monetary policy may be quite short, just the opposite seems to be true with regard to the outside lag.[11] This assertion should not be too surprising. A simple lowering of the discount rate may take a good bit of time to be effective. A lower rate of interest will tend to increase the level of investment, but new investment projects take a good bit of time to get moving. Contracts take time for builders to sign. Thus, there can be a considerable delay.

The outside lag in fiscal policy appears to be rather short, however.[12] Unfortunately this shorter outside lag need not make up for the rather long inside lag.

As a result of the duration of the inside and outside lags for both monetary and fiscal policy, it is difficult to *fine tune* the economy. That is to say, it is difficult to make changes in any policy that will have rapid effects. At best, fiscal policy can be used to correct large disturbances only. Congress seems reluctant to give the President

---

[11] See, for example, M. Friedman and A. J. Schwartz, "Money and Business Cycles," *Review of Economics and Statistics,* Vol. 45 (February 1963).

[12] See R. H. Rasche and H. T. Shapiro, "The F.R.B.-M.I.T. Econometric Model: Its Special Features," *American Economic Review,* Vol. 58 (May 1968).

standby powers to introduce temporary tax cuts and temporary public works programs. Monetary policy, on the other hand, can be used to stabilize prices over the long run only. The inside lag in monetary policy, though potentially short, is fraught with problems of judgment on the part of the members of the Open Market Committee and the Board of Governors. Consequently, it is frequently possible that erroneous policies are suggested; or that, due to the outside lag, by the time the policies become effective, just the opposite policy is required. The result is that fine tuning is a will o'-the-wisp.

CONCLUSION

In this book, we have examined the essentials of macroeconomic analysis. Our examination has been largely theoretical, with some policy applications discussed at the appropriate points. In this final chapter, we looked more closely at recent macroeconomic policy. In the process, we made several predictions about future levels of real output and employment, and future rates of price inflation. We even predicted the form of the most appropriate monetary policy. After having committed ourselves, we must admit that making predictions is perhaps the worst thing that an economist can do—time and politics always work against the prediction. On this note of warning, it is wise to end our discussion of macroeconomics.

Selected references

Chapter 1

Ackley, Gardner. *Macroeconomic Theory*. (New York: Macmillan Co., 1961), chap. 1.

Crouch, Robert. *Macroeconomics*. (New York: Harcourt, Brace and Jovanovich, Inc., 1972), chap. 1.

Friedman, Milton. "The Methodology of Positive Economics." in *Essays in Positive Economics*. (Chicago: University of Chicago Press, 1955).

Lindauer, John. *Macroeconomics*. 2d ed. (New York: John Wiley and Sons, 1971), chap. 1.

Shapiro, Edward. *Macroeconomic Analysis*. 2d ed. (New York: Harcourt, Brace, and World, Inc., 1970), chap. 1.

Chapter 2

Dernburg, Thomas, and Duncan McDougall. *Macroeconomics*. 3d ed. (New York: McGraw-Hill, Inc., 1968), Chaps. 2, 3, and 4.

Glahe, Fred R. *Macroeconomics: Theory and Policy*. (New York: Harcourt, Brace and Jovanovich, Inc., 1973), chap. 1.

McKenna, Joseph. *Aggregate Economic Analysis*. 3d ed. (New York: Holt, Rinehart and Winston, Inc., 1969), chap. 2.

National Bureau of Economic Research. *A Critique of the United States Income and Product Accounts*, Studies in Income and Wealth. vol. 22 (Princeton, N.J.: Princeton University Press, 1958).

Ruggles, Richard, and Nancy Ruggles. *National Income Accounts and Income Analysis.* 2d ed. (New York: McGraw-Hill, Inc., 1956).

Chapter 3

Shapiro, Edward. *Macroeconomic Analysis.* 2d ed. (New York: Harcourt, Brace, and World, Inc., 1970), chap. 6.

Sirkin, Gerald. *Introduction to Macroeconomic Theory.* rev. ed. (Homewood, Ill.: Richard D. Irwin, Inc., 1965), chap. 2.

Walker, Franklin. *Growth, Employment, and the Price Level.* (Englewood Cliffs, N.J.: Prentice-Hall, Inc., 1963), chap. 5.

Chapter 4

Ackley, Gardner. *Macroeconomic Theory.* (New York: Macmillan Co., 1961), chap. 1.

Dernburg, Thomas and Duncan McDougall. *Macroeconomics.* 3d ed. (New York: McGraw-Hill, Inc., 1968), chap. 5.

Glahe, Fred R. *Macroeconomic Analysis: Theory and Policy.* (New York: Harcourt, Brace, Jovanovich, Inc., 1973), chap. 3.

McKenna, Joseph. *Aggregate Economic Analysis.* 3d ed. (New York: Holt, Rinehart and Winston, Inc., 1969), chap. 4 and 6.

Samuelson, Paul. "The Simple Mathematics of Income Determination." In *Income, Employment, and Public Policy.* (New York: W. W. Norton and Co., Inc., 1948). Reprinted in M. G. Mueller, ed., *Readings in Macroeconomics.* 2d ed. (New York: Holt, Rinehart and Winston, Inc., 1971).

Shapiro, Edward. *Macroeconomic Analysis.* 2d ed. (New York: Harcourt, Brace, World, 1970), chap. 7.

Sirkin, Gerald. *Introduction to Macroeconomic Theory.* rev. ed. (Homewood, Ill.: Richard D. Irwin, Inc., 1965), chap. 4.

Chapter 5

Baird, Charles W. *Macroeconomics: An Integration of Monetary, Search, and Income Theories.* (Chicago: Science Research Associates, Inc., 1973), chap. 7.

Dusenberry, James S. *Income, Saving, and the Theory of Consumer Behavior.* (Cambridge, Mass.: Harvard University Press, 1949).

Glahe, Fred R. *Macroeconomics: Theory and Policy.* (New York: Harcourt, Brace and Jovanovich, Inc., 1973), chap. 5.

Sirkin, Gerald. *Introduction to Macroeconomic Theory.* rev. ed. (Homewood, Ill.: Richard D. Irwin, Inc., 1965), chap. 4.

Chapter 6

Dernburg, Thomas and Duncan McDougall. *Macroeconomics.* 3d ed. (New York: McGraw-Hill, Inc., 1968), chap. 7.

Glahe, Fred R. *Macroeconomic Analysis: Theory and Policy.* (Harcourt, Brace and Jovanovich, Inc., 1973), chap. 6.

Knox, A. D. "The Acceleration Principle and the Theory of Investment: A Survey." *Economica* vol. 19 (1952). Reprinted in Mueller, ed., *Readings in Macroeconomics.* 2d ed.

McKenna, Joseph. *Aggregate Economic Analysis.* 3d ed. (New York: Holt, Rinehart and Winston, Inc., 1969), chap. 7.

Samuelson, Paul. "Interactions between the Multiplier Analysis and the Principle of Acceleration." *The Review of Economic Statistics* vol. 21 (1939). Reprinted in Mueller, ed., *Readings in Macroeconomics,* 2d ed.

Sirkin, Gerald. *Introduction to Macroeconomic Theory.* rev. ed. (Homewood, Ill.: Richard D. Irwin, Inc., 1965), chap. 5.

White, W. H. "Interest Inelasticity of Investment Demand." *American Economic Review,* vol. 46 (1956).

Chapter 7

Bailey, Martin. *National Income and The Price Level.* 2d ed. (New York: McGraw-Hill, Inc., 1971), chap. 9.

Dernburg, Thomas and Duncan McDougall. *Macroeconomics.* 3d ed. (New York: McGraw-Hill, Inc., 1968), chap. 6.

Gurley, John. "Fiscal Policies for Full Employment: A Diagrammatic Analysis." *Journal of Political Economy* vol. 60 (1952).

Haavelmo, Trygve. "Multiplier Effects of a Balanced Budget." *Econometrica* vol. 13 (1945).

Sirkin, Gerald. *Introduction to Macroeconomic Theory.* rev. ed. (Homewood, Ill.: Richard D. Irwin, Inc., 1965), chap. 6.

Chapter 8

Baumol, William. "The Transactions Demand for Cash: An Inventory Theoretic Approach." *Quarterly Journal of Economics* vol. 66 (1952).

Bronfenbrenner, Martin and Thomas Mayer. "Liquidity Functions in the American Economy." *Econometrica* vol. 28 (1960).

Dernburg, Thomas and Duncan McDougall. *Macroeconomics*. 3d ed. (New York: McGraw-Hill, Inc., 1968), chap. 8.

Friedman, Milton. "The Demand for Money—Some Theoretical and Empirical Results." *Journal of Political Economy* vol. 67 (1959).

Lindauer, John. *Macroeconomics*. 2d ed. (New York: John Wiley and Sons, 1971), chap. 9.

Shapiro, Edward. *Macroeconomic Analysis*. 2d ed. (New York: Harcourt, Brace, and World, 1970), chap. 18.

Chapter 9

Baird, Charles W. *Macroeconomics: An Integration of Monetary, Search, and Income Theories*. (Chicago: Science Research Associates, Inc., 1973), chap. 12.

Dernburg, Thomas and Duncan McDougall. *Macroeconomics*. 3d ed. (New York: McGraw-Hill, Inc., 1968), chap. 9.

Hicks, John. "Mr. Keynes and the 'Classics': A Suggested Interpretation." *Econometrica* vol. 5 (1937). Reprinted in Mueller, ed., *Readings in Macroeconomics*, 2d ed.

McKenna, Joseph. *Aggregate Economic Analysis*. 3d ed. (New York: Holt, Rinehart and Winston, Inc., 1969), appendix to chap. 9 and appendix to chap 10.

Chapter 10

Bailey, Martin. *National Income and the Price Level*. 2d ed. (New York: McGraw-Hill, Inc., 1971), pp. 28–32.

Dernburg, Thomas and Duncan McDougall. *Macroeconomics*. 3d ed. (New York: McGraw-Hill, Inc., 1968), chap. 11.

Patinkin, Don. "Price Flexibility and Full Employment." *American Economic Review* vol. 38 (1948). Reprinted in Mueller, ed., *Readings in Macroeconomics*. 2d ed.

Chapter 11

Baird, Charles W. *Macroeconomics: An Integration of Monetary, Search, and Income Theories*. (Chicago: Science Research Associates, Inc., 1973), chap. 14.

Bailey, Martin. *National Income and the Price Level.* 2d ed. (New York: McGraw-Hill, Inc., 1971), pp. 32–41.

Crouch, Robert. *Macroeconomics.* (New York: Harcourt, Brace, Jovanovich, Inc., 1972), chap. 8.

Dernburg, Thomas and Duncan McDougall. *Macroeconomics.* 3d ed. (New York: McGraw-Hill, Inc., 1968), chaps. 11 and 12.

Tobin, James. "Money Wage Rates and Employment." In Seymour E. Harris, ed., *The New Economics.* (New York: Alferd A. Knopf, Inc., 1947). Reprinted in Mueller, ed., *Readings in Macroeconomics,* 2d ed.

Chapter 12

Ackley, Gardner. *Macroeconomic Theory.* (New York: Macmillan Co., 1961), chap. 14.

Crouch, Robert. *Macroeconomics.* (New York: Harcourt, Brace and Jovanovich, Inc., 1972), chaps. 7 and 8.

Smith, Warren. "A Graphical Exposition of the Complete Keynesian System." *Southern Economic Journal* vol. 23 (1956). Reprinted in Mueller, *Readings in Macroeconomics,* 2d ed.

Chapter 13

Bailey, Martin. *National Income and the Price Level.* 2d ed. (New York: McGraw-Hill, Inc., 1971), pp. 52–56.

Lindauer, John. *Macroeconomics.* 2d ed. (New York: John Wiley and Sons, 1971), pp. 250–52.

Patinkin, Don. *Money, Interest, and Prices.* 2d ed. (New York: Harper and Row, Publishers, 1965), chap. 2.

Walker, Franklin. *Growth, Employment, and the Price Level.* (Englewood Cliffs, N.J.: Prentice Hall, Inc., 1963), chap. 8.

Chapter 14

Bailey, Martin. *National Income and the Price Level.* 2d ed. (New York: McGraw-Hill, Inc., 1971), pp. 56–62.

Crouch, Robert. *Macroeconomics.* (New York: Harcourt, Brace and Jovanovich, Inc., 1972), chap. 5.

Patinkin, Don. *Money, Interest, and Prices,* 2d ed. (New York: Harper and Row, Publishers, 1965), pp. 213–21.

Chapter 15

Lindauer, John. *Macroeconomics.* 2d ed. (New York: John Wiley and Sons, 1971), chap. 5.

Meade, J. "The International Monetary Mechanism." *The Three Banks Review* no. 63 (1964).

Mundell, Robert. "Flexible Exchange Rates and Employment Policy." *Canadian Journal of Economics and Political Science* vol. 27 (1961).

Timberlake, Richard. "The Fixation with Fixed Exchange Rates." *Southern Economic Journal* vol. 36 (1969).

Walker, Franklin. *Growth, Employment, and the Price Level.* (Englewood Cliffs, N.J.: Prentice Hall, Inc., 1963), chap. 9.

Chapter 16

Glahe, Fred R. *Macroeconomics: Theory and Policy.* (New York: Harcourt, Brace and Jovanovich, Inc., 1973), chap. 2.

Lindauer, John. *Macroeconomics.* 2d ed. (New York: John Wiley and Sons, 1971), chap. 12.

McKenna, Joseph. *Aggregate Economic Analysis.* 3d ed. (New York: Holt, Rinehart, and Winston, Inc., 1969), chap. 13.

Shapiro, Edward. *Macroeconomic Analysis.* 2d ed. (New York: Harcourt, Brace, and World, 1970), chap. 16.

Wells, Paul. "Keynes' Aggregate Supply Function." *Economic Journal,* vol. 42 (1960).

Chapter 17

Bailey, Martin. *National Income and the Price Level.* 2d ed. (New York: McGraw-Hill, Inc., 1971), chap. 4.

McKenna, Joseph. *Aggregate Economic Analysis.* 3d ed. (New York: Holt, Rinehart and Winston, Inc., 1969), chap. 16.

Samuelson, Paul and Robert Solow. "Analytical Aspects of Anti-Inflation Policy." *American Economic Review* vol. 50 (1960). Reprinted in Mueller, ed., *Readings in Macroeconomics.* 2d ed.

Selden, Richard. "Cost-push vs. Demand-pull Inflation, 1955–1957." *Journal of Political Economy* vol. 67 (1959).

Sirkin, Gerald. *Introduction to Macroeconomics.* rev. ed. (Homewood, Ill.: Richard D. Irwin, Inc., 1965), chap. 9.

Chapter 18

Ackley, Gardner. *Macroeconomic Theory.* (New York: Macmillan Co., 1961), chap. 15.

Clower, Robert. "Keynes and the Classics: A Dynamical Perspective." *Quarterly Journal of Economics* vol. 74 (1960).

Crouch, Robert. *Macroeconomics.* (New York: Harcourt, Brace and Jovanovich, Inc., 1972), chap. 15.

Klein, Lawrence. *The Keynesian Revolution.* (New York: Macmillan Co., 1947), chaps. 3, 4, and 5.

McKenna, Joseph. *Aggregate Economic Analysis.* 3d ed. (New York: Holt, Rinehart and Winston, Inc., 1969), chap. 14.

Chapter 19

Dernburg, Thomas, and Duncan McDougall. *Macroeconomics.* 4th ed. (New York: McGraw-Hill, Inc., 1968), chap. 16.

Phillips, A. W. "Employment, Inflation, and Growth." *Economics,* vol. 29, (1962). Reprinted in Mueller, ed., *Readings in Macroeconomics.* 2d ed.

Shapiro, Edward. *Macroeconomic Analysis.* 2d ed. (New York: Harcourt, Brace, and World, 1970), chap. 21.

Yeager, Leland. "Some Questions about Growth Economics." *American Economic Review* vol. 63 (1954).

Chapter 20

Dernburg, Thomas, and Duncan McDougall. *Macroeconomics.* 3d ed. (New York: McGraw-Hill, Inc., 1968), chaps. 19–21.

Friedman, Milton, and Anna J. Schwartz. *A Monetary History of the United States, 1867–1900.* (New York: National Bureau of Economic Research, Inc., 1963).

Glahe, Fred R. *Macroeconomics: Theory and Policy.* (New York: Harcourt, Brace and Jovanovich, Inc., 1973), chap. 15.

Shapiro, Edward. *Macroeconomic Analysis.* 2d ed. (New York: Harcourt, Brace, and World, 1970), chap. 24.

Index

A

Absolute Income Theory (AIT), 63–64
Accelerator
 analysis, 87–89
 definition of, 84
 effect, 86
 and growth, 296
Ackley, Gardner, 272 n
Aggregate demand; *see also* Aggregate expenditure
 and capital output ratio, 297–98
 Classical view, 258
 derivation, with price Level, 241–42
 and employment level, 242
 equilibrium level of, and
  full employment, 251
 as a function of the price level, 241–42
 inflation pressure, 193
 investment, 292
 investment function, 185
 monetary authority, 324–25
 net foreign investment, 223–24
 and price level, 256
 function
  Classical, 243–44
  defined, 243
  Keynesian, 244
  and real output, 254–55
 Keynesian
  and productive capacity, 238
  and real cash balances, 244
 real
  and level of investment, 222
  and level of real consumption, 222

Aggregate expenditure; *see also* Aggregate demand
 curve, and net foreign investment, 225
 function, and real cash balances, 283
Aggregate investment function, 90
Aggregate supply
 definition of, 169, 236
 function, definition of, 237
 curve, derived, 237–39
 and Classical assumption, 239
 equilibrium, with inflexible money wages, 248
 and fixed wage rate, 239
 full-employment, equilibrium, 236
 and Keynesian assumption, 239
 as a price-quantity relationship, 236–37
AIT; *see* Absolute Income Theory
Allen, R.D.G., 301 n
APC; *see* Average Propensity to Consume
APS; *see* Average Propensity to Save
Average Propensity
 to Consume (APC), 59, 64–65, 69, 71, 73
 definition of, 33
 to save (APS), 294

B

Bailey, M. J., 100 n, 154 n
Balances
 cash, supply of, and price level, 283–84
 nominal, and national income, 251

338 Index

Baumol, W.J., 118 n
Bischoff, C.W., 93 n
Bonds
  demand for, 124
    real, 213–14
  demanders of, 213
  market, 122, 173, 213–17
    equilibrium curve, 215–16
      derivation of, 213–16
    and IS curve, 217
    and LM curve, 217
    and money market, 285
    and rate of interest, 310
    and real cash balances, 214
    and real national income, 213–14
  supply of, 124
Brennan, Michael J., 55 n
Brunner, K., 129 n
Budget
  balanced, 100–101
  surplus, real value of, 311–12
Business transfer payments, 13

C

Cambridge, K., 142–43, 150
  and cash balances, 120–21
Capacity, and investment, 297
Capital
  consumption allowances, 11
  gain, 123
  loss, 122–23
  stock,
    and accelerator, 85
    growth rate of, 292, 308
Capital-output ratio, 296
  constant, 297
  definition of, 86
Cash balances
  demand for, and change in equilibrium level of national income, 152
  and rate of interest, 269–70
  real, demand curve for, 156–57
  supply of, and interest rate, 186–87
Circular flow of goods & services, 4–5
Classical demand for money, 120–21
  definition of, 121
Constant tax receipts, 105–8
Consumption
  current, 69
  and disposable income, 55
  and government sector, 102, 105–6, 109
  level of
    dependent upon level of income, 54
  Keynesian analysis, 62

Consumption—*Cont.*
  and real income, 269
  permanent
    income, defined by, 70
    proportional to permanent income, 71
  present, 72–73
  real, 154
    and rate of interest, 203, 213
    and real income, 154
  transitory, 70, 73
Consumption function
  and Absolute Income Theory, 62–63
  defined, 62
  classical analysis, 61–62
  and coefficient,
    of correlation, 55–56
    of determination, 57 n
  definition, 32
  and growth, 298
  long-run, 55, 62, 74–75
  and non-proportional expenditures, 62, 64
  and Permanent Income Theory, 62
  and proportional expenditures, 66
  Relative Income Theory, 64–68
    definition of, 62–63
  short-run, 58–59, 74
Contractionary effect and budget deficit, 311
Currency confiscation, 221

D

Deficit
  budgetary, 311
  definition of, 314
  spending, 104
  and Monetorists, 287–88
Deflation
  budgetary surplus, 313
  and price indexes, 20
Deflationary gap, 49, 99, 313
Demand curve for labor, 165
Demand deposits, 129
Devaluation, 228
Diminishing returns
  law of, 165
  and output, 299
Diminishing returns to scale, 237–38
  and aggregate production function, 237
Discount rate, 326
  definition of, 78–79
Disposable personal income, definition of, 13
Domar, E., 295
Domestic currency, and exports, 226

Duesenberry, J.S., 64 n
Dynamic analysis, 84
Dynamic economic analysis, and growth, 296

E

Easy money policy, 150
Economic growth, and technical progress, 307–8
Economic stagnation, 298
Economic theory
  dynamic, definition, 5
  static, definition, 5
Effective demand, defined, 252
Elasticity
  definition of, 119 n
  and demand for money, 124
  and equilibrium level of national income, 147
Employment
  and cost push inflation, 262
    less than full equilibrium, 279–80
  and easy money policy, 275
  and price level, 264–65
  and real wage rate, 275
Employment function
  definition of, 250–51
  derivation of, 250–54
Employment rate and price inflation, 265–66
Employment sector
  curve, and aggregate supply, 217
  equilibrium curve, 198
  and real balance effect, 212–13
Equilibrium
  adjustments in, 28–29
  aggregate, 5
    definition of, 5
  for consumers, 25
  definition of, 25
  in economy as a whole, 26
  in employment sector, 164
  expenditure sector, 29
  inflationary, 269
  interest rate, 131–32
  level of income,
    national, 43
    permanent, 46
  macroeconomic, 24–27
  market
    and exchange rates, 227
    in money market, 139
    defined, 131
  partial, 5
  process of, in money market, 29
  for producers, 25
  stability of, 28

Evans, Michael K., 61 n
Ex-ante investment; *see* Investment, intended
Ex-ante savings; *see* Savings, intended
Excess reserves, 130
Exchange rate, 226
  defined, 226
  differences in, 226–27
  fixed
    adjustment of, 229–32
    and stabilization, 229
    and foreign demand, 225–26
    official, 226–27
Expansion
  permanent, 43
  temporary, 43–46
Expansionary effect, budget deficit and, 311
Expansionary gap, 49
  and multiplier, 50
Expected rate of return, 76
Expenditures
  consumption
    exogenous increases, 43–44
    and rate of interest, 61–62
  current, 44–45
  curve, 39
  equilibrium curve,
    function, real and equilibrium value, 281
    slope of, 206
  sector
    disturbances in, 173–74
    equilibrium, 212
      with bonds sector, 218
Exports
  control of, 223
  level of, and flexible exchange rates, 232
  real, value of, 225
Ex-post investment; *see* Investment, actual
Ex-post savings; *see* Savings, actual

F

Factors of production, 9
Federal Reserve System
  and Great Depression, 318
  and inflation, 321
  and interest rate, 319
Fiscal
  drag, 315
  effect, definition of, 310
  lags, definition, 326
  policy, 5, 311
    and action lag, 326
    and changes in equilibrium, 144

Fiscal—*Cont.*
   expansionary, 287, 313, 317
   and flexible exchange rates, 232
   and full employment, 232–33, 324
   and national income, 310
   and national output, 286
   and outside lag, 326–27
Friedman, M., 69 n, 127 n, 327 n
   and Monetarists, 286
Full employment
   definition of, 167
   and equilibrium rate of interest, 195
   and falling wage rate, 179–80
   and flexible wage rate, 248–49
   and level of, 311–12
      output, 298
      real income, 233–34
   and productive capacity, 292
   and real balance effect, 250
Full-employment equilibrium, 167–69
   and exports, 225
   less than
      cost of, 315
      definition of, 240
      and price inflation, 266
      and real balance effect, 250
Full-employment surplus, 322
   budget
      definition of, 314
      level of, 313
      and deficit, 324

G

Gallaway, L.E., 202 n
GNP; *see* Gross national product
Government
   expenditure
      and accelerator effect, 88–89
      and IS, LM analysis, 143–144
   purchases, level of, 95–96
   Real and shifting real IS curve, 196–97
   sector, 96–97
   spending, and the multiplier, 107–11
   transfer payments, definition of, 314
Gross investment, definition of, 11
Gross national product (GNP)
   in current and constant dollars compared, 15–17
   potential, 324
   predicability of, 289
Growth
   and dynamic process, 308–9
   economic, definition of, 291
      rate of, 297
         constant, and productive capacity, 295

Growth—*Cont.*
   required, definition of, 295
   sustained, 298
   warranted, derivation, 296–97
   rate of national ouput, 301
Gurley, J.G., 202 n

H–I

Harrod, R., 296 n
Income
   absolute value of, 63
   current, 69
      temporary deviations from, 68
   equilibrium level of, 46
      determination of, 143
   interest, and present consumption, 204
   level of
      current, 69
      full-employment, defined, 50
      and multiplier, 39–40
   real
      and consumption, 203
      and exports, 223
   national and real consumption, 204
   nominal
      definition of, 161
      and price level, 250–51
   peak, 65, 66
   permanent, 68–69
      definition of, 69
      level of, 68–69
      rachett effect on, 68
   transitory, 70, 73, 74
   velocity, 242–43
   wind fall, and Permanent Income Theory, 73
Indirect business taxes, 13
Inflation, 323
   and aggregate demand, 257
   cost push, 261–64
      definition of, 262
   definition, 257
   demand pull, 257
   and economic growth, 272
   and fixed exchange rates, 231
   and fixed income, 271
   and income distribution, 271
   and money supply, 324
   and price indexes, 20
   and price level, 271
   and purchasing power, 271
   rate of, 320, 324
Inflationary gap, 50
   and multiplier, 50
Inside Lag, Definition of, 326

Interest rate, 131
  and accelerator, 86
  and bonds, 118–19, 214
  classical view, 183
  demand for money, 125–26
  determined, 132–33
  effect, 203
  equilibrium, 142–43, 183, 186
    and price level, 158–59
  and exchange rates, 231
  and full employment level of output, 169–70
  and level of investment, 79–82
  and level of national income, 135
  as monetary phenomenon, derived, 186–88
  and price changes, 153
  as a real phenomenon, 184–86
  and speculative demand of money, 121–22
  and supply of money, 128–29, 259
  world, 229
International Sector, and determination of the level of national income, 222
Inventories
  unintended, 278
  and Classical Theory, 278
Investment
  actual autonomous, 86
  as a capital asset, 25
  as a constant, 36
  cycle, 89–90
  definition of, 25
  diminishing returns, 299
  elasticity of, 92–93
    definition of, 92–93
  gross, 86
  induced, 86
  intended, 25, 36
    and exogenous change in consumption expenditure, 44
  level of
    and capital stock, 292
    and interest rate, 76
    and multiplier, 41–42
    and technology, 91–92
  net, and Economic Prosperity, 292
  real
    as function of the level of real income, 205–6
    and real wage rate, 209–10
IS curve
  adjustment, stable, 208–9
  definition of, 136
  derivation of, in real terms, 155
  equilibrium condition, 136
  and exports, 225

IS curve—*Cont.*
  and flexible exchange rates, 227
  and government expenditures, 143–44
  positively sloped, 208
    adjustment of, 208–9
  real
    and real balance effect, 212 n
    and real rate of interest, 270
  and unstable equilibrium, 208–9

K–L

Keynes, John Maynard, 79 n, 250, 250 n
  and wage stop, 276
Keynesian less-than-full-employment equilibrium, 247–48
Labor
  demand curve, 90
  exploitation of, 261
  and sustained growth, 298
Labor market, 29
  classical, 273
    adjustments in, 277–78
    in equilibrium, 280–81
    and IS curve, 274
  Keynesian, 273
    adjustments in, 277
    and LM Curve, 274–75
Labor supply, 167
  curve, 90–91
  and money wage rate, 273
Labor Unions
  and Phillips curve, 267
  and prices, 262
Lag
  action, definition of, 326
  outside, definition of, 326
  recognition, definition of, 326
Laidler, D., 128 n
Liquidity trap, 124, 145
  and Keynesian aggregate demand function, 245–46
  and monetary policy, 149
  and price level, 246
  and real balance effect, 249
  and wage stop, 279
LM Curve
  definition of, 139
  derived in real terms, 138–42, 157–60
    with full multiplier, 145
    positive sloped and aggregate demand, 244
  real, 157

M

Machlup, F., 24 n
Macroeconomic policy, 310

Macroeconomic policy—*Cont.*
  in the form of fiscal policy, 5
  in the form of monetary policy, 5
Macroeconomic theory, 1
Marginal efficiency of capital, definition of, 79
Marginal product, 238
  of capital, 300
  of labor, 166, 300
  physical, of labor curve, 237
Marginal propensity
  to consume (MPC), 32, 59–60
    definition of, 32
    and output produced, 277–78
    to import, 223
  to save (MPS), 294, 297
    definition of, 34–35
Market value of assets, 117
Meltzer, A.H., 127 n, 129 n
Microeconomic analysis and employment sector, 164
Microeconomic theory, 1
Monetarists
  and aggregate demand, 286–87
  and money supply, 287
Monetary authority
  and exchange rates, 228
  and inflation, 260
  and price level, 322
    response to changes in price level, 157
  and wage price freeze, 322
Monetary control program
  and inflation, 324
  and wage and price controls, 325
Monetary policy
  and action lag, 327
  easy, and aggregate demand, 256
  and economic activity, 286
  and equilibrium changes, 147–51
  and fixed exchange rates, 231
  and inflation, 324
  and inside lag, 327
  and interest rates, 286–87
  and outside lag, 327
Monetary and real sector, relationship between, 188
Monetary rule, and stabilization of economy, 288
Money
  creation, 220–21
  demand for
    and absolute price, 201
    and bonds, 213–14
    and relative prices, 201
    easy, policy to raise national income, 230

Money—*Cont.*
  illusion
    definition of, 276
    in labor market, 276, 279
    and quantity theory, 284
    in speculative demand for money, 285
  market, 29, 131–32
    in equilibrium, 215
      Keynesian and Classical differences, 280–81
    and price level, 157
  quantity theory of, 280–86
    definition of, 242
    and equation of exchange, 242–43
  stock of, 281–83
  supply, 128–30, 132 n
    and aggregate demand, 243
    and bonds market equilibrium, 219–20
    definition of, 128–29
    and full employment, 275
    and level of income, 29
    and price level, 219–20, 259, 270, 321, 322–23
    and rate of interest, 324
    and real balance effect, 191
    real value of, and Price Level, 163
  Wage Rate, flexible, and level of employment, 239–40
MPC; *see* Marginal Propensity to Consume
MPS; *see* Marginal Propensity to Save
Multiplier
  algebraically viewed, 51–53
  balanced budget, 102
  constant tax receipts, 107–11
  cumulative effect on income, 45–46
  and fluctuating tax receipts, 111–15
  and government spending, 98–100
  and IS curve, 138
  IS, LM analysis, 144–45
  and macroeconomic policy, 47
  permanent expansion and, 46
  positively sloped LM curve, 151–52
  productive capacity, 294–95
  simple, 38–42
  and tax revenue changes, 112–13
  with transaction-precaution demand for money, 147

N

National income, 1, 4, 13–15
  definition of, 7
  dollar value of, 19
  equilibrium level of, 135
  and fiscal policy, 148–49

Index 343

National income—Cont.
 interpreted, and income accounts, 23
 level of equilibrium, 145–46
 and money supply, 151
 potential, definition of, 315
 and real cash balances, demand for, 158
 in real terms, 154
 real value, and price level, 154
National product, 7
Neo-Classical growth theory, 292
Neo-Keynesians
 definition of, 286
 and economy, 286
Net foreign investment, definition of, 222
Net foreign balances, definition of, 8
Net investment, definition of, 11
Net national product (NNP), 7–9
 definition of, 8
 measurement of by income approach, 8
Neutral technological progress, defined, 307–8
Nixon administration, and wage price controls, 322
Nominal balances
 and aggregate demand function, 259
 and real balance effect, 200
Numeraire, definition of, 172

O

Okun, Arthur, 315 n
Open Market Committee, 327
Opportunity cost, 118
Output-capital ratio, 295, 303, 305, 308
Output
 current, 44–45
 national
  at full-employment, 169, 220
  per capita, 292
  real, distribution of, 292
 real
  growth rate, and inflation, 320
  and employment, 325
  and interest rate, 216–17
  and price level, 325

P

Patinkin, D., 280 n
Permanent Income Theory (PIT), 68–74
Perry, G.L., 267 n
Personal income, 13–15
 definition of, 13

Phillips curve, 264
 and expansionary policy, 322
 long-run, 267
 stability of, 266
Pigou effect, 190
PIT; see Permanent Income Theory
Planned investment; see Investment, intended
Planned savings; see Savings, intended
Policy measures, predicability of, 213
Population
 control, 306–7
 growth rate of, 305
Precautionary demand for money, 120
Present value, 76–77, 77 n
Price
 flexibility, 181
 index
  construction of, 17–20
  consumer, 18
  definition of, 17
  to deflate national income, 19
  weaknesses of, 20–22
  wholesale, 20
 inflation, and interest rate, 320
 level, 153
  and aggregate demand, 186
  and aggregate supply, 239
  bonds market equilibrium curve, 219–20
  definition, 20
  equilibrium, 247
  and expenditure sector, in relation to, 160–61
  at full employment, 169–70
  and interest rate, 186
  and Keynesian aggregate demand, 244
  and LM curve, 170–71
  and monetary sector
   adjustments in, 162–63
   variables, 160–63
  and money stock, 319–20
  and money wage rate, 239, 256
  and quantity of money, 280
  rate of increase in, 323
  and real balances, 191
  relative, Definition of, 153
  stable, 259
Production function
 aggregate, 300–301
 and diminishing returns, 304
 homogenous, 300
 shift in, 210–11
 short-run, 165
Productivity, Real, Long-Run, 325
Profit maximization, 238

Q–R

Quantity theory
  and Keynesian framework, 280
  Keynesian rejection of, 280
  and less-than-full-employment, 280
  and money illusion, 280
  and price level, 280
  and rigid wage rate, 284
  and speculative demand for money, 280
Rasche, R.H., 327 n
Real balance effect, 188, 190
  and consumption function, 210
  and demand curve for real cash balances, 193–94
  and employment sector, 196–97
  in expenditure sector, 248–49
  and full employment, 196–97
  as link between monetary and real sectors, 196
  and monetary sector, 199
  Derived, 199
Real cash balances, 158
Real output
  and employment, 255
  equilibrium level of, and level of Employment, 254–55
Real rate of return, 269
Regression analysis
  and consumption, 55
  and demand for Money, 127
  and investment, 92–93
Relative Income Theory (RIT), 62, 64–68
Reserve requirement, 130
Resource allocation, and wage-price controls, 323
Resources, and sustained growth, 298
RIT; see Relative Income Theory
Rittler, L.S., 121 n

S

Samuelson, P.A., 264 n
Shapiro, H.T., 327 n
Savings
  actual as a capital asset, 26
  definition of, 25
  to finance investment expenditures, 294
  function, description of, 37–38
  intended, 25, 37–38
  level of, in equilibrium, 303–4
  real, and budgetary surplus, 313
  target level of, 205
Say's law
  and absolute prices, 201–2

Say's law—*Cont.*
  definition of, 200–201
  and full employment, 201
  and money market, 201
  and real output, 200–201
Schwartz, Anna J., 318
Shortages, and wage-price controls, 323
Short run, defined, 165
Smith, P.E., 202 n
Smithies, A., 63 n
Solow, R.M., 264, 300 n
Speculative demand for money, 121
  definition of, 121–24
  and interest rate, 185
  and IS curve, 141
Stable economic system, 219
Static analysis, 84
  and growth, 296
Stationary state, 298
  and diminishing returns, 298
Supply function, and income, 252
Supply of money, and price level, 194 n
Swan, T. W., 307 n

T

Taylor, Lester D., 204
Tax revenue and budget surplus, 312
Taxes
  and budgetary surplus, 313
  and multiplier, 107–8
Technical progress and growth, 307
Technology
  and aggregate supply, 325
  and productivity of capital, 299
Tobin, J., 118 n, 121 n, 128 n
Total demand for money, 124–26
Total product, 9
Total wage bill, 210
Transactions cost, 118
Transactions demand for money, 118–19
Transactions-precautionary demand for money, 121, 124–25, 185, 243, 285
  and IS Curve, 218
Transfer cost, 118

U

Unemployed
  frictionally, defined, 266
  structurally, defined, 266
Unemployment
  and GNP, 321
  and government policy, 262–63
  involuntary, 102, 276–77
  natural rate of, 267
  and price inflation, 264–65

Unemployment—*Cont.*
and wage-price controls, 324
Utility
  maximization of, 61
  and output distribution, 292

V–W

Value added, 9–10
Velocity
  income, 242
  and monetarists, 287
  and Neo-Keynesians, 288
  and rate of growth, 320
Wage and price controls, 310, 322–25
Wage rate, 90–91
  equilibrium and less-than-full-employment, 250

Wage rate—*Cont.*
  flexible, 273
  and liquidity trap, 249–50
  inflexible, and inflation, 260
  and investment, 155
  minimum, 273–74
  real, 165
  rigidity of, 261
Wage stop, 279
  defined, 261, 274
Walras' law
  and bonds Market, 213
  definition of, 171–72
  and equilibrium, 171–73
  Analysis, 217
Wealth, nonmonetary, 220
Weber, W.E., 205
Welfare of society, 292

This book has been set in 11 and 10 point Baskerville, leaded 2 Points. Chapter numbers are 30 point Helvetica, and chapter titles are 16 point Helvetica. The size of the type page is 26 $\times$ 45 picas.